John Bowlby and Attachment Theory

John Bowlby (1907–1990) has been described as 'one of the three or four most important psychiatrists of the twentieth century'. In this book Jeremy Holmes provides a focused and coherent account of Bowlby's life and work, based on his writings and those of the 'post-Bowlbians', as well as interviews with members of his family and with psychoanalysts who knew him.

Bowlby's Attachment Theory is one of the major theoretical developments in psychoanalysis this half-century. Combining the rigorous scientific empiricism of ethology with the subjective insights of psychoanalysis, it has had an enormous impact in the fields of child development, social work, psychology, psychotherapy and psychiatry. Jeremy Holmes examines the origins of Bowlby's ideas, and presents the main features of Attachment Theory and their relevance to contemporary psychoanalytic psychotherapy. He looks at the processes of attachment and loss, and reviews recent experimental evidence linking secure attachment in infancy with the development of 'autobiographical competence'. He also provides fascinating insights into the history of the psychoanalytic movement, and considers the ways in which Attachment Theory can help in understanding society and its problems.

John Bowlby and Attachment Theory will be essential reading for all students of psychotherapy, counselling, social work, psychology and psychiatry, and for professionals working in those fields.

Jeremy Holmes is Consultant Psychiatrist/Psychotherapist at the North Devon District Hospital.

The Makers of Modern Psychotherapy
Series editor: Laurence Spurling

This series of introductory, critical texts looks at the work and thought of key contributors to the development of psychodynamic psychotherapy. Each book shows how the theories examined affect clinical practice, and includes biographical material as well as a comprehensive bibliography of the contributor's work.

The field of psychodynamic psychotherapy is today more fertile but also more diverse than ever before. Competing schools have been set up, rival theories and clinical ideas circulate. These different and sometimes competing strains are held together by a canon of fundamental concepts, guiding assumptions and principles of practice.

This canon has a history, and the way we now understand and use the ideas that frame our thinking and practice is palpably marked by how they came down to us, by the temperament and experiences of their authors, the particular puzzles they wanted to solve and the contexts in which they worked. These are the makers of modern psychotherapy. Yet despite their influence, the work and life of some of these eminent figures is not well known. Others are more familiar, but their particular contribution is open to reassessment. In studying these figures and their work, this series will articulate those ideas and ways of thinking that practitioners and thinkers within the psychodynamic tradition continue to find persuasive.

Laurence Spurling

John Bowlby and Attachment Theory

Jeremy Holmes

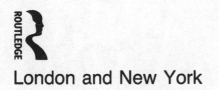

London and New York

First published 1993
by Routledge
11 New Fetter Lane, London EC4P 4EE

Simultaneously published in the USA and Canada
by Routledge
29 West 35th Street, New York, NY 10001

© 1993 Jeremy Holmes

Phototypeset in Times by Intype, London
Printed and bound in Great Britain by
Mackays of Chatham PLC, Chatham, Kent

British Library Cataloguing in Publication Data

A catalogue record for this book is available from the British Library

Library of Congress Cataloging in Publication Data

Also available

ISBN 0–415–07729–X
      0–415–07730–3 (pbk)

To Jacob, Matthew, Lydia and Joshua; also to Ben, Polly, Matilda and Flora; and in memory of Tabitha.

By the same author

The Values of Psychotherapy (with R. Lindley), (1991 [1989]), Oxford University Press.
A Textbook of Psychotherapy in Psychiatric Practice (Editor), (1991), Churchill Livingstone.
Between Art and Science: Essays in Psychotherapy and Psychiatry (1992), Routledge.
The Good Mood Guide (with R. Holmes), (1993), Orion.

Contents

List of illustrations   ix

Acknowledgements   x

1 Introduction   1

Part I Origins

2 Biographical   13

3 Maternal deprivation   37

Part II Attachment Theory

4 Attachment, anxiety, internal working models   61

5 Loss, anger and grief   86

6 Attachment Theory and personality development: the
  research evidence   103

Part III Implications

7 Bowlby and the inner world: Attachment Theory and
  psychoanalysis   127

8 Attachment Theory and the practice of psychotherapy   149

9 Attachment Theory and psychiatric disorder   177

10 Attachment Theory and society   200

11 Epilogue   210

Glossary of terms relevant to Attachment Theory   217
Chronology of John Bowlby   225
Bibliography   228
Index   244

Illustrations

FIGURES

3.1 Developmental pathways from maternal deprivation   52

4.1 The attachment behavioural system   76

4.2 Patterns of insecure attachment   80

6.1 The evolution of attachment patterns   118

6.2 Anna and the holding environment   121

7.1 The anxiously attached infant   142

TABLES

6.1 The continuity of secure and insecure attachment   115

7.1 Classical, Object-Relations and Attachment Theories compared   133

8.1 Clinical aspects of insecure-avoidant and dismissive attachment   163

Acknowledgements

The origins of this book can be traced to a phone call from Laurie Spurling asking me whom I would like to write about. John Bowlby sprang instantly to mind – so I must start by acknowledging my gratitude to him for that invitation, and for his subsequent editorial help and suggestions.

The next 'without whom . . .' is to the Wellcome Trust, who granted me a six-month Research Fellowship which enabled me to concentrate exclusively on the book, free from my clinical and administrative responsibilities. Sabbaticals are becoming rare enough in universities, and in the National Health Service are almost unheard of. Mine was a blissful period which not only enabled me to devote myself to the book, but also provided a perspective from which I realised how stressful and exhausting most NHS consultant posts are. So the Wellcome has saved me from burn-out (or postponed it for a while) as well as enabling the book to get written. Never was a psychotherapist so professionally indebted to a pharmaceutical firm!

Next I must express my gratitude to my colleagues in the Department of Psychiatry at North Devon District Hospital, and especially to Drs Roberts, Sewell and Van Buren, who gave their blessing to my absence, even though it meant more work for them, also to Dr Simon Nicholson, who cheerfully and efficiently took my place while I was away.

I am grateful to the Institute of Psycho-Analysis for granting me access to their archives.

Much gratitude is due to the many friends and colleagues who have given up time and effort to discuss Attachment Theory and to read all or part of the manuscript and have made many helpful suggestions which have improved its quality: Anthony Bateman,

Mary Boston, Peter Fonagy, Dorothy Heard, Matthew Holmes, Sebastian Kraemer, Brian Lake, Richard Lindley, Pat Millner, Oliver Reynolds, Glenn Roberts, Charles Rycroft, Anthony Storr, and Robert and Lorraine Tollemache. Needless to say, the defects of the book are entirely my responsibility.

I am very grateful for the help and encouragement I have had from members of the Bowlby family. By agreeing to be interviewed, and with their written comments, Ursula Bowlby, Mary Gatling, Sir Henry and Lady Evelyn Phelps Brown, Juliet Hopkins and Marjorie Durbin gave me a fascinating window of reminiscence into their family and social life in the early part of the century.

My secretary, Patricia Bartlett, helped as always in countless ways to lighten the burden of my work and made my absence from the hospital possible by her combination of good humour, vigilance and efficiency.

Alison Housley and her staff in the library at North Devon District Hospital have been tireless in the promptness and enthusiasm with which they responded to my endless requests for references. Their contribution to making our hospital a true 'periphery of excellence' is incalculable.

Finally, I am grateful to Ros and Joshua Holmes, who, by providing me with a loving and secure base, enabled me to explore the world of Attachment Theory, and by expecting – without demanding – me to provide one for them, offered the necessary distraction without which one's work becomes stale and unbalanced.

Chapter 1

Introduction

When people start writing they think they've got to write something definitive . . . I think that is fatal. The mood to write in is 'This is quite an interesting story I've got to tell. I hope someone will be interested. Anyway it's the best I can do for the present.' If one adopts that line one gets over it and does it.

(Bowlby in Hunter 1991)

This book has four main aims. The first, and simplest, is to present John Bowlby's story of attachment – and we shall hear much about stories in the course of the book – in a condensed and coherent way. Bowlby was a lucid and prolific exponent of his own views, but the very comprehensiveness of his work, described by one critic as having a 'Victorian monumentality about it' (Rycroft 1985), can be daunting. Despite the clarity of his thought and the charm and epigrammatic flair of his literary style, the 1,500 pages of the *Attachment and Loss* trilogy (Bowlby, 1969b, 1973a, 1980), covering as they do every aspect of the subject in immense detail, are hard going for the faint-hearted reader. His later works, *The Making and Breaking of Affectional Bonds* (Bowlby 1979) and *A Secure Base* (Bowlby 1988), are more accessible, but as collections of essays they do not necessarily pull all his theories together into a whole. So there is a need for a survey of Bowlby's work, and also – here is a second objective – given that it is well over half a century since he published his first papers, a need to take an historical perspective on the evolution of his ideas.

The past thirty years have seen a second, and more recently a third, generation of researchers stimulated by Bowlby's seminal ideas first published in the 1960s. The 'post-Bowlbians' – Ainsworth, Main, Bretherton, Marris and Sroufe in the United States; the Grossmanns in Germany; Parkes, Hinde, Byng-Hall and Heard in Britain – have developed Attachment Theory into a major framework of developmental psychology in ways that are highly relevant to psychotherapy. Many of their findings have been collected into two important research symposia (Parkes and Stevenson-Hinde 1982; Parkes *et al.* 1991), but there is no single volume explicitly devoted to the exposition of contemporary Attachment Theory and little concerted effort has been made to consider its implications for psychotherapeutic theory and practice. The need for such a work is a third objective and justification for the present work.

A fourth and more compelling reason than these worthy but perhaps mundane considerations informs much of the purpose of this book. This is the attempt to come to grips with a curious enigma which surrounds Bowlby and his work. Apart from Freud and Jung, Bowlby is one of the few psychoanalysts who have become household names and whose ideas have entered the vernacular. The ill effects (or otherwise) of maternal deprivation; the importance of bonding between parents and children; the need for a secure base and to feel attached; the realisation that grief has a course to run and can be divided into stages – these are concepts with which people far removed from the worlds of psychology and psychotherapy are familiar. All may be traced, in whole or in part, to the work of John Bowlby.

Yet Bowlby's familiarity and acceptance by the general public and his influence in a number of specialist fields such as pediatrics, developmental psychology, social work and psychiatry have never been matched within the domain of psychotherapy. In his chosen profession of psychoanalysis his influence is honoured more often in the breach than the observance. Between his papers delivered in the late 1950s and early 1960s to psychoanalytic societies in Britain and the States, and polite obsequies of the early 1990s, there has for the most part been a resounding silence from the psychoanalytical movement in response to the challenges and opportunities which his work represents. A major aim of this book is to try to understand this discrepancy between public recognition and professional avoidance, and the attempt to remedy it by showing how Attachment Theory can inform the practice of adult psychotherapy.

The details of the relationship between Bowlby and psycho-analysis will emerge gradually in the course of the book but, as an overture, a brief summarising overview will now follow. The answers to the riddle of Bowlby's rift with the psychoanalytic movement can be found at three distinct but interrelated levels: Bowlby's own personality, background and outlook; the atmosphere within the psychoanalytic society just before and in the aftermath of Freud's death; and the social and intellectual climate in the years surrounding and including the 1939–45 world war.

John Bowlby, described in an obituary as 'one of the three or four most important psychiatrists of the twentieth century' (Storr 1991), came from a conventional upper-middle class background. Cambridge educated, very 'English' in his reserve and empiricism, a 'nineteenth century Darwinian liberal' (Rycroft, 1985), he entered a psychoanalytical society in the 1930s that was riven between two warring factions led by Melanie Klein on the one hand and Anna Freud on the other (Grosskurth 1986). Melanie, a Berliner, divorced and separated from her children, the great innovator, faced the unmarried Viennese Anna, devoted to the orphans in her Hampstead nursery, defender of the true Freudian faith. Klein was powerful and domineering, but with a helpless side that meant that she depended on utter loyalty from her supporters. Anna Freud was shy and diffident, but with a steely determination not to be done down, and the confidence of her father's blessing.

The battle between the two women was ostensibly about theory. For Freud the Oedipus complex was the 'kernel of the neuroses' and he had had little to say about the early mother–infant relationship. Klein put the mother on the psychoanalytic map, arguing for the importance of phantasy in the early weeks and months of life; the primacy of the death instinct as an explanation for infantile aggression; and the need in therapy to lay bare and put into words these primitive impulses of infancy. Anna Freud – Antigone to her father's Oedipus – questioned Klein's speculations about the mind of the infant, continued to see the Oedipus complex arising at the age of two to three years as the starting point for the neuroses, and saw the role of therapy as strengthening the ego in its efforts to reconcile id and superego. Bowlby struggled to find his bearings in the charged atmosphere of the psychoanalytic society created by the rivalrous antagonism of these two daughters of the psychoanalytical movement, each vying for supremacy. With characteristic independence he steered a course between them, trying to work things out for himself. He took his stand on two main battlefields: the scientific status of psychoanalysis, and the role of the environment in the causation of neurosis.

Although both sides invoked the name of science in support of their ideas, this was, in Bowlby's view, little more than a genuflection to Freud's insistence that psychoanalysis should take its place as a new science of the mind. Bowlby saw both women and most of their followers as hopelessly unscientific. Neither Klein nor Anna Freud had any kind of scientific background. Both argued from intuition and authority rather than subjecting their claims to empirical testing. Neither had made any attempt to keep abreast of contemporary developments in science, or to revise Freudian metapsychology in the light of the emerging ideas about information processing and feedback which were to have such an impact on academic psychology and ethology. In rejecting Bowlby, his psychoanalytic critics on the other hand felt that by restricting himself to a narrow definition of science – to what could be observed and measured – Bowlby was missing the whole point of psychoanalysis. Any so-called 'science' of the mind which did not take account of the inner world of phantasy was worthless and certainly had no place within psychoanalytic discourse.

A similar polarisation took place around the role of the environment in the causation of neurosis. Bowlby was struck by the extent to which his patients had suffered from privation and loss, and horrified by the apparent disregard of real trauma as compared with an emphasis on the importance of autonomous phantasy in the Kleinian approach. Matters came to a head when Bowlby presented to the psychoanalytic society his famous film made with James Robertson (Robertson 1952; Bowlby and Robertson 1952b) documenting the distress shown by a small girl when separated from her parents on going into hospital. While Anna Freud endorsed Bowlby's views, the Kleinians in the audience were unimpressed, and felt that the girl's distress was due more to her unconscious destructive phantasies towards her pregnant mother's unborn baby than to the separation itself.

Bowlby was in an unusual position within the psychoanalytic society in that he was someone with non-Kleinian views who had been analysed and supervised by members of the Kleinian group (Joan Riviere and Miss Klein herself). Finding himself stuck in his analysis he decided to change to a non-Kleinian analyst, but extreme pressure was placed on him not to do so, to which, uncharacteristically, he submitted (Grosskurth 1986). He was cited by the Kleinians as evidence that they were not out to brainwash or convert all psychoanalytical candidates to their persuasion. As someone with evident ability and reputation he would have been quite a catch for whichever group he chose to join.

But both sides had reckoned without Bowlby's originality and ambition and preparedness to go out on a limb on his own. His discovery of ethology in the early 1950s provided the opportunity he was looking for to put psychoanalysis on a sound scientific footing. His World Health Organisation monograph (Bowlby 1951) and later observations of children separated from their parents enabled him to establish once and for all the importance of environmental trauma as a cause of neurosis and character disturbance. Attachment Theory was born, but rather than illuminating and strengthening Object Relations Theory as Bowlby had hoped, it was perceived by many analysts as a threat or even a betrayal. Bowlby had hoped to reconcile the warring factions within the society with his new theory, but instead they were for the most part united in either outright opposition or polite indifference to his ideas. Bowlby gradually drifted away from the society, and Attachment Theory came to stand as a discipline in its own right, owing much to psychoanalysis, but with links also to systems theory and cognitive psychology, and making a contribution as much to family and cognitive therapies as to psychoanalysis.

In retrospect the splits within the British Psycho-Analytical Society seem comparatively trivial. As Pedder (1987) puts it:

> an innocent might . . . ask what all the fuss was about. Because really it could be argued that there was not a lot of disagreement. They argued about phantasy: how wide the concept should be. . . . They argued about . . . how early the Oedipus complex starts, whether at two or three or sooner. . . . They argued about the emphasis that should be placed on aggression and the death instinct, and whether neurosis is precipitated by the frustration of libido, as the Viennese thought, or [as the Kleinians saw it] by the awakening of aggression. . . . All these could be seen as matters of degree which you might think reasonable people could well discuss.
>
> (Pedder 1987)

But as every psychotherapist should know, things are rarely that simple. The psychoanalytical movement was still struggling with the death of its founder, searching for a direction in which to go. The polarisation between those who idealised the dead leader (the Anna Freudians) and those who dealt with their depression by a kind of manic triumphalism, a celebration of the new (the Kleinians), can be understood in terms of the very concepts that those two groups espoused. A female principle was needed to balance the phallocentrism of the earlier Freudian movement. 'The King is dead, long live the Queen' might have been their slogan. But which queen should it be? The battle for psycho-analysis was going on against a backdrop of world war, of death, dislocation and genocide. The Kleinian emphasis on autonomous phantasy, on the death instinct, on the power of psychoanalysis to heal, irrespective of environmental factors, can be seen as a desperate attempt to bring some sense of order and the possibility of control – at times omnipotently – into a world in which one could not but feel powerless and helpless. Anna Freud's emphasis on the need to strengthen the ego was an effort to hold on to reason and sanity in the face of the irrational destructiveness unleashed by war.

Bowlby was perhaps the perfect scapegoat, with his cool Eng-lishness, his social and intellectual powers, his espousal of a narrow version of science that could not encompass the cultural breadth of the Jewish-European intelligentsia, his comparative insulation from the full horrors of war, and his Whiggish belief in the possibilities of progress based on social and scientific reason. His attempt to open out psychoanalysis to ethology and contemporary science was premature. He threatened the closed world of psychoanalysis and, offered a cold shoulder, like others before him (Jung, Adler, Ferenczi, Reich), he gave up the fight after a while and moved away to follow his own interests.

The loss was both his and that of psychoanalysis. There is something in the kernel of psychoanalysis which Bowlby seems not to have fully assimilated. In comparison with Freud's and Klein's passionate world of infantile sexuality, Attachment Theory appears almost bland, banal even. An appreciation of the power of phantasy, and the complexity of its relationship with external reality, is somehow lacking in his work. It is not loss alone that causes disturbance, but the phantasies stirred up by loss – the lack of this appreciation makes Bowlby appear at times simplistic in his formulations. But in eschewing the scientific rigour which Bowlby saw it so badly needed, psychoanalysis was held back in its development as a discipline and a therapy, a setback from which it is only just beginning to recover (see Peterfreund 1983; Stern 1985). Perhaps there was something in the climate of the 1950s which made such a split inevitable. The divide between the 'two cultures' epitomised by the belief in the possibility of progress based on science advocated by C. P. Snow, and Leavis's moral condemnation of an illiterate and degenerate society was just too great to bridge (Holmes 1992). Psychoanalysis became increasingly identified with 'culture' – with the imagination, linguistics and the moral and aesthetic dimension (Rycroft 1985; Rustin 1991), while Attachment Theory gathered momentum as a part of scientific psychology, taking root in the United States in a way that seemed less possible in a Britain that was so split in its educational and bureaucratic structures between art and science.

But times have changed. The old certainties no longer hold. Psychoanalysis has lost its dogmatism and is much more open to empirical evidence and to cross-disciplinary influence. The Berlin wall which separated psychoanalysis from the superficiality but also the stimulus of other disciplines has come down. The debate about the scientific status of psychoanalysis, and the role of the environment in neurosis, continues, but it is no longer a matter of life and death. Each side can claim partial victories. Klein was right in her emphasis on the early weeks and months of life – there is abundant evidence of psychic life from the moment of birth (Stern 1985). She was probably wrong in her insistence on the universality of the paranoid-schizoid position – it seems likely that splitting and projection predominate only in anxiously attached infants. She was right to emphasise loss and separation as central themes in character formation from the earliest years, but wrong in the concreteness of her thinking – she believed that bottle feeding could never substitute for the breast and that the events surrounding weaning were critical determinants of character. It seems likely that it is the style and general handling of the infant that matters, not the specific events, unless these are overwhelmingly traumatic. In therapy she was right to emphasise the central importance of the relationship between therapist and patient, but wrong in her belief that only 'deep', 'Kleinian' interpretations would be effective: the strength of the therapist–

chment is a crucial determining factor in the outcome
, but the nature of the interpretations, as long as they
nably sensible, coherent and brief, is not (Holmes 1991).
easing evidence of early trauma appears in the histories
of patients with major character disorder (Grant 1991), Bowlby's
emphasis on the importance of the environment as a determinant
of pathology appears to be vindicated, but he also tended to be
too concrete and specific in his hypotheses – it is not the loss of
a parent in itself that is traumatic but the family discord or
disruption surrounding it that causes the damage (Rutter 1981).

Klein showed how an individual's inner world shapes their
perception of the object, and how, through projective identification, the object is coerced into feeling and behaving according
to the projections it receives. In contrast with this near solipsistic
account, Bowlby is concerned primarily with the impact of the
object on the self. The self, which in his theories tends to be
almost passive, is moulded by the inadequacies and absences of
the object. We shall explore how the *interactive* view of self
and object postulated by Winnicott (1965) and Bion (1978) and
observed by developmental psychologists like Stern (1985) and
Brazelton and Cramer (1991) offers the possibility of a long
overdue climate of reconciliation and new understanding.

Bowlby was always careful to distinguish between the scientific
and therapeutic aspects of psychoanalysis. As a scientist he was
struggling for simplicity and clarity and for general principles,
while therapy inevitably concerns itself with complexity and concreteness of the individual case. Much of the disagreement
between Bowlby and psychoanalysis appears to rest on a confusion of these two aspects. Bowlby's main concern was to find
a firm scientific underpinning to the Object Relations approach,
and Attachment Theory, with its marrying of ethology to the
developmental ideas of psychoanalysis, can be seen in that light.
Although couched in the language of science, psychoanalytic
therapy has come increasingly to be seen as a hermeneutic discipline, more concerned with meanings than mechanism, in which
patient and therapist collaboratively develop a coherent narrative
about the patient's experience. Such objectification and coherence
are in themselves therapeutic, irrespective of the validity or otherwise of the meanings that are found. An extreme illustration of
this comes from the finding that schizophrenic patients with complex and coherent delusional systems are better able to function

socially than those who lack such meanings, however idiosyncratic (Roberts 1992). Bowlby's work has ensured that clinical hypotheses based on Object Relations Theory with a scientific underpinning of Attachment Theory are unlikely to be far removed from the truth, or to be tainted by totally unjustified speculation.

As we shall see in Chapter 6, recent developments in Attachment Theory suggest an exciting bridge between the narrative approach of contemporary psychoanalysis and the science of developmental psychology. There is a strong link between the kinds of attachment patterns found in infancy and the narratives that people tell about themselves several years later. Put briefly, securely attached children tell coherent stories about their lives, however difficult they have been, while insecurely attached children have much greater difficulty in narrative competence, either dismissing their past or remaining bogged down in it, and in neither case being able to talk objectively about it. The therapeutic implications of this are self-evident. Good therapy, like good parenting, provides the security and space within which a healing narrative can begin to emerge.

Psychoanalysis, perhaps more than it would care to admit, is influenced by the prevailing cultural climate. The Oedipus complex with its emphasis on castration anxiety reflected the patriarchy of its day. With the weakening of paternal power within the family came the rise of the female principle within psychoanalysis. The Society which Bowlby joined in the 1930s was dominated by strong women: Melanie Klein, Anna Freud, Joan Riviere, Sylvia Payne, Susan Isaacs, Paula Heimann and many others. Ernest Jones's power was waning, and Glover's grip on the Society was gradually being loosened. The main theorists of the post-war period – Klein, Bion, Winnicott and Bowlby – were all concerned with the role of the mother. A new phase of deconstruction has begun which emphasises the reciprocities of reader and writer, social, cultural and racial pluralism. We are entering an era of therapeutic co-constructionism – far removed from the *ex-cathedra* interpretations of classical therapy – where therapist and patient collaboratively build up a picture of their world and history. We have moved, perhaps, from the father principle, through the maternal, to the era of the sibling, in which, however different in their roles, there is a fundamental symmetry between patient and therapist.

This brings us to a concluding note about the nature of biography. A biographer is, in a sense, both patient and therapist in relation to the person he chooses to write about. As Gathorne-Hardy (1992) points out, there is an inevitable positive transference to one's subject; how else could one justify the long hours spent (far exceeding any psychoanalysis, however interminable) reading, studying, thinking about them? Biographers identify with their subjects, just as patients identify with their therapists, and see them in a way that is inevitably influenced and may be biased by their own themes and preoccupations. At the same time, biographers as 'therapists' have an opportunity to see their subjects as they really are: but with that privilege must also take into account their own counter-transferential tendencies towards voyeurism, prurience, envy, denigration and idealisation. Biographers should approach their subjects in the same spirit in which therapists see their patients: compassionately without becoming over-involved, with objectivity but without excessive detachment, with a sense of the uniqueness and specialness of the individual but without indulgence. The aim of this book is to form a working alliance with Attachment Theory and its originator – to see them in their strengths and limitations, their possibilities and blind spots. Although this book is not primarily a biography, some biographical preliminaries are therefore inevitably needed and it is to them that we must now turn.

Part I

Origins

Chapter 2

Biographical

> Parents, especially mothers, are much-maligned people.
>
> (Bowlby 1988a)

A family photograph, taken just before the First World War, shows Lady Bowlby surrounded by her six children. Her husband, Sir Anthony, the King's surgeon, is not there – he is, as usual, at work. She is flanked by her two favourite sons, John and Tony, aged about four and five, looking boldly and brightly into the camera. On her lap sits the baby Evelyn. The two older girls, aged eight and eleven, stand dutifully and demurely to one side. Finally there is two-year-old Jim, the weak member of the family, dubbed a 'late developer', lacking the physical and intellectual vigour of his brothers and sisters. A hand appears around his waist, partly propping him up. But whose hand can it be? Is it his mother's? No, hers are firmly around the baby – a rare moment of physical closeness, as it turned out. Can it be one of his older sisters? No, their hands are politely by their sides. It is in fact the hand of an invisible nurse, crouching behind the tableau vivant, the tiny and perfectionist 'Nanna Friend' who, with the nursemaids and governess, provided the child care in this fairly typical example of the English *haute bourgeoisie* on the threshold of the modern era.

Bowlby was notoriously reticent about his background and early family life. In the Adult Attachment Interview (see Chapter 6) he might have been rated as 'dismissive', giving the kind of response in which a person describes their childhood as 'perfectly all right' and refuses to be drawn further – a pattern that is strongly correlated with an insecure-avoidant pattern of attachment. But, as his book on Darwin testifies, Bowlby found the task of psychobiography worthwhile, making a strong case for considering Darwin's recurrent anxiety attacks as a manifestation of his inability to grieve loss, the pattern for which was set by his mother's death when he was eight. Whereas the main purpose of this book is an exposition of Attachment Theory, the aim of this chapter is to consider Bowlby's life and personality as a background to his ideas and to explore the relationship between them. The chapter is divided into three parts: the first is a chronological account of his life and career, touching on much that will be developed in subsequent chapters; the second consists of an assessment of his character, based on reminiscences of his family, friends and colleagues; and the third considers some of the major personal themes and preoccupations which inform Bowlby's work.

BOWLBY'S LIFE

Childhood and youth

Edward John Mostyn Bowlby was born on 26 February 1907. His father, whom he resembled in many ways, was Major-General Sir Anthony Bowlby (1855–1929), a successful London surgeon who had operated on one of Queen Victoria's sons, and was rewarded with a knighthood for his appointments as Royal Surgeon to King Edward VII and King George V, and a baronetcy on becoming President of the Royal College of Surgeons in 1920. John's grandfather, 'Thomas Bowlby of *The Times*', was a foreign correspondent for *The Times* who was murdered in Peking in 1861 during the Opium Wars when Sir Anthony was a small child. Anthony felt responsible for his mother, who did not remarry, and he only began to look for a wife after her death when he was forty. He was introduced by a mutual friend at a house party to the well-connected May Mostyn, then thirty, and pursued her (mainly on bicycles – they shared a love of the countryside and outdoor life) until they were married less than a year later. The train of May's wedding dress was embroidered with violets in deference to her dead mother-in-law as the statutory period of mourning had not yet passed. May was the eldest daughter of the Hon. Hugh Mostyn, who, despite grand origins (he was the youngest child, of ten, of Lord Mostyn of Mostyn in North Wales), was content to be a country parson in a remote Huntingdonshire village for all his working life. Bowlby's mother revered her father ('Grampy' in the Bowlby household) and invoked him as a model for all acceptable behaviour. She had little time for her mother, whom, when she was not having babies (May resented her numerous younger brothers and sisters and considered that first-borns were the only ones who really mattered) she described as 'always in the kitchen'.

John's parents were well into middle age by the time he was born: his mother forty, his father fifty-two. Each had had a special relationship with one parent and may have found the very different atmosphere of a large and vigorous family overwhelming. May had resented the demands of her younger brothers and sisters, and Sir Anthony was used to his bachelor ways. In any case, like many parents of their class and generation, they mainly entrusted the upbringing of their children to their numerous servants.

The children fell into three groups by age: the two older girls, Winnie and Marion, who were talented musicians from an early age; Tony and John, only 13 months apart; then Jim and Evelyn. Tony was their mother's clear favourite and could get away with almost anything. He later became a successful industrialist, and as eldest son inherited his father's title. John and Tony were close in age and temperament, good friends, but extremely rivalrous. They were treated as twins – put in the same clothes and in the same class at school. This meant that John was always making superhuman efforts to overtake his brother, who was equally as keen to retain his advantage. (Years later as a parent John would be renowned in the family for resisting his children's clamouring demands with the phrase, 'Now, don't bully me, don't *bully* me'.) They both teased and were concerned about their slightly backward brother Jim. John read delightedly in a newspaper about the miraculous effects of 'monkey gland extract' (presumably thyroxine), hoping that it would be the answer to their brother's difficulties, but of course they were disappointed. Jim struggled throughout his life, farmed not very successfully for a while and never married. It seemed contrary to the Bowlby spirit to have a family member who was not a 'success'. John's combination of competitiveness and his concern for disadvantaged and sick children may be not unrelated to his position between these two very different brothers. At fifteen he fought and defeated Tony when he discovered that he had destroyed a picture that Jim had made out of dried flowers. The two older sisters did not marry. According to John, 'the men they might have married were killed in the First World War' (Bowlby *et al*. 1986) – a curiously unpsychological explanation. Evelyn shared her brother's interest in psychoanalysis. She married the distinguished economist Professor Sir Henry Phelps Brown. Their daughter Juliet Hopkins is a child psychotherapist at the Tavistock Clinic.

Bowlby describes his family as a 'straightforward, fairly close – not all that close – but fairly close, professional class family living a pretty traditional lifestyle, with nurses of course' (Bowlby in Hunter 1991). Nanny Friend, whose hand appears in the photograph, joined the family when John's older sister Winnie was one month old and after the children were grown up stayed with Lady Bowlby until she died at the age of ninety-seven. She was highly intelligent and well read, a disciplinarian, whose firm regime would occasionally be lightened by her capacity for entrancing and elaborate story-telling and by reading Dickens to the children in the nursery.

Evelyn remembers life in their London house in Manchester Square as rather joyless – regulated by order, innumerable clocks, a sense of propriety, humourless governesses, and interminable slow processional walks in nearby Hyde Park. Tony, in contrast, describes a happy childhood. The reality perhaps was that they had two childhoods – one in the country and one in the town. Lady Bowlby boasted that she *never* worried about her children and, especially in London, left them mostly to their own devices. She would visit the nursery to receive a report from Nanny after breakfast every day, and the children, clean and brushed, would come down to the drawing room from 5 to 6 p. m. after tea, where she would read to them, especially from her beloved *Children of the New Forest*. May Mostyn had vowed that she would never marry a 'city man', and Sir Anthony loved fishing and shooting. Every spring and summer there was a ritual of family holidays. At Easter the children were dispatched to Margate with the nurses while Sir Anthony and Lady Bowlby went to Scotland for fishing. In July May would take the children to the New Forest, in those days a wild and idyllic place. For the whole of August and half of September the entire family decamped to Ayrshire in Scotland, travelling by train in a specially hired railway carriage. (Sir Anthony and Lady Bowlby never owned a car: he used a brougham for his rounds in London and after his death she would travel around Gloucestershire in pony and trap well into the 1950s.)

On holiday John's mother seemed to come alive and, as 'Grampy' had done with her, ensured that her children were well versed in nature and country sports. From her and 'Grampy' they learned to identify flowers, birds and butterflies, to fish, ride and shoot, and John and Tony became and remained passionate naturalists. Sir Anthony seemed to be a fairly remote and intimidating figure, especially in London, but he gave the children special animal nicknames: John was known as 'Jack' the jackal (other nursery nicknames for John were 'Bogey' and the prophetic 'Admiral Sir Nosey Know-all'); Tony was 'Gorilla'; Evelyn 'Cat'. They saw little of him during the week but would walk with him in family procession across Hyde Park most Sundays to church, when he would instruct and occasionally amuse them with his deep factual knowledge about the world and its ways.

The war came in 1914 when John was seven. John and his elder brother were immediately dispatched to boarding school, because of the supposed danger of air raids on London. John later maintained that this was just an excuse, being merely the traditional first step in the time-honoured barbarism required to produce English gentlemen. The English preparatory school system took its toll: John was beaten for defining a 'cape' in a geography lesson as a cloak rather than a promontory, but, a resilient and self-assured little boy, he flourished. Sir Anthony was away in France as a surgeon-general for most of the war. When the war came to an end, John went as naval cadet to Dartmouth where he learned to sail, and gained a discipline and organisation which lasted a lifetime. Tony was destined to follow in his father's footsteps and become a surgeon, but he decided against this in his teens, feeling that it would mean 'failure' since he could never equal his father's eminence. This left the way clear for John to go into medicine, who, despite having passed out top in his Dartmouth exams, was already dissatisfied with the narrow intellectual horizons and rigidity of the Navy (as he was to become two decades later with the British Psycho-Analytical Society), as well as suffering badly from seasickness! Somewhat to John's surprise, Sir Anthony agreed to buy him out. Although not driven by a strong vocational pull, John felt that a medical career would be least unacceptable to his father and, together with a close Dartmouth friend, applied to Cambridge and duly entered Trinity college as a medical student in 1925. His intellectual distinction was already in evidence at university where he won several prizes and gained a first class degree in pre-clinical sciences and psychology.

Already mature and independent-minded, with an 'inner calm' (Phelps Brown 1992) that was to stand him good stead throughout his life, John's next move proved decisive. Rather than going straight on to London to study clinical medicine, which would have been the conventional thing to do, he got a job instead in a progressive school for maladjusted children, an offshoot of A. S. Neill's Summerhill. His father, who would undoubtedly have opposed such a move, had, in John's words 'fortunately' already died when John was twenty-one, so he was free to chart his own course. At the school he had two sets of experiences which were to influence the whole course of his professional life. The first was the encounter with disturbed children, with whom he found he could communicate, and whose difficulties seemed to be related to their unhappy and disrupted childhood. Like one of Lorenz's (1952) greylag geese, who were to play such an important part in the development of Attachment Theory, one boy followed Bowlby round wherever he went:

> There I had known an adolescent boy who had been thrown out of a public school for repeated stealing. Although socially conforming he made no friends and seemed emotionally isolated – from adults and peers alike. Those in charge attributed his condition to his never having been cared for during his early years by any one motherly person, a result of his illegitimate birth. Thus I was alerted to a possible connection between prolonged deprivation and the development of a personality apparently incapable of making affectional bonds and, because immune to praise and blame, prone to repeated delinquencies.
>
> (Bowlby 1981a)

The second seminal encounter at the school was with another man working there, John Alford, who had had some personal therapy, and who advised John to go to London to train as a psychoanalyst.

Psychoanalytical training

In the autumn of 1929, aged twenty-two, John came to London, to start his medical studies. He found these so tedious and wearisome that he started and managed 'Bogey's Bar', a sandwich bar patronised by his friends. While at University College Hospital (which was, and has remained, a home for would-be psychoanalysts wanting to acquire a medical degree) he entered the Institute of Psycho-Analysis, going into analysis with Mrs Riviere, a close friend and associate of Melanie Klein. His intention was to become a child psychiatrist, a profession which was then just emerging. After medical qualification in 1933, he went to the Maudsley to train in adult psychiatry, and then was appointed in 1936 to the London Child Guidance Clinic, where he worked until he became an Army psychiatrist in 1940.

The 1930s were a time of intellectual ferment. Progressive thought centred on Freud and Marx. Bettelheim vividly captures the atmosphere of debate:

> In order to create the good society, was it of first importance to change society radically enough for all persons to achieve full self-realisation? In this case psychoanalysis could be discarded, with the possible exception of a few deranged persons. Or was this the wrong approach, and could persons who had achieved full personal liberation and integration by being psychoanalysed create such a good society? In the latter case the correct thing was to forget for the time being any social or economic revolution and to concentrate instead on pushing psychoanalysis; the hope was that once the majority of men had profited from its inner liberation they would almost automatically create the good society for themselves and all others.
>
> (Bettelheim 1960)

Although by nature irreverent and at times iconoclastic, Bowlby tempered his rebelliousness with a belief in science and the need for evidence to back up ideas. He shared a house with his friend the Labour politician and academic Evan Durbin, who challenged his newly acquired psychoanalytic ideas – as did Aubrey Lewis at the Maudsley. While he believed in the practical efficacy of psychoanalysis, he was always sceptical about its theoretical basis. He came into conflict with his first psychoanalytical supervisor, 'a rather prim old maid . . . we never seemed to be on the same wavelength' (Bowlby 1991), but got on very well with his next, Ella Sharpe, who supported Anna Freud against Klein in the 'Controversial Discussions', 'a warm hearted middle-aged woman who had a good understanding of human nature and a sense of humour' (Bowlby 1991). He qualified as an analyst in 1937, and immediately started training in child analysis with Mrs Klein as his supervisor. Here too there was conflict, especially when Bowlby felt that she paid insufficient attention to the part played by the environment in causing his patient's disturbance – in this case a hyperactive little boy of three whose mother was having a breakdown and had been admitted to mental hospital.

Meanwhile, Bowlby was beginning to develop his own ideas, based mainly on his experience at the Child Guidance Clinic. There he worked with two analytically orientated social workers who introduced him to the idea of the transgenerational transmission of neurosis in which unresolved problems from a parent's own childhood can play a large part in causing and perpetuating the problems of their children.

> I was particularly struck by two cases, one of sibling rivalry in which the mother had herself been intensely jealous of her sister, and the other in which a father was deeply troubled by his seven-year-old son's masturbation and had dipped him under a cold tap whenever he found him touching his genitals, and who, it transpired, had himself fought an unsuccessful battle against masturbation all his life.
>
> (Bowlby 1977)

With his stress on the role of the environment in causing psychological difficulty, Bowlby was aligned with a group of British psychiatrists who, while influenced by Freud and sympathetic to the analytic cause, also maintained some distance from it. These included David Eder, a left-wing intellectual associated with the Bloomsbury Group; Bernard Hart, psychiatrist at University College Hospital, whose influential *Psychology of Insanity* Bowlby would certainly have read; W. H. Rivers, famous as an anthropologist as well as psychiatrist, who had applied Freud's ideas to victims of shell-shock in the First World War and who felt that the self-preservative instinct was as important as Freud's sexuality; and, above all, Ian Suttie, whose *Origins of Love and Hate* proposed a primary bond between mother and child, unrelated to infantile sexuality (Heard 1986; Pines 1991; Newcombe and

Lerner 1982), an idea which, as we shall see in Chapter 4, Bowlby was to develop and put at the heart of Attachment Theory.

In order to qualify as a full member with voting rights in the analytic society Bowlby had to read a paper. Many of his later ideas are to be found in embryonic form in 'The influence of the environment in the development of neuroses and neurotic character', which was published in the *International Journal of Psycho-Analysis* in 1940. It consists of a description of cases treated in the Child Guidance Clinic. He emphasises the scientific value of such one-weekly 'clinic cases' to complement more intensive analytic work. He boldly puts forward a 'general theory of the genesis of neurosis', in which environmental factors in the early years of a child's life are causative, especially separation from the mother through death or 'broken home'. He explicitly challenges the Kleinian view – actually something of a caricature, a product of the polarisation within the Society at that time, since Kleinians have never entirely denied the importance of the environment – that childhood phantasy is unrelated to actual experience: 'Much has been written about the introjection of phantastically severe parents, an imaginary severity being itself the product of projection. Less perhaps has been written recently about the introjection of the parents' real characters' (Bowlby 1940a). He cautions against unnecessary separation of children from parents – 'if a child must be in hospital the mother should be encouraged to visit daily' – and insists that

> If it became a tradition that small children were never subjected to complete or prolonged separation from their parents in the same way that regular sleep and orange juice have become nursery traditions, I believe that many cases of neurotic character development would be avoided.
>
> (Bowlby 1940a)

He advocates working with the mothers of disturbed children so as to elucidate their own childhood difficulties which are interfering with their role as parents, and thereby helping them to feel less guilty. A second paper, 'Forty-four juvenile thieves, their characters and home life' (which led to Bowlby's wartime nickname of Ali Bowlby and his Forty Thieves), was also based on his work in the Child Guidance Clinic and continues the same ideas in a more systematic way. His capacity for coining a telling phrase emerges in his notion of the 'affectionless psychopath' –

a juvenile thief for whom the lack of good and continuous childhood care has created in him (it almost always is a him) an
absence of concern for others.

In this early work Bowlby shows a strong reforming drive: he
saw psychotherapy as preventative medicine which would help to
change not just individuals but also society. But he would not
have accepted Bettelheim's view that one had to choose between
Marx or Freud, nor was he prepared to swallow either whole.
His attitude towards extremism, whether Kleinian or communist,
might be compared with A. S. Neill's account of a wedding he
had attended:

> Filled with followers of Melanie Klein . . . they can't laugh;
> Melanie has evidently shown them humour is a complex which
> no normal man should have. To my asking what Klein was
> doing to prevent complexes there was a silence. I said: you
> can't analyse humanity but you can attempt to get a humanity
> that won't need analysis. No answer. Gott, they were a dull
> crowd. . . . Rather like talking to communists with a blank
> curtain that you could not penetrate.
>
> (Grosskurth 1986)

Several of John's friends of both sexes were acquired through his
more sociable older brother. Tony shared a 'staircase' at Oxford
with Evan Durbin, later to become a minister in the post-war
Attlee labour administration. Similar in physique, intelligence
and temperament, he and John soon struck up a close friendship,
based on shared intellectual interests and a love of walking (it
was hard to keep up with them as they strode rapidly through
the Cotswolds, deep in conversation). They collaborated in their
book *Personal Aggressiveness and War* (Durbin and Bowlby
1938). In Bowlby's contribution we see again later talents and
themes prefigured. He introduces psychoanalytic ideas in a common-sense (if slightly old-fashioned) way: in exemplifying the
concept of unconscious aggression he ways, 'It is impossible to
criticise some maids without paying for it in breakages. Plates
"come apart in my hands" far more frequently after the maid
has been reprimanded than when she has been praised' (Durbin
and Bowlby 1938). He surveys the literature on aggression in
apes and other higher mammals drawing parallels with human
behaviour, just as he was to do in the 1950s when he applied
ethological ideas to mother–infant behaviour. He also subjects

Marxist ideas about war to the same critical scrutiny with which he had approached psychoanalysis as an ideology, pointing out the dangers of any global theory of human behaviour.

Bowlby's friendship with Durbin continued until the latter's untimely death by drowning while on holiday in Cornwall in the late 1940s. Bowlby, who was on holiday nearby, was called in to help and in his typically practical way immediately organised with Durbin's close parliamentary colleagues a trust fund which supported the Durbin children through their education. Durbin's death was the most overwhelming loss of John's life, and certainly influenced his interest in the themes of grief and loss which were to figure so centrally in his work.

The war years

Bowlby volunteered in 1940 at the age of thirty-three, but was not called up and joined instead a group of Army psychiatrists whose main job was, by using statistical and psychotherapeutic methods, to put officer selection on a scientific footing – to put, as it was said, the 'chi' into psychiatry. His organisational and intellectual qualities soon showed themselves and he worked closely with members of the 'invisible college' (Pines 1991) of psychoanalytic soldiers like Wilfred Bion, Eric Trist and Jock Sutherland on the selection boards.

By 1944 the War Office had established a Research and Training Unit in Hampstead, of which Bowlby was a member. This enabled him to continue active participation in the affairs of the Psychoanalytic Society, riven at that time by factional fighting between the Kleinian and Freudian groups. Emerging from the 'Controversial Discussions' these differences were contained by the 'gentlemen's agreement' between the two ladies, Anna Freud and Melanie Klein. This established two training streams: 'A', the Freudians, and 'B', which comprised the Kleinians and 'Independents' (who later split off as a separate 'middle group' of which Bowlby was a member). The President of the Society, Sylvia Payne, herself an Independent, proposed Bowlby as Training Secretary in 1944, and despite not being a Training Analyst, and against strong opposition from Melanie Klein, his balance and organisational ability were recognised, and he was duly elected. Bowlby's passionate and uncompromising feelings were much in evidence at meetings of the Psycho-Analytic Society during that period. As well as the Klein–Freud split there was a more general division about the aims and methods of the Society. Under Jones's and later Glover's leadership the Society had adopted something of the features of a secret cell: purist, esoteric, autocratically led, unwilling to sully itself with anything but the 'pure gold' of psychoanalysis, and refusing to have anything to do with the analytic fellow travellers represented by the Tavistock Clinic, who included several Christian psychiatrists like J. R. Rees and Suttie, and which was referred to contemptuously by the psychoanalysts as the 'parson's clinic' (Pines 1991). All this was anathema to Bowlby, who believed in democratic methods and was appalled by what he saw as the Society's indifference towards the emergence of a National Health Service which was clearly going to be established after the war. He advocated full participation in the discussions between the Government and the medical profession:

> We find ourselves in a rapidly changing world and yet, as a Society, we have done nothing, I repeat nothing, to meet these changes, to influence them or to adapt to them. That is not the reaction of a living organism but a moribund one. If our Society died of inertia it would only have met the fate it had invited.
>
> (King and Steiner 1990)

Bowlby and the progressives carried the day, and Bowlby was delegated as a member of the Government's Mental Health Standing Committee, where he proceeded to have the same effect on the civil servants as he did on the older members of the Society, and he was described in a Whitehall report as 'a "live" member, with embarrassing enthusiasm for his own speciality. An advanced theorist who does not always give weight to practical considerations' (Webster 1991).

Family life

Tony Bowlby married young: a beautiful musician and actress whom he met through his sisters who were at the Royal Academy of Music. John had had several tempestuous liaisons, but as his analysis progressed and he approached his thirties, began to wish to settle down. On holiday in the New Forest he encountered the Longstaffs, a family of seven attractive daughters living with their pipe-smoking mother whose father, Dr Longstaff, the famous alpinist, had abandoned her for a younger woman. Ursula, the third daughter, intelligent and beautiful but more diffident than her older sisters, attracted his interest. On a shooting holiday in Ireland she and John fell for each other. They were married in 1938. John, like his father, was some ten years older than his bride. Ursula proved a devoted and loyal companion. Although highly intelligent and literate, she had no knowledge of psychology, and claims not to have read any of his books except the biography of Darwin on which she collaborated extensively. She also helped to supply the quotations for the chapter headings in the 'trilogy'.

The Bowlbys had four children, the day-to-day care of whom John left almost entirely to Ursula. The family was afflicted by dyslexia, a condition unrecognised at the time, and his children's academic difficulties were a source of some sorrow and frustration to their father, although they were fully compensated by their practical and technical abilities. John had had little experience of close parent–child relationships, and found fatherhood a difficult role. He was, by contrast, in his daughter Mary's words, a 'brilliant grandfather' ('Grampy's' good influence making itself felt again) – tolerant, funny and adoring. John and Ursula's grandson, Ben, in the Bowlby tradition of independence and originality, received first-class honours in engineering for designing and building his own racing car – an 'external working model' (see Chapter 4). John, a slightly remote father, followed his own father's tradition of hard work and long holidays, so much so that his eldest son asked, around the age of seven, 'Is Daddy a burglar? He always comes home after dark and never talks about his work!' Family holidays were in Scotland, and a house was first rented and then bought on Skye where John, Ursula and the children could enjoy the walking, boating, bird-watching, shooting and fishing in beautiful and remote surroundings that repeated the pattern of his own childhood.

The Bowlbys and the Durbins had shared a house in York Terrace (where Adrian and Karen Stevens and Ernest Jones had their consulting rooms). This pattern was continued after the war when John's democratic ideas and recognition of the benefits of an extended network of friends and family when bringing up small children were realised, when he and Ursula and their growing family shared a large house in Hampstead with the Sutherlands (Jock Sutherland was soon to become director of the Tavistock Clinic) and with a young psychologist, later to become Mrs Mattie Harris, who became organising tutor of the child psychotherapy training programme at the Tavistock (Sutherland 1991).

The post-war years: the Tavistock Clinic

Immediately after the war the 'invisible college' of Army psychoanalysts re-grouped themselves around the Tavistock Clinic, hitherto ruled out of bounds by the autocratic Jones. An election was held and, although neither had previously worked there, Jock Sutherland was elected Director, with Bowlby as Deputy, given the specific task of developing a Department for Children.

John went about this with his usual energy, efficiency and determination. He established a clinical service, treating patients, seeing mothers and children together, spending one day a week in a well-baby clinic, supervising, and chairing case conferences. Together with Esther Bick he set up the child psychotherapy training and continued to support it, even when its Kleinian orientation began to diverge sharply from his own views.

About a third of his week was devoted to clinical and administrative duties. The rest was for research. One of John's unsung qualities was his ability to raise research funds. On the basis of his pre-war experiences in the Child Guidance Clinic, he had decided to make a systematic study of the effects of separation on the personality development of young children. He recruited James Robertson, a conscientious objector in the war who had worked as a boilerman in Anna Freud's Hampstead residential children's nursery, and who later became an analyst and film-maker. Mary Ainsworth, later to become the co-founder of Attachment Theory, also joined the team, as did Mary Boston. The outcome of Bowlby's collaboration with Robertson was the famous film *A Two-year-old Goes to Hospital*, which showed the intense distress of a small child separated from her mother, made with a hand-held cine-camera without artificial light, almost impossible to watch dry-eyed, and which did so much to liberalise hospital visiting rules. As mentioned in the previous chapter, the film met with a mixed reception when shown to the Psycho-Analytical Society, the Kleinians being particularly unimpressed, a foretaste of the response Bowlby was to meet when he presented his breakthrough papers on Attachment Theory a few years later.

Bowlby's research interests, together with his Forty-four Thieves paper, made him an obvious choice when the World Health Organisation was looking for an expert to prepare a report on the mental health of homeless children. Bowlby travelled widely in Europe and the United States, meeting the leading figures in child development, and combined their views with his own in a review of the world literature, *Maternal Care and Mental Health* (Bowlby 1951). This was published in a popular edition as *Child Care and the Growth of Love* (Bowlby 1953), which became an instant best-seller, selling 450,000 in the English edition alone, and was translated into ten different languages.

Bowlby's reputation was by now secure and he was able to follow his innovative instincts without anxiety. He was keen to break down the ivory towerism of the Tavistock and to foster links with local health visitors, GPs and social workers. His efforts to establish liaison were blocked until the Minister of Health issued a directive asking the London County Council to pay more attention to mental health. The Chief Medical Officer of the LCC invited Bowlby to give a lecture on the subject. He refused, saying that mental health could not be properly taught by didactic methods, but offering to join a study group if one were set up. A week later he received a message from the Chief Medical Officer: 'Your "study group" is ready. When would you like to start?' (Mackenzie 1991).

Ainsworth (1982) believes that the idea of attachment came to Bowlby 'in a flash' when in 1952 he heard about and then read Lorenz's and Tinbergen's work in ethology, having been lent an advance copy of *King Solomon's Ring* by Julian Huxley. The ethological approach provided the scientific grounding that Bowlby believed was needed to update psychoanalytic theory. Seen psychobiographically, Attachment Theory might be seen as a return by Bowlby to the values of his mother which he had rejected when he became a psychoanalyst. Disappointed with his mother's self-preoccupations and favouritism, he turned to the many mothers of psychoanalysis – Klein, Riviere, Payne. But these too, partly through their own limitations, partly because they contained his hostile projections, disappointed in their turn. By marrying the biology of ethology with Freudian theory, he managed to reconcile the discordant elements in his personality:

his country-loving mother with her respect for nature, and the intimidating urban medical father whose success and intelligence were inspirational but whose Gradgrindian devotion to fact and duty dominated his life. Bowlby soon organised regular attachment seminars which were attended by a talented and eclectic group including the ethologist Robert Hinde and, for a time, R. D. Laing. A year as a fellow at the Centre for Behavioural Sciences in Stanford, California, gave him an opportunity to re-read Freud and to prepare the breakthrough papers of the late 1950s, starting with 'The nature of the child's tie to his mother' (Bowlby 1958).

Bowlby remained active in the Psycho-Analytical Society in the post-war years. He was Deputy President to Donald Winnicott between 1956 and 1961, responsible for 'everything administrative' (Bowlby 1991). He set up and chaired the Research Committee, and initiated several other committees, including the Public Relations Committee; a committee to look at indemnity insurance for non-medical members (typical of Bowlby to be alert to the possible hazards to members uncushioned by the secure base of medicine); and the Curriculum Committee (set up to prevent trainings becoming interminable – another typically practical move).

While the society was happy to benefit from his organisational skills, Bowlby's theoretical papers, presented between 1957 and 1959, excited considerable discussion but little enthusiasm, and were received by the Kleinians with outright hostility. Typical comments were: from Guntrip, 'I think it is very good for an eminent psychoanalyst to have gone thoroughly into the relation of ethology to psychoanalysis, but my impression is that he succeeds in using it to explain everything in human behaviour except what is of vital importance for psychoanalysis' – (1962, letter to Marjorie Brierley, in Archives, Institute of Psychoanalysis); from Winnicott, although generally friendly and sympathetic to Bowlby's contribution (Malan 1991), 'I can't quite make out why it is that Bowlby's papers are building up in me a kind of revulsion although in fact he has been scrupulously fair to me in my writings'; and, from an anonymous analyst, 'Bowlby? Give me Barabbas' (Grosskurth 1986). The analysts found his patrician manner and 'orotund' (Rycroft 1992) delivery offputting, although these may well have been exaggerated in the intimidating atmosphere of the Psycho-Analytical Society at the time. Bowlby had an impish quality and a capacity for amusing tomfoolery which was clearly not evident to the analysts. Whether Bowlby did indeed betray psychoanalysis, or breathed new life into it, will form much of the discussion in subsequent chapters.

The trilogy

Partly no doubt because of his hostile reception, and partly because of his growing reputation elsewhere, Bowlby spent little time in the Psycho-Analytical Society after the mid–1960s although, unlike other distinguished dissidents such as Rycroft and Meltzer, he did not discontinue his membership. While continuing his clinical role at the Tavistock, in 1963 he became a part-time member of the Medical Research Council, which enabled him to devote yet more time to writing. The years 1964 to 1979 were devoted to his monumental trilogy *Attachment* (1969b), *Separation* (1973a), and *Loss* (1980). These have also been best-sellers, with the first volume selling well over 100,000, the second 75,000, and the third 45,000 (Bowlby *et al.* 1986). Colin Murray Parkes and Dorothy Heard joined him at the Tavistock in the 1960s. Like Bowlby, Parkes had been struck by the relevance of Darwin's ideas about grief to abnormal mourning, and a fruitful partnership developed (Parkes 1964, 1971, 1975). Bowlby was much in demand as a lecturer, especially in the United States where, through the work of Ainsworth (1969), Attachment Theory was exciting increasing interest.

Bowlby held numerous important positions and consultancies, and received many honours, including the CBE, Honorary Doctorates at Cambridge and Leicester, Honorary Fellowships of the Royal Society of Medicine and College of Psychiatrists, Fellowship of the British Academy, and several Distinguished Scientist awards and medals in the United States, including that of the American Psychological Association. As befits an innovator and original thinker, he was probably slightly more honoured abroad than at home, and, unlike his follower, Michael Rutter, neither received a knighthood nor became an FRS, both of which many thought were his due (Kraemer 1991). He did, however, do 'better' than his lifelong friend and rival, his brother Tony.

He retired from the NHS and the MRC in 1972, but remained at the Tavistock Clinic, dividing his time between London and his beloved Skye. He continued to encourage students and to receive many foreign visitors. During 1980 he was Freud Memorial Professor of Psychoanalysis at University College London, a post which gave him great satisfaction. His lectures from there and his trips abroad were collected in *The Making and Breaking of Affectional Bonds* (1979c) and *A Secure Base* (1988a). Mentally and physically active as ever, he began an entirely new project in his seventies, a psychobiography of Darwin (Bowlby 1990), which was published a few months before his death, and was well reviewed.

His eightieth birthday was celebrated in London with a conference with many distinguished speakers from around the world. The affection he inspired was palpable, as, garlanded with flowers, he embraced his many friends and colleagues to loud claps and cheers. A few weeks later he collapsed unconscious with a cardiac arrhythmia, but made a complete recovery, and was able to finish the Darwin biography. Three years later he suffered a stroke, while in Skye with his family, who had gathered as they did every year for the Skye Ball, where John had been a skilled exponent of Scottish reels. He died a few days later on 2 September 1990, and was buried at Trumpan on the Waternish peninsula, a hillside graveyard overlooking the cliffs of Waternish and the Ardmore peninsula. It was a favourite spot, wild and remote, from which John, with his great feeling for nature, often used to walk, and he had asked to be buried there. He had a traditional Skye funeral with three 'lifts' from the hearse to the grave. His friend Hyla Holden, a former Tavistock colleague, one of the bearers, concludes: 'his funeral and burial were in keeping with the straight-forward and loving simplicity which lay behind his formidable intellect' (Trowell 1991). His constancy and steadfastness of purpose are celebrated in the inscription on the headstone of pale grey Aberdeen granite, which reads: 'To be a pilgrim'.

BOWLBY THE MAN

What was John Bowlby like? In his work his greatest achievement was his bringing together of psychoanalysis and, via ethology, evolutionary biology. A similar capacity to reconcile divergent elements is to be found in his personality which, although remarkably coherent and consistent, contained many contradictory aspects: reserved, yet capable of inspiring great affection; quintessentially 'English' and yet thoroughly cosmopolitan in outlook; conventional in manner yet revolutionary in spirit; equally at home with the sophistication of Hampstead and in the wilds of Skye; outstandingly intelligent and yet not in a conventional sense an intellectual; a man of action who devoted his life to the inner world; determined in his convictions and yet without overt aggression; an explorer of the psyche who mistrusted the purely subjective; someone who believed passionately in the importance of expressing emotion, whose own feelings were an enigma; an *enfant terrible* who was always slightly formal.

It is hard to get an impression of Bowlby as a therapist because personal clinical material is so sparse in his writings. He is fierce in his opposition to rigid and punitive methods of child-rearing, detests the way in which children are deprived of love and affection in the name of not 'spoiling' them, and insists on the enduring nature of dependency which he refuses to see as a childlike quality to be outgrown, but rather an essential aspect of human nature. One guesses that he had first-hand experience of the child-rearing philosophy he rejects so vigorously. He consistently advocates flexibility and acceptance:

> An immense amount of friction and anger in small children and loss of temper on the part of their parents can be avoided by such simple procedures as presenting a legitimate plaything before we intervene to remove his mother's best china, or coaxing him to bed by tactful humouring instead of demanding prompt obedience, or by permitting him to select his own diet and eat it in his own way, including, if he likes it, having a feeding bottle until he is two years of age or over. The amount of fuss and irritation which comes from expecting small children to conform to our own ideas of what, how, and when they eat is ridiculous and tragic.
>
> (Bowlby 1979c)

The dangers of suppressing feelings is repeatedly emphasised by Bowlby:

> a main reason why some find expressing grief extremely difficult is that the family in which they have been brought up, and with which they still mix, is one in which the attachment behaviour of the child is regarded unsympathetically as something to be grown out of as soon as possible . . . crying and

other protests over separation are apt to be dubbed as babyish, and anger and jealousy as reprehensible.

(Bowlby 1979c)

Bowlby describes one such patient:

I well remember how a silent inhibited girl in her early twenties given to unpredictable moods and hysterical outbursts at home responded to my comment 'it seems to be as though your mother never really loved you' (she was the second daughter, to be followed in quick succession by two much wanted sons). In a flood of tears she confirmed my view by quoting, verbatim, remarks made by her mother from childhood to the present day, and [describing] the despair, jealousy, and rage her mother's treatment roused in her.

(Bowlby 1979)

Bowlby himself came from a family in which there were two daughters, to be followed in quick succession by two much wanted sons, with a mother whose love her children may well have doubted (with the possible exception of Tony), so he probably knew what he was talking about. Even if he did not have a particularly loving mother, Bowlby had learned enough from her, and perhaps from his much-loved nursemaid Minnie who left when he was no more than four, to know what it takes to be one. In adult life he relied greatly on his wife Ursula's intuition and sensitivity. In a posthumously published self-portrait Bowlby modestly asserts:

I am not strong on intuition. Instead, I tend to apply such theories as I hold in an effort to understand the patient's problems. This works well when the theories are applicable but can be a big handicap when they are not. Perhaps my saving graces have been that I am a good listener and not too dogmatic about theory. As a result several of my patients have succeeded in teaching me a great deal I did not know. . . . I often shudder to think how inept I have been as a therapist and how I have ignored or misunderstood material a patient has presented. Clearly, the best therapy is done by a therapist who is naturally intuitive and also guided by the appropriate theory. Fortunately, nowadays I meet many such people in clinical seminars, and among supervisees.

(Bowlby 1991)

One such was Victoria Hamilton, who confirms Bowlby's listening skills, painting a vivid portrait:

a very unassuming person who at the same time displayed an unusual acuity. . . . My most constant image of John Bowlby . . . is of him sitting back in a chair, his legs crossed indicating an expression of relaxed concentration, and a very alert face. He had penetrating but responsive eyes, beneath raised eyebrows which expressed both interest and a slight air of surprise and expectation . . . a remarkable ability to listen to the thoughts and beliefs of others, combined with a capacity for objectivity and a rare facility with the English language. He could step back from an idea and reformulate it in a succinct articulate way. . . . Despite his somewhat military manner, expressed in a certain abruptness and stiffness very far from 'small talk', he was perfectly able to 'take turns', the essential ingredient of conversation.

(Hamilton 1991)

A lifelong friend, Jock Sutherland (1991), describes his first encounter with John during the war, in which he appeared 'somewhat formal and even aloof'. Sutherland and Eric Trist, another of John's half-century friends, speculated that Bowlby's description of the 'affectionless character' was based on empathic understanding (rather as Freud's discovery of the Oedipus complex was based on his own rivalry with his father):

We speculated that John's own early experience must have included a degree, if not of actual deprivation, of some inhibition of his readiness to express emotional affection . . . so that he developed in some measure a protective shell of not showing his feelings as readily as many people do. . . . John's slightly formal and even detached manner struck many people on first knowing him Eric Trist and I were always convinced he was the possessor of a deep and powerful fund of affection – the source of his intensely caring concern for those who worked with him.

(Sutherland 1991)

John Byng-Hall, another Tavistock colleague, sees Bowlby as a perfect embodiment of his idea of the secure base, capable of holding together family therapists and child psychotherapists despite their very different philosophies, alert to real dangers faced by patients and therapists, and above all 'very reliable. I have images of him, even last winter [i.e. in his eighty-second year], shaking the rain off his green mackintosh and hat as he arrived on time for some evening meeting; while others sent their apologies' (Byng-Hall 1991).

Those clocks that Bowlby had grown up with did have their uses.

SPRINGS OF ACTION AND THOUGHT

It seems to be a characteristic of many outstanding men and women that they retain the freshness and innocence of childhood, however clothed it is with responsibility and the burdens of maturity. This was certainly true of Bowlby's great hero, Darwin (Bowlby 1990), with whom he strongly identified, and had much in common, although he would have been embarrassed by the comparison. Like Darwin, Bowlby had a boyhood love of outdoor sports, of the countryside and of exploration, with a keenness of intellect that was not precociously evident. Like Darwin, Bowlby had a strong and successful medical father; both seem to have aroused in their sons a rebelliousness hedged about with caution. Both were younger sons, with clever and rather overshadowing older brothers and sisters. Darwin's mother died when he was eight; Bowlby's was (at least in her London life) remote and self-centered. Both lived in times of social turmoil and had a strongly held but restrained sense of social justice, and of the responsibilities of the fortunate towards the disadvantaged, in the best Whig tradition. They both believed passionately in the power of reason to illuminate both the natural and social world. Bowlby admired Darwin's openness to all available evidence, as shown by the long hours he spent in smoke-filled public houses discussing breeding methods with pigeon fanciers in search of support for his theory of natural selection. Bowlby, too, mixed with mothers in nurseries and baby clinics, ever observant of patterns of attachment. Both showed generosity towards their supporters, and lacked rancour towards their detractors. Finally, it might be said of their theories that they have the quality of immediacy and 'obviousness' – of which it might be said, 'Why on earth did no one think of that before?' In retrospect it seems obvious that species have evolved by natural selection, that people are attached to one another and suffer when they separate – but it took child-like simplicity of vision combined with mature determination and attention to detail to root out the obvious and to create for it a secure theoretical base.

Bowlby describes an early boyhood memory of Darwin's concerning showing off:

> He recalls 'thinking that people were admiring me, in one instance for perseverance, and another for boldness in climbing a low tree, and what is odder, a consciousness, as if instinctive, that I was vain, and a contempt for myself'. This reference to self-contempt for being vain thus early in his life is of much significance, since we find it persisting as a major feature of his character into his final years.
>
> (Bowlby 1990)

Here we see Bowlby's extreme sensitivity to the uncertainties, miseries and vulnerability of childhood, to the gulf between a child's fragile self-esteem and a potentially hostile or indifferent world. Bowlby cared intensely about the mental pain of children, and his life's work was directed towards trying to prevent, remove and alleviate it. Behind the disturbed child's tough, 'affectionless' carapace Bowlby had a sixth sense for the sadness and sense of betrayal. Apparently bolder than Darwin, Bowlby kept his vulnerability well hidden. But in his rebelliousness we see perhaps the protest of the child who has been hurt and neglected. In his application and indefatigability we find the attempt to make good the unthinking damage the adult world so often does to children.

Many of Bowlby's metaphors were medical. Famously, 'mother-love is as important for mental health as are vitamins and proteins for physical health' (Bowlby 1953); 'deprived children . . . are a source of social infection as real and serious as are carriers of diphtheria and typhoid' (Bowlby 1953); 'the basic fact that people really do want to live happily together . . . gives confidence [to the family therapist], much as a knowledge of the miraculous healing powers of the body gives confidence to the surgeon' (Bowlby 1948).

Bowlby's ideas were forged in the era of two world wars. Millions died in the first war. The enormity of the loss went unmourned by society in the triumphalism of Versailles and the manic activity of the twenties. The second war saw the horror of the Holocaust, countless more deaths, and the disruption of the lives of children throughout Europe. As early as the 1930s,

Bowlby saw loss and separation as the key issues for psychotherapy and psychiatry. It was the men – the fathers, sons,
brothers, husbands, lovers – who died; it was a men's world that
went to war. And yet in Bowlby's work men are conspicuous by
their absence. It is *maternal* deprivation that made Bowlby's
name. Bowlby's strong identification with his much-absent father
comes through in his medical imagery, but he does not emerge
as a live figure in the family drama as depicted by Bowlby, or
indeed by the other outstanding analysts of his generation, Klein
and Winnicott. Bowlby's contribution, and that of his contempor-
aries, has been to rehabilitate the female principle, the missing
mother who until then was absent from social and psychoanalytic
discourse (Freud's main preoccupation was with fathers and their
children). In his concept of maternal deprivation it is as though
Bowlby was simultaneously reproving and idealising his neglectful
mother. Unlike Winnicott he seems uncertain of his intuitive
feminine side, just as he may have mistrusted his mother with
her fickle and uneven affections. In his theories of motherhood
it is as though Bowlby is *enacting* the male role – the guardian
of evidence and objectivity – without really examining it. His
father is there in the metaphors but not at the meal table. Bowlby's maleness is in the counter-transferential blind spot through
which he sees mother and child, but not himself seeing them –
a typical example of the modern 'patriarchal but father-absent'
family (Leupnitz 1988). To consider these and other issues we
must now turn to the topic for which Bowlby is best known, that
misnamed miscreant, maternal deprivation.

Chapter 3

Maternal deprivation

[The] evidence is now such that it leaves no room for doubt . . . that the prolonged deprivation of a young child of maternal care may have grave and far reaching effects on his character and so on the whole of his future life. It is a proposition exactly similar in form to those regarding the evil aftereffects of German measles before birth or deprivation of vitamin D in infancy.

(Bowlby 1953)

Statements implying that children who experience institutionalisation and similar forms of privation in early life *commonly* develop psychopathic or affectionless characters are incorrect.

(Bowlby, Ainsworth, Boston and Rosenbluth 1956)

Psychotherapy can be seen as a branch of social psychiatry, using psychological methods to reverse or mitigate the damaging effects of environmental failure. This immediately raises two questions. First, given that the damage is already done, how can mere talk undo past miseries? Second, given that many people survive unhappy childhoods without developing psychiatric disorder, are therapists justified in attributing present difficulty to previous trauma? The two quotations from Bowlby above illustrate the transition between his career as a clinician and psychoanalyst to that of a researcher and theorist. The therapist, faced with the patient in front of him, naturally attributes his difficulties to the history of environmental failures he recounts. The researcher, with a control group and a sense of a population at risk rather than just one individual, is forced to more cautious conclusions.

The answer to both questions, in brief, lies in the fact that environmental failure is not merely impressed on a passive organism, but is *experienced* and given meaning by the afflicted individual. Psychotherapy is concerned with the way that stress is mediated psychologically – with why this person succumbs while others survive – and, by altering psychological responsiveness and the attribution of meanings, to change not the facts of history, but their context and significance. In this chapter I shall approach these issues through a discussion of 'maternal deprivation', and its corollary, 'that maternal care in infancy and early childhood is essential for mental health' (Bowlby 1952). However self-evident it may seem to us now – and this is largely the result of Bowlby's work – the idea of maternal deprivation as a cause of mental illness was in its day a revolutionary concept which became a paradigm (Kuhn 1962), setting the terms of debate and research in social psychiatry for the ensuing forty years.

CHILD CARE AND THE GROWTH OF LOVE

As Rutter (1981) points out, the phrase 'maternal deprivation', the central concept of Bowlby's WHO report *Maternal Care and Mental Health*, is a misnomer. His report was concerned primarily with privation (the absence of something which is needed), rather than de-privation (the removal of something that was previously there). The distinction is important because, as we shall see, the results of the complete lack of maternal care are almost always damaging to the child and have severe long-term consequences, while deprivation is less easy to define and much less predictable in its impact.

In its popular edition, *Maternal Care and Mental Health* was retitled *Child Care and the Growth of Love* – a significant shift, since it suggests a universal message about mothers and children rather than confining itself to questions of mental health. The book is far more than a scientific work (and indeed has been criticised for its handling of the evidence – Andry 1962), and is perhaps best seen as a landmark social document, comparable to the great nineteenth-century reports such as Elizabeth Fry's account of sanitary conditions in prisons, or Mayhew's descriptions of the plight of the London poor.

What marks *Child Care and the Growth of Love* out in the history of social reform is its emphasis on *psychological* as opposed to economic, nutritional, medical or housing difficulties as a root cause of social unhappiness:

In a society where death rates are low, the rate of employment high, and social welfare schemes adequate, it is emotional instability and the inability of parents to make effective family relationships which are the outstanding cause of children becoming deprived of a normal family life.

(Bowlby 1952)

The evidence

The central thrust of Bowlby's work is the effort to substantiate this claim and to consider its clinical, professional, ethical and political consequences. The evidence upon which the book is based includes Bowlby's own studies of juvenile delinquents, Goldfarb's comparison of institution-raised children in the United States with those who had been placed in foster homes, and the accounts of Anna Freud and Dorothy Burlingham from their residential nursery in Hampstead. All these studies strongly support the view that children deprived of maternal care, especially if raised in institutions from under the age of seven, may be seriously affected in their physical, intellectual, emotional and social development. Institution-raised children grow less well, and are retarded in their acquisition of language, and as they become older show evidence of impaired ability to form stable relationships – often tending to be superficially friendly but promiscuous (either metaphorically or literally) in their relationships. Based on his own finding that only two out of fourteen 'affectionless psychopaths' had not had prolonged periods of separation from their mothers in early childhood Bowlby asserts that 'prolonged separation of a child from his mother (or mother substitute) during the first five years of life stands foremost among the causes of delinquent character development' (Bowlby 1944; Bowlby 1952). It is worth noting that Bowlby was making very sweeping conclusions based on studies which had often only looked at relatively small numbers of cases – in his case fourteen, in Goldfarb's only fifteen, juvenile delinquents. By present-day standards these studies would also not be acceptable in that they often included no control groups, or, if they did, they were not rated blind by the researchers, who had a vested interest in establishing a link between deprivation and depravity. Bowlby was aware of these difficulties and, anticipating the modern vogue for 'meta-analysis' (based roughly on the Maoist principle that '600 million

Chinese people cannot be wrong'), suggested that, by combining many small studies, an overall trend emerges which is likely to have some validity.

Family care versus institutional care

Having established to his satisfaction that children without maternal care are indeed gravely disadvantaged, Bowlby goes on to contrast the quality of life in a family with that in an institution:

> All the cuddling and playing, the intimacies of suckling by which a child learns the comfort of his mother's body, the rituals of washing and dressing by which through her pride and tenderness towards his little limbs he learns the values of his own, all these have been lacking.
>
> (Bowlby 1952)

The tinge of sentimentality in this lyrical account has, as we shall see, been much criticised by feminist writers, as has his hymn of praise to what Winnicott was later to call the 'ordinary devoted mother':

> The provision of constant attention night and day, seven days a week, 365 days in the year, is possible only for a woman who derives profound satisfaction from seeing her child grow from babyhood, through the many phases of childhood, to become an independent man or woman, and knows that it is her care which has made this possible.
>
> (Bowlby 1952)

These much-quoted and sometimes derided overstatements have to be seen in context. The world was horrified in the 1990s by the revelation of the squalor and emotional deprivation in the orphanages of Romania. This was not just the result of a dictatorship but of an ideological devaluation of family life, and a belief in the power of public provision to overcome individual poverty. Bowlby was reacting against a similar trend to be seen throughout Europe and the United States in the post-war era, and indeed to a long tradition among the British middle classes, of which he had first-hand experience, of turning their sons and many of their daughters over first to nannies and then to institutional care in boarding schools from the age of seven! To the extent that Bowlby idealises motherhood – as opposed to offering a realistic appraisal of its central importance in child-rearing – this must be seen at least in part as a reflection of the deprivations which he and other members of his class had experienced in the nursery and at school. The long hand of the otherwise invisible nanny reached far.

The impact of Bowlby's advocacy has been enormous, and continues to the present day. It is now taken for granted, and enshrined in the 1989 Children Act, that individual care in foster homes is preferable to group care in nurseries, that 'bad homes are better than good institutions' (Bowlby 1952). The battle to replace institutional care for the mentally ill and mentally handicapped with care within the family, or at least provision of a family-type home atmosphere, is still being waged.

The need for professionalisation of child care

Critics have accused Bowlby of wanting to 'pin women down in their own homes' (Mead 1962). While it is true that he criticises cavalier attitudes towards elective separations of mothers from children under the age of three, he could rather be seen as arguing for a much greater valuation by society of motherhood – indeed, as being recruited in support of the feminist demand for state provision of 'wages for housework'. Whatever his views on housewives, he puts a strong case for the professionalisation for all child-care workers, including workers in day nurseries and children's homes, foster mothers and (we would now add, since this argument has also not been fully won) child minders. These workers must be skilled in understanding a deprived child's overwhelming needs: the craving for parental love; the need to idolise parents however flawed they are in reality; the importance of maintaining contact with absent parents, however fragmentary; the right to express pain, protest about separation, and to grieve loss. They must also be able to help parents in turn to recognise their children's and their own ambivalent feelings. He is intensely critical of case workers who 'live in the sentimental glamour of saving neglected children from wicked parents' (Bowlby 1952) (a comment still relevant today to the dilemmas presented by working with sexually abused children), and of actions which 'convert a physically neglected but psychologically well-provided child into a physically well-provided but emotionally starved one' (Bowlby 1952). All these principles are now enshrined at least in the theory of child-care practice, and for this too Bowlby is largely responsible.

Government action

Much of the debate about the de-institutionalisation of the mentally ill has centred on the question of funding. It was thought that community care must be cheaper than institutional care, and partly for this reason it received governmental support. Bowlby puts forward similar economic arguments in favour of family support for troubled children:

> There are today governments prepared to spend up to £10 per week [this was 1952!] on the residential care of infants who would tremble to give half this sum to a widow, an unmarried mother, or a grandmother to help her care for her baby at home. . . . Nothing is more characteristic of both the public and voluntary attitude towards the problem than a willingness to spend large sums of money looking after children away from their homes, combined with a haggling stinginess in giving aid to the home itself.
>
> (Bowlby 1952)

Although, thanks to Bowlby and others, much has changed, much remains the same. For some things may be worse than in 1952: the haggling stinginess has returned, but is now accompanied by an *un*willingness to spend large sums on public provision. The 1989 Children Act creates a partnership between parents and the local authorities to provide for 'children in need', à la Bowlby, with cash payments if necessary, but no extra funding has been made available for this.

Vicious and benign circles

A major idea which emerges in *Child Care and the Growth of Love* is that of cycles of deprivation: 'the neglected psychopathic child growing up to become the neglectful psychopathic parent . . . a self-perpetuating social circle' (Bowlby 1952). Today's emotionally deprived child becomes tomorrow's neglectful parent: adverse experiences become internalised by the growing child in a way that leads on to further adverse experiences, thus perpetuating the vicious circle of neurosis. Writing in an era of social optimism, and with what, sadly, in hindsight must be seen as some naïvety, Bowlby argued that, with concentrated social, economic and psychological effort, society could put these vicious circles into reverse, so that 'it may, in two or three generations, be possible to enable all boys and girls to grow up to become men and women who, given health and security, are capable of providing a stable and happy life for their children' (Bowlby 1952).

Psychoanalytical principles

One of the impressive features of *Child Care and the Growth of Love* is the way it presents psychoanalytical principles in an accessible and simple form. It is infused with the belief that it is always better to speak the truth, however painful, than to suppress it, and that to try to wipe the slate of the past clean is misguided and in any case impossible. Bowlby believed that children should be involved in any decisions about their welfare, and their own views and wishes taken into account – a principle which has only reached the statute book half a century later in the Children Act of 1989. He thought that children should be encouraged to express their ambivalent feelings about their parents. Children often believe themselves responsible for the calamities which befall them and their families, and child-care workers need to be aware of this and help put these feelings into perspective. For a child away from home 'the lack of a sense of time means that separation feels like an eternity', and this too needs to be understood. In a remarkable quotation from his psychoanalytic colleague Winnicott, a case is made that every child has a right to a primary home experience:

> without which the foundations of mental health cannot be laid down. Without someone specifically oriented to his needs the infant cannot find a working relation to external reality. Without someone to give satisfactory instinctual gratifications the infant cannot find his body, nor can he develop an integrated personality. Without one person to love and to hate he cannot come to know that it is the same person that he loves and hates, and so cannot find his sense of guilt, and his desire to repair and restore. Without a limited human and physical environment he cannot find out the extent to which his aggres-

sive ideas actually fail to destroy, and so cannot sort out the difference between fantasy and fact. Without a father and a mother who are together, and who take joint responsibility for him, he cannot find and express his urge to separate them, nor experience relief at failing to do so.

(Winnicott and Britton in Bowlby 1952)

These principles are as relevant today as they were when they were written. The tragedy of contemporary 'community care' is that, while the need to avoid the negative aspect of institutions has been grasped, the primary home experience as described by Winnicott remains elusive.

Bowlby's outrage

Perhaps the greatest single thread in Bowlby's work, one which comes through strongly in *Child Care and the Growth of Love*, is his pain and outrage at the unnecessary separation of children from their parents. He could take heart at the changes in pediatric and obstetric practice it has led to. The book ends with this passionate outcry at a 'developed' society which has forgotten the fundamental importance of human attachment:

Finally let the reader reflect for a moment on the astonishing practice which has been followed in obstetric wards – of separating mothers and babies immediately after birth – and ask himself whether this is the way to promote a close mother–child relationship. It is hoped that this madness of western society will never be copied by so-called less developed societies.

(Bowlby 1952)

Sadly, there is increasing evidence that Bowlby's fears are being realised.

Bowlby's work has excited considerable reaction, ranging from uncritical acceptance to outraged dismissal. His critics can be divided into two groups. First, there are those who question the social and political implications of his work, mainly from a feminist perspective. A rather different group of researchers have examined the factual basis of the concept of maternal deprivation. These workers, who include Bowlby himself, have modified and

refined our understanding of the short- and long-term implications of maternal separation and mishandling for the developing
child.

THE FEMINIST CRITIQUE

Feminists have aimed three broad kinds of criticism at the idea of
maternal deprivation. The first, and most simple, merely accuses
Bowlby of overstating his case. The studies upon which he bases
his conclusions were of children who had experienced almost
complete lack of maternal care. To generalise from these to the
view that *any* separation of mother from child in the first three
years of life is likely to be damaging is unwarranted (Oakley
1981). There is abundant evidence, they claim (and, as we shall
see later, the facts support this view), that when a mother entrusts
her child for part of the day to the care of a trusted and known
person – whether a grandmother, a *metapalet* in a kibbutz, or a
responsible baby minder – no harm is done. They argue, on the
contrary, that *exclusive* care by the mother alone can lead to less
rather than greater security for the child, and that Bowlby was
wrong in his concept of 'monotropism' (that is, exclusive attachment of the child to one preferred figure). The reality is that the
child has a hierarchy of attachment figures, of whom the mother
is usually the most important, but that fathers, grandparents,
siblings and other relations and friends also play a part, and that
in the absence of one, the child will turn to another in a way that
does not equate with the emotional promiscuity of the institution-
raised child. They also point to the emotional burden on the
mother alone with her child, who, despite (or because of) 24-
hour proximity to her child may be emotionally neglectful even
if she is physically attentive (Chodorow 1978). The dangers which
Bowlby repeatedly identifies in his later work – role reversal
between mother and child, threats of suicide, or saying the child
will be sent away – can all be seen in part as consequences
of this burden and the exclusivity which he advocates for the
mother–child bond.

The second plank upon which the feminist critique rests is
more complex, and consists of an attempt to locate Bowlby's
ideas in an historical, anthropological and sociological context. It
starts from the historical context of post-war Europe where, as
New and David (1985) put it, Bowlby

got an audience: women who had been working in munitions factories, obliged to send their children for nine or ten hours daily into indifferent nurseries, men who for years had been equating peace with the haven of the family, governments which saw the social and financial potential of idealizing motherhood and family life.

The collective sense of loss, and guilt, and desire for reparation found an answer in the idea of maternal deprivation. Children had suffered terribly as a result of the war, and this needed to be faced, as had the 'internal children' of the adults who had witnessed the horrors of war. The valuation and at times sentimentalising of the mother–child relationship in post-war Europe could be compared with a similar process in the nineteenth century in the face of the brutality of the Industrial Revolution. Bowlby's tenderness towards little children carries echoes of Blake and Wordsworth, Dickens and Kingsley. There had to be a safe place which could be protected from the violence of the modern world, and the Christian imagery of mother and child reappears, in his work, as an icon for a secular society.

A slightly different slant was offered in the suggestion that governments welcomed the idea of maternal deprivation in that it appeared to let them off the hook of providing child care, pushing it back to individual and family responsibility. Winnicott wrote to Bowlby warning him that his views were being used to close down much-needed residential nurseries (Rodman 1987). Bowlby had not, of course, argued that money should be withdrawn, but rather transferred from institutional care to home care, but, as in the more recent case of the mentally ill and handicapped, governments were less keen on this part of the argument.

The heart of the feminist case against Bowlby is that, like Freud, he had wrongly assumed that anatomy is destiny. Implicit, they argue, in the concept of maternal deprivation is a view of the biological 'naturalness' of an exclusive mother–child relationship which, as Margaret Mead (1962) puts it, is a 'reification into a set of universals of a set of ethnocentric observations on our own society'. Anthropology shows that what is normal is for child care to be shared by a stable *group* of adults and older children, usually, but not always, related, and usually, but by no means always, female. Maternal care is an important but certainly not exclusive part of this. For infants to survive in non-industrial countries such shared care is essential. As an Object-Relations theorist Bowlby rejects Freudian drive theory, but, once attachment theory was developed, offered an evolutionary-ethological account of the mother–child bond. Feminists object that he is using biology to justify what is essentially a cultural product of our own 'patriarchal but father-absent' society (Leupnitz 1988), with its nuclear families, small numbers of children, weakened kinship networks, mobile population, and fathers who are away from home for long periods, or absent altogether.

A more tenuous sociological argument (Mitscherlich 1963; Parsons 1964) suggests that the family structure which Bowlby implicitly advocates, with strong, closely bonded mothers and children, and peripheral fathers, fits the needs of modern capitalist society. Paternal authority has been replaced by that of the headmaster or boss in school, office and factory, producing a docile workforce, while the mother controls her children by bribes and threats, thus preparing them for the social manipulations of advertising and manufactured need which an ever-expanding consumerist economy requires. This pattern is offered as the norm for 'adequate' family functioning, as it is in the functionalist account offered by such influential writers as Parsons (1964). Leupnitz, from a feminist family therapy perspective, sees this as enshrining a state of affairs that suits men, but leaves wives who are obese, sexually dissatisfied, psychosomatically ill, and prone to depression (Leupnitz 1988).

Child Care and the Growth of Love was written about children who had lost their mothers, usually for good, and described the psychological consequences of that privation. Until recently, Europe has enjoyed an unprecedented period of peace and stability (warfare, starvation, genocide and mass migration have continued apace, exported to the developing world). The problems facing the modern family are not so much maternal deprivation as of paternal deprivation due to weak, absent or abusive fathers, and 'implosion' of the children onto unsupported mothers. Chodorow (1978) and other feminist psychotherapists have written about the psychological consequences of these changes. In summary, they lead to identity difficulties for both men and women. Lacking a strong father with whom to identify, boys differentiate themselves from their mothers and sisters by a disparagement of women, which conceals a dread of their phantasised omnipotence. It is this, according to Horney (1924), not Freud's castration anxiety, which underlies male fear of women and their difficulties in intimacy. The elusive search for 'success' is an attempt to please and appease the all-powerful mother. Girls, on the other hand, remain tied into their mothers, often taking on their pain and depression, and feeling intense guilt if they try to assert their independence and autonomy. The absent or seductive father makes a move towards him difficult or dangerous. Motherhood provides a temporary relief, but the girl again may feel caught in a mother–child dyad from which she still cannot escape, while the boy, now a father, feels excluded and jealous. As we shall see in later chapters, the Bowlbian concepts of avoidant and ambivalent attachment capture roughly these male and female patterns of anxious attachment in the modern family.

In summary, the feminist critique has questioned the logic of the implicit Bowlbian argument (one which in its simplistic form Bowlby would have been the first to repudiate) that since absent mothers lead to disturbed children, ever-present mothers will produce happy children. The feminists – in so far as it is possible to group them together – in turn have tended to overstate their case and failed to appreciate the importance which Bowlby has established for the role of the mother in her child's emotional development, both as a scientific fact and as a social and ethical principle. Bowlby's advocacy of the vital importance of mothers in the care of children, and the implications of his studies that good day-care facilities should be available for mothers who want or are forced by economic necessity to work, funded so that children can have individual and continuous relationships with care workers, should be seen as a step towards the liberation of women, increasing their range of choices and valuation by society.

Although it is still in print, it is now nearly fifty years since *Child Care and the Growth of Love* was first published. The terms of the debate have changed, so that, with less physical absence, but with ever-increasing difficulties in managing their lives, mothers are subject to enormous social pressures and their children are often the first casualties of this. For a more detailed examination of maternal deprivation from a contemporary perspective, and to a discussion of how children may be helped to escape or may remain ever more deeply trapped in deprivation we must turn now to the work of Michael Rutter.

MATERNAL DEPRIVATION REASSESSED

Rutter's monograph (Rutter 1981) and numerous papers (for example, Rutter 1972; Rutter 1979) comprise the definitive empirical evaluation and update of Bowlby's work on maternal deprivation. His contribution has been to amass further evidence, and, based on this, to begin to tease out the many different social and psychological mechanisms which operate under the rubric of maternal deprivation.

Bowlby, it will be recalled, claimed that maternal deprivation produced physical, intellectual, behavioural and emotional damage. He further argued that even brief separations from the mother in the first five years of life had long-lasting effects, and in general that these problems perpetuated themselves in a cycle of disadvantage as such children themselves became parents. Rutter has examined each of these points in turn.

On the question of intellectual and physical disadvantage, and the effects of brief separation, it seems that Bowlby was only partially right, and often for the wrong reasons. While it is true that institution-raised children are intellectually disadvantaged, this is mainly in verbal as opposed to performance intelligence, and this is a consequence of the child's 'verbal environment', not the lack of parents *per se*. Children brought up in large families are similarly disadvantaged. It is lack of verbal stimulation that is the problem for the deprived children, not lack of mother. A similar picture emerges with 'deprivation dwarfism', which has been shown to be due, as might be expected, to lack of food intake rather than some mysterious emotional factor, and can be rapidly reversed by attentive feeding, whether by a nurse or mother.

Acute separation distress is also probably less damaging, and more complex than Bowlby first saw it. Preparation and care by known figures reduces distress, and even without these there is no evidence of long-term effects from a single brief separation however painful it may be at the time. An important point comes from Hinde's rhesus monkey studies (Hinde and McGinnis 1977), which show that the effects of separation depend on the mother–child relationship *before* the event: the more tense the relationship, the more damaging the separation. These kinds of findings indicate a move towards a more subtle appreciation of the nature of bonds, and away from simplistic event-pathology models. What matters is not so much the separation itself but its meaning and the context in which it happens.

A similar conclusion applies to the relationship between anti-social behaviour and maternal deprivation. First, as Rutter (1979) puts it, 'the links are much stronger looking back than they are looking forward'. In 'Forty-four juvenile thieves', Bowlby found that a quarter of the thieves had had major separations from their parents in infancy, and in the sub-group of 'affectionless psychopaths' only two out of fourteen had not experienced maternal deprivation. In his later follow-up study of children who had been in a tuberculosis sanatorium he found that, compared with controls, the differences in social adjustment, while in the *direction* of less good adjustment for the sanitorium children, were not all that marked, and that at least half of the deprived children had made good social relationships (Bowlby *et al.* 1956). Second, the implication of the phrase 'maternal deprivation' is that antisocial behaviour is specifically linked to the loss of mother. Rutter's work (1971) suggests that antisocial behaviour is linked not to maternal absence as such, but to family discord which in divorcing families is often associated with temporary separations from mother. Children who have lost their mothers through death have a near-normal delinquency rate, while the rate is much raised when parents divorce, especially where there is a combination of active discord and lack of affection. Here too, presumably, it is the way in which the loss is handled, its antecedents (how secure the child has been with the separating parents), and meaning for the child that matter.

The importance of these refinements of the maternal deprivation hypothesis is that they mark a move away from Bowlby's medical analogy, exemplified by the Vitamin D-rickets comparison, to a psychological model which takes account of an individual's history, and of the way untoward events are 'processed' psychologically. It seems more plausible that maternal deprivation should act as a general 'vulnerability factor' (cf. Brown and Harris 1978) which raises a child's threshold to disturbance rather than as a causative agent in any simple sense. Delinquency is such a complex phenomenon, dependent on non-psychological issues such as policing policy, quality of schools and housing that it would be unlikely to be the result of any one single factor, however important childhood deprivation may be.

For children unfortunate enough to be entirely deprived of

maternal care, recent research has served to confirm Bowlby's original claims. Tizard's (1977) follow-up studies on institution-raised children have shown that, as the maternal deprivation hypothesis predicted, these eight-year-olds were more attention-seeking, restless, disobedient and unpopular compared with controls, while as infants they had shown excessive clinging and diffuse attachment behaviour. Her studies also indicate that, as Bowlby suggested, the period six months to four years may be critical for the capacity to form stable relationships, since children who had been adopted after four, despite forming close and loving bonds with their adoptive parents, remained antisocial in their behaviour at school.

DEVELOPMENTAL PATHWAYS THROUGH CHILDHOOD

Subsequent studies have also generally confirmed Bowlby's concept of cycles of disadvantage. People brought up in unhappy or disrupted homes are more likely to have illegitimate children, become teenage mothers, make unhappy marriages and to divorce. Parents who physically abuse their children tend to have had childhoods characterised by neglect, rejection and violence. Girls from disrupted homes when they become mothers tend to talk less to their babies, touch them less and look at them less (Wolkind et al. 1977). But not all children from unhappy homes suffer and fail in this way. A complex model is needed to explain individual differences that takes into account the child, the parent, events and their appraisal, and the social environment. This can be conceptualised as a series of pathways through childhood that lead in a more or less positive direction. A number of varied influences will determine which path a particular child takes (Rutter 1981). Figure 3.1 attempts to summarise these.

As will be discussed in more detail in Chapter 6, there is good evidence that parents' own childhood experiences are important in influencing the way they respond to their child. Events around the birth are also important: mothers separated from their babies soon after birth are less confident and competent as mothers in the subsequent months. The sex and birth position of the child matter: parents are more relaxed and less punitive with second children than with first-borns. Male children are generally more vulnerable to family discord than are females. The death of a parent is more damaging for a same-sex child than if they are

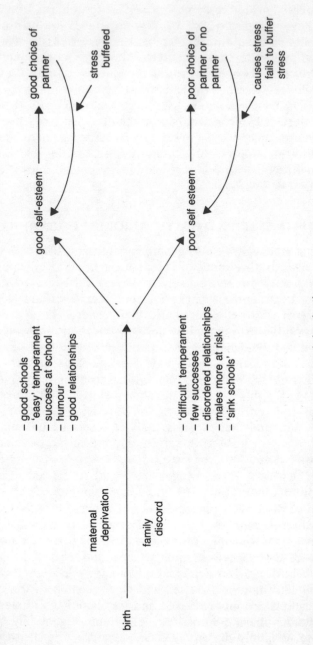

Figure 3.1 Developmental pathways from maternal deprivation

the opposite sex. Temperament plays an important part too: children who are less adaptable and more prone to negative moods are more likely to be targets of parental criticism than their more easy-going siblings, and are more likely to develop a childhood psychiatric disorder. Even in discordant homes, if the child has a good relationship with one parent or with a grand-parent, this acts as a protective factor against conduct disorder. Finally, the social environment is important. Inner-city areas have much higher rates of childhood psychiatric disorder than country or small-town areas, and even within inner cities some schools are much more successful in helping their pupils to avoid delin-quency than others.

IMPLICATIONS FOR PSYCHOTHERAPY

Key issues for adult psychotherapists are the need to clarify more precisely the links between early childhood difficulty and emotional disorder in later life (Rutter 1986); the question of how some people survive and are even strengthened ('steeled') by adversity, while others go under (Rutter 1985); and the need for a model that will suggest at what points in the process psycho-therapeutic intervention is likely to produce change (Holmes 1991).

Social psychiatry tends to emphasise present adversity in the causation of neurosis, while psychoanalytic explanations stress the past. The evidence suggests that both current and past dif-ficulties are important, and that *self-esteem* is a crucial factor linking the two. Looking at adverse experiences in childhood, those who, despite loss or difficulty, manage to maintain a sense of self-esteem do well. Self-esteem in turn rests on two main foundations: self-efficacy and good relationships. Success at school – in social relationships (especially the capacity to generate humour), athletic prowess, musical ability or scholastic achieve-ment – is correlated with better adjustment in institution-raised children in adult life (Rutter and Quinton 1984). There are likely to be a series of interlocking benign or vicious circles here. Good self-esteem means a child will be likely to cope with deprivation – chronic illness in a parent, for example – and the fact of coping will in itself enhance self-esteem, and give the individual a feeling that they will be able to cope in the future. This in turn will influence their choice of partner and the kind of relationship they have with them. Conversely, as Beck *et al.* (1979) and Ryle (1990) argue, depressed people will expect themselves to cope badly, will perceive themselves as doing so, may do so in fact, all of which will be experienced as depression-reinforcing 'failure'.

Apart from coping and competence, the second important childhood component of self-esteem derives from good relationships. Psychotherapists have long suggested that a history of at least one good relationship in the past predicts good outcome in therapy (Malan 1976), and this too is confirmed by empirical studies. An important point about both self-efficacy and good relationships is that they can generalise, so that one positive feature will lead to good self-esteem, despite an otherwise gloomy picture. The opposite is the case in depression (Brown and Harris 1978), where adverse experiences are generalised into a global feeling of hopelessness.

Bion mocked the early psychoanalytic fellow travellers like Suttie for their simplistic overemphasis on past trauma: 'doctor put it in the past' (Pines 1991). Equal in importance to past influences in the adult outcome of maternal deprivation is, as several studies have shown, the quality of a person's current intimate relationships. Vulnerable women who experience loss are protected from depression by the presence of a confiding relationship with a spouse or partner (Brown and Harris 1978). Parker and Hadzi-Pavlovic (1984) found that people whose parents die in childhood are less prone to depression in adult life if they have an affectionate spouse. Rutter and Quinton (1984) report similar findings for institution-raised women, who in general have more psychosocial difficulties than controls, and were much more likely to react badly to stress, unless they had a supportive husband in a harmonious marriage. This suggests another important vicious circle, since maternally deprived girls are more likely to marry unstable and similarly deprived men: childhood difficulty leads to low self-esteem, which makes for poor choice of sexual partner, which in turn leaves women unprotected from stress in adult life. As Bowlby (1952) puts it, there are 'strong unconscious drives which lead husbands and wives to create the very problems of which they complain', and so produce 'the distorted light in which they see the behaviour of their spouse'.

There are important implications of these findings for psychotherapy. There is an implicit contradiction in the psychoanalytic emphasis on the overwhelming importance of early experience – and even more so phantasies in early childhood – in determining adult difficulty and the claims for the efficacy of psychoanalytic therapy. If continuity between childhood and adult life is so strong, how is psychoanalysis likely to reverse it? The recent evidence suggests a much more subtle relationship between past and present, in which a person's partner plays a crucial role in determining outcome. Caspi and Elder (1988) found that 'difficult' children were more likely to demonstrate ill-tempered parenting and poor social control in adult life, but this only emerged if they were married to non-assertive men. Difficult behaviour in childhood made it more likely that these women *would* marry non-assertive men, but when they did not, then poor parenting was avoided. As we shall see in Chapter 8, therapy, through empathy and limit-setting, may play a similar role to marriage in helping to modify maladaptive behaviours. This may be particularly applicable to those whose early experiences have made it hard for them, despite a longing for intimacy, to sustain close relationships at all (Parker *et al.* 1992).

Apart from very severe cases, there is no simple one-to-one correlation between childhood mental states and adult difficulty. There are a number of environmental, and to some extent accidental, mediating factors which determine whether outcomes are favourable or not: the area a person grows up in, the school they go to, whether or not they happen to meet the right person at the right time. Nor is there a simple relationship between environmental stress and disturbance; the meaning and context of a particular event is critical. A teenager who storms out of the house after a row about what time he should come home, followed by the threat of 'You'll be the death of me', and who returns to find that his father *has* died suddenly is going to be more vulnerable to difficult relationships (perhaps characterised by avoidance and inhibition of anger and therefore poor conflict resolution), than one whose parent dies peacefully over several months with good opportunities for grieving. Also, it is important to see the 'victim' of deprivation not as a passive recipient of stress, but as an active agent, in a dynamic relationship with his environment, trying to make sense of experience, to master it and to cope as best he can, but also, via the benign and vicious circles of neurosis, as an active participant in his own downfall or deliverance.

CONCLUSIONS

Maternal deprivation emerges from this account not as the cause of neurosis, but as one, albeit vital, vulnerability factor among many in a complex web of developmental influences. Because nothing succeeds like success, and nothing fails like failure, these influences may summate in retrospect to give the impression of a simple choice between primrose or thorny paths, but there are in fact many roads less travelled (Frost 1954) and it is the psychotherapists' task to explore these. The circularity of neurotic patterns both in the present and over time is a central unifying concept, and suggests how and why many different kinds of intervention may be effective. Analytic therapy may be an example of how one good relationship can counteract many adverse influences: the nature of that good relationship will be considered further in Chapter 8. Cognitive-behavioural therapy concentrates on increasing a person's sense of self-efficacy, and reducing generalisation of bad feelings so that self-esteem remains intact despite loss. Family and marital therapy tackle relationships directly, thereby enhancing the buffering against stress. All types of time-limited therapy assume that if a person can be helped to re-engage with the benign cycles of normal life (although feminists argue that the definition of what constitutes a 'normal' family needs to be contested), then outcomes will be good, since, in Bowlby's (1952) words, 'there is in almost all families a strong urge to live together in greater accord, and this provides a powerful motive for favourable change'.

We have moved from simple privation to the complexities of relationships, from loss to the nature of the bond that is broken, from a simple model of environmental trauma to a consideration of its psychological impact. The stage is set for Bowlby's move from maternal deprivation to Attachment Theory, and after a short literary diversion, we shall, in the next and following two chapters, follow him there.

OLIVER TWIST: AN INTERLUDE

Dickens' *Oliver Twist*, with its mixture of realism, caricature, and fairy-tale, can be seen as a classic account of maternal deprivation. Oliver, orphaned at birth, brought up 'by hand' for the first few months of his life, spends his childhood in the 'parochial' orphanage, 'where twenty or thirty other juvenile offenders against the poor-laws rolled about the floor all day, without the inconvenience of too much food or too much clothing'. Protesting against the 'tortures of slow starvation', he 'asks for more', is sent out to work for his pains, and, after running away from further cruelty, falls among thieves and so begins his career as a delinquent, much as Bowlby would have predicted. But here, despite many reversals and cruel twists, his fortunes change. He is rescued first by the kindly Mr Brownlow, and a second time by the loving Rose Maylie. He is recognised as being in some way different from the run of juvenile thieves. In two crucial passages he is watched over by these parental figures in his sleep:

> The boy stirred, and smiled in his sleep, as though these marks of pity and compassion had awakened some pleasant dream of a love and affection he had never known . . . some brief memory of a happier existence, long gone by.

Later, anticipating Winnicott's (1965) concept of 'being alone in the presence of the mother', Oliver once again sleeps after a terrifying escapade of attempted robbery in which he is wounded, watched over by the tender Rose Maylie:

> It is an undoubted fact, that although our sense of touch and sight be dead, yet our sleeping thoughts, and visionary scenes that pass before us, will be influenced . . . by the *mere silent presence* of some external object. [Italics in the original]

The book ends, of course, happily, with Oliver's affluent parentage established, evil (in the shape of Monks, Sykes and the Bumbles) vanquished, and with the beginning of secure attachment:

> Mr Brownlow . . . from day to day filling the mind of his adopted child with stores of knowledge, and becoming *attached* to him, more and more, as his nature developed itself. . . . [My italics]

The universality of Dickens' message means that each generation can bring to the story its own themes and preoccupations. For the Victorians it was a social tract documenting the iniquities of the poor laws, and a contrast between the cruelties of the bad father and the benign love of Mr Brownlow. But this is no sentimental Victorian morality tale. The powers of good and evil are evenly balanced. Mr Brownlow's benign Bowlbian view of the perfectibility of human nature is contrasted with the cynical realism of his friend Mr Grimwig, who, at least in the short run, wins his wager that Oliver will take Mr Brownlow's money and run.

A Kleinian reading might see in its exaggerations and description of unbearable hunger an account of the 'bad breast' and the projection into it of the child's hatred and rage. As Oliver's bad feelings are balanced by good 'therapeutic' experience, so he becomes strengthened in his resolve to escape from the clutches of Fagin and Sikes, and sees them and the Bumbles no longer as phantasmagoric creatures of enormous power but as the seedy petty criminals which they are.

The Bowlbian perspective on *Oliver Twist* starts with the mystery of Oliver's parentage. The book opens with the description of a *place* – the orphanage where Oliver was raised. It ends with a *name* – Agnes, Oliver's mother, a name on a tomb:

> There is no coffin in that tomb. . . . But, if the spirits of the dead ever come back to earth, to visit spots hallowed by the love – the love beyond the grave – of those whom they knew in life, I believe that the shade of Agnes sometimes hovers round that solemn nook.

In finding his story, Oliver has found his lost mother even though he has never met her in reality, and can never do so, not even in her coffin. The movement from the concrete attachment to person and place of childhood to the possession as adults of a story, of a name which has been internalised, is a theme common to literature and to psychotherapy. The book is closed, the parents who nurtured (and failed to nurture) us are no longer there, but their characters remain with us – for good or ill. Therapy recreates past attachments so that they can live inside us again. The progress from attachment to narrative is part of the Bowlbian story too: we shall examine it more closely in the final section of the book.

Part II

Attachment Theory

Chapter 4

Attachment, anxiety, internal working models

> All of us, from the cradle to the grave, are happiest when life is organised as a series of excursions, long or short, from the secure base provided by our attachment figures.
>
> (Bowlby 1988)

In this and the following chapter we shall outline the main features of Attachment Theory, starting with the first of the two great themes described poetically by Bowlby as the 'making and breaking of affectional bonds'.

Bowlby was in some ways, like Freud, a late starter. Although he had a substantial body of related work behind him, it was not until around his fiftieth year, in a series of papers published between 1958 and 1963 (Bowlby 1958, 1960, 1961), that he began to formulate the main outlines of Attachment Theory. Perhaps psychological theorising, like novel writing, but unlike poetry or mathematics, requires a certain maturity; perhaps, like Freud too, Bowlby's revolutionary spirit was combined with a cautiousness of personality that meant that he needed to be absolutely certain of his ground before attempting to challenge the heavens. Bowlby had always felt some unease about the scientific status of psychoanalysis: his discovery of ethology in the 1950s provided him with the scientifically secure base from which to make his conceptual advance: 'The time is already ripe for a unification of psychoanalytic concepts with those of ethology, and to pursue the rich vein of research which this unification suggests' (Bowlby 1953c).

THE THEORETICAL AND EXPERIMENTAL
BACKGROUND TO ATTACHMENT THEORY

Bowlby's earlier work had shown that separated or bereaved children experienced, no less than adults, intense feelings of mental pain and anguish: yearning, misery, angry protests, despair, apathy and withdrawal. He had shown too that the long-term effects of these separations could sometimes be disastrous, leading to neurosis or delinquency in children and adolescents, and mental illness in adults. In separating parent from child a delicate mechanism had been disrupted, a fundamental bond broken linking one human being to another. What is the nature of that bond, and how does it develop? These were the questions Bowlby set out to answer.

He had at his disposal two sets of theories. The first was psychoanalysis which, as we have seen, he had embraced and struggled with for the preceding twenty years. The second was ethology, to which his attention had only recently been drawn, when he read the English translation of Konrad Lorenz's *King Solomon's Ring* (1952) in draft form; soon after, he encountered Tinbergen's (1951) work, and began to collaborate with Robert Hinde (1982b, 1987). Other important influences were the ideas of Kenneth Craik (1943) who, like Bowlby, was a product of the Cambridge Psychology Department, and Ian Suttie (1935), whose book *The Origins of Love and Hate* was influential in the thirties and had contributed to Bowlby's views on social psychology.

Psychoanalysis offered two different accounts of the infant–mother bond: drive theory and object-relations theory. Both of these were, in Bowlby's eyes, seriously flawed. The first, 'classical', drive-theory account came from Freud's early formulations. Here the bond which links mother to infant is libido, or psychical energy. The newborn infant lives in a solipsistic world of 'primary narcissism' and experiences a build-up of tension – the need to feed, to suck the breast as an expression of his infantile sexuality. The mother provides the vehicle for the discharge of this libido. If she, or her breast, is absent, tension arises due to undischarged libido which is felt by the infant as anxiety. The baby learns to love the mother because she feeds him, and so reduces the inner tension which is felt as anxiety. Bowlby calls this the 'cupboard love' theory of relationships.

In *Inhibitions, Symptoms, and Anxiety*, Freud (1926) changed his theory of anxiety from one of dammed-up libido to the theory of *signal anxiety*. Here anxiety is felt whenever there is actual or threatened separation 'from someone who is loved and longed for'. The basis of this love, however, remains satisfaction of physiological need:

> The reason why the infant in arms wants to perceive the presence of its mother is only because it already knows by experience that she satisfies all of its needs without delay. The situation, then, which it regards as a 'danger' and against which it wants to be safeguarded is that of non-satisfaction, of a *growing tension due to need*, against which it is helpless.
>
> (Freud 1926)

Despite this retention of a physiological substratum to relationships, Freud now emphasises that 'it is the absence of the mother that is now the danger'. This shift towards regarding anxiety as based on object-loss is a decisive move towards the *Object-Relations* viewpoint that has become the predominant psychoanalytic paradigm, especially in Britain (Greenberg and Mitchell 1983). For Melanie Klein, the infant is linked psychologically as well as physiologically to the mother and her breast from birth. She sees an intimate link between the physiological processes of feeding and elimination, and the beginnings of mental and ethical structures in the mind of the infant. The satisfying, nourishing, comforting breast is the prototype of the 'good object'; the absent, withholding, empty breast is the 'bad object', containing not only the actual failures and unresponsiveness of the mother, but also the infant's reactions to those failures, projected into and attributed to the 'bad breast'.

For Bowlby, both Freud and Klein failed to take the all-important step of seeing attachment between infant and mother as a psychological bond in its own right, not an instinct derived from feeding or infant sexuality, but *sui generis*:

> The young child's hunger for his mother's love and presence is as great as his hunger for food. . . . Attachment Theory provides a language in which the phenomenology of attachment experiences is given full legitimacy. Attachment is a 'primary motivational system' with its own workings and interface with other motivational systems.
>
> (Bowlby 1973a)

He based his new theory of attachment partly on the findings of ethology, partly on his theoretical critique of psychoanalysis.

As a keen naturalist Bowlby had been particularly struck by the phenomenon described by Lorenz (1952) of following responses in some avian species. Newly hatched goslings follow their mother (or a mother-surrogate), and exhibit analogues of 'anxiety' (cheeping, searching) when separated from her, despite the fact that she does not directly provide them with food. Here bonding seems to be dissociated from feeding. The converse example is provided by Harlow's (1958) monkey studies, which became available around the time Bowlby was publishing his first papers on Attachment Theory. Harlow, in an article with the tongue-in-cheek title 'The nature of love', described how he separated infant rhesus monkeys from their mothers at birth and reared them with the help of surrogate 'wire mothers'. In one series of experiments the infant monkeys were presented with a wire 'mother' to which a feeding bottle had been attached, and another 'mother' without a feeding bottle, but covered with soft terry nappy material. The infant monkeys showed a clear preference for the 'furry' mother, spending up to 18 hours per day clinging to her (as they would with their real mothers) even though they were fed exclusively from the 'lactating' wire mother – a finding which Harlow, arguing as forcibly against a behavioural 'derived drive' theory of bonding as did Bowlby against the psychoanalytic 'secondary drive' hypothesis, concluded, 'is completely contrary to any interpretation of derived drive in which the mother form becomes conditioned to hunger-thirst reduction'.

Geese demonstrate bonding without feeding; rhesus monkeys show feeding without bonding. Thus, argues Bowlby, we must postulate an attachment system unrelated to feeding, which, adopting a biological approach from which psychoanalysis had increasingly become divorced, makes sound evolutionary and developmental sense.

By thinking in terms of primary attachment and bringing the ideas of neo-Darwinism to bear on psychoanalysis, Bowlby identified what he saw as some fundamental flaws in psychoanalytic metapsychology. First, it overemphasises internal dangers at the expense of external threat. The biological purpose of the attachment system is protection from predators which would have been a vital necessity in the environmental conditions in which early man evolved. Infants and small children need to stay close to their mothers at all times, and to signal separation if they are to remain safe from predation. Suttie (1935) called this an 'innate need for companionship which is the infant's only way of self-preservation'. Bowlby criticises psychoanalysts for their over-civilised view of man in which they discount environmental threat, and emphasise instead the projection of 'internal' dangers (feelings of rage and hatred, for example) onto a neutral or benign environment. Even in an urban setting external dangers are far from negligible and children who are victims of injuries in the home or from traffic accidents and sexual attacks are likely to be unprotected and unaccompanied.

Second, Bowlby is critical of the psychoanalytical picture of personality development in which each 'phase' – oral, anal, phallic and genital – succeeds each other in a linear fashion. He questions the idea that normal development can be derived from considering pathological states, and is unhappy with the idea of regression to fixation points as an adequate model of psychological illness. He contrasts Freud's 'homuncular' model in which each stage is predetermined according to some pre-existing plan of development, with an 'epigenetic' model (Waddington 1977) in which several lines of development are possible, the outcome of which depends on an interaction between the organism and its environment. Thus, although the developing child has a propensity to form attachments, the nature of those attachments and their dynamics will depend on the parental environment to which he or she is exposed. Also, the development of the attachment dynamic can be considered as a process in its own right independent of other dynamics – for example, sex or feeding – just as the different organs of the body develop relatively independently of one another.

Bowlby also rejects the teleological 'Lamarckian' view in which the 'purpose' of psychological functions can be determined by some *a priori* goal: for example, the 'purpose' of attachment is not the reduction of physiological need, but, in evolutionary terms, to increase the fitness of those possessed of it, so protecting them from predators. Finally, he is critical of 'hydraulic' models of drive-discharge, seeing human behaviour rather in terms of control theory whose aim is the maintenance of homeostasis. Infant monkeys separated from their mothers respond with a rise in pulse rate and a fall in body temperature. In humans,

Brazelton and Cramer (1991) have shown that mothers who have to return to work within a year after giving birth show higher levels of physiological disturbance than those who are able to stay with their babies, and that there is a correspondingly higher incidence of infection in the infants. Secure attachment provides an external ring of psychological protection which maintains the child's metabolism in a stable state, similar to the internal physiological homeostatic mechanisms of blood-pressure and temperature control.

The group of analysts to whom Bowlby felt his ideas were closest were the 'Hungarian School', especially Ferenczi (1955) and Michael Balint (1964). Ferenczi, originator of the famous phrase 'it is the physician's love which cures the patient', had fallen out with Freud over his emphasis on Freud's insistence on the 'real' (as opposed to transferential) nature of the relationship between patient and therapist, and his rather dubious propensity to kiss and hug his patients when he felt it necessary. Balint, his pupil, had postulated a 'primary love' and a primitive clinging instinct between mother and child that are independent of feeding. Bowlby also saw an affinity between his ideas and those of Fairbairn (1952) who, like Bowlby, had jettisoned drive theory in favour of primary object-seeking, and who refused to see adult dependency as a relic of orality, but rather conceived of development as a movement from infantile to mature dependence.

As described in the Introduction, the reaction of the analytic world to Bowlby's challenge was, on the whole, unfavourable. The Kleinians saw him as having betrayed analytic principles, contaminating psychoanalysis with behaviourism, trying to expunge the heart of psychoanalysis – its account of the inner world of phantasy. Anna Freud and her supporters could hardly fail to notice that the Oedipus complex and infantile sexuality – for them, the cornerstones of the psychoanalytic edifice – played virtually no part in Bowlby's writings. What started out as an attempt by Bowlby to modernise psychoanalytic metapsychology and to find a sound biological underpinning for Object-Relations Theory became, in the face of the rejection of his ideas by his psychoanalytic colleagues, increasingly to look like a new psychological paradigm. As we shall see in Chapters 6 and 8, recent developments in 'post-Bowlbian' research have opened out the possibility of reconciliation. But first we must focus more clearly on the nature of attachment theory.

WHAT IS ATTACHMENT THEORY?

Attachment Theory is in essence a *spatial* theory: when I am close to my loved one I feel good, when I am far away I am anxious, sad or lonely. The child away from home for the night plays happily until she hurts herself or bedtime approaches and then feels pangs of homesickness. The mother who leaves her child with a new baby minder thinks endlessly about her baby and misses her dreadfully. Attachment is mediated by looking, hearing and holding: the sight of my loved one lifts my soul, the sound of her approach awakes pleasant anticipation. To be held and to feel her skin against mine makes me feel warm, safe and comforted, with perhaps a tingling anticipation of shared pleasure. But the consummation of attachment is not primarily orgasmic – rather, it is, via the achievement of proximity, a relaxed state in which one can begin to 'get on with things', pursue one's projects, to *explore*.

Definitions

It is useful to distinguish between the interrelated concepts of attachment, attachment behaviour, and the attachment behavioural system (Hinde 1982a), which represent roughly the psychodynamic, the behavioural and the cognitive components of Attachment Theory.

'*Attachment*' is an overall term which refers to the state and quality of an individual's attachments. These can be divided into secure and insecure attachment. Like many psychodynamic terms, 'attachment' carries both experiential and theoretical overtones. To feel attached is to feel safe and secure. By contrast, an insecurely attached person may have a mixture of feelings towards their attachment figure: intense love and dependency, fear of rejection, irritability and vigilance. One may theorise that their lack of security has aroused a simultaneous wish to be close and the angry determination to punish their attachment figure for the minutest sign of abandonment. It is though the insecurely attached person is saying to themselves: 'cling as hard as you can to people – they are likely to abandon you; hang on to them and hurt them if they show signs of going away, then they may be less likely to do so'. This particular pattern of insecure attachment is known as 'ambivalent insecurity' (see below and Chapter 6).

Attachment behaviour is defined simply as being 'Any form of behaviour that results in a person attaining or retaining proximity to some other differentiated and preferred individual'. Attachment behaviour is triggered by separation or threatened separation from the attachment figure. It is terminated or *assuaged* by proximity, which, depending on the nature of the threat, may vary from being in sight, to physical closeness and soothing words without touching, to being tightly held and cuddled.

Attachment and attachment behaviour are based on an *attachment behavioural system*, a blueprint or model of the world in which the self and significant others and their interrelationship are represented and which encodes the particular pattern of attachment shown by an individual. The ambivalently attached person we have described might have a working model of others as desirable but unreachable, and of themselves as unworthy of support and love, and/or of an unreliable and rejecting attachment figure with a protesting, attacking self.

An attachment relationship can be defined by the presence of three key features (Weiss 1982).

1 Proximity seeking to a preferred figure

As parents of toddlers well know, small children have a maddening propensity to follow their attachment figures wherever they go. The distance at which the child feels comfortable depends on such factors as age, temperament, developmental history, and whether the child feels fatigued, frightened or ill, all of which will enhance attachment behaviour. Recent separation will lead to greater proximity seeking, or 'mummyishness', as Robertson's (1952) film so beautifully demonstrates. The extent of the proximity required will also depend on circumstances. A three-year-old collected from playgroup after her first day may rush up to the parent and bury her head in his lap and want to be held and cuddled for a long time. A month later she may be content to slip her hand quietly into that of her collecting parent and continue chatting to her friends as she walks down the road.

Of central importance to attachment theory is the notion that attachment is to a *discriminated* figure (or small group of figures).

Bowlby originally explained this by analogy with the phenomenon of imprinting in which young birds will attach themselves to any mobile figure to which they are exposed at the 'sensitive period' in their development. Studies on primates suggest that imprinting does not occur in the same way as in birds, and that attachment, rather than being an all-or-none phenomenon, develops as a result of a gradual process of genetically programmed development and social learning (Rutter 1981; Bretherton 1991b).

The fact that attachment is, in Bowlby's word, 'monotropic' – that is, occurs with a single figure, most usually the mother – has profound implications for psychological development and psychopathology throughout the life cycle.

> It is because of this marked tendency to monotropy that we are capable of deep feelings, for to have a deep attachment to a person (or a place or a thing) is to have taken them as the terminating object of our instinctual responses.
>
> (Bowlby 1988a)

Monotropy is by no means absolute: a small child's attachments can best be thought of as a hierarchy usually, but not necessarily, with the mother at the top, closely followed by the father (or, rarely, the father followed by the mother), grandparents, siblings, godparents and so on. Inanimate objects such as transitional objects are also important.

Attachment Theory accepts the customary primacy of the mother as the main care-giver, but there is nothing in the theory to suggest that fathers are not equally likely to become principal attachment figures if they happen to provide most of the child care. The theory is a two-person psychology and has little to say directly about the different roles of mother and father, and of sexuality in psychological life. This has the advantage that its findings are perhaps more generally applicable across cultures than mainstream psychoanalysis, but means that it does not address the fact that individuals' identity is intimately bound up with their sexual roles.

Three-person psychology enters into Attachment Theory via separation and loss. The growing child has to learn that the figure to whom he is attached must also be shared with her sexual partner and other siblings, which forms the basis for the Oedipal situation, and makes separation and loss an inherent part of the attachment dynamic. For Melanie Klein (1986), the 'depressive position' represents the realisation that the loved and gratifying breast/mother and the hated and rejecting breast/mother are one and the same. For Bowlby, the human dilemma turns on the central importance of an attachment that cannot be entirely reliable, must perforce be shared, and will be lost, eventually (and often prematurely). The capacity to separate from attachment figure(s) and to form new attachments represents the developmental challenge of adolescence and young adulthood. The cycle repeats itself as parents attach themselves to their children only to let them go as *they* reach adolescence. Finally, as death of one's loved ones, and one's own death approaches, the 'monotropic' bond to life itself has gradually to be relinquished.

2 The 'secure base' effect

Mary Ainsworth (1982) first used the phrase 'secure base' to describe the ambience created by the attachment figure for the attached person. The essence of the secure base is that it provides a springboard for curiosity and exploration. When danger threatens we cling to our attachment figures. Once danger passes, their presence enables us to work, relax and play – but only if we are sure that the attachment figures will be there if we need them again. We can endure rough seas if we are sure of a safe haven. Anderson (1972) made a naturalistic study of mothers and their toddlers in a London park. The mothers sat on the park benches, reading or chatting while their children toddled and played on the surrounding grass. He found that each child had an invisible radius – a Maginot line – beyond which it would not venture to go. When it neared the limit it would begin to look anxiously towards the mother. Attachment exerted an invisible but powerful pull on the child, just as heavenly bodies are connected by gravitational forces. But unlike gravity, attachment makes its presence known by a *negative* inverse square law: the further the attached person is from their secure base, the greater the pull of attachment. The 'elastic band' which constitutes the attachment bond is slack and imperceptible in the presence of a secure base. If the secure base becomes unreliable or the limits of exploration are reached, the bond tugs at the heart-strings.

The example of the mother who leaves her child with the child minder and then worries about and misses her dreadfully suggests that attachment behaviour is not confined to infancy and applies to care-givers as well as care-seekers. Heard and Lake (1986) have extended the secure base concept in their model of an adult attachment dynamic in which they postulate a fundamental need for 'companionable interaction' based on 'preferred relationships in the attachment network'. These comprise, as in parent-child attachment, a mixture of support and exploration, with a sense of psychological proximity as the precondition for such companionship. Where no secure base exists, the individual is in a state of 'dissuagement', and resorts to defensive manoeuvres (such as splitting off anger; inhibition of sexuality; or conversely compulsive sexualisation of relationships) in order to minimise the pain of separation anxiety, and, if needs be, to manipulate support at the expense of truly reciprocal companionship.

Violence and a social facade

Jennifer, a successful painter, was forty when she entered psychotherapy. Her complaint was that she could never be her 'real self' in close relationships. In social situations she could be jolly and cheerful and was well liked; by herself she often felt depressed and anxious, but could cope, especially when she was painting. In her marriages (she had had two) she never felt at ease, unable to share feelings openly or to feel relaxed with her husbands. She had rather desperately sought some affirmation of herself through affairs, but in the end these left her feeling empty and valueless. Naturally enough these patterns were repeated transferentially in therapy and she bent her best efforts towards trying to please, seduce and sometimes (via projective identification) to exclude her therapist. She dated the death of her straightforward 'companionable self' and the shattering of her secure base to an incident where her much-feared father (who had been away at the war for the first three years of her life) was playing with her older brother and sister when Jennifer was about four. She tried to gain his attention but was ignored; she pinched his leg harder and harder until suddenly and terrifyingly he threw her across the room. From that day (and similar episodes were repeated in various ways throughout her childhood) she could only get attention, playfulness, support from others by means of pleasing them, controlling them, or vicariously caring for herself through her care for them (this characterised her relationship with her mother, herself chronically depressed). This illustrates in an extreme form a typical family pattern of absent-father/depressed-mother that so often underlies the lack of a secure base, and leads to defensive postures by the children who grow up in such an atmosphere. Progress in therapy only began when this woman had tested her therapist again and again for his reliability and had, inevitably, found him wanting, but still felt safe enough to reveal the extent of her disappointment and rage towards him.

3 Separation protest

Try to prise a limpet away from its rock and it will cling all the harder. The best test of the presence of an attachment bond is to observe the response to separation. Bowlby identified protest as the primary response produced in children by separation from their parents. Crying, screaming, shouting, biting, kicking – this 'bad' behaviour is the normal response to the threat to an attachment bond, and presumably has the function of trying to restore it, and, by 'punishing' the care-giver, of preventing further separation. The clinical implications of separation protest are very important and will be dealt with in subsequent chapters. For example, Ainsworth used it in devising her 'strange situation', the basic tool used for classifying the quality of attachment in children (see Chapter 6), and the analysis of patient responses to weekend and holiday 'breaks' are a basic theme in analytic psychotherapy (see Chapter 8).

A remarkable feature of attachment bonds is their durability. The persistence of attachment in the face of maltreatment and severe punishment has enormous implications for child and adult psychopathology. Harlow's monkeys clung ever more tightly to their cloth 'mothers' even when 'punished' by them with sudden blasts of compressed air (Rutter 1980)! It is hard to explain this phenomenon on the basis either of the psychoanalytic 'cupboard love' theory, or of reward-reinforcement learning theory. It is explicable along the ethological lines of Attachment Theory since stress will lead to an enhancement of attachment behaviour even when the source of that stress is the attachment figure itself. The 'frozen watchfulness' of the physically abused child is eloquent proof of the phenomenon of ambivalent attachment and its inhibition of normal exploration and playfulness.

THE DEVELOPMENT OF THE ATTACHMENT SYSTEM

The human infant is born in a state of great immaturity (a consequence, evolutionary biologists suggest, of the need to get the
huge human brain through the pelvic floor before it is too late!).
It is not surprising therefore that, unlike in ducks, monkeys and
other animals, the human attachment system takes several
months to develop. Only after six months does the baby begin
to exhibit the full triad of proximity seeking, secure base effect
and separation protest that we have described. The ontogeny of
the attachment system can be conveniently divided into four
phases.

1 0–6 months: orientation and pattern recognition

Although newborn babies cannot distinguish one person from
another, they are highly responsive to human contact. Centrally
important in this process is the sight of the human face, which
evokes intense interest. The onset of the smiling response around
four weeks marks the beginning of the cycles of benign interaction
that characterise the relationship between the baby and his care-
givers. The baby's smile evokes a mirroring smile in the mother;
the more she smiles back the more the baby responds, and so
on. As we shall see in Chapter 6, maternal *responsiveness* is a
key determinant of the quality of attachment as development
proceeds. Winnicott (1971) famously states: 'What does the baby
see when he or she looks at the mother's face? I am suggesting
that ordinarily what the baby sees is him or herself.' He goes on
in the same paper to suggest that what happens in psychotherapy
is 'a long term giving the patient back what the patient brings.
It is a complex derivative of the face that reflects what is there
to be seen' (Winnicott 1971).

Daniel Stern (1985), from a perspective of developmental psychology, and Kenneth Wright (1991), from a psychoanalytical
viewpoint, both see the mutual looking between mother and baby
as a key element in the development of an internal world in which
attachment can be represented and regulated. The invariability of
the mother's face, the recognition of it as a pattern, give the
baby a primitive sense of *history*, of continuity through time that
is integral to the sense of self. To evoke her smile provides a
sense of *agency* and effectiveness. Her mirroring response is the

first link between what is perceived *out there*, and what is felt *in here*.

For Wright the mother's face is the first symbol; her face is not part of the self and yet, because it is responsive, feels intimately connected to the self. In the Kleinian account of the origin of symbol formation – based on Freud's idea of hallucinatory wish-fulfilment – images are thought to arise as a consequence of *loss* or absence: 'no breast; so imagine a breast', thinks the Kleinian infant. Wright proposes a more harmonious theory in which the separation is simply spatial: the face is *over there, held off* and so is available for thinking about, contemplation, meditation. To watch a 3-month-old baby at the breast is to get *visible* proof of the rhythm of feeding and mutual gazing that constitutes the mother–child relationship at this stage. Freud, in his discussion of Leonardo (Freud 1910), seems to see looking as a sort of visual incorporation, a drinking in with the eyes, rather than a modality of relating with its own dynamic. The complexity and specificity of the visual world, as opposed to the gustatory world, is what makes looking the basis of attachment: 'Wine comes in at the mouth, love comes in at the eyes.' The world is mapped through the visual system: the mother's face is imaged on the retina and visual cortex before it is imagined in the inner world. We shall consider later some of the implications of the failure of this mirroring process.

As with looking, so with holding, a term used by Winnicott (1971) in his phrase 'the holding environment' to denote not just the physical holding of the baby by the mother but the entire psychophysiological system of protection, support, caring and containing that envelops the child, without which it would not survive physically or emotionally. The reliability and responsiveness of the holding environment form the nucleus of the emergent attachment patterns as the child begins the process of separation-individuation.

In the second half of the first six months the beginnings of an attachment relationship starts to be evident. The baby becomes much more discriminating in his looking. He listens out for and responds differently to his mother's voice; cries differently when she departs compared with other people; greets her differently; and begins to put his arms up towards her in a request to be picked up. She in turn responds to the physiological and social cues from her baby in a way that leads to the establishment of a mutual system of feedback and homeostasis. An interactive matrix is established, felt as a mutual 'knowing' of each other that is the hallmark of a secure mother–infant relationship.

2 6 months–3 years: 'set-goal' attachment

In the second half of the first year several developmental changes occur which mark the onset of attachment proper. Children removed from foster homes into permanent adoptive homes before 6 months show little distress, whereas after that watershed they show increased crying, clinging, apathy, and feeding and sleep disturbance (Bretherton 1985). Around 7 months the baby will begin to show 'stranger anxiety', becoming silent and clingy in the presence of an unknown person (Spitz 1950).

These changes coincide with the onset of locomotion in the child, which entails a much more complex system of communication if the baby is to remain in secure contact with the mother. The immobile baby is bound to remain where he is. The mother of the mobile baby needs to know that the child will move towards her at times of danger, and the child needs to be able to signal protest or distress when necessary to a mother who now feels she can put him down for a few minutes.

Bowlby conceives the attachment system at this stage as being based on 'set-goals', which he compares to the setting on a thermostat, maintained by a system of feedback control. The 'set-goal' for the infant is to keep 'close enough' to the mother: to use her as a secure base for exploration when environmental threat is at a minimum, and to exhibit separation protest or danger signalling when the need arises.

Figure 4.1 attempts to summarise the features of the attachment system at this stage. Several points should be made about this diagram. First, attachment behaviour, although usually discussed from the point of view of the attached person, is a *reciprocal relationship*. The parent is simultaneously offering complementary care-giving behaviour that matches, or should match, the attachment behaviour of the child. For example, when put in a new situation the child will, through *social referencing*, make eye contact with the mother, looking for cues which will sanction exploration or withdrawal. Second, and as a consequence, parent–child attachment systems can be seen in terms of continuously monitored *distance-regulation* (Byng-Hall 1980),

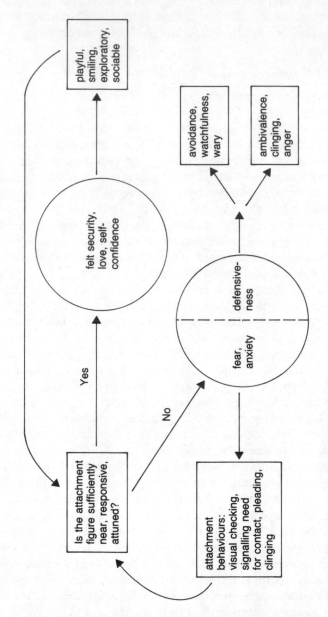

Figure 4.1 The attachment behavioural system

with many opportunities for problematic variants. The over-anxious parent may inhibit the child's exploratory behaviour, making them feel stifled or smothered; conversely, the neglectful parent may inhibit exploration by failing to provide a secure base, leading to feelings of anxiety or abandonment. Third, inherent in the model is the notion of an internal map or 'internal working model' which represents the relative whereabouts of the self and attachment figure. To the analytically minded psychotherapist this may seem like a rather uninteresting predominantly 'cognitive' map, but this would be mistaken. What is stored in the 'internal working model' is not so much an ordnance survey picture but an *affective* model which, if it could be translated into words, might be along the lines of 'I feel tense when my mummy goes out of the room so I must keep a good eye out for her and scream if necessary', or 'when my mummy comes so close to me while I am playing I feel uncomfortable, so I'll try to move away a bit, without discouraging her so much that she loses interest' (cf. Beebe and Lachmann 1988).

We have moved from a discussion of set-goals which keep toddler and parent in eyesight and earshot of each other to the idea of a *relationship*, and to a consideration of what internal processes might regulate it. This brings us to the attachment system in its fully fledged form which, Bowlby maintains, is established by the third birthday and persists from then on throughout life.

3 3 years onwards: the formation of a reciprocal relationship

As Bowlby first conceived it, the attachment system in the toddler was something like a 'homing device' in which the child was programmed to focus on the parent with the 'set-goal' of maintaining proximity. With the advent of language and the expanding psychological sophistication of the three- to four-year-old a much more complex pattern arises that cannot be described in simplistic behavioural terms. The child now can begin to think of his parents as separate people with their own goals and plans, and to devise ways of influencing them. If the mother is going to leave the child for the evening he may plead, bribe, charm or sulk in an attempt to maintain attachment, rather than crying or clinging as he would have done a year or two earlier. Attachment Theory at this point merges into a general theory about relationships (or 'affectional bonds', as Bowlby likes to call them) and how they are maintained, monitored and may go wrong.

INTERNAL WORKING MODELS

A key concept here is that of the 'internal working model'. This is Bowlby's way of describing the internal world of the psychoanalysts, but couched in characteristically practical terms. The idea of an internal 'model' of the world derives from Kenneth Craik's (1943) influential *The Nature of Explanation*, in which he argues that

> Thought models, or parallels reality . . . the organism carries a 'small-scale model' of external reality and its own possible actions within its head which enable it to react in a fuller, safer, and more competent way to the emergencies which face it'.

Wright (1991) has remarked how, until the advent of Winnicott's influence, the *work* ethic dominated the language of psychoanalysis: *working* through, getting the patient to *work* on their problems, forming a *working* alliance, and Bowlby's internal *working* models. Wright sees Winnicott as representing the female, maternal influence, a reaction against the paternal force of Freud. Bowlby in turn was in part reacting against the powerful women who had trained him, his analyst Joan Riviere, and supervisor, Melanie Klein. The idea of a 'working model' implies a practical mechanism, a down-to-earth title which he claimed 'allows for greater precision of description and provides a framework that lends itself more readily to the planning and execution of empirical research' (Bowlby 1981c).

Although derived from the psychoanalytic perspective, the idea of internal working models is perhaps closer to that of cognitive therapy (Beck *et al.* 1979) (itself also a development of and a reaction against the psychoanalytic paradigm). The developing child builds up a set of models of the self and others, based on repeated patterns of interactive experience. These 'basic assumptions' (Beck *et al.* 1979), 'representations of interactions that have been generalised' (Stern 1985), 'role relationship models' and 'self–other schemata' (Horowitz 1988), form relatively fixed representational models which the child uses to predict and relate to the world. A securely attached child will store an internal working model of a responsive, loving, reliable care-giver, and of a self that is worthy of love and attention and will bring these assumptions to bear on all other relationships. Conversely, an insecurely attached child may view the world as a dangerous place in which other people are to be treated with great caution, and see himself as ineffective and unworthy of love. These assumptions are relatively stable and enduring: those built up in the early years of life are particularly persistent and unlikely to be modified by subsequent experience.

Bowlby wished to recast psychoanalytic theory in terms of a systems approach in which feedback loops are a key element. They underlie the 'epigenetic' stability of psychological phenomena: the benign circles of healthy development, and the vicious circles of neurosis in which negative assumptions about the self and others become self-fulfilling prophecies.

THEORIES OF NEUROSIS: AVOIDANT AND AMBIVALENT ATTACHMENT

Bowlby uses the notion of faulty internal working models to describe different patterns of neurotic attachment. He sees the basic problem of 'anxious attachment' as that of maintaining attachment with a care-giver who is unpredictable or rejecting. Here the internal working model will be based not on accurate representation of the self and others, but on *coping*, in which the care-giver must be accommodated to. The two basic strategies here are those of *avoidance* or *adherence*, which lead to avoidant or ambivalent attachment (see Figure 4.2).

In avoidant attachment the child tries to minimise his needs for attachment in order to forestall rebuff, while at the same time remaining in distant contact with the care-giver whose rejection, like the person's own neediness, is removed from consciousness by what, based on Dixon's (1971) concept of perceptual defense, Bowlby calls 'defensive exclusion'. The ambivalent strategy involves clinging to the care-giver, often with excessive submissiveness, or adopting a role-reversal in which the care-giver is cared for rather than vice versa. Here feelings of anger at the rejection are most conspicuously subjected to defensive exclusion. A third pattern of insecure attachment, 'insecure disorganised', less common than the first two but probably associated with much more severe pathology, has also been delineated. All three patterns will be discussed in more depth in Chapter 6.

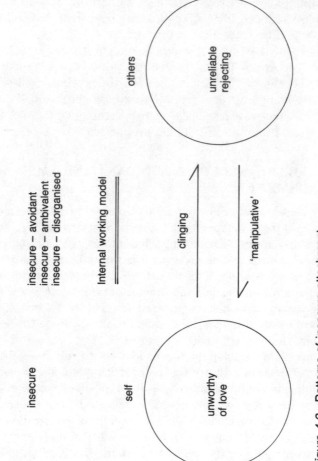

secure

insecure

insecure – avoidant
insecure – ambivalent
insecure – disorganised

Internal working model

self

others

unworthy
of love

unreliable
rejecting

clinging

'manipulative'

Figure 4.2 Patterns of insecure attachment

Although these strategies have the function of maintaining attachment in the face of difficulties, a price has to be paid. The attachment patterns so established are clearly restricted and, if repeated in all relationships, will be maladaptive. Also, defensive exclusion means that models cannot be updated in the light of new experience. Bowlby visualises the coexistence of incompatible models – for example, 'the good mother who lets me come near to her (if I look after her)', and the 'bad mother who rejects me and makes me angry (and who I'll try not to think about)' – which lead to sudden changes of mood and poor adaptation. A central problem created by defensive exclusion is the lack of opportunity for emotional processing of painful affect, particularly evident in pathological mourning, which leads to the persistence of primitive feelings of hate and abandonment and restricts emotional growth and development.

ATTACHMENT IN ADULT LIFE

This consideration of internal working models has been a necessary diversion in our discussion of attachment across the life cycle. It is through internal working models that childhood patterns of attachment are carried through into adult life and, as we shall discuss in Chapter 6, are transmitted to the next generation.

As children grow older and begin to reach adolescence they tolerate increasing periods of separation from their parents. Does this mean that the attachment 'phase' has been outgrown, to be superseded by, say, 'adult genitality'? According to Bowlby's 'epigenetic' model, emphatically not! As he sees it, attachment and dependency, although no longer evident in the same way as in young children, remain active throughout the life cycle. For adolescents the parental home still remains an important anchor point, and the attachment system will become re-activated at times of threat, illness or fatigue. The turbulence of adolescence can be seen in Bowlbian terms as springing from the complexity of detachment and re-attachment which the adolescent must accomplish. To disengage from parental attachments, to mourn that loss, to move on via the transitional phase of peer group attachment to the pair-bonding of adult life is no easy task.

Bowlby saw marriage, or its equivalent, as the adult manifestation of attachment whose companionship provides a secure base allowing for work and exploration, and a protective shell in times of need. Like Fairbairn (1952), but unlike Freud (1929) for whom affection was 'aim-inhibited sexuality', Bowlby saw bodily pleasure not as an aim in itself but as a 'signpost to the object', and so tends rather to downplay the role of sexuality in marriage. Just as the mother–infant relationship cannot, in Bowlby's eyes, be understood as primarily based on feeding, so adult pair-bonding cannot be adequately explained by sexuality. Sex without attachment and sexless marriages are both all too common, and suggest that the attachment system and sexual behaviour are separable psychological entities, however much society might wish that this were not so. 'In sickness and in health' is a reminder that the psychological purpose of marriage is to provide a secure base and an attachment system which can be awakened in times of need. The unconscious operation of the attachment system via internal working models probably plays an important part in the choice of marital partner and relationship patterns in marriage. Holmes (1993) has described a pattern of 'phobic-counterphobic' marriage in which an ambivalently attached person will be attracted to an avoidant 'counter-phobic' spouse in a system of mutual defence against separation anxiety.

The steeplejack's wife

A young woman developed multiple phobic symptoms soon after the birth of her first baby. At first her fears were of harming the baby; later she became severely agoraphobic, and took to phoning her mother several times a day for reassurance. She insisted on moving house so as to be within easy reach of her mother. Her mother 'helped' by looking after the baby for much of the day, and would herself telephone frequently to check if the baby was 'all right'. When the patient told her mother of a dream in which her son had fallen under a lorry, the mother (who was unlikely to have read Freud) told her that this meant that she wanted to kill her son! As a child the patient had lacked a secure base with this mother whom she felt neglected her in favour of two younger sisters, one of whom had been chronically ill with kidney disease, while the other was epileptic, and to whom she had devoted all her attention.

In an initial phase of individual therapy she was able to link her fears of harming the baby with aggressive feelings towards her younger sisters and her angry dependency on her mother, but her symptoms persisted. Marital therapy was then offered. At the first session she proudly announced that her husband – unlike herself – was afraid of nothing. He accepted the compliment rather diffidently, but confirmed that he had been more or less self-reliant since the age of ten, when his parents had divorced and he and his younger brother had been left to fend for themselves on the rough estate where they lived. He worked as a scaffolder on high buildings. When asked if it was true, as his wife believed, that he was frightened of nothing, he confessed that he had slipped on a plank that morning and had been very scared, and that since the birth of the baby he had been much less of a daredevil. His wife seemed surprised at this revelation, but visibly relaxed and perked up. He then admitted that he saw it as his task to conceal his fears and worries from his wife because of her 'illness'. For example, he resented his mother-in-law's intrusions into their family life, but was petrified by the idea of confronting her. Given the task of answering the phone when she rang, and explaining that his wife was too busy to speak, he became quite shaky and said that he would much rather be asked to go up a chimney-stack in a high wind! The patient was asked to rehearse him in this by role-playing her mother, and the session ended in laughter, with a much less anxious patient and subsequent good clinical improvement.

This example shows how attachment patterns are stored as internal working models. The patient saw herself as uncared for, unworthy of care and therefore unable to care for her baby, whom she perceived, in a sense correctly, as in danger of neglect or attack. Lacking a secure base inside herself she was unable to provide one for others, and her anger and frustration about this lack of care interfered with her capacity to look after her baby. The intrusiveness of her mother and the detachment of her husband (due in turn to their own faulty attachment patterns) served to reinforce her sense of an absent secure base. Her demandingness and dependency represented a desperate effort to create an ideally safe attachment, and her protest about the lack of it. Giving her an opportunity to nurture her husband made her feel better about herself, and the affective release of anger and laughter in the sessions enabled her to revise her internal working models towards a more realistic assessment of her capacities.

We shall discuss in Chapter 6 important evidence showing how, as Winnicott (1965) suggested, the advent of parenthood calls into being the new parent's own attachment history. As the life cycle unfolds, each parent is presented with new challenges to their capacity to hold, respond to, attune with and release their children. With increasing age the depth and strength of attachment bonds increases. At the same time losses begin to accumulate. Divorce, and separation and death begin to take their toll. We shall see in the next chapter how Attachment Theory provides a schematic map of the painful terrain of depression, disappointment and bereavement.

CONCLUSION: THE MEDIATION AND PSYCHOPATHOLOGY OF ATTACHMENT

Bowlby's original mission was to find links between major life events such as parental loss or neglect and the development of psychiatric symptoms in children and adults. In 'Forty-four juvenile thieves' he linked such disruptions with the two major psychiatric disorders of childhood: conduct disorders and phobias. He anticipated that there would be connections between problems of attachment in childhood and adult conditions such as depression, agoraphobia and psychopathic disorders. He made a fundamental distinction between *secure* and *anxious* attachment, seeing the latter as the precursor of developmental difficulty and adult psychiatric disease.

In his early formulations he saw anxious attachment as resulting from gross disruptions of parenting such as parental death or divorce. He also incriminated major qualitative difficulties in parenting which included depression and unresponsiveness on the part of a parent; threats of suicide directed at the child; threats to send or give the child away; and situations of role reversal in which the child is expected to 'mother' the parent and be a caregiver for her, either overtly, or as in the case of the steeplejack's wife, by becoming an 'ill' child to whom the anxious parent can cling.

Bowlby the systematiser and theoretician relied greatly on collaborators to provide the experimental evidence upon which his ideas rested. James Robertson's (1952) research and films confirmed his ideas about maternal deprivation, and Mary Ainsworth (1982, 1989) is generally seen as the co-author of Attachment Theory. Since his original formulations the research of Ainsworth and her students has extended and to some extent modified Bowlby's original ideas. In particular, the focus has shifted away from gross disruptions of care such as bereavement, which, as discussed in Chapter 3, do not in themselves necessarily result in psychopathology if conditions are otherwise favourable. The contemporary emphasis is much more on the subtleties of parent–child interaction which contribute to the qualitative features of the attachment bond. Maternal *responsiveness* and the ability to *attune* to her child are seen as key features in determining the security or otherwise of attachment bonds.

We have assumed in this chapter that the mother is likely to be the primary care-giver in the first year of life. Changing patterns of family life mean that this is not necessarily the case. The evidence, such as it is (Brazelton and Cramer 1991), suggests that fathers are as capable of providing responsive attunement as mothers, and for the purposes of the arguments presented in this and subsequent chapters mothers and fathers should for the most part be considered as interchangeable. But here too there are subtle differences. Mothers are more likely to offer a containing 'envelope' for infant activity, while fathers tend to interact more intensely but for much shorter periods, in which can be found the beginnings of organised play as development proceeds.

Other important new themes to emerge from the work of the post-Bowlbians have been the emphasis on narrative and 'autobiographical competence' (Holmes 1992) as manifestations of secure attachment. These and other research findings relevant to Attachment Theory will be reviewed in Chapter 6. But we must turn now to the second of Bowlby's great themes, the breaking of affectional bonds, and the need for affective processing so as to mitigate the psychological impact of separation and loss.

Chapter 5

Loss, anger and grief

A liability to experience separation anxiety and grief are the ineluctable results of a love relationship, of caring for someone.

(Bowlby 1973a)

Towards the end of his long life Bowlby advised one of his former research students: 'Always choose a central topic when doing research. That way you know you can get sufficient data. That's why I studied separation. You can't miss it. Whatever people say, it is there in the data' (Hamilton 1991). As we have seen in Chapter 3, Bowlby's insistence that people *had* missed the significance of separation and loss as a cause of unhappiness, delinquency and psychiatric illness met a receptive audience in the post-war era of recuperation and reparation. The early work of Bowlby and his associates on loss comprised a systematic description of the psychological reactions to separation and bereavement in children and adults (Bowlby 1953b: Bowlby *et al.* 1952; Parkes 1964); once Attachment Theory was in place, he could then go on to develop a theoretical account of mourning, based on psychoanalysis but supplemented by the insights of ethology (Bowlby 1980).

EARLY STUDIES

Bowlby's first attempts to understand the effects of separation on psychological development were retrospective studies based on the histories of children and adolescents referred to the child guidance clinics where he worked. In his study of 'Forty-four juvenile thieves' (Bowlby 1944), 40 per cent of the offenders had

had prolonged separations of 6 months or more from their mothers or foster-mothers during the first five years of their life, compared with only 5 per cent of controls. Of the 'affectionless' thieves, twelve out of fourteen had had prolonged separations, compared with only five of the remaining thirty. Bowlby saw two main factors as being of etiological significance. First, the separation itself:

> Thus the essential factor which all these separations have in common is that, during the early development of his object-relationships, the child is suddenly removed and placed with strangers. He is snatched away from the people and places which are familiar and whom he loves and placed with people and in surroundings which are unknown and alarming.
>
> (Bowlby 1944)

This must have struck many a sympathetic chord in readers who had survived six years of wartime evacuation, enforced separation and bereavement.

The second factor connecting delinquency and the 'affectionless character' with separation was the 'inhibition of love by rage and the phantasies resulting from rage'. The separated child responds to the absence of his parent with feelings of fury and destructiveness. Normally, as Klein and later Bion described, the soothing presence of the parent would enable these phantasies to be modified by reality, and therefore to give up their dominance in the child's mind. But if the mother is absent, or is herself aggressive and liable to retaliate rather than accept her child's anger, the growing child may be left harbouring phantasies of revenge and hatred which then become manifest in delinquent behaviour. This may be accompanied by an indifference born of

> [the] determination at all costs not to risk again the disappointment and resulting rages and longings which wanting someone very much and not getting them involves . . . a policy of self-protection against the slings and arrows of their own turbulent feelings.
>
> (Bowlby 1944)

We see in this early work the prefigurings of three of Bowlby's most insistent themes: the centrality of loss as a determinant of disturbance, the importance of the mother in neutralising and defusing the destructive effects of rage in response to loss, and the use of affective withdrawal as a defense against the pain of unmet longing or anger faced alone. Bowlby had already identified the importance of *expression* of anger, rather than its repression, and the role of the parents in fostering or holding this back, in his pre-war study of aggression:

> Take the child away from the fire, deny it a second piece of cake, but avoid being angry or hurt or disapproving if a scream of rage or a kick on the shins is the immediate consequence of thwarting a child's will to happiness. To permit children to express their *feelings* of aggression, whilst preventing *acts* of irremediable destruction is, we suggest, one of the greatest gifts that parents can give to their children.
>
> (Durbin and Bowlby 1938)

As we saw in Chapter 3, Bowlby's own retrospective findings were buttressed by his review of the world literature on the effects of separation, and here too he emphasises the importance of *active protest* as a mark of a positive response to separation: 'a violent reaction is normal and an apathetic resignation a sign of unhealthy development' (Bowlby 1965).

PROSPECTIVE STUDIES: CHILDREN IN HOSPITAL

Together with James Robertson (Robertson and Bowlby 1952b), Bowlby was next able to establish by direct observation the effects on children of temporary separation from their parents. They studied the reactions of children who were taken into hospital, which in those days required almost complete absence of contact with parents during the admission (for fear of cross-infection), and a series of constantly changing carers in the hospital ward. Profound effects were noted, especially in the younger age groups. The children initially became tearful, crying and calling bitterly for their parents, and rejecting the staff's attempts to mollify or distract them. Later, bored indifference and apathy seemed to take over, with the children isolating themselves from their peers, sitting listlessly staring into space, playing and eating little. Finally, children appeared to 'recover' and to become active once more, but if hospitalisation was prolonged their relationships with adults and other children appeared superficial and self-centered compared with before.

These three phases were described by Bowlby as the stages of *protest, withdrawal* and *detachment*. Feelings of protest re-emerged when these separated children were reunited with their parents, who were subjected to a mixture of rejection (even to the point of failing to recognise them), angry attacks and clinging in the days following return from hospital. Some of these changes were long-lived and could be detected up to two years later. They also found that the effects of separation could be mitigated by a number of common-sense measures including regular hospital visiting by parents, preliminary reconnaissance visits to the hospital ward, allowing children to take familiar comforting objects like teddy-bears with them when they went into hospital, and in the case of separations not involving hospital, placing them with adults who were previously known and trusted. All of these moves have by now become part of routine parental and pediatric practice.

AN ANATOMY OF MOURNING

The 1960s saw two important developments in the understanding of the psychological impact of loss. First, Bowlby was joined at the Tavistock by Colin Murray Parkes who undertook a systematic study of bereavement in adults which complemented and confirmed Robertson's (1952) earlier work with children (Parkes 1975). Second, the crystallisation of Attachment Theory provided a theoretical basis on which to understand these empirical findings.

Bowlby's theory of bereavement is essentially an extension of his theory of separation anxiety which we have considered in the previous chapter. He sees anxiety as realistic response to separation or threatened separation of a vulnerable individual from his care-giver. Since care-seeker and care-giver form a reciprocal partnership, and since the attachment dynamic continues throughout adult life, separation anxiety will arise whenever the parent–child, adult–spouse or adult–companion relationship is threatened. The components of separation anxiety include a subjective feeling of worry, pain and tension; angry protest, whose function is to register displeasure and to punish the errant partner so as to prevent repetition; and a restless searching for the missing person.

Bowlby sees the grief reaction as a special case of separation anxiety, bereavement being an irreversible form of separation. He believes that the psychological response to the trauma of separation is biologically programmed in the same way that the inflammatory response is an orderly sequence of physiological responses to physical trauma – redness, swelling, heat and pain. The early phases of grief consist of an intense form of separation anxiety. The later phases result from the confusion and misery that arise from the realisation that the secure base to whom the bereaved individual would turn for comfort in distress is the very person who is no longer available. With this in mind, let us look now at the four phases of mourning (Bowlby 1980, 1982a, 1988a) in more detail.

Stage 1: numbing

A soldier wounded on the field of battle may feel no pain and continue to fight until help is at hand. In the same way, perhaps, the very earliest response to a sudden bereavement may be an apparent calmness based on emotional shutdown in which all feelings are suppressed, or reality denied, until the bereaved person is in a safe enough situation to let go a little.

A bereaved wife in the casualty department

A young scaffolder was brought into the casualty department dead, having fallen from a tall building. There were no external signs of injury. When his wife arrived she was completely and chillingly calm, expressing no emotion, simply saying: 'Oh, but he's not dead, he's asleep, doesn't he look beautiful and peaceful.' It was only when, several hours later, her mother arrived that she began to sob and wail uncontrollably.

Stage 2: yearning, searching, anger

Bowlby places the *search for the lost object* at the centre of the mourning response. There may be physical restlessness and wandering as the bereaved person goes from room to room, from place to place, scanning, looking, hoping that their lost loved one may reappear. A similar process goes on psychologically in which the bereaved person goes over in their mind every detail of the events leading up to the loss, in a kind of compulsive 'action replay', hoping that some mistake may have been made and that past events can be made to turn out differently.

Freud (1917) saw the purpose of this mental searching as that of detachment: 'Mourning has a quite precise psychical task to perform: its function is to detach the survivor's memories and hopes from the dead.' Bowlby, by contrast, sees purpose in evolutionary rather than teleological terms, and views the mental searching of the bereaved as an attempt to recover and be reunited with the lost object. Similarly, Bowlby's understanding of the prevalence of visual images of the dead person that so often haunt the bereaved is of an intense 'perceptual set' towards the sight and sound of the lost person that can lead to misinterpretation of auditory and visual clues. Just as the 3-month-old infant quickens at the sound of his mother's footsteps and scans his visual field anxiously until he can meet her greeting smile with his, so the bereaved person is desperately trying to track down his missing attachment figure. Following Darwin (1872), Bowlby sees the facial expressions and crying of the bereaved as a resultant of the tendency to scream in the hope of awakening the attention of a negligent care-giver, and the social inhibition of such screaming.

Anger too is part of the normal response to separation: 'almost every separation has a happy ending, and often a small or large dash of aggression will assist this outcome' (Bowlby 1961c). Bowlby emphasises again and again the importance of the expression of anger if the bereaved person is to recover:

> Only if he can tolerate the pining, the more or less conscious searching, the seemingly endless examination of why and how the loss occurred, and anger at everyone who might be responsible, not even sparing the dead person, can he gradually come to realise and accept that loss is in truth permanent and that his life must be shaped anew.
>
> (Bowlby 1982a)

The anger so often seen towards potential comforters whose aim is to help the bereaved person 'come to terms' with the loss, or towards doctors responsible for the care of the dead person, can be understood in this light too. They represent the loss of hope that the loved one might somehow be alive. Their cold comfort can trigger an angry outburst in one who, already weakened by the stress of loss, wants nothing less than to be reminded that the loss is indeed irrecoverable. If only someone can be blamed then this allows the 'secret hope that perhaps in some miraculous way to seek out the villain will lead to recovery of loss' (Bowlby 1961c).

The lonely widow

Marion was fifty-five when her husband died suddenly of a heart attack. Childless, they had been married for thirty years and had returned to the United Kingdom after years of living over-seas, having lost all their possessions in a fire. Marion had relied on her husband for everything, sheltering behind his competence and social confidence. She 'coped' well at first after his death, but then was admitted to hospital after taking a large overdose. She had only been found in time because the milk-man had noticed uncollected bottles and raised the alarm. When she recovered she explained how furious she had felt when her doctor (who had failed in her eyes to save her husband's life) had summoned her for a cervical smear test, without appar-ently realising that she had had a hysterectomy some years pre-viously.

Therapy with her meant withstanding a torrent of fury about the unfairness of life. She blamed the doctors, the laxity of modern society (the England she had returned to was such a different place from the one she had left), the insurance compan-ies, the Government – everyone. She agreed reluctantly to try not to kill herself, although she continued to insist that life with-out her husband was futile and meaningless. Contrary to expec-tation, exploring her childlessness, of which the GP's summons had reminded her, did not lead to feelings of sadness about her lack of children. Instead she revealed how she, unlike her hus-band, had never wanted children since she feared that this would divert his care and attention from her, as she felt had happened with her mother in her family (she, like Bowlby's mother, was the oldest of six) when her younger siblings were born. A history of excessive dependency and exclusive monotropism is a signifi-cant predisposing factor towards prolonged grief reactions (Parkes 1975).

Stages 3 and 4: disorganisation and despair: reorganisation

The diagram of the attachment relationship (Figure 4.1) shown in the previous chapter depicted a dynamic equilibrium between care-seeker and care-giver, constantly monitored, quiescent at times of exploration, activated at times of stress. Bowlby (1980) likens the shock of loss to a see-saw in which one person is suddenly removed, and quotes C. S. Lewis on his widowerhood: 'So many roads once; now so many culs-de-sac.' The basic dilemma of the bereaved is, as we have said, that the loss removes not only the loved one, but also the secure base to which the bereaved person would expect to turn in their hour of need.

Loss throws the inner world of the sufferer into turmoil. All the assumptions and expectations which depended on the presence of the loved one are now thrown into question. Where can the bereaved person find hope and comfort in the face of his inner turmoil and confusion? The quasi-depressive state which marks the third stage of grief can be understood in a number of ways. Freud (1917) recognised that some internal work was occurring which was necessary before the person could begin to form new attachments. For him the key feature was *identification* with the lost object; in Klein's (1986) word, the lost person is 'reinstated' in the inner world in the course of healthy grief so that he or she forms part of a composite internal representation of reality.

Melanie Klein (1986) sees the depression and apathy and withdrawal of the bereaved as a regression to infancy, a result of the assault on the security of the inner world which has been so painstakingly built up through childhood. For Klein grief is 'shot through with persecutory anxiety and guilt' (Bowlby 1961a) because the bereaved person is thrown back to the abandonments and failures of early childhood. During the phase of disorganisation the bereaved person is constantly questioning and questing, but 'reality passes its verdict – that the object no longer exists – upon each single one of the memories and hopes' (Klein 1986). Just as the infant, through maternal tolerance and capacity to process conflict and negative affect learns that the lost breast will reappear, that his anger has not destroyed his mother's love, so the bereaved person begins once more to build up his inner world:

> every advance in the process of mourning results in a deepening in the individual's relation to his inner objects, in the

happiness of regaining them after they were felt to be lost. This is similar to the way in which the young child step by step builds up his relation to external objects, for he gains trust not only from pleasant experiences, but also from the ways in which he overcomes frustrations and unpleasant experiences, nevertheless retaining his good objects.

(Klein 1986)

Bowlby is critical of Klein for what he sees as her overemphasis on the persecutory aspect of normal (as opposed to abnormal) grief, and for her neglect of the *reality* of the danger to which the bereaved person is exposed (widowers die of a broken heart more frequently than comparable non-bereaved men). Nevertheless, her account of the impact of death on the internal world is entirely compatible with the Bowlbian view that the work of grief consists of rebuilding a secure inner base, that the building of secure attachment depends on a secure holding environment which in the past has been reliable enough to withstand and process hostility, and that new attachments can only be formed once old ones are relinquished.

A widower – at twenty-six

Jock was a tough shipbuilder from the Clyde. At twenty-six his wife died suddenly of a cerebral haemorrhage, leaving him with six children aged eight to 6 months. He tried for a few weeks to carry on as normal but suddenly took all the children to his sister and brother-in-law and set off for London. There he led the life of a tramp, living on the streets and in doss houses, drinking heavily, fighting a lot and moving on. Eventually he was brought to the emergency clinic of the hospital, where he told his story. He spoke of his feelings of rage and fury towards his wife for abandoning him, about which he felt intensely guilty and about his incomprehension that God (he was a devout Catholic) should have allowed such a thing to happen to him; of the despair and chaos which he felt inside; of his wish to smash anyone and everyone who thwarted or tried to control him; and of his need to drink to blot out the pain of losing the wife whom he loved so much. His drinking and way of life continued, but he went on coming to the clinic to talk. Then, suddenly and without warning he disappeared. A few weeks later he wrote saying that he had returned to Glasgow, had stopped drinking and was now happily looking after the children. A further letter about a year later confirmed that things continued to go well.

Perhaps Jock felt sufficiently 'held' (in the Winnicottian sense) by his weekly contact with the therapist at the hospital to be able to rebuild his inner world so that he could become once more a secure base for his children – leaving his therapist as abruptly as his wife had 'left' him. For Bowlby the opportunity for emotional release is an essential ingredient in healthy mourning, avoiding the defensive manoeuvres which unexpressed emotion requires:

> The behaviour of potential comforters plays a large part in determining whether a bereaved person is sad, perhaps dreadfully sad, or becomes despairing and depressed as well . . . if all goes well, since he will not be afraid of intense and unmet desires for love from the person lost, he will let himself be swept by pangs of grief and tearful expressions of yearning, and distress will come naturally.
>
> (Bowlby 1982a)

MOURNING AND ADULT PSYCHOPATHOLOGY

Bowlby's early studies had convinced him of the far-reaching effects of separation and bereavement in childhood. He was convinced that much of adult psychiatric disability could be traced back to such traumata. This view is supported by recent psychophysiological findings that early separation can have long-lasting effects on the sensitivity of brain receptors, leading to permanently raised anxiety levels (Van de Kolk 1987; Gabbard 1992). Post (1992) has similarly argued that depression in adult life may originate with environmental trauma that is encoded in brain changes in protein and RNA, on the analogy of the 'kindling' phenomenon in epilepsy in which the sensitivity of brain cells becomes progressively greater with each seizure, so that what starts as a response to an environmental stimulus becomes eventually an intrinsic feature of the brain.

Bowlby was also convinced that the response of the adult world to a child's distress had a decisive influence on the outcome of loss. He was implacably opposed to the stiff-upper-lip attitude, and disparagement of 'childishness' which epitomised his generation, class and profession. Love, tenderness, encouragement of emotional expression even if hostile, and acceptance of the life-long imperative for mutual dependency were his watchwords.

Recent epidemiological research (Tennant 1988) suggests that the influence of childhood bereavement *per se* on adult psychiatric disorder is probably less significant than Bowlby imagined. Parental disruption and disturbance is a much more potent cause of difficulty and depression than loss in itself. But, as we shall see in Chapters 6 and 9, the current evidence suggests that Bowlby was right to emphasise the real nature of environmental influence and to make quite sharp distinctions between normal and abnormal developmental patterns, a point which he felt the psychoanalysts consistently fudged. His hunch that loss was a key research issue has been proved right, but in a more subtle way than he might have imagined, and one which is compatible with the Kleinian view from which he was so careful to distance himself. The manner in which a child's carers respond to her or his reactions to loss, whether major or minor – to the anger and pining and demandingness – may crucially influence that child's subsequent development. The establishment of a secure internal base, a sense that conflict can be negotiated and resolved, the avoidance of the necessity for primitive defences – all this depends on parental handling of the interplay between attachment and loss that is the leitmotiv of the Bowlbian message.

COMPANIONSHIP AND ATTACHMENT: A POETIC POSTSCRIPT

Being highly intelligent, very well-organised and slightly obsessional, Bowlby was a master of any topic to which he put his mind: for example, he re-read the whole of Freud during his Stanford fellowship in 1957. The corollary of this was that he tended to avoid those few subjects of which he had only passing or partial knowledge, one of which was English literature (U. Bowlby 1991). Having no such scruples – perhaps to my discredit – I conclude this chapter by considering three classic poems of grief from the English canon, which in their non-scientific way lend some support to Bowlby's thesis on mourning.

Milton's *Lycidas* and Tennyson's *In Memoriam* are both poems by young men about the loss of loved and valued fraternal comrades. It is debatable whether friendship (and sibship) fulfil the criteria of proximity seeking, secure-base effect and separation protest which are the hallmarks of a full-blown attachment relationship. Weiss (1982) distinguishes the companionship provided by friends from the intimacy of adult attachment typically to be found in a sexual partnership. He showed how wives who move because of their husband's job to new towns felt cut off from their friends and bored, but did not experience the specific empty loneliness that widows or separated people feel when loss of a spouse first hits. Similarly, Heard and Lake (1986) write about the need for 'like-minded companions of similar experience and stamina with whom to engage in mutually interesting and enjoyable activities' as part of the 'attachment dynamic'. A cursory glance at any lonely hearts column will attest to the reality of this need. The prime role of friendship seems to facilitate exploratory activity rather than to provide a secure base, although without a secure base no exploration is possible, and many intimate relationships, especially marriage, provide both. It seems likely that friendship or sibship does have a more central role as a source for a secure base in certain circumstances: in adolescence; among comrades in intense and isolated circumstances such as the armed services or mountaineering expeditions; and between siblings when the parental relationship is difficult or defective. The latter was certainly the case for Tennyson, who had an extremely unhappy and tormented childhood which he survived mainly through his writing and intelligence (Hamilton 1986), and, from his teenage years, through his friendship with Arthur Hallam who, although two years younger, became his mentor, sponsor and champion. Hallam's premature death when Tennyson was only twenty-four led to near-breakdown for the poet. *In Memoriam* was started within weeks of the loss, but was only completed and published some thirteen years later.

Milton's *Lycidas* 'bewails' the death of a 'learned friend' (Edward King) drowned in the Irish Sea – like Tennyson's Hallam, a childhood companion and one who shared Milton's radical anti-clericalism. Milton's mother had died a few months earlier; numbed, Milton had apparently been unable to write anything to mark her loss. The scene is pastoral and the two friends are depicted as shepherds. The need at times of grief to return to the good object (breast-hill) is evoked:

For we were nursed upon the self-same hill,
Fed the same flock by fountain, shade, and rill.

The centrepiece of the poem is the attack on the 'corrupted clergy then in their height', drawn as self-serving, ignorant shepherds. Like so many prematurely bereaved people, Milton rails against the injustice of fate: why has *my* loved one died, who did not deserve it, and not those undeserving souls who live on?

'How well could I have spared for thee, young swain,
Enow of such as for their bellies' sake
Creep, and intrude, and climb into the fold! . . .
Blind mouths! that scarce themselves know how to hold
A sheep-hook . . .
The hungry sheep look up, and are not fed,
But swoln with wind, and the rank mist they draw,
Rot inwardly, and foul contagion spread.'

The inner world is contaminated and fouled by the anger and despair of the poet, then projected onto the corrupt priests who are held to blame for the loss.

The action of the poem takes place in a single night in which the poet passes through the stages of sadness, despair, anger, blame and depression until he reaches acceptance, with the help of two images from the natural world. The first are the garlands of flowers with which to 'strew the laureat hearse where Lycid lies', and which serve to link the loss of Lycidas with the natural transience of beauty. In the second he pictures the sun setting over the ocean where Lycidas is drowned, only to rise again the next morning,

and with new spangled ore
Flames in the forehead of the morning sky.

An image of setting and rising, of separation and reunion, has replaced the sense of irretrievable loss. A secure base is re-established, mirroring perhaps the regular appearance and disappearance of the feeding mother. The poet can begin once more to explore, no longer enshrouded, but enveloped by a cloak that moves and lives:

At last he rose, and twitched his mantle blue:
To-morrow to fresh woods and pastures new.

In *In Memoriam* we see many of the same themes. In recalling his love for Hallam, Tennyson is taken back to pre-verbal paradisial times before the loss, reminiscent of the mother's attunement to her baby's needs, which leads, in Winnicottian terms, to the opening out of a transitional space between them. The poet describes the two friends' sense of intuitive, empathic understanding:

> Dear as the mother to the son
> More than my brothers are to me . . .
>   Thought leapt out to wed with Thought
> Ere thought could wed itself with speech.

But then the dreadful boat brings the dead body home. Tennyson contrasts his own empty hands and those reunited with their attachment figures:

> Thou bring'st the sailor to his wife
>   And travelled men from foreign lands
>   And letters unto trembling hands
> And, thy dark freight, a vanished life.

Tennyson tackles the tragic implications of monotropism: attachments are not transferable, or only so by a slow and painful process of withdrawal and re-attachment. By contrast, nature becomes an indifferent mother who cares equally and indiscriminately for all her 'children' and has no special affection for any one of them.

> Are God and Nature then at strife,
>   That Nature lends such evil dreams?
>   So careful of the type she seems,
> So careless of the single life?

Despair strikes, meaning is destroyed, when the interplay of attachment, with its mutual reinforcement, its linking of inner world and outer reality is disrupted:

> 'So careful of the type'? But no.
>   From scarped cliff and quarried stone
>   She cries, 'A thousand types are gone;
> I care for nothing, all shall go.'

Loss throws us back to our childhood, to our primary attachments:

> but what am I?
> An infant crying in the night:
> An infant crying for the light:
> And with no language but a cry.

Tennyson begins to think on a new time-scale and to see the possibility of new attachments, as one generation succeeds another:

> Unwatch'd, the garden bough shall sway,
>   The tender blossom flutter down . . .

> Till from the garden and the wild
> A fresh association blow,
> And year by year the landscape grow
> Familiar to the stranger's child.

Finally he returns to the image of mother and child, to the hatching of individuality from their symbiotic mixed-upness (Balint 1964). The mother's 'roundness' takes him round the corner of his developmental pathway towards a less despairing separation in which the inner world is strengthened and clarified:

> The baby new to earth and sky
>   What time his tender palm is prest
>   Against the circle of the breast
> Has never thought that 'this is I'

> So rounds he to a separate mind
>   From whence clear memory may begin
>   As through the frame that binds him in
> His isolation grows defined.

So it is with grief where, if all goes well, can come a strengthening of the inner world, of memory and definition. As we shall argue in Chapter 8, the importance of telling a story, of 'clear memory' is central to the poet's (and the psychotherapist's) mission.

John Donne's 'A Valediction: forbidding mourning' also concerns a sea voyage, and also uses the image of a 'round' or circle as an antidote to the abyss of loss and separation. This is a poem about anticipatory grief, given by Donne to his wife before setting sail for France in November 1611 (Gardner 1957).

He starts by advocating a slipping away on parting, which he compares with death, rather than an abrupt and emotional separation:

As virtuous men pass mildly away,
  And whisper to their soules to goe
Whilst some of their sad friends doe say
  The breath goes now, and some say no.

He contrasts their love which that of 'dull sublunary lovers', who
lack a secure inner base and who therefore are dependent on
one another's physical presence. They

    cannot admit
Absence, because it doth remove
  Those things which elemented it.

But we . . .
Interassured of the mind,
  Care lesse, eyes, lips, and hands to misse.

He pictures the invisible but precious bonds which link carer and
cared-for, lover and beloved in an attachment relationship as
slender threads of gold:

Our two souls therefore, which are one,
  Though I must goe, endure not yet
A breach, but an expansion,
  Like gold to ayery thinnesse beate.

Then, in another brilliant metaphysical metaphor, he imagines
the internal working model of self and other as the two ends of
a pair of compasses:

Thy soule the fixt foot, makes no show
  To move, but doth, if th'other doe.

And though it in the center sit,
  Yet when the other far doth rome,
It leanes, and hearkens after it,
  And growes erect, as it comes home. . .

Thy firmnes makes my circle just,
  And makes me end, where I begunne.

We have mentioned how Bowlby says little about sexuality and
is at pains to separate 'mating behaviour' from 'attachment
behaviour'. The sexual imagery of this poem – despite appear-
ances to the contrary ladies *do* move, perhaps 'grow erect' even,
the lover 'ending' (that is, in orgasm) where he 'begun' (namely,

was born) – combines in a profound way sexuality and attachment. The rhythm of sexuality, of coming together and separating, is linked both with death and the parting of soul from body at the start of the poem, and with birth at the end. They are held together by the central image of the secure base or 'interassurance' of lover and beloved. Seen in this way, attachment is a unifying principle that reaches from the biological depths of our being to its furthest spiritual reaches. The inevitability of loss means that for Bowlby grief sometimes outshines attachment in importance, that his criticisms of psychoanalysis sometimes outweigh his praise, just as for the republican Milton, Satan and the underworld were more vibrant and interesting than the kingdom of God.

Chapter 6

Attachment Theory and personality development: the research evidence

> It is just as necessary for analysts to study the way a child is really treated by his parents as it is to study the internal representations he has of them, indeed the principal form of our studies should be the interaction of the one with the other, of the internal with the external.
>
> (Bowlby 1988a)

One of Bowlby's main reasons for re-casting psychoanalysis in the language of Attachment Theory was the hope that this would make it more accessible for empirical testing. This hope has been fully justified. The past thirty years have seen an explosion of research in infant and child development, a major part of which has arisen directly from the work of Bowlby and Mary Ainsworth in the 1950s and sixties. The aim of this chapter is to show how these findings point to a remarkably consistent story about the emergence of personality, or 'attachment style', out of the matrix of interactions between infant and care-givers in the early months and years of life. The issue of how what starts as interaction becomes internalised as personality is a key question for developmental psychology. Object-Relations Theory rests on the assumption that early relationships are a formative influence on character. I hope to demonstrate in this and the following chapter that Bowlby's movement away from psychoanalysis has come full circle and produced ideas that are highly relevant to, and provide strong support and enrichment for, the psychoanalytic perspective.

As a scientific discipline, Attachment Theory has two great advantages over psychoanalysis. First, it rests on direct observation of parent–child interaction, rather than on retrospective reconstructions of what may or may not have gone in a person's past. Second, it starts from the observation of normal development, which can then be used as a yardstick against which to understand psychopathology, rather than building a theory of normal development from inferences made in the consulting room. It is perhaps no accident that the psychoanalyst with whom Bowlby has most in common, Winnicott, was also keenly aware of normal developmental processes through his earlier work as a pediatrician. Winnicott and Bowlby both believed that their observations of normal development were relevant to psychotherapy, for by getting a picture of what makes a good parent, we are likely to be in a better position to know what makes a good psychotherapist.

MARY AINSWORTH AND THE STRANGE SITUATION

There is an intimate relationship between technology and scientific advance. Galileo's observations depended on the expertise of the sixteenth-century Italian lens grinders; Darwin's discoveries sprang from the navigational and cartographic skills of Victorian maritime imperialism. Ainsworth's 'Strange Situation', 'a miniature drama in eight parts' (Bretherton 1991a) for mother, one-year-old infant and experimenter, has established itself as an indispensable tool in developmental psychology.

Ainsworth devised the Strange Situation in the late 1960s as part of her studies of mother–child interaction in the first year of life. She had worked with Bowlby in the 1950s, then moved to Uganda where she had made naturalistic studies of mothers with their babies, and finally settled in Baltimore, Maryland. Influenced by Attachment Theory, although at first wary of its ethological bias, she was interested in the relationship between attachment and exploratory behaviour in infants, and wanted to devise a standardised assessment procedure for human mothers and their children which would be both naturalistic and could be reliably rated, comparable to the methods used by animal experimenters like Harlow (1958) and Hinde (1982b).

The Strange Situation (Ainsworth *et al.* 1978) consists of a twenty-minute session in which mother and one-year-old child are first introduced into a playroom with an experimenter. The mother is then asked to leave the room for three minutes and to return, leaving the child with the experimenter. After her return and the re-union with the child, both mother and experimenter go out of the room for three minutes, leaving the child on its own. Mother and child are then once more re-united. The whole procedure is videotaped and rated, focusing particularly on the response of the child to separation and re-union. The aim is to elicit individual differences in coping with the stress of separation. Initially three, and later four, major patterns of response have been identified:

1 *Secure attachment* ('B')   These infants are usually (but not invariably) distressed by the separation. On re-union they greet their parent, receive comfort if required, and then return to excited or contented play.
2 *Insecure-avoidant* ('A')   These children show few overt signs of distress on separation, and ignore their mother on re-union, especially on the second occasion when presumably the stress is greater. They remain watchful of her and inhibited in their play.
3 *Insecure-ambivalent (insecure-resistant)* ('C')   They are highly distressed by separation and cannot easily be pacified on re-union. They seek contact, but then resist by kicking, turning away, squirming or batting away offered toys. They continue to alternate between anger and clinging to the mother, and their exploratory play is inhibited.
4 *Insecure-disorganised* ('D')   This small group has recently been demarcated. They show a diverse range of confused behaviours including 'freezing', or stereotyped movements, when re-united with their parent.

In Ainsworth's original middle-class Baltimore sample the proportions were 'B' (secure) 66 per cent, 'A' (avoidant) 20 per cent, and 'C' (ambivalent) 12 per cent. 'D' had not been identified at that stage. Since her original publication, the Strange Situation has been used in well over thirty different studies (Ijzendoorn and Kroonenberg 1988), and is generally accepted as a reliable and valid instrument – comparable perhaps to the widespread use of the Expressed Emotion scales in psychiatry (Leff and Vaughn 1983; see Chapter 9). There are significant cross-cultural variations, so that 'A' (avoidant) classifications tend to be commoner in Western Europe and the United States, while 'C' (ambivalent) is commoner in Israel and Japan. Intra-cultural variation between different socio-economic groups and between disturbed and non-disturbed families is greater than inter-cultural variance.

A whole set of research and theoretical questions follows from the establishment of this robust research tool. What is the meaning of the different patterns of response? Are they stable over time, and if so for how long? Do they predict disturbed behaviour later in childhood? Do they, as psychoanalytic theory might assume, persist into adult life? Can they be related to patterns of maternal–infant interaction in the early months of life? If maternal handling is relevant to classification pattern, what is the relationship between this and the mother's *own* experience of being mothered? If so, what are the psychological mechanisms by which attachment patterns are carried over from one generation to the next? Can patterns be altered by therapeutic intervention? The remainder of this chapter will be devoted to a discussion of these and related questions.

THE ROOTS OF SECURE AND INSECURE ATTACHMENT

Bowlby saw personality development primarily in terms of environmental influence: relationships rather than instinct or genetic endowment are primary. Differing patterns of attachment result from differing patterns of interaction, rather than being a reflection of infant temperament, or instinct. Sroufe (1979) makes an important distinction between 'emergent patterns of personality organisation' as revealed in the Strange Situation, and temperament, the latter representing quasi-physiological styles of behaviour, while the former reflect much more complex habitual relationship patterns. Thus babies may be sluggish, or active, 'cuddly' or non-cuddly, slow or fast, but still be classified as secure. Even more telling is the finding that children have different, but characteristic, attachment patterns with their two parents, and may be classified as secure with one and insecure with the other. This argues strongly that attachment patterns are a feature of the parent–child *relationship*, as yet not 'internalised' at one year, although by 18 months patterns have become more stable, with maternal patterns tending to dominate over paternal.

The Strange Situation research was part of a much larger study in which Ainsworth and her colleagues visited mothers and their infants regularly for periods of observation and rating during the whole of the first year of life. She found that attachment status at one year correlated strongly with the maternal relationship in the preceding twelve months, and this finding has been replicated in several other centres (Main and Weston 1982; Grossman *et al.* 1986; Sroufe 1979). In summary, prospective studies show that mothers of secure one-year-olds are *responsive to their babies*, mothers of insecure-avoidants are *unresponsive*, and mothers of insecure-ambivalents are *inconsistently responsive*.

The key to secure attachment is active, reciprocal interaction (Rutter 1981), and it seems that it is quality of interaction more than quantity that matters – a finding that contradicts Bowlby's earlier view on the causes of maternal deprivation. Passive contact alone does not necessarily promote attachment. Many babies are strongly attached to their fathers even though they spend relatively little time with them, and kibbutzim-reared children are more strongly attached to their mothers than to the nurses who feed them and look after them during the day, but often without much active interaction. In the first three months, mothers of secure infants respond more promptly when they cry; look, smile at and talk to their babies more; and offer them more affectionate and joyful holding. Mothers of avoidant children tend to interact less, and in a more functional way in the first three months, while mothers of ambivalents tend to ignore their babies' signals for attention and generally to be unpredictable in their responsiveness. By the second half of the first year, clear differences can be detected in the babies, and those who will be classified as secure at one year cry less than the insecure group, enjoy body contact more, and appear to demand it less (Bretherton 1991b).

The factor which mothers of insecurely attached children have in common can be understood in terms of Stern's (1985) concept of maternal *attunement*. He shows how sensitive mothers interacting with their children modulate their infant's rhythms so that when activity levels fall and the infant appears bored the mother will stimulate them, and when the child becomes overstimulated the mother will hold back a little so as to restore equilibrium. In *cross-modal attunement* the mother follows the baby's babbling, kicking, bouncing and so on with sounds or movements of her own that match and harmonise with those of the baby, although they may be in a different sensory mode. As he bounces up and down she may go 'Oooooh . . . Aaaaah . . .', matching the tempo and amplitude of her responses to the baby's movements.

This helps, as Stern sees it, in the development of the infant's sense of integrated selfhood. These processes of attunement are impaired in mothers of insecurely attached infants, leading to 'derailment' or mismatching in maternal response (Beebe and Lachmann 1988): thus mothers of ambivalently attached children can be observed to force themselves on their children when they are playing happily, and ignore them when they are in distress.

Brazelton and Cramer (1991) propose a similar model in which they break down the components of secure mother–child inter-active patterns into four main features: synchrony (temporal attunement), symmetry (matching of actions), contingency (mutual cueing), and 'entrainment' (the capturing of each other's responses into a sequence of mutual activity). On the basis of this, play, and later infant autonomy, begins to emerge. Insecure attachments result from intrusiveness or under-responsiveness. They have developed an experimental model of the latter in their 'still face' experiments in which the infant is momentarily presented with an unmoving image of the mother, who is pro-hibited from picking up the baby or responding to it. The baby shows disappointment, gaze aversion and self-soothing strategies, which match those seen in the children of clinically depressed mothers.

As we have seen in the previous chapter, aggression is a major component of the initial response to threatened separation. Both patterns of insecure attachment can perhaps be understood in terms of the interplay between the need for attachment and the aggressive response to the threat of separation. The ambivalently attached child shows overt aggression towards the inconsistent mother who, in the Strange Situation, has just 'abandoned' him for two successive periods (albeit only for 3 minutes – but how was the one-year-old to know that?). It is as if he is saying, 'Don't you dare do that again!', but clinging on at the same time since he knows from experience that she will. The avoidant child shows little overt aggression in the Strange Situation, although these children do show outbursts of unprovoked aggression at home. It may be that the avoidant response is a way of dampening aggression and so appeasing the mother to whom the child needs desperately to feel close, but whom he fears will rebuff him if he reveals his needs too openly, or shows her how angry he feels about being abandoned (Main and Weston 1982).

The clock-watcher

A clinical example of avoidant attachment in adulthood is provided by a patient who, although faithfully reliable in her attendance at therapy, found it difficult to enter affectively into sessions
which consisted mostly of a catalogue of the preceding week's
events. She was meticulous about timekeeping, kept a close eye
on her watch throughout the sessions, because, she said, she was
terrified to overrun by a single second. As a solicitor she knew
how annoying it was when clients outstayed their allotted time.
The effect of this clock-watching was quite irritating to her therapist, who commented that timekeeping was *his* responsibility and
tried to persuade her to remove her watch for sessions. It then
emerged that her phantasy was that without her watch she would
get 'lost' in the session, lose control of her feelings and at just
that moment the therapist would announce that it was time to
stop; she would then get so angry she would 'disgrace' herself,
the therapist would not tolerate this and would break off the
treatment. She had been a rather 'good' if distant child who had
spent a lot of time on her own, while her older sister had been
renowned for her tantrums and angry outbursts. By keeping
her distance in a typically avoidantly-anxious pattern, she had
maintained some sort of contact with her therapist (and presumably as a child, her parents), while avoiding the danger of threat-
ening her tenuous attachments with her rage. She also kept some
sort of coherence in the face of fear of disintegration. The price
she paid for this adaptation was affective distancing, low self-
esteem ('He would not tolerate me if he knew what I was really
like') and the lack of a sense of movement and growth in her
life.

THE STRANGE SITUATION AS A PREDICTOR OF SOCIAL ADJUSTMENT

The idea that anxious attachment patterns represent an adaptation or compromise to a sub-optimal environment is borne out
by follow-up studies of children classified at one, and tested at
pre-school, on school entry and again at ten (Bretherton 1985).
At two years, securely attached children have a longer attention
span, show more positive affect in free play, show more confidence in using tools, and are more likely to elicit their mother's

help in difficult tasks compared with anxiously attached children. Their nursery teachers (blind to attachment status) rate them as more empathic and compliant and higher on positive affect. In peer interaction avoidants are hostile or distant, while ambivalents tend to be 'inept' and to show chronic low-level dependency on the teacher, and to be less able to engage in free play by themselves or with peers.

Evidence that the patterns of behaviour defined by the Strange Situation behaviour carry forward into subsequent development comes from the Grossmans (1991), who have shown that patterns of behaviour on re-union were 87 per cent predictable between one year and six years. They also showed that six-year-olds classified at one year as secure played concentratedly and for longer, were more socially skillful in handling conflict with their peers, and had more positive social perceptions, compared with children who had been rated as insecure as infants. Sroufe (1979) sees secure-rated children as having greater *ego control* and *ego resiliency* than those who were insecure. Secure children were rated by their teachers as neither overcontrolled nor undercontrolled, while avoidants were overcontrolled, ambivalents undercontrolled. Resiliency was inferred from such statements as 'curious and exploring', 'self-reliant, confident'. Sroufe concludes: 'What began as a competent caregiver-infant pair led to a flexible resourceful child. . . . Such predictability is not due to the inherently higher IQ of the securely attached infant, or, apparently, to inborn differences in temperament.'

LANGUAGE, NARRATIVE, COHERENCE

So far we have confined our account to attachment behaviour. As we look now at older children and their mothers, we turn to the trickier but psychotherapeutically more salient topics of the nature of attachment experience, its internal representation and how it manifests itself in language.

Main *et al.* (1985), Bretherton (1991b) and Cassidy (1988) have tried to tap into the child's experience of attachment by the use of play techniques such as a picture completion task, story completion, and puppet interview and story all depicting in different ways episodes of separation and re-union. Children tend to reveal their attachment histories through their play and imaginative activity. Avoidant children at six tend to draw figures with blank faces and no hands, suggesting a lack of responsiveness and holding in their lives. Secure children in response to a picture-story task give coherent, elaborated responses, including references to their own separation experiences, and are able to suggest positive ways in which separated figures could resolve their difficulties. Avoidant children, by contrast, describe separated children as sad, but cannot think of ways to help them. Secure children at six were more able to give a balanced view of themselves as good, but not perfect, while insecure children saw themselves as either faultless or bad. It should be noted that these results were much more consistent for the avoidant than the ambivalent group who gave very varied responses to the play tasks, without a clear pattern emerging. The disorganised group ('D') emerged more clearly in these as opposed to previous studies, showing bizarre or disorganized responses to picture- and story-completion tasks.

Main (1991) presents some remarkable preliminary findings of a follow-up study in which ten- and eleven-year-olds, who had been classified in the Strange Situation at one year, were asked for a spoken autobiography. There was a 75 per cent correspondence between classification at one and at ten. Compared with the insecurely attached, the secure children's stories were consistently more coherent, had greater access to memories, especially of their pre-school years, and showed more self-awareness and ability to focus in on their own thought processes, a phenomenon Main calls 'megacognitive monitoring' – the ability to think about thinking.

The findings so far, which represent more than a decade of 'post-Bowlbian' research into Attachment Theory, can be summarised as follows. Relationship patterns established in the first year of life continue to have a powerful influence on children's subsequent behaviour, social adjustment, self-concept and autobiographical capacity. These effects last for at least ten years. Mother–infant relationships characterised by secure holding (both physically and emotionally), responsiveness and attunement are associated with children who are themselves secure, can tolerate and overcome the pain of separation, and have the capacity for self-reflection.

These results undoubtedly support the view that the early years of life play a crucial part in character formation, and show in a fascinating way the continuity between the pre-verbal infant self and the social self as we commonly conceive it. But two important qualifications need to be noted. First, since the parent–child relationship operates continuously as development proceeds, what we are seeing is not so much the *result* of some irreversible early events as an ongoing relationship with its own 'epigenetic' stability. There is evidence that if a mother's circumstances change – for example, a single parent entering into a stable relationship with a partner – then attachment status for her child may change, in this case from insecure to secure. Similar changes can occur, as we shall see later in the chapter, when mother and infant are both treated with psychotherapy (Murray and Cooper 1992). Second, in presenting these findings the emphasis has been on the contribution of the parent, especially the mother, with the infant's role being relatively passive. Clearly this is a gross oversimplification, and temperamental, or even neurological, factors in the child will play their part in the relationship with the parent, and subsequent social adjustment. Attachment status is quite a crude classification and clearly there will be a spectrum of subtle characterological features within it. Nevertheless, the evidence seems to be that the parent is the determining factor and that a 'good' mother even with a 'difficult' baby will, by one year, be likely to have a securely rather than insecurely attached child. For example, the amount a child cries at one year seems to depend more on the mother than the child: there is a strong correlation between prompt and sensitive maternal *responsiveness* to infant crying in the first three months of life and reduced (as compared with children of less responsive mothers) crying at one year, whereas there is no correlation between the extent of infant crying itself in the first three months and the amount of crying at one year.

This leads us directly to the issue of the inter-generational transmission of attachment. If relationships are in some way internalised by the growing child as 'character', what happens when that child grows up and becomes a parent? We know from Harlow's (1958) experiments that infant monkeys separated from their mothers show, when they become sexually mature, gross abnormalities in mating and parenting behaviour. Can we trace in the infinitely more complex language- and experience-based world of the human primate, connections between a mother's capacity to provide secure attachment for her child, and her experiences with her own mother when she was a child?

THE ADULT ATTACHMENT INTERVIEW

The Adult Attachment Interview (AAI) was devised by Main and her co-workers (1985) as a tool for assessing the working models or inner world of the parent with respect to attachment. It is a semi-structured interview conducted along the lines of a psychotherapy assessment aiming to 'surprise the unconscious' into self-revelation (Main 1991). The subject is asked to choose five adjectives which best describe the relationship with each parent during childhood, and to illustrate these with specific memories; to describe what she did when she was upset in childhood; to which parent she felt closer and why; whether she ever felt rejected or threatened by her parents; why she thinks her parents behaved as they did; how her relationship with her parents has changed over time; and how her early experiences may have affected her present functioning.

The interviews are audiotaped and then rated along eight scales: loving relationship with mother; loving relationship with father; role reversal with parents; quality of recall; anger with parents; idealisation of relationships; derogation of relationships; and coherence of narrative. The 'state of mind with respect to attachment' of the interviewees can then reliably be assigned to one of four categories: *Autonomous-secure, Dismissing-detached, Preoccupied-entangled* and *Unresolved-disorganised*.

The Autonomous-secure parents give accounts of secure childhoods, described in an open, coherent and internally consistent way. Attachments are valued, and even if their experiences have been negative there is a sense of pain felt and overcome. The Dismissing-detached group give brief, incomplete accounts, professing to having few childhood memories and tending to idealise the past with such remarks as 'I had a perfect childhood'. Preoccupied-entangled parents give inconsistent, rambling accounts in which they appear to be overinvolved with past conflicts and difficulties with which they are still struggling. The Unresolved-disorganised category is rated separately and refers specifically to traumatic events such as child abuse which have not been resolved emotionally.

Several independent studies have shown remarkably consistent correlations between the attachment status of infants in the Strange Situation, and that of their mothers in the AAI. A number of retrospective studies have shown a 70–80 per cent correspondence between infant security and parental attachment status on the AAI. Thus Main and Goldwyn (1984) found that 75 per cent of secure infants had mothers who were rated Secure-autonomous, while mothers of avoidant infants tended to be Dismissing-detached, and ambivalent infants had Preoccupied-entangled parents. The Grossmans found 77 per cent correspondence, and Ainsworth 80 per cent. Even more striking are the findings of Fonagy and his co-workers (Fonagy *et al.* 1991), who administered the AAI to prospective parents during pregnancy and found that the results predicted infant attachment status in the Strange Situation at one year with 70 per cent accuracy. Of insecure infants 73 per cent had insecure mothers, and only 20 per cent of secure infants had insecure mothers, while 80 per cent of secure mothers had secure infants. The influence of fathers appeared to be less: 82 per cent of secure fathers had secure infants, but 50 per cent of insecure fathers still had secure infants. This supports the view that attachment status is a function of the infant–parent relationship, rather than of temperament, and also suggests that maternal, rather than paternal, insecurity is the more potent transmitter of insecure attachment across the generations.

Prospective findings were less clear-cut for the preoccupied parent–ambivalent infant correlation. Many ambivalent children had mothers who were apparently secure when given the AAI in pregnancy. However, Fonagy *et al.* (1992), on reviewing these interviews, found evidence of a certain 'fragility' in the replies of these mothers, suggesting a tendency to idealisation which could easily be mistaken for security. There is some evidence that ambivalent children may have shown physiological immaturity at birth, or are the products of difficult labours, and it is possible that immaturity in the infant may have exposed the mother's 'fragility' in such a way as to produce an ambivalent attachment status at one year.

THEORETICAL INTERLUDE

The findings of this new generation of post-Bowlbian researchers are summarised in Table 6.1 and produce a coherent picture of benign and vicious cycles of security and insecurity. Secure mothers are responsive and attuned to their babies and provide them with a secure base for exploration. They are able to hold

Table 6.1 The continuity of secure and insecure attachment

	Pregnant Mothers	Babies 0–1	Infants 1 year	2-year-olds	6-year-olds	6-year-olds	10-year-olds
Classification	Secure	Responsive mothers – look more, pick up more quickly	Secure	Call for mother when needed, use tools confidently	Concentrated play, socially resilient	Can cope with idea of separation, finds resolution	Coherent memories, stories of conflict resolved
	Insecure-entangled	Inconsistent mothers	Insecure-ambivalent	Inept, low-level dependency	Under-controlled	Varied response	Incoherent stories, no resolution of sadness
	Insecure-dismissive	Unresponsive mothers, 'functional' handling	Insecure-avoidant	Hostile and distant with peers	Over-controlled	Draw pictures with blank faces, no hands, sadness unresolved	Poor recall and poor self-awareness
Test	AAI	Observation of mothers and infants	Strange Situation (SS)	Nursery-school observations	Direct observation, repeat SS	Play tasks picture completion	Spoken autobiography
Reference	Fonagy et al. (1991)	Ainsworth et al. (1978)	Ainsworth et al. (1978)	Bretherton (1985)	Grossman and Grossman (1991)	Main et al. (1985)	Main (1991)

them, delight in them, and cope with their discontent and aggression in a satisfactory way. These mothers have a balanced view of their own childhoods which, even if unhappy, are appraised realistically. Their children, secure as infants, grow up to be well-adjusted socially and to have a realistic self-appraisal and a sense that separation, although often sad and painful, can be responded to positively. Secure mothers and secure children have a well-developed capacity for self-reflection and narrative ability, and convey a sense of coherence in their lives.

Insecure children, by contrast, especially if avoidant, tend to have mothers who found holding and physical contact difficult, who were unresponsive to their infant's needs and not well attuned to their rhythms. These mothers tended to be dismissing about their relationships with their parents and to be unable to tell a vivid or elaborated story of their own childhoods. As they grow up, avoidant children tend to be socially isolated, to show unprovoked outbursts of anger, to lack self-awareness and to be unable to tell a coherent story about themselves.

Are we seeing in these insecure children the roots of adult personality difficulty and neurosis? If so, what can we learn about the mental mechanisms that may underlie these disorders, and do they provide clues as to how psychotherapy might help to reverse them? We shall discuss in the next two chapters the parallels between avoidant strategies in infancy and some of the features of borderline personality disorder, and the possible links between phobic and dependency disorders in adults and patterns of ambivalent attachment in infancy. Our concern here is to try to conceptualise how maternal handling becomes internalised as infant psychology. In Fraiberg's (Fraiberg et al. 1975) telling metaphor: 'In every nursery there are ghosts. These are the visitors from the unremembered pasts of the parents; the uninvited guests at the christening.' How do the parental ghosts get incorporated into the internal working models of the infant? Three inter-related ideas can be used to clarify this: avoidance of painful affect (Grossman and Grossman 1991), consistency and coherence of internal working models (Bretherton 1991a), and self-reflection (Fonagy 1991; Fonagy et al. 1991, 1992).

As we have seen in the previous chapter, Bowlby views the capacity to 'process' negative affect – to feel and resolve the pain of separation and loss – as a central mark of psychological health. Parents of insecure infants fail to respond appropriately to their infant's distress, either ignoring it (avoidants) or becoming over-involved, panicky and bogged down in it (ambivalents). It seems possible that because these parents have not been able to deal with or 'metabolise' (Bion 1978) their own distress they cannot cope with pain and anger in their infants and so the cycle is perpetuated. The infant is faced with parents who, due to their own internal conflicts or ego weakness, cannot hold (Winnicott 1971) the child's negative feelings of distress or fear of disinte gration. The child is therefore forced to resort to primitive defense mechanisms in order to keep affects within manageable limits. Aggressive feelings may be repressed or split off, as in the avoidant child who does not react to his mother's absence but then shows overt aggression towards toys or siblings: or the insecure-ambivalent child who may show overcompliance based on 'identification with the aggressor'. Behavioural manifestations of these parent–child malattunements include such phenomena as gaze aversion, self-injury (such as head banging), freezing or fighting. They may also, as we shall consider further in Chapter 9, be related to such adult maladaptive behaviours as social avoidance, self-injurious behaviour such as wrist cutting, overdosing and substance abuse.

One can imagine continuities between infant physiological experience and psychological structures which evolve through childhood into adult life (see Figure 6.1). From maternal consistency comes a sense of history: the reliability of the mother's response to the infant becomes the nucleus of autobiographical competence. From maternal holding comes the ability to hold one's self in one's own mind: the capacity for self-reflection, to conceive of oneself and others as having minds. The insensitivity and unresponsiveness of the mother of the insecure infant is not necessarily mean or abusive, but rather a failure to see the world from the baby's point of view, to 'take the baby's perspective' (Bretherton 1991a). The mother who cannot act as an 'auxiliary ego' for her child exposes him or her to inchoate and potentially overwhelming feelings when that child is faced, as will be inevitable (and in the case of an insecure mother to an excessive degree), with loss and separation anxiety.

Fonagy (Fonagy *et al.* 1991) sees *coherence* as a central feature of parents classified as Secure-autonomous on the AAI:

The coherence of the parent's perception of his past derives

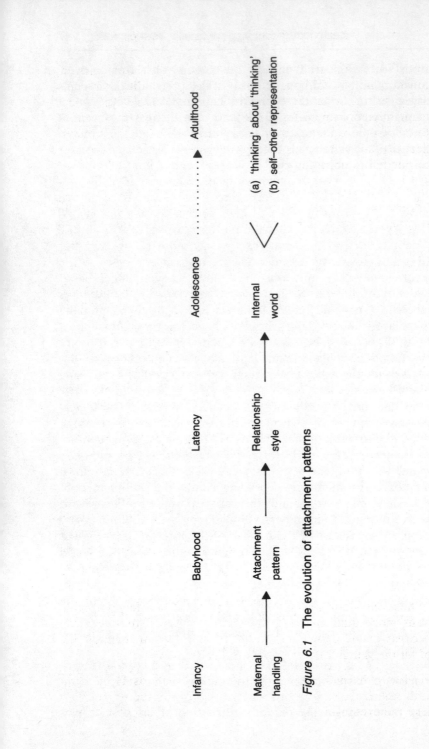

Infancy   Babyhood   Latency   Adolescence   Adulthood

Maternal   →   Attachment   →   Relationship   →   Internal
handling   pattern   style   world

(a) 'thinking' about 'thinking'
(b) self–other representation

Figure 6.1 The evolution of attachment patterns

from his unhindered capacity to observe his own mental functioning. . . . This coherence is the precondition for the caregiver to be able to provide an 'expectable' or 'good enough' environment for the infant. . . . A child may be said to be *secure* in relation to a caregiver to the extent that his or her mental state will be appropriately reflected on and responded to accurately.

Without some sense of coherence and benignity towards oneself, self-reflection becomes distorted or even impossible, as the following case of borderline personality disorder illustrates.

'*I hate myself*'

Anna was a single parent in her mid-twenties. She became depressed and suicidal when her child was 6 months old. Her mother had been in hospital a lot when Anna was a small child because of TB, and at one point (when Anna was ten) had left the home for a while to live with another man. Despite this neglect Anna saw her mother as 'perfect', someone whose standards she could never match, and herself as hateful. She had two distinct 'selves': one competent, intelligent, well-organised, cheerful, compliant, pretty; the other dark, despairing, longing to die. In hospital at times she avoided eye-contact, secreted razor blades and frequently cut herself, was morose and monosyllabic, and would occasionally have outbursts of rage. At other times she was a model patient and collaborated enthusiastically with her therapeutic programme. She was discharged from hospital and started weekly analytic therapy, but once more became suicidal and was readmitted. She complained that she found psychotherapy very difficult because it meant that she had to *think about herself*. That entailed getting in touch with her self-hatred:

> 'Whenever I look into myself I come across the feeling that I want more than anything to die. I am forced to stay alive because of my daughter. Coming to talk to you reminds me of all the things I don't want to think about.'

Her wish to harm herself arose whenever she was faced with painful feelings of separation; for example, when she was on her own in the evenings. The origins of an almost unbridgeable split between her compliant and defiant selves, and the difficulty in reaching her real pain and hope could be seen in terms of insecure-avoidance, and the feeling that she had never felt securely held by her mother as a child, and was reminded of the anxiety and pain of this whenever she was on her own. She needed to be held by the hospital ward – sometimes actually – before she could begin to think about holding herself in mind in therapy, and to feel secure about her capacity to be a mother to her daughter. As suggested by Figure 6.2, her mental state could be represented by a series of parallel concentric circles of holder and held.

Borderline patients like this provide adult examples of the insecure infant with a deficient holding environment, whose mother has been unable to reflect on and so metabolise her infant's feelings of pain on separation, who survives as best she can, using splitting, isolation and self-harm as ways of coping, and who, when she becomes a parent, is in great danger of perpetuating the cycle of insecurity. Ward staff and therapists may then counter-transferentially re-enact a repetition of the unresponsiveness and breaks in care that the patient experienced as a child. Thus Anna became passionately involved with one male nurse – paralleling her long-repressed desire to have an exclusive relationship with her mother – and did very well until he was transferred to another ward, whereupon she took a huge overdose of drugs.

Bowlby depicted healthy internal working models as subject to constant revision and change in the light of experience. Anna exemplified how in pathological mental states there is often a sense of repetitiousness and stuckness in therapy. Bretherton (1987) has speculated about why it might be that internal working models in insecure attachment are particularly resistant to change. She sees mental structures as organised hierarchically from low-level 'event-scripts' (Shank 1982), such as 'When I hurt myself my mother comes to comfort me', through intermediate generalisations like 'My mother is usually there when I need her', to basic assumptions: 'My mother is a loving person. I am lovable and loved.' Insecure individuals not only may have negative core assumptions, but because communication between different levels of the hierarchy is distorted and restricted, may not be able to revise these models in the light of experience. Anna's basic assumption – 'I am hateful' – remained impervious to contrary

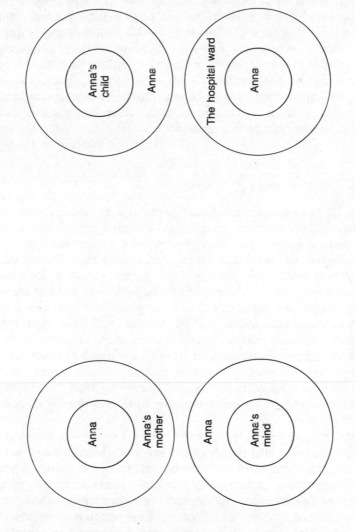

Figure 6.2 Anna and the holding environment

evidence provided by the love of her boyfriend and the care of her therapists:

> What seems to differentiate the Internal Working Models of secure and insecure individuals is in part their content, but also their internal organisation and relative consistency within and across hierarchical levels. . . . Reconstruction of working models cannot be achieved [simply] by 'lifting repression' or removing barriers which allow well-encoded, but hitherto inaccessible information to come into conscious awareness. Something much more akin to complete reorganisation and reinterpretation may be necessary.
>
> (Bretherton 1991a)

THERAPEUTIC IMPLICATIONS

From the perspective of Attachment Theory the process of therapy will require the provision of a secure base, comprising reliability, responsiveness and the capacity to process negative affect, especially in relation to separation and loss. Out of this should emerge an individual with a greater capacity for self-reflection, increased coherence of mental structures and enhanced autobiographical competence. The implications of this for psychotherapy with adults will be considered in the next two chapters. It is beyond the scope of this book to consider the full implications of Attachment Theory for psychotherapy with children, and the reader's attention is drawn to the considerable literature on the subject (Belsky and Nezworski 1988; Greenberg et al. 1988). Three important areas of work will briefly be mentioned.

Lieberman and Paul (1988) have shown that a clinical classification of neurotic disturbance in pre-school children fits well with the categories suggested by Attachment Theory research. They found three basic groups of problematic behaviours: excessive danger seeking, such as wandering off unaccompanied in children whose mothers appeared to discount the attachment needs of their offspring; excessive danger fleeing with punitive mothers who discouraged exploration and illustrated the paradox of clinging to a punitive attachment figure; and children who were 'hypercompetent', equivalent to Bowlby's category of 'compulsive caregiving' (Bowlby 1980) in which there was role-reversal between children and their mothers and inhibition of expression of painful affect.

Informed by attachment theory, several groups have attempted preventive psychotherapy with depressed mothers by working directly with the mother and her infant. Murray and Cooper (1992) describe one such case.

'Uppie . . . uppie'

Following a puerperal depression, Joan had felt unable to get emotionally close to her 18-month-old daughter Sophie, and was frightened that the pattern of distance and lack of trust which characterised her relationship with her own mother was repeating itself. Tested on the Strange Situation, Sophie showed a typical pattern of insecure-avoidance. In the course of brief exploratory-supportive therapy in which Sophie and Joan were seen together, their relationship changed dramatically. In place of distant watch-fulness, Sophie began to approach her mother, asking to be picked up and cuddled, saying 'Uppie, uppie', and was responded to with warmth and affection. At the same time negative feelings became less problematic for both of them. When Sophie cried or was difficult and rejecting, Joan could tolerate this without feeling guilty, and could also allow herself to become irritable with her daughter at times. In parallel with these changes Joan reported an improvement in her relationship with her own mother: here too she could be both affectionate and cross instead of, as before, maintaining a cool distance. At termination, Sophie's re-test on the Strange Situation now showed a pattern of secure attachment. In place of a rigid and restricted pattern of relating, each was able to respond to the other in a more fluid and spontaneous way. This movement from inflexibility towards 'give' and play illustrates Winnicott's (1965) well-known dictum that the essence of psychotherapy is learning to play.

In view of the increasing numbers of adult psychotherapy patients who report sexual and/or physical abuse in childhood, mention must also be made of studies which have approached familial abuse from the perspective of Attachment Theory. 'High risk' (that is, low socio-economic status) parents do not have dispro-portionate numbers of insecure children. The A/B/C ratios remain roughly the same: B, 65 per cent; A, 20 per cent; C, 15 per cent. The proportion of A/C families rises sharply among mothers with major depressive illness, and in families where there is proven sexual or physical abuse. With depressed mothers, 40 per cent of children were insecure-avoidant, and in abusive families 50 per cent are avoidant and 30 per cent disorganised, with only 10 per cent classified as secure (Belsky and Nezworsky 1988). The apparent compliance and conformity sometimes seen in adult patients who have been abused can be understood in the light of Crittenden's (1988) comment that

> Attachment Theory proposed that the maintenance of affectional bonds . . . is essential to the survival of the human species and a compelling individual need. . . . Those people who are most at risk for destroying their love relationships altogether devote the most intense effort towards maintaining the semblance of bonds; inept mothers and their children scrap and feud; mildly abusing mothers and their children are hostile and difficult; but many severely maltreating mothers do not dare challenge the durability of their relationships . . . it is as though they fear that a simple dispute could become an uncontrollable attack on the relationship.

CONCLUSION

Bowlby's grafting of the experimental methods of ethology to the insight of psychoanalysis has born rich fruit. The research we have surveyed in this chapter has begun to lay bare some of the relational elements which provide the foundations of psychological health: a sense of security, of efficacy, of being loved and having the capacity to love, of being a person in the world like others and yet with one's own unique biographical trajectory, of being able to withstand the failures, losses and disappointments that are the inevitable consequence of the 'thousand natural shocks that flesh is heir to'. We have learned about some of the ingredients that make up good parenting: responsiveness, attunement, holding. We turn now to the implications of these findings for psychotherapy, and to further exploration of the relationship – at times avoidant, at times ambivalent – between Attachment Theory and psychoanalysis, in the hope of finding a more secure and coherent synthesis.

Part III

Implications

Chapter 7

Bowlby and the inner world: Attachment Theory and psychoanalysis

> [The] early formulations of psychoanalytic theory were strongly influenced by the physiology of the day . . . cast in terms of the individual organism, its energies and drives, with only marginal reference to relationships. Yet, by contrast, the principal feature of the innovative technique for treating patients that Freud introduced is to focus attention on the relationships patients make with their therapist. From the start, therefore, there was a yawning gulf between the phenomena with which the therapist was confronted, and the theory that had been advanced to account for them.
>
> (Bowlby 1990)

Bowlby was primarily a theorist rather than a therapist. Although trained psychoanalytically, and active in the Psycho-Analytical Society from the late 1930s until the late 1950s, where he held high office, he saw himself mainly as a researcher and administrator. Case reports and clinical illustrations are to be found throughout his writings, but, with the exception of his earliest papers, these are almost all based on the work of colleagues or on published articles by other authors. Dreams are nowhere to be found in his work, and he is, for the most part, concerned with observable behaviour rather than the inner world. Nevertheless, Attachment Theory is a child of psychoanalysis and has much to contribute to the theory and practice of psychotherapy. Towards the end of his career Bowlby (1991) wrote, 'my theoretical work has always been directed primarily to my colleagues in the International [Psychoanalytical] Association'. The aim of this chapter is to consider in some detail the relationship between Attachment

Theory, psychoanalysis and contemporary psychoanalytic psychotherapy.

Bowlby's reservations about psychoanalysis come under four
main headings: its neglect of real experience and environmental
influence in favour of overemphasis on autonomous phantasy;
an atmosphere of dogmatism inimical to scientific enquiry; an
outmoded metapsychology; and a lack of experimental observation to underpin its unbridled theorising. All of these objections
may seem to the contemporary observer somewhat overstated,
and we must first place them in an historical context.

HISTORY: BRITISH PSYCHOANALYSIS 1935–60

The atmosphere in the British Psycho-Analytical Society when
Bowlby started training in the mid–1930s was one of ferment and
controversy. The heady excitement of a new science of mind that
went straight to the heart of twentieth century men's and women's
discontents seemed to have generated a hotbed of intrigue, back-
biting, gossip and jockeying for position. The climate resembled
less that of a scientific society than of a family in which a patriarch
was n(aring the end of his life with the terms of his inheritance
still unuecided.

Ernest Jones had invited Melanie Klein to practise in London
and had entrusted his own two children to her for child analysis
based on her new technique of play therapy. Until the advent of
Klein, the focus of analytical work was predominantly the Oedipus complex. She insisted on the importance and the analysability
of much earlier stages of development, and in particular on the
phantasies and anxieties of the infant in its first two years of life.
As we saw in Chapter 1, Freud tended to regard Klein's views
with some disfavour (Steiner 1985), especially as her ideas about
child analysis differed from those of his daughter Anna, who
saw splitting and other primitive defence mechanisms such as
projective identification proposed by Klein as belonging to a
much later stage of development.

At the time of the arrival of Freud and Anna in London in
the late 1930s the British Society comprised a group of highly
talented and intelligent people, including James Strachey,
Edward Glover, Sylvia Payne, Melanie Klein (Bowlby's supervisor) and Joan Riviere (Bowlby's analyst). A leadership struggle
broke out with an increasing schism between the Kleinian camp,

who were accused of dogmatism and attempts to win students exclusively onto their side, and the more orthodox Freudians, represented by Anna and her followers, together with a third group, who remained non-aligned. Eventually, in 1944, a compromise was reached with the 'gentleman's agreement' (in fact made between three women, Klein, Payne and Anna Freud) between the parties to form separate 'streams' of training and scientific discussion, while remaining united within one society.

Although Bowlby's organisational and intellectual talents were recognised early on – he was appointed Training Secretary of the Society in 1944 (Melanie Klein opposed this on the grounds that he was not a Training Analyst) – he was somewhat at variance with the mainstream of the analytic milieu. His strong commitment to the scientific method, his quintessential Britishness and reserve, his decision to work in child guidance clinics rather than in private practice, set him apart. These very qualities, as well as the fact that he was the son of a famous surgeon, may also have given him the credibility with the medical establishment that was needed for his successful popularisation of psychoanalytic ideas about the importance of infancy, and the mother–child relationship, as a determinant of later mental health.

From early in his psychoanalytic career Bowlby had had misgivings about the way in which analysts downplayed the importance of the environment in the origins of psychological disturbance. Although Freud has been accused of a deliberate and cowardly retreat from his original hypotheses about the adverse effects of childhood seduction (Masson 1985), there is no doubt that he continued to believe that childhood trauma was important, but as the pioneer of a new 'science' he emphasised the primacy of the inner world as the proper domain of psychoanalytic discourse, and this lead was certainly adhered to by his followers. Bowlby writes:

> During . . . 1936–39 I was slowly waking up to the fact that my ideas were developing in a direction very different from those that were accepted truths in the British Psycho-Analytical Society . . . under the influence of Ernest Jones and Melanie Klein it was held that an analyst should concern himself only with the patient's internal world and that to give attention to his real life experiences could only divert attention from what really matters. My experiences in the Child Guidance

Clinic . . . were leading me to an opposite conclusion . . . that one can only understand a person's internal world if one can see how [it] has come to be constructed from the real-life events to which he has been exposed.

(Bowlby 1991; Rayner 1992)

A marked copy of a paper by Bowlby's analyst Joan Riviere contains the following passage:

Psychoanalysis is Freud's discovery of what goes on in the imagination . . . it has no concern with anything else, it is not concerned with the real world . . . it is concerned simply and solely with the imaginings of the childish mind.

(Quoted in Rayner 1992)

In the margin Bowlby has pencilled 'Role of the environment = zero' (Rayner 1992). Bowlby was particularly distressed when the mother of his first training patient in child analysis, a hyperactive little boy of three, was admitted to mental hospital:

When I reported this to Melanie Klein [his supervisor], however, her only concern seemed to be that, since it was no longer possible for me to continue the boy's analysis, another patient must be found for me. The probability that the boy's behaviour was a reaction to the way his mother treated him seemed altogether to escape her.

(Bowlby 1991)

Bowlby consistently stressed the range of environmental traumata to which a developing child can be exposed: actual separations and disruptions in care; threats of separation or suicide by parents; being unwanted, or the 'wrong' sex; suppression of the true facts about parentage (for example, grandfather or uncle the true father, or sister the true mother); role reversal and the 'parentification' of children. His views have been thoroughly vindicated by the recent disclosure of the extent of physical and sexual abuse of children. The evidence that more subtle forms of environmental failure such as parental unresponsiveness and mis-attunement underlie childhood and probably adult psychopathology has been reviewed in the previous chapter. These findings make the polarisation between Bowlby's characterisation of the Kleinians as wholly uninterested in the environment and exclusively concerned with phantasy, and his own insistence on the primacy of environmental failure rather artificial. The Kleinian account is a phenomenological description of mental states found in adult patients, particularly those with borderline pathology, inferring from these what may have gone on in the minds of infants and small children. The Kleinian account contains no clear causal model to account for the phenomena she describes. Bowlby and the post-Bowlbians offer the outlines of an explanation of how such pathological states come about. They suggest that the *capacity* to phantasise and to symbolise, as opposed to resorting to defensive enactments of unmanageable feelings, is itself environmentally sensitive. Parents who can contain and attune to their children have children who can put their feelings into words and who are able to resolve conflict. Those who cannot contain and attune are more likely to have children who are at risk of dealing with their feelings by splitting and projective identification, and so being afflicted by a sense of emptiness and meaninglessness. It is worth noting that Klein, like Freud, assumes that there may be constitutional differences between infants, a point which Bowlby tends to overlook. Westen (1990) has suggested that some babies may have reduced inborn capacities for self-soothing, which would make them more vulnerable to parental deficiencies in containing and calming.

A second area of difficulty about psychoanalysis for Bowlby was its atmosphere of dogmatism and authoritarianism. Peterfreund (1983), who is approvingly cited by Bowlby in several places, decries what he calls the 'stereotyped', dogmatic, 'alogarithmic' approach of traditional psychoanalytic formulation and interpretation. He compares this with the 'heuristic' approach which he and Bowlby advocate, in which patient and therapist find things out for themselves rather than imitating Talmudic scholars burrowing in the obscure texts of the psychoanalytic testament. There is no doubt that at its worst psychoanalysis can degenerate into a mouthing of clichéd formulas by an omniscient analyst who, faced with the pain and complexity of suffering, offers some certainty, however ill-founded, to a confused patient who has no choice but to grasp at straws. The relentless interpretation of the transference may hypnotically open the patient up to layers of regression and dependency which make such interpretations self-fulfilling prophecies. There has been a move towards a much more tentative approach to interpretation in contemporary psychoanalysis (Casement 1985), in which Keats's 'negative capability' – the capacity to allow oneself to be 'in uncertainties, mysteries, doubts, without any irritable reaching after fact and reason' – is valued, and indeed is seen as the hallmark of the 'depressive position' with its emphasis on compromise and reconciliation rather than splitting and false certainties.

Bowlby writes that

> I was dissatisfied with much of the [psychoanalytic] theory . . . being a somewhat arrogant young man . . . I was in no mood to accept dogmatic teaching. My analyst was not altogether happy with my critical attitude and complained on one occasion that I would take nothing on trust and was trying to think everything out from scratch, which I was certainly committed to doing.
>
> (Bowlby 1991)

Bowlby's re-thinking of psychoanalytic metapsychology and terminology has been discussed in the preceding three chapters. Attachment Theory is perhaps best seen as a variant of Object-Relations Theory, using updated terminology and informed by neo-Darwinism. Attachment comprises a distinct motivational system – which includes drive, affect, cognition and behaviour – that parallels and complements sexuality. The main differences between classical Freudian theory, the Object-Relations Theory of Klein, Fairbairn and Winnicott, and Attachment Theory are summarised in Table 7.1. For Bowlby the important issue is not, as the orthodox Freudians thought, sex, but security. Attachment is primary, not a derivative of orality. The organism is not an isolated drive-driven creature in search of an object on whom to discharge his accumulated tension, but a person relating to other persons. Homeostatic and other cybernetic control systems govern his behaviour, just as they do that of other mammals. His relationship to the world is determined not just by unconscious phantasy but also by internal working models which include affective, cognitive and behavioural elements. Aggression is a response to frustration and loss, not an intrinsic property of an individual dominated by the death instinct.

Bowlby's fourth cavil at psychoanalysis was its neglect of direct observation of normal and abnormal children. He felt that reconstructions based on childhood recollections of disturbed patients, while valuable in themselves, did not qualify as a scientific account of what really goes on in real children. He therefore set

Table 7.1 Classical, Object-Relations and Attachment Theories compared

	Classical Freudian theory	Object-Relations Theory	Attachment Theory
Main authors	S. Freud A. Freud	Melanie Klein Donald Winnicott Ronald Fairbairn Wilfred Bion Michael Balint Margaret Mahler	John Bowlby Daniel Stern
1 Models of normal development			
(a) Attachment	Drive-based Aim of drive is 'discharge' Attachment is a 'secondary drive'	Attachment to breast which gratifies But NB Balint's 'clinging instinct'	Intra-personal Primary attachment – continues throughout life
(b) Stages	(i) Pre-Oedipal → Oedipal (ii) oral → anal → (phallic) → genital	(i) 1 person → 2 person → 3 person (Balint) (ii) Infantile autism → symbiosis → separation – individuation → rapprochement (Mahler) (iii) Paranoid-schizoid position → depressive position (Klein)	Pattern-recognition → maternal differentiation → set-goal attachment → relationship

Table 7.1 (cont.)

(c) Role of parents in normal development	?inherently traumatic: love of mother versus castration anxiety	inherently traumatic: split between gratifying and frustrating breast, but overcome by (i) holding (Winnicott) (ii) transmuting, 'metabolising' (Bion)	Attunement Responsiveness Secure base } overcome frustration of separation
2 *Model of Mind*	conscious/unconscious → id, ego, superego	(i) good object/bad object → whole object (guilt, reparation) (Klein) (ii) libidinal object/anti-libidinal object, libidinal self/anti-libidinal self (Fairbairn)	Internal working models Hierarchical coherence Representation of self and other
3 *Roots of psychopathology*			
(a) Early	Parental 'seduction' Early loss Regression/fixation } trauma of over-excitement	Failure of holding transmuting	Lack of responsiveness attunement secure base Failure to cope with loss, separation (based on mother's own experience as a child)

Table 7.1 (cont.)

(b) Later	The Oedipal situation: sibling rivalry, over-involvement with mother, lack of identification with father Regression/fixation	Failure to progress from paranoid → depressive position Lack of reparation	Environmental disruption: loss, inconsistency, abuse
(c) Defences	Primitive: Splitting, repression Intermediate: Isolation, undoing Mature: Sublimation, humour	Kleinians emphasise splitting and projective identification	'Defensive exclusion' ⎱ strategies Avoidant ⎰ Ambivalent
(d) Theory of anxiety and aggression	Surplus libido (e.g. Oedipal) → Signal anxiety (loss)	Projection Aggression Fear of damage to object	Separation anxiety Aggression is response to threatened separation
(e) Theory of depression	Identification with lost object. Guilt	Loss Guilt Identification with lost object	Loss Lack of experience of 'metabolising' separation – i.e. depression is abnormal grief
(f) Theory of borderline states	Regression to infantile narcissism	Splitting Projective identification Narcissistic defenses	Avoidant anxious attachment Failure to attune by mother → no self-reflection, lacks coherence

out to study systematically the effects of separating infants and children from their parents, and it was on the basis of those findings that Attachment Theory was born.

BOWLBY AND THE POST-FREUDIANS: THE POST-WAR PERIOD

To continue with our historical account, Bowlby was of course not alone in his dissatisfaction with the state of psychoanalysis in the 1940s and early fifties. During the post-war period several divergent responses can be found within psychoanalysis and psychotherapy in response to the difficulties – dogmatism, obsolete metapsychology and anti-empiricism – with which Bowlby was struggling. The first was the development of Object-Relations Theory, epitomised by the work of Winnicott, Fairbairn and Balint, all of whom were influenced by the Kleinian emphasis on the early infant–mother relationship, but, taking the decisive step of abandoning drive theory altogether, posited *relationships* as primary. Mahler's (1975) direct observations of mothers and infants from a psychoanalytic perspective combined object relations with a degree of empiricism.

A quite different tack was to reject the pseudo-scientific determinism of classical Freudianism altogether, seeing psychoanalysis more as a hermeneutic discipline concerned with meanings rather than mechanisms and emphasising the importance of the creative imagination and spontaneity as the wellspring of the psychoanalytic process (Rycroft 1985). Meanwhile, neo-Kleinian developments concentrated on delving deeper and deeper into the mysteries of the infant–mother relationship in the early stages of life and relating these to the findings of psychoanalysis with psychotic patients (Bion 1978). Finally, there were moves away from the psychoanalytic paradigm altogether, adopting either a family systems approach derived from cybernetics and anthropology (Bateson 1973), or a 'cognitive' approach, based on Piaget and Kelly, in which the logical operations of the mind and the way in which they are organised hierarchically form the basis of psychotherapeutic theory and practice (Beck *et al.* 1979).

Bowlby and Winnicott

Bowlby as a researcher responded to the problems of the psycho-analytic paradigm by moving in the direction of observable behaviour. Attachment, whether secure or insecure, avoidant or ambivalent, can be observed, rated, measured, correlated. By basing his ideas on ethology Bowlby sidestepped the dehumanis-ation and absurdities of stimulus–response behaviourism, while remaining within the framework of conventional science. Winni-cott, an outstanding clinician but an elusive theorist, was wrest-ling with the same problems but from the perspective of the inner world, developing in his idiosyncratic but highly original way a language of experience directly applicable to the therapeutic situation.

Winnicott and Bowlby had much in common. Both were very 'English' in their background and outlook, in contrast to the European/Jewish/Celtic atmosphere of the Psycho-Analytical Society. Both had had a Cambridge scientific education and were deeply influenced by Darwin. They shared an analyst, Joan Rivi-ere, who, despite her later Kleinian orthodoxy, was firmly inter-personal in her philosophy. With an echo of John Donne, she wrote:

> There is no such thing as a single human being, pure and simple, unmixed with other human beings. Each personality is a world in himself, a company of many. That self . . . is a composite structure . . . formed out of countless never-ending influences and exchanges between ourselves and others. These other persons are in fact therefore part of ourselves . . . we are members of one another.
>
> (Riviere 1927; reprinted 1955)

Winnicott (1965) was therefore paraphrasing Riviere in his famous dictum, 'there is no such thing as an infant . . . wherever one finds an infant one finds maternal care and without maternal care there would be no infant'. Like Bowlby, Winnicott was primarily concerned with the welfare of children, and wrote to an American enquirer about his wartime experiences:

> I became involved with the failure of the evacuation scheme and could therefore no longer avoid the subject of the anti-social tendency. Eventually I became interested in the etiology of delinquency and therefore joined up quite naturally with

John Bowlby who was at that time starting up his work based on the relationship that he observed between delinquency and periods of separation at significant times in the child's early years.

(Rodman 1987)

When Winnicott later was offered the presidency of the Psycho-Analytical Society he accepted, on condition that he have a deputy who would take care of the detailed administrative work. The ever-efficient Bowlby was an obvious choice. They make sparse but polite references to each other's work in their writings. There are many similarities between their theoretical viewpoints, despite the radically different language which each uses. Rycroft's (1985) remark that 'I've always had a phantasy that Bowlby and I were burrowing the same tunnel, but that we started at opposite ends', would be equally true of Bowlby and Winnicott.

Winnicott and Bowlby's responses to the Kleinian domination of the Psycho-Analytical Society can be seen in terms of avoidant and ambivalent attachment. Bowlby, in an avoidant way, distanced himself, expressing neither warmth nor anger, but having little to do with the Society after the 1960s. Winnicott clung ambivalently to his alma mater, and, in his theory of hate, emphasised how identity can be forged through opposition and reaction.

Bowlby and Winnicott's overall view of the infant–mother relationship, and what may go wrong with it, is very similar. Winnicott postulates a 'holding environment' provided by the mother, in which, on the basis of her 'primary maternal preoccupation', she can empathise with the needs and desires of the growing child. The main job of the holding environment is, like attachment, protection, although, in contrast to Bowlby, Winnicott describes this in existential rather than ethological terms: 'The holding environment . . . has as its main function the reduction to a minimum the impingement to which the infant must react with resultant annihilation of personal being' (Winnicott 1965). Winnicott sees 'handling' and 'general management', equivalent to the Bowlbian concept of maternal responsiveness, as the framework within which need can be met. The mother's actual physical holding and handling are primary:

The main thing is the physical holding and this is the basis of all the more complex aspects of holding and of environmental provision in general. . . . The basis for instinctual satisfaction and for object relationships is the handling and general management and care of the infant, which is only too easily taken for granted when all goes well.

(Winnicott 1965)

'Good-enough' holding leads to integration of the infant personality, to a 'continuity of going-on-being', which prefigures Stern's (1985) idea of a 'line of continuity' that is the germ of the sense of coherent self. Where there is such continuity the growing child can cope with temporary separations without resorting to maladaptive defences. Like Bowlby, Winnicott sees the seeds of pathology in failures of the holding environment. Separations may provide the nucleus of later delinquency:

Separation of a one or two year old from the mother produces a state which may appear later as an anti-social tendency. When the child tries to reach back over the gap [i.e., created by the separation] this is called stealing.

(Winnicott 1965)

Although Bowlby and Winnicott are saying something very similar about juvenile theft there is a subtle difference in their language and focus. For Bowlby theft is a sociological phenomenon, which can be well accounted for by the disrupted lives and maternal separations of the thieves' early childhood. Winnicott is reaching towards an understanding of the symbolism of the act of theft itself. He is suggesting that the stolen object stands in for the missing mother which the youth is using to bridge the emotional gap left by her absence. Bowlby is reaching for explanation, Winnicott for meaning. Both, incidentally, tend to ignore other possible aspects of the problem: Bowlby looks exclusively at the childhood experiences of his thieves, and ignores contemporary influences such as housing and unemployment, while Winnicott leaves little room for the many other possible symbolic meanings that an act of theft might represent.

Winnicott goes on to describe how the good mother empathically understands what stage the child's object constancy has reached and so knows how to handle separations: 'She knows she must not leave her child for more minutes, hours, days than the child is able to keep the idea of her alive and friendly' (Winnicott 1965). If this is unavoidable she will have to resort to therapeutic 'spoiling': 'If she knows she must be away too long

she will have to change from a mother into a therapist in order
to turn the child back into a state in which he takes the mother
for granted again' (Winnicott 1965).

Like Winnicott, Bowlby is insistent in his opposition to the
notion that children can be 'spoilt' by too much love, and reminds
therapists who are working with adults who weep and cling: 'It
is perhaps too often forgotten by clinicians that many children
when they become distressed and weepy and are looking for
comfort are shooed off as intolerable little cry-babies' (Bowlby
1988a).

Winnicott visualises 'two mothers' in the early months of life.
The first protects the child from 'impingement' and acts as an
'auxiliary ego' which enables him gradually to build up his own
autonomous ego. He calls this the 'environment mother' who
offers 'affection and sensuous coexistence'. Within the ambiance
created by the environment mother the child then relates to the
'object mother' who can be sucked and bitten, loved and hated.
Her response will have far-reaching consequences: overintrusive-
ness can in a seductive way be as traumatic as neglect, and both
can lead to defensive moves such as 'self-holding', disintegration
and the development of a false self.

For Bowlby there are also two mothers. The first is equivalent
to Winnicott's 'environment mother', the provider of the secure
base. The second mother is the companion with whom the child,
once a secure base has been established, engages in exploratory
play. This 'third mother' is different from Winnicott's second
'object mother' with whom the child engages in orgiastic play.
Bowlby seems less interested in orgasmic activities, although the
sexual foreplay of trusting adults can be seen as a form of mutual
exploration (analogous to the sensuous intimacy of mother and
child), which enables a greater build-up of intense pleasure than
orgasm not preceded by exploration.

In Winnicott's sophisticated theory of the origins of play he
sees the emphatic responsiveness of the mother helping to create
a necessary illusion of omnipotence in the infant so that, as a
wish begins to form in the child's mind so she begins to answer
it – just as the baby begins to feel hungry, the breast appears,
as though by magic. In this transitional zone of overlapping phantasy are to be found the origins of playfulness, creativity and,
ultimately, culture. Bowlby's 'companion mother' can be seen in
similar, if less mystical terms. The post-Bowlbians emphasise

the collaborative nature of exploration, the 'zone of proximal development' (Vygotsky 1962), where parent and child interact and in which learning takes place. Stern (1985) sees the task of the mother as maintaining an internal 'line of continuity' for the child, so that she will unobtrusively stimulate the child when his imagination begins to flag, back off when he is playing happily, and dampen his excitement when it threatens to get out of hand. The differing languages of Winnicott and Bowlby reflect the differing foci of their thought. For the Bowlbian, child play and exploration take place 'out there' in the world, while Winnicott's child is concerned with inner exploration, with the world of the imagination 'in here'. The real child is of course engaged in both at the same time. The toddler building and breaking and building again his tower of bricks is simultaneously acquiring Piagetian knowledge of physics – the properties of materials, the mathematics of cubes, the nature of gravity – and in a Freudian sense exploring potency and castration, and the interplay of destruction and reparation of the inner world.

Klein's depressive position becomes in Winnicottian terminology the 'stage of concern'. Here the 'environment mother' and the 'object mother' come together as one person. The environment is necessarily defective: the mother cannot always be perfectly responsive: there will be gaps and breaks and discontinuities of care. The child responds with aggression and rage directed at the 'object mother': she survives the attacks and continues to love her child, and the balance is restored. He now realises that the mother who lets him down is also the one he loves. Clouds of guilt and anxiety appear on his horizon, but also the seeds of gratitude and reparation. For Bowlby, too, the good mother can withstand her child's aggressive onslaughts, and these early experiences lead to a mental set in later life (based on internal working models) that feelings can be expressed and 'processed', conflicts successfully resolved. The anxiously attached child is caught up in a vicious circle (see Figure 7.1) in which he lacks a secure base; feels angry and wants to attack the attachment figure for premature separation; doesn't dare to do so for fear of retaliation or pushing the attachment figure even further away; and so suppresses his feelings of anxiety and rage thereby increasing the sense of insecurity; leading ultimately to an expectation of lack of care, and danger in emotional expression with potentially disastrous implications for self-esteem and intimate

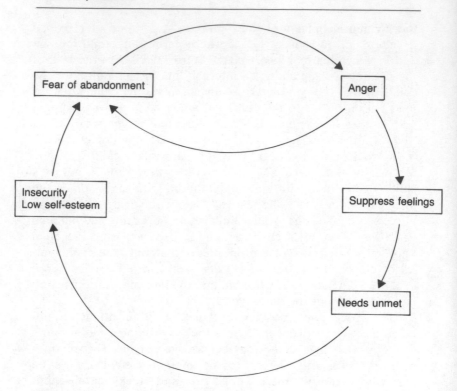

Figure 7.1 The anxiously attached infant

relationships. There is, in this 'Winnicott-type theory' (Bowlby 1988b)

> a massive block against expressing or even feeling a natural desire for a close trusting relationship, for care, comfort and love – which I regard as the subjective manifestations of a major system of instinctive behaviour.

Like Bowlby, Winnicott also repudiates the linear 'monorail' model of development in which the child progresses from oral to anal to genital phases of development:

> Most of the processes that start up in early infancy are never fully established and continue to be strengthened by the growth that continues in later childhood and indeed in adult life, even in old age.
>
> (Winnicott 1965)

Bowlby and Kohut

Bowlby's conviction that attachment needs continue throughout life and are not outgrown has important implications for psychotherapy. It means that the therapist inevitably becomes an important attachment figure for the patient, and that this is not necessarily best seen as a 'regression' to infantile dependence (the developmental 'train' going into reverse), but rather the activation of attachment needs that have been previously suppressed. Heinz Kohut (1977) has based his 'self psychology' on a similar perspective. He describes 'selfobject needs' that continue from infancy throughout life and comprise an individual's need for empathic responsiveness from parents, friends, lovers, spouses (and therapists). This responsiveness brings a sense of aliveness and meaning, security and self-esteem to a person's existence. Its lack leads to narcissistic disturbances of personality characterised by the desperate search for selfobjects – for example, idealisation of the therapist or the development of an erotic transference. When, as they inevitably will, these prove inadequate (as did the original environment), the person responds with 'narcissistic rage' and disappointment, which, in the absence of an adequate 'selfobject' cannot be dealt with in a productive way.

BOWLBY AND CONTEMPORARY PSYCHOTHERAPEUTIC THEORY

There is an inherent dualism in the Freudian project. Freud saw psychoanalysis as a science, and wanted his accounts of psychopathology to have the same status and explanatory power as those of physical medicine. At the same time, as Rycroft (1985) points out, he called his *magnum opus The Interpretation*, not *The Cause of Dreams*, and

> It can indeed be argued that much of Freud's work was really semantic and that he made a revolutionary discovery in semantics, namely that neurotic symptoms are meaningful, disguised communications, but that, owing to his scientific training and allegiance, he formulated his findings in the conceptual framework of the physical sciences.
>
> (Rycroft 1985)

The scientific-explanatory and the semantic-hermeneutic poles of Freud's thought are epitomised in contemporary psychotherapy on the one hand by Kleinian and Lacanian psychoanalysis and on the other by cognitive therapy. In this section I shall first give a brief account of these apparently irreconcilable approaches and then suggest that Attachment Theory provides a possible bridge between them.

Rustin (1991) has described the history of psychoanalysis as moving through the three Kantian categories of truth: scientific, ethical and aesthetic. Freud saw himself as a natural scientist, looking for general truths about normal and abnormal psychology; Melanie Klein's theories were essentially ethical – about destructiveness and splitting and the reconciliation of good and bad in the depressive position; Rustin sees current psychoanalysis as predominantly aesthetic in its orientation. Kant distinguishes aesthetic from scientific or moral judgement in having to do with 'disinterested contemplation of objects of experience, related neither to the goal of interpersonal knowledge of causes, nor to issues of conformity with the moral law' (Rustin 1991). The discovery of meanings is central to this aesthetic sensibility, the prototype of which is to be found within the mother–infant relationship. The mother 'contains' or 'binds' (Bion 1978) infantile sense experiences and mental images; she points, and shapes and names, and so gives meaning to them. Maternal attunement (Stern), secure base provision (Bowlby) and holding environment (Winnicott) are all reaching towards the same idea. The function of the parent, of the therapist and of cultural objects can all be understood in this framework of containment and structuring of inchoate experience.

To illustrate his point Rustin contrasts classical and contemporary psychoanalytic accounts of *Hamlet*. Ernest Jones (1949) saw the play as a quintessentially Oedipal drama in which Hamlet is wracked by his ambivalence towards the father-figures (the Ghost, the King, Polonius), and his simultaneous yearning and rage towards his mother. Williams (Meltzer and Williams 1988) sees the problem of the play centring on Hamlet's search for a vehicle with which to express his grief, anger and ambition. The corrupt world of the court, of institutional power cannot contain this intimacy of the imagination. The play-within-a-play 'catches the conscience of the king', but action – as opposed to thought – spills over into murder and intrigue. Throughout the play

Hamlet, like a patient in therapy, has been struggling to write his story, to find, in Williams' words, an 'aesthetic correlative to image the idea of a new prince' (that is, one not caught up in power and corruption). Dying, he enjoins his faithful Horatio to

Absent thee from felicity awhile,
And in this harsh world draw thy breath in pain
To tell my story.

In this neo-Kleinian perspective, *narrative* becomes a key feature of the psychotherapeutic process. The therapist provides a setting in which thought rather than action can happen, and in which the patient can begin to tell himself his own story, undistorted by repression, splitting and affective distancing. In the Lacanian (Bowie 1991) account too, narrative is central, although a 'story', spoken in words, is seen as the imposition of the *logos*, of phallo-centric culture on the primal, pre-verbal unity of mother and child. For the Kleinians there is no such radical rupture with the onset of language: integration is achieved at the advent of the depressive position, rather than thwarted by the insertion of the paternal order.

The aesthetic perspective provides perhaps a much-needed cultural location for psychoanalysis, but what of its claim to be a science, and how do we evaluate one narrative account against another? Are all 'stories' equally valid, or are some more 'true' than others? And what of Bowlby's own comment:

I believe that our discipline can be put on to a scientific basis. A lot of people think you can't or don't know how to. There are people who think psychoanalysis is really a hermeneutic discipline. I think that's all rubbish quite frankly.

(Bowlby *et al*. 1986)

Bowlby wanted to make psychoanalysis more scientific, claiming to be truer to Freud's intentions and more in touch with his later ideas than were Klein and her followers. He did so at a time when psychoanalysis, partly in spite of itself, was gradually moving away from science and in the direction of hermeneutics and meanings. Attachment theory, like one of Darwin's Galapagos islands, became isolated from the mainland of psychoanalysis, so developing its own ideas and language.

However, to continue the analogy, continental drift has occurred: previously separate areas are now beginning to overlap.

It is here that the recent work of Main (1991), Fonagy (1991) and Bretherton (1991a and b) are so intriguing. As we showed in the previous chapter, the Adult Attachment Interview is a standardised instrument by which an individual's autobiographical narrative *account* of their childhood and attachment history can be linked with their behaviour as parents, and with the security of their children. Clear, coherent stories correlate with securely attached children. Narrative incompetence – inability to tell any sort of story, or embroilment in a muddled and incoherent one – is linked with insecure attachment. The narrative dimension in psychotherapy – helping patients to gain a clearer picture of their life and their early attachments – can be supported on scientific as well as aesthetic grounds. The polarisation between hermeneutics and science implicit in Bowlby's rather intemperate dismissal now looks a lot less clear-cut. Psychoanalysis provides a system of meanings for helping to decode patients' symptoms, but, if we step back from the specific meanings, we find good scientific evidence that narrative capacity, the ability to make meanings out of the inchoate flow of an 'unstoried' life – especially out of loss and disappointment – is associated with healthy psychological functioning.

If hermeneutics is 'rubbish' – a view which, had he lived long enough to consider the implications of Main and Fonagy's work, Bowlby might well have revised – what then of the opposing scientific tendency within psychotherapy? Cognitive therapy, devised by Beck *et al.* (1979), works primarily with cognitions, as opposed to the emotions that are the raw material of psychoanalysis. It is based on the idea that cognitions determine feelings (rather than vice versa), and that if the faulty cognitions which underlie neurotic states can be unearthed and corrected, then psychological health will ensue. There are strong echoes of Bowlbian metapsychology in this model. Mental structures are visualised in a hierarchy of expectations and assumptions, from specific assumptions such as 'When I am distressed I will receive help', to core beliefs such as 'I am lovable and can love'. The internal working models of Attachment Theory are similarly visualised as a set of guiding affective and cognitive models of the world that are more or less subject to revision and updating. Cognitive therapy assumes that in neurosis the normal process of testing and modifying assumptions about the world breaks down, so that, for example, if the core belief in depression is 'I am unworthy

of love and deserve rejection', when a fortuitous reb
serves to reinforce the faulty belief and to deepen the

In Ryle's (1990) modification of cognitive therapy,
analytic therapy (CAT), he considers that the underly.
beliefs have their origins in disturbed attachment patte.
infancy and early childhood, later perpetuated in adult rela..on-
ships by a vicious circle of self-fulfilling negative assumptions
about the self and the world. Ryles's model of therapy requires
a much more active collaborative attitude on the part of the
therapist than in traditional analytic therapy. The therapist sets
tasks for the patient, such as encouraging them to keep a 'mood
diary' and to rate their progress on visual scales, as well as
offering the patient a written formulation of the problem and its
dynamics and a farewell letter when therapy (which is brief –
typically sixteen sessions) comes to an end.

CAT is 'Bowlbian' in three important ways. First in its theoretical eclecticism: Ryle happily marries cognitive science with
psychoanalysis in an information-processing model that is very
similar to Bowlby's attempt to re-write psychoanalytic defense
mechanisms in terms of control theory. Second, Ryle's active
therapist is engaging in 'companionable interaction' with the
patient just like the secure base mother who actively plays with
her child, and meeting the need for affiliation postulated by
Heard and Lake (1986). Third, like cognitive therapy, CAT
focuses on the need for self-reflection by the patient. This links
with Fonagy's account of narrative capacity discussed above. In
his model the good mother accurately reflects the moods and
wishes of her infant. This mirroring is then internalised as self-
reflexive capacity, as the child gradually comes to know about his
own internal states. This in turn manifests itself, as development
proceeds, in the capacity to verbalise these states, and to 'tell a
story' about oneself. The main themes of this autobiographical
skill are the history of one's attachments, separations and re-
unions. Being a brief therapy, CAT highlights and tries to acceler-
ate the emergence of autobiographical competence in a deliberate
way rather than assuming that it will be an automatic part of the
therapeutic process. Post-Bowlbian research provides a rationale
for this in that there is a demonstrable link between the capacity
to 'tell one's story' and the development of secure attachment
which is an overall goal of psychotherapy.

In summary, Attachment Theory has shown that the emphasis

on narrative and hermeneutics in contemporary psychotherapy can be justified on good developmental grounds. Good mothers help their infants towards personal meanings, which in turn are a basis and mark of secure attachment. Cognitive therapy, although apparently opposed to the narrative approach in its concern with here-and-now cognitions, is also, in its way, a story about the internal world. Its 'basic assumptions' are not far removed from Bowlby's internal working models or the 'representational world' of psychoanalysis.

Freud (1911) always insisted that there were *two* principles of mental functioning, the primary and secondary processes – the visual and the verbal, the imaginative and the rational – and that healthy functioning required a balance between the two. In Humphrey's (1992) re-working of this model there are two channels of information available to the organism, sensation and perception, which tell it about its own internal states and the state of the world respectively. Out of the post-war schisms of psychoanalysis there emerged an unhealthy polarisation between the concern of psychoanalysis with the primary processes and the focus of attachment and cognitive theory on secondary processes. The paradigm of narrative, a blending of sensation and perception, in which the inner world can be described objectively, while the subjective colouring of the outer world is also held up for inspection, is exciting increasing interest in psychotherapy (see Spence 1982; Shafer 1976). The question arises whether a secondary-process type verbal *encouragement* towards self-observation and narrative capacity is likely in itself to be effective, or whether primary-process ingredients, especially the arousal of affect through transference, are also needed. To consider this and other more practical questions we must now turn to a consideration of the specific implications of the Bowlbian perspective for the practice of psychotherapy.

Chapter 8

Attachment Theory and the practice of psychotherapy

The therapeutic alliance appears as a secure base, an internal object as a working, or representational, model of an attachment figure, reconstruction as exploring memories of the past, resistance as deep reluctance to disobey the past orders of parents not to tell or not to remember. . . . Whilst some traditional therapists might be described as adopting the stance 'I know; I'll tell you', the stance I advocate is one of 'You know, you tell me' . . . the human psyche, like human bones, is strongly inclined towards self-healing. The psychotherapist's job, like that of the orthopaedic surgeon's, is to provide the conditions in which self-healing can best take place.

(Bowlby 1988a)

We come now to the core of the book: an attempt to describe Attachment Theory's distinctive contribution to the theory and practice of psychotherapy. Two related concepts have emerged. The first, starting from Object-Relations Theory, but going beyond it, is the idea of the *core state with respect to attachment*. Bowlby sees a person's attachment status as a fundamental determinant of their relationships, and this is reflected in the way they feel about themselves and others. Neurotic patterns can be seen as originating here because, where core attachments are problematic, they will have a powerful influence on the way someone sees the world and their behaviour. Where there is a secure core state, a person feels good about themselves and their capacity to be effective and pursue their projects. Where the core state is insecure, defensive strategies come into play.

Bowlby's concept of defence is different from that of classical psychoanalysis (Hamilton 1985) in that it is not primarily intrapsychic – a way of reducing the internal disruption created by unmanageable feelings – but interpersonal. Secure attachment provides a positive 'primary' defence; 'secondary', pathological defences are methods of retaining proximity to rejecting or unreliable attachment figures. The two main patterns can be formulated along the lines of 'I need to be near to my attachment figures in order to feel safe, but they may reject my advances, so I will suppress my needs both from myself and them, and remain on the emotional periphery of relationships' (avoidant strategy), or 'I need to be near to my attachment figures but they may fail to respond to me or intrude on me in a way I can't control, so I will cling to them and insist on their responding to and caring for me' (ambivalent strategy). Both can be formulated in terms of dilemmas (Ryle 1990) arising out of the need to get close and the imagined dangers of so doing: rejection, abandonment or intrusion. Both lead to inhibition of vital parts of personality functioning. In avoidance, aggression tends to be displaced or split off; in ambivalence, exploration is held back.

The second central concept to have emerged from Attachment Theory is that of *narrative*. A person's core state is a condensate of the history of their primary relationships. If this history is available to them in the form of a personal narrative, then they are likely to feel secure. We have seen in Chapter 6 the evidence that 'autobiographical competence' (Holmes 1992) both results from and contributes to secure attachment. The word 'narrative' derives from *gnathos* or knowing. Psychotherapy is based on the Delphic injunction (Pedder 1982): know thyself. Making the unconscious conscious can be re-formulated as knowing and owning one's story. Attachment Theory has shown that self-knowledge in the form of narrative is associated with a core state characterised by secure attachment. Narrative turns experience into a story which is temporal, is coherent and has meaning. It objectifies experience so that the sufferer becomes detached from it, by turning raw feeling into symbols. It creates out of fragmentary experience an unbroken line or thread linking the present with the past and future. Narrative gives a person a sense of ownership of their past and their life.

Contemporary psychotherapy is characterised by a myriad of different schools and models of the therapeutic process. Attachment Theory should not be seen as yet one more form of psychotherapy, but rather as defining features that are relevant to therapy generally – individual, group, family – akin to Frank's (1986) common factors or 'metamodel' approach to the diversity of therapies. He proposes certain key elements which are shared by all therapies. These include a *relationship* with the therapist, which provides hope or 'remoralisation' – in Bowlbian terms a secure base from which to start to explore the problem; a coherent *explanation* for the patient's difficulties – a shared narrative; and a *method* for overcoming them. Holmes and Lindley (1989) saw the overall goal of psychotherapy as 'emotional autonomy' – the capacity to form relationships in which one feels both close and free, corresponding with Attachment Theory's picture of a secure base facilitating exploration.

This chapter will be devoted to a discussion of five key themes which determine an individual's core state of attachment, and how psychotherapy may help, via the development of a therapeutic narrative, to create secure rather than neurotic (that is, insecure) attachments. These are: the need for a secure therapeutic base; the role of real trauma (as opposed to phantasy) in the origins of neurosis; affective processing, especially of loss and separation; the place of cognitions in therapy; and the part played by 'companionable interaction' between therapist and patient. The main focus will be on individual therapy, but the principles are equally applicable to group therapies, and the chapter ends with a consideration of Attachment Theory in relation to family therapy, of which Bowlby was one of the founding fathers.

1 ATTACHMENT AND THE SECURE BASE IN PSYCHOTHERAPY

Attachment Theory predicts that when someone is faced with illness, distress, or threat they seek out an attachment figure from whom they may obtain relief. Once a secure base is established attachment behaviour is assuaged, and they can begin to explore – in this case, the exploration will be of the situation which has caused the distress and the feelings it has aroused. This would be a simple account of many episodes of brief counselling, and of psychotherapy generally were it not for the question of the nature of the secure base. The establishment of a base depends on the interaction between help-seeker and help-giver. The very fact that someone seeks psychotherapeutic help implies that they will have had difficulty in establishing such a base in the past.

The patient brings with him into therapy all the failures and suspicions and losses he has experienced through his life. The defensive forms of insecure attachment – avoidance, ambivalence, disorganisation – will be brought into play in relation to the therapist. There will be a struggle between these habitual patterns and the skill of the therapist in providing a secure base – the capacity to be responsive and attuned to the patient's feelings, to receive projections and to transmute them in such a way that the patient can face their hitherto unmanageable feelings. To the extent that this happens, the patient will gradually relinquish their attachment to the therapist while, simultaneously, an internal secure base is built up inside. As a result, as therapy draws to a close, the patient is better able to form less anxious attachment relationships in the external world and feels more secure in himself. As concrete attachment to the therapist lessens, so the qualities of self-responsiveness and self-attunement are more firmly established in the inner world.

Freud wrote in 1913: 'The first aim of the treatment consists in attaching . . . [the patient] to the treatment and to the person of the physician.' Psychoanalysts have worried about two aspects of this attachment. First, can healthy, conscious, therapeutic attachment be distinguished from unconscious phantasy-based transferential feelings aroused in the patient by being in treatment? Second, is it the secure base of this relationship and the 'new beginning' (Balint 1968) which provide the main vehicle of cure, or are interpretations and the insight they produce the crucial factors?

The therapeutic alliance and the 'real' relationship

Zetzel (1956) was the first to use the phrase the 'therapeutic alliance' to describe the non-neurotic, reality-based aspect of the therapist–patient relationship (Mackie 1981), a term which is usually used interchangeably with that of the 'working alliance'. Greenson (1967) sees the 'reliable core of the working alliance in the "real", or non-transference relationship'. By 'real' is meant both genuine and truthful as opposed to contrived or phoney, and also realistic and undistorted by phantasy.

In practice these distinctions are not so easy to make. The patient may well have a genuine desire to get better and to collaborate with the therapist in doing so, and at the same time be concealing feelings of despair and disappointment behind an idealising transference. It is certainly the therapist's task to provide a secure base for the patient: to be available regularly and reliably; to be courteous, compassionate and caring; to be able to set limits and have clear boundaries; to protect the therapy from interruptions and distractions; and not to burden the patient with his own difficulties and preoccupations. Since Attachment Theory presupposes that a distressed individual will naturally seek security, the distinction between the 'real' and the transferential relationship becomes less problematic. Dependency on the therapist is not seen as inherently neurotic, but as an appropriate response to emotional distress. The issue is whether the patient has formed a secure or an anxious type of attachment, and if anxious, what pattern. If, for example, there has been major environmental trauma in the patient's life (prolonged separation from parents, or physical or sexual abuse, for example), then the patient is unlikely to find it easy to form a secure base and may in an avoidant way approach therapy and the therapist with suspicion and reserve, and detach himself at the faintest hint of a rebuff, and the 'real' relationship may hang by a thread.

The question of whether attachment to the therapist is merely a necessary first step for the initiation of transference or whether it constitutes a therapeutic element in its own right is usually understood in terms of stages of development. Balint's 'basic fault' patient (that is, one who is severely damaged by early environmental failure) needs a new kind of empathic experience with the therapist which can then be internalised and so provides an inner sense of security which is the precondition of autonomy. In a less damaged 'Oedipal' patient, attachment to the therapeutic environment can be more taken for granted, and the focus will be on the way that the person of the therapist is viewed and treated. Kohut (1977) and Guntrip (1974) have pointed to the difference in technique required for these two types of patient, arguing that more damaged 'borderline' patients require greater acceptance and environmental provision. Kernberg (Bateman 1991) has questioned this, claiming that limit setting and interpretive understanding is even more vital if these patients are to be helped towards adaptation to reality.

Bowlby rejected a simplistic 'stage'-based model of development, but the distinctions which attachment therapy makes between ambivalent, avoidant and disorganised patterns of insecure attachment are relevant here. The disorganised pattern may represent the most disturbed patients who are threatened by too close attachment of any sort, and need a low-key supportive approach (Holmes 1992). The ambivalently attached need a combination of absolute reliability and firm limit setting to help with secure attachment, combined with a push towards exploration. The avoidant group associate close contact with pain and rejection and may experience interpretations as intrusive assaults, and so benefit from a more flexible and friendly therapeutic relationship.

Balint's (1968) distinction between 'ocnophils' (clingers) and 'philobats' (avoiders) corresponds closely with Bowlby's classification of insecure attachment into ambivalent and avoidant patterns. Balint sees many psychoanalysts as 'ocnophilic', clinging to their patients with their interpretations. Like Meares and Hobson (1977) in their discussion of the 'persecutory therapist', he argues that attachment must be sought and accepted as a goal in its own right with more disturbed patients, and that too much interpretation can inhibit a patient's exploration.

Spying or seeking

Annabel was a disturbed young woman living away from home in a bedsitter. She had always felt that her mother favoured her brother over herself. This feeling of exclusion was compounded when, during her teens, her mother became ill and her previously neglectful father had tenderly looked after his sick wife. Annabel confessed to her therapist that one day when alone in the house she had crept into her landlady's part of the house and, searching through her desk, had found some love-letters from her husband and had read them avidly.

A Kleinian interpretation might have focused on the envious 'attack on linking' implicit in this act, trying to help her to get in touch with the angry and destructive impulses which made her feel responsible for her mother's illness. A Bowlbian approach, however, would see the need to maintain a line of attachment as paramount, and would therefore interpret this act as a search for a secure base in her parents' marriage (and by transference in the therapy). Only once this secure base was firmly established would it be appropriate to look at her protest about loss and separation.

As we mentioned in Chapter 3, Attachment Theory is essentially a spatial theory in which the care-seeker is constantly monitoring and adjusting his distance from the care-giver depending on the level of perceived anxiety and the strength of the drive to explore. Balint also emphasises the importance of getting the right distance from the patient, especially if words fail and the patient falls silent. The therapist must be

> felt to be present but must be all the time at the right distance – neither so far that the patient feels lost or abandoned, nor so close that the patient might feel encumbered and unfree – in fact at a distance that corresponds to the patient's actual need.
>
> (Balint 1986)

Therapists and parents

Post-Bowlbian research has begun to provide a picture of the kinds of mother–infant interaction that are likely to give rise to a secure base experience for the growing child. The children of parents who are responsive and attuned and see their infants as separate are likely to be better adjusted socially, more able to reflect on their feelings and to weave their experience into a coherent narrative. The capacity to handle loss and separation with appropriate anger, sadness and reconciliation is associated with secure attachment. These findings can be compared with the Rogerian view that effective therapists show empathy, honesty and non-possessive warmth (Truax and Carkhuff 1967). The good therapist acts, mainly at an unconscious and non-verbal level, like a good parent with his patients. Empathy corresponds with attunement and responsiveness; honesty ensures that negative feelings, especially those connected with loss and separation based on the inevitable failures of the holding environment in therapy (therapist's illness, holidays, memory-lapses and so on), are dealt with openly and without prevarication; non-possessive warmth means that the therapist gets the attachment distance right which means they are containing to the patient without being intrusive.

Based on Attachment Theory research we can identify three component elements which go to make up the secure base phenomenon in therapy: attunement, the fostering of autobio-

graphical competence and affective processing (Holmes 1992).
Two case examples will now be given to illustrate the phenomena
of attunement and autobiographical competence in therapy.
Affective processing will be considered in a later section of the
chapter.

Attunement

Stern (1985) sees attunement as the basis for the emerging sense
of self in the pre-verbal infant:

> Tracking and attuning . . . permit one human to be with
> another in the sense of sharing likely inner experience on an
> almost continuous basis. . . . This is exactly our experience of
> feeling-connectedness, of being in attunement with another. It
> feels like an unbroken line. It seeks out the activation contour
> that is momentarily going on in any and every behaviour and
> uses that contour to keep the thread of communication
> unbroken.
>
> (Stern 1985)

For Stern, the emotionally disturbed patient is one whose early
experiences lacked this attunement. There is perhaps a faint echo
of Hamlet's farewell to Horatio when he compares the need for
an attuning parent (or therapist) with

> the continuing physiological need for an environment contain-
> ing oxygen. It is a relatively silent need of which one becomes
> aware sharply only when it is not being met, when a harsh
> world compels one to draw one's breath in pain.
>
> (Stern 1985)

Brazelton and Cramer's (1991) detailed description of secure
parent–infant interaction similarly delineates the components of
responsive interaction: synchrony, symmetry, contingency and
'entrainment', from which mutual play and infant autonomy begin
to emerge (see Chapter 6). These features are equally applicable
to therapist–patient interactions. Good therapists find themselves
automatically mirroring their patients' levels of speech volume
and their posture. Malan's (1976) concept of 'leapfrogging'
between patient and therapist is very similar to the idea of contingency and entrainment in which parent and child hook onto
each other in sequences of mutual responsiveness. This can be

demonstrated immediately in videotapes of therapy, but is less easy to convey in a written account.

Sarah's 'ums' and 'aahs'

Despite marriage, parenthood, a profession and a circle of good friends, Sarah had reached her fiftieth year almost without any sense of who she was or what the meaning and direction of her life should be. In her social self she played the part of a cheerful and active woman constantly fighting off feelings of depression and the wish to end her life. In therapy she returned again and again to the question, 'Who *am* I?'.

She had been brought up in a 'progressive' children's home where her parents were the proprietors. She had always felt that her mother was 'so near and yet so far': she could *see* her, but was expected, from the age of three, to fit in and share a dormitory with the other children, and was not allowed to have any kind of special relationship with her. Her father was harsh, distant, controlling and physically and sexually abusive. She dated the origin of the split between her 'social' and her 'real' self to the age of eight, when she had naïvely tried to disclose her father's abuse but had been disbelieved, and punished by him for what to her was quite inexplicable 'wickedness'. Any attunement between her inner world and the external one was fractured from then on. Peer Gynt-like, she complained that however much she peeled away the onion skin of her existence she could never find her real self.

As therapy progressed she found the 'attuning' sounds of the therapist – the 'ums' and 'aahs', grunts, inhalations and exhalations – immensely comforting. 'They give me a sense that somehow *you know* how I feel, however much you appear distant, rejecting or uninterested (all words she had used about her parents) in your verbal comments.' In fact, it was extremely difficult to tune into this patient, who varied between desperate attempts to draw the therapist into her pain and misery, complaining ('Why aren't you *angry* about the terrible things that happened to me as a child?'), demanding ('I need to know that you *like* me'), and excluding him with a self-absorbed, miserable monologue. Nevertheless, the fact that she *could* complain, demand and moan was, for her, in itself a considerable achievement. She dreamed of the therapist looking at her and knowing, without her having to put it into words, how she felt, and of his gently putting an arm around her in a gesture of protection.

Autobiographical competence

Winnicott (1965) described psychotherapy as 'an extended form of history-taking'. The patient comes with a story, however tentative and disjointed, which is then worked on by therapist and patient until a more coherent and satisfying narrative emerges, which provides an objectification and explanation of the patient's difficulties, and a vehicle or symbolisation which links inner and outer experience (Spence 1982; Shafer 1976). Tulving (Eagle 1988) distinguishes between 'semantic' memory, which is propositional and influences behaviour but which need not necessarily be conscious, and 'episodic' memory, which has a narrative structure and consists of stored chunks of remembered experience. The process of therapy can be seen as one of making 'semantic' memory episodic, of weaving a narrative out of the unconscious attitudes, assumptions and affects which the patient brings to the therapy in the transference, so that they feel they now own them.

The avoidant patient with a dismissing autobiographical style begins to allow some of the pain of separation into consciousness, the ambivalent patient with a preoccupied style can start to feel safe enough to let go of their past anguish. Out of narrative comes meaning – the 'broken line' of insecure attachment is replaced by a sense of continuity, an inner story which enables new experience to be explored, with the confidence that it can be coped with and assimilated. The next example tries to illustrate the immediacy of this process by presenting material from a single session.

Peter: stringing a story together

Peter is a man in his late fifties, now in his second year of weekly therapy. He has a very strong presence: powerful, pugnacious, a self-made man who grew up in the Gorbals, he is now a ship's captain, away from home for long stretches of time. His problems are depression, marital conflict and suicidal feelings which have been present for many years but which came to the surface after the birth of his youngest child.

He starts the session by talking about money. 'I'm like my

father, always worrying about money. I'm feeling good today, I've bought a car cheap, and I've got some work.' But that means another break away from home and from therapy. A lot of therapeutic effort has gone into helping him recognise how he detaches himself from feelings of loss when he goes away. 'I used to pride myself on not bothering to ring home or to miss them when I was away – it's only two weeks, why make a fuss.'

I take up the implication that in one sense therapy has made things more difficult for him now that he is in touch with feelings of loss and separation rather than cutting off from them, and remind him of the misery which he described when as a child he was evacuated to the country during the war, away from the bombs but also from his mother.

'Yes, it was terrible. After a few weeks my mother came to collect me. *Did* she dote on me or what? Everyone says that she did, but I just can't remember.' He then goes on to list a string of incidents which we have already unearthed and discussed from his childhood – playing truant at the age of five without his mother knowing, feeling an outsider among his playmates, learning to establish himself through fighting – 'Who *is* that little boy, I just don't recognise him; *is* that me?' He jokes: 'Oh well, like my father used to say, nostalgia's like neuralgia.'

I suggest that he can't piece himself together, can't identify with the little boy that he was because his mother wasn't there to string the episodes of his life together for him, just as I won't be there when he goes off to work next week.

He protests: 'But I can get what I like from women', and gives several examples to prove his point. I reply by wondering if he feels these women really *know* him, whether he feels that I or his wife know him, if his mother really knew his sadness and fear. Perhaps it was his vitality and strength that she doted on, like the women he can get what he likes from, not his vulnerability.

He then recounts some new history about his mother's childhood, how she was illegitimate, the offspring of his grandmother's second 'husband', how his grandfather had been quite well off, loved opera (as he does) and had taught his mother to play the piano, how she had been only eighteen when she became pregnant by his father and they 'had' to get married.

I suggest that his confusion about whether or not his mother 'doted' on him was perhaps because she was depressed during his infancy, confused in her new 'legitimate' identity, just as he had become depressed after the birth of his youngest child.

There was a pause: it seemed that this had struck a chord. '*Click:* they always used to say what a difficult feeder I was as a baby. My father' (the father who had always told this highly intelligent man what a dunce he was) 'had to buy special milk for me.'

I said: 'So money goes to the heart of your identity. He worked to keep you alive, just as you see me working to keep you alive now.'

He began to weep. I wondered if his sadness was to do with the coming break. 'No,' he said, 'It's gratitude – you seem to *recognise* what I am like.'

Seen from this post-Bowlbian perspective the tension between attachment and interpretation as curative factors in psychotherapy becomes less problematic. The responsiveness of the therapist begins to restore the 'broken line' of the patient's internal world and forms the basis of a secure therapeutic base. This enables the beginnings of exploration which in the setting of therapy takes the form of a narrative in which the therapist's interpretations are an attempt to modify, expand and lend coherence to the patient's story. But the narrative is not just the patient's 'case history'. It is also the history of the therapeutic relationship itself, of the movement from what Balint (1968) calls the 'mixedupness' of patient and therapist to a state of differentiation in which the patient detaches himself from the external support of the therapist and comes to rely on his own internal secure base, with a less fractured line of self.

2 REALITY AND TRAUMA

The notion of the 'broken line' brings us to the question of trauma in the genesis of neurosis. We saw in the last chapter how Bowlby's psychoanalytic education took place in an atmosphere in which the role of external reality was seen as largely irrelevant, compared with the influence of phantasy in mental life. Bowlby found this incomprehensible and reprehensible, and in one sense his life's work could be seen as an attempt to prove Klein wrong on this point.

His model was a rather simple, common-sense one, based on

Freud's early views, in which neurosis is the result of trauma, the facts or emotional implications of which have been repressed. The task of therapy is primarily that of undoing this repression in a non-judgemental and accepting atmosphere. This must be contrasted with Freud's mature views and those of contemporary psychoanalysts. Here the crucial factor is the *interaction* between environmental failure and the child's phantasy life. What makes trauma traumatic is, as Symington (1986) puts it, 'when reality confirms the phantasy'. In the Oedipal situation the child feels that his attachment to the mother is threatened by her relationship with his father. He may harbour feelings of hatred towards him, and have angry outbursts at home or at school. If he is then in reality beaten by his father – say, because of this recalcitrance (or, conversely, there is no father to help him detach himself from his mother) – then his internal world will be deformed and he is likely to be mistrustful of attachment while secretly yearning for it. This will affect his subsequent relationships, which may be characterised by demandingness, violence or detachment. If, on the other hand, his original feelings of fear and rage were accepted by the parents, the outcome will be favourable. A similar story can be imagined about the frustrations of infancy: a mother's actual unreliability and inability to accept the child's protests without retaliation will solidify rather than modify an already split inner world, and lay the foundations for 'borderline' patterns of relationships in which good and evil are kept unstably apart and compromise and balance are inaccessible (see Chapter 9).

Bowlby's own research and the accumulating evidence that parents do indeed abandon, neglect, physically and sexually abuse their children, and often deny that they do so and prohibit protest about the distress they have caused, seems to support his position that trauma and loss are central to the genesis of neurosis. Against this must be set several important qualifications. First, as we saw in Chapter 3, there are not a few resilient children who, despite apparently appalling environmental traumata, appear to come through without major psychological damage (Rutter 1985). Second, seeing people merely as victims of their circumstances, although valid at one level leaves out the idea of *agency*, which is a vital ingredient of psychological health. It also fails to comprehend the way in which pathological patterns, once internalised, are perpetuated by the sufferers themselves: the vicious circles of neurosis in which mistrust breeds disappointment, avoidance invites neglect, clinging provokes rejection, depressive assumptions lead to negative experiences which confirm those assumptions (cf., for example, Beck *et al*. 1979; Strachey 1934; Ryle 1990). Third, merely commiserating with a patient about the ways in which they have been damaged by their parents or by traumatic events does not in itself necessarily produce a good therapeutic outcome. For that to happen there has also to be some re-living (before relieving) of the emotional response to the trauma, and it is a central task of psychotherapy to provide the setting in which this affective processing can take place.

3 AFFECTIVE PROCESSING

Bowlby's early work seemed to imply that separation, at least in the first five years of life, was inherently a bad thing, and that a major task of preventive psychiatry would be to minimise the occurrence and affects of such separations. In his later work, however, there is a shift of perspective so that it is not just the facts of loss and separation, but the nature of a person's emotional response to them that matters. The Adult Attachment Interview findings (Bretherton 1991b) suggest that loss that is either denied (dismissive pattern) or cannot be transcended (pre-occupied pattern) is associated with insecure attachment (see Table 8.1). The way a parent handles a child's response to separation is a key factor here – whether by accepting and encouraging the expression of feelings of anger and sadness, or by sweeping them under the carpet. Bowlby saw the task of the therapist both to encourage appropriate emotional response to past trauma, and to be alert to the ways in which the patient is reacting to the losses and separations in therapy and to encourage discussion and ventilation of feelings about them. His views are well illustrated in his discussion of Charles Darwin's lifelong symptoms of anxiety and psychosomatic illness.

Charles Darwin: loss denied

Bowlby (1990) explained Darwin's lifelong intermittent psychosomatic symptoms of palpitations, paraesthesia, exhaustion and faintness in terms of unmourned loss. His mother died when he was eight. His father, a busy and irascible country doctor, whose

Table 8.1 Clinical aspects of insecure-avoidant and dismissive attachment

	Narrative style	Parenting	Core anxiety	Secondary defense	Transference	Counter-transference	Therapeutic strategy
INSECURE ATTACHMENT — Avoidant	Dismissive	Functional Pushing away	Abandonment	Splitting Denial	Terrified of contact	Bored Angry	Acceptance of rage
Ambivalent	Enmeshed	Inconsistent Intrusive	Impingement	False self Compliance	Terrified of separation	Stifled	Containment

own mother had died when he was a child, handed Charles over
to the care of his older sisters, who forbade any mention of their
mother's death. So powerful was the effect of this prohibition
that, at the age of thirty-three, in a letter of condolence to a
friend sympathising about the death of his young wife, he wrote:
'I truly sympathise with you though never in my life having lost
one near relation, I daresay I cannot imagine how severe grief
such as yours must be.'

Another instance of the repression of painful affect in Darwin's
life comes from his granddaughter's account of a family word
game in which words are 'stolen' by one player from another if
they can add a letter so as to create a new one. On one occasion
Darwin saw someone add an 'M' to 'other' to make 'Mother'.
Darwin stared at it for some time, objecting: 'There's no such
word as MO-THER'! (An unpsychological explanation such as
Bowlby's parents might have offered was that Darwin was a
notoriously bad speller – Raverat 1952.)

Bowlby sees Darwin's chronic ill health as reflecting two sets
of unresolved conflict. The first was his inability to grieve, to
bear the pain of the many losses in his life, starting with that of
his mother, and including his wife's many pregnancies (sources
of great anxiety to Darwin) and the loss of their beloved eldest
daughter in 1851. The second was his ambivalent relationship
with his overbearing father, whom Charles both revered and
feared. Bowlby sees his hesitancy about publication of *The Origin
of Species* (it took nearly twenty years between writing the original draft and publication, which was spurred on eventually by
competition from Wallace) as reflecting this compliance and
defiance in relation to authority. Bowlby's recipe for helping
Darwin to overcome his difficulties would have been to 'recognise
and gradually counteract the powerful influence . . . of the
strongly entrenched Darwin[ian] tradition that the best way of
dealing with painful thoughts is to dismiss them from your mind
and, if possible, forget them altogether'. Thus does Bowlby
recruit Freud to help with the Englishman's Achilles' heel – his
fear of feelings.

Bowlby and Winnicott: to commiserate or not?

It is interesting to compare Bowlby's ideas with those of Winnicott on this point. Winnicott opposes any reassurance or com-

miseration about trauma from the analyst, on the grounds that they may inhibit the affective processing that is needed if therapy is to succeed. He bases this on a rather subtle argument about the infant's necessary illusion of 'omnipotence', based on the mother's sensitive anticipation of his needs so that just as he is, as it were, thinking he might be hungry, the breast miraculously appears, as though by magic. For Winnicott the origins of creativity are to be found in this interplay between mother and child. Like Bion (1978), he also sees the mother helping the infant to deal with bad feelings through her containing and transmuting functions. If the baby feels that his protest and anger are accepted and held, then the environment does not 'impinge' in a traumatic way: 'The ego-support of the maternal care enables the infant to live and develop in spite of his not yet being able to control or feel responsible for what is good and bad in the environment' (Winnicott 1965).

Like Bowlby (but unlike Klein), Winnicott seems to acknowledge that the environment can let the child down, but argues that the child needs to have felt that everything is under his control before he can come gradually to accept his vulnerability:

> The paradox is that what is good and bad in the infant's environment is not in fact a projection, but in spite of this it is necessary . . . if the infant is to develop healthily that everything shall seem to him to be a projection.
>
> (Winnicott 1965)

This viewpoint enables Winnicott to argue the case for an analytic attitude in which the trauma is re-experienced in the transference in such a way that it comes within the area of 'omnipotence':

> In psychoanalysis there is no trauma that is outside the individual's omnipotence. . . . The patient is not helped if the analyst says 'your mother was not good enough . . .'. Changes come in an analysis when the traumatic factors enter the psychoanalytic material in the patient's own way, and within the patient's omnipotence.
>
> (Winnicott 1965)

Winnicott's phrase, 'bringing into omnipotence', is an example of the combination of clinical accuracy with theoretical fuzziness that Bowlby was keen to remedy in psychoanalysis. It also reflects Winnicott's ambivalence about Klein. He is straining both to be true to his clinical experience (that what is good and bad is *not* a projection) and to remain faithful to Kleinian theory (which emphasises the 'omnipotence' of infantile thought). A behavioural way of looking at this is to see it as an example of 'state-dependent learning' – that is, the observation that some things can only be learned, or unlearned, when the emotions associated with them are re-experienced. Humphrey's (1992) recent distinction between perception, an appreciation of the state of the world 'out there', and sensation, the state of things 'in here', is also helpful. While perception is a mirroring of external events that happens willy-nilly if the organism is to survive, and can be conscious or unconscious, Humphrey sees sensation as an active process in which the subject, as it were, presents his feelings to himself and that this is quintessentially a conscious process. One can imagine that sensation is, in the early stages of life, a shared activity between parent and child as the experiences of holding, seeing, feeding and touching are presented to the growing child. As Garland (1991) argues, traumatic events overwhelm the 'stimulus barrier' so that, although perceived, they cannot be sensed. The subject is paralysed by them and cannot actively present them to themselves, while the parent or protector who might help to do so is inevitably absent. The task of therapy then is to 'represent' these traumatic events – via a narrative transformation from 'semantic' to 'episodic' memory – in such a way that they can be sensed, and therefore, by definition, made conscious. This process could possibly be described as 'omnipotent' in so far as any representation or map, including the cerebral 'map' of feelings, is 'omnipotent'. Thus a grain of sand could be said omnipotently to 'contain all heaven'. Here is an example of such emotion recollected in (comparative) tranquillity:

The tonsillectomy

A man in his thirties entered therapy because of his feelings of depression and a failed marriage. His relationships were characterised by avoidant attachment. He was always seemingly throwing away the very things that he wanted. He knew what he did *not* want, but not what he wanted. Whenever his career threatened to take off he would leave his job. A similar pattern affected his relationship with his partner: the closer they became the more likely there was to be a violent argument. He was an only child whose father had been killed in the war, and the origins of this pattern seemed to go back to his mother, on whom he was very dependent, but whom he experienced as intrusive and interfering.

One winter's day as he was waiting for his therapy session he saw the therapist through the closed window breathing steam into the cold air. He found himself worrying that the therapist might have something wrong with his lungs. Suddenly a flood of memories returned a tonsillectomy he had undergone when he was five. Visiting was restricted (these were normal regimes in those pre-Bowlbian days), but he was able to see his mother through a glass window twice a week (it may not have been that bad – this was how he recalled it). He remembered his fury at not being able to go home with her, throwing the toys she had left for him, shouting 'I want my mummy . . .'. As the memories returned so he began to cry profusely. This session was a turning point, enabling him to move from a position of 'I don't want . . .', to 'I want . . .'. The traumatic separation had been re-experienced in the therapy, and no longer needed to be enacted via projective identification (doing to his employers and girlfriend what as a child he had felt had been done to him by his mother) but could be symbolised and so become part of the therapeutic narrative.

Therapists out of touch?

Attachment Theory throws an interesting light on the dilemma posed by the problem of touch in therapy. Bowlby emphasises the importance of real attachment of patient to therapist. Because attachment needs are seen as distinct from sexual or oral drives there is no intrinsic danger of gratification or seduction. Attachment provides a quiet background atmosphere of security within which more dangerous feelings can be safely explored. The patient who asks to touch the therapist, to hold a hand or be hugged, is wanting to get hold of the 'environment mother' who let him down or was absent in childhood, and it may be legitimate in certain circumstances, and with appropriate ethical safeguards (Holmes and Lindley 1989) for the therapist to respond to such a request (Balint 1968). In 'Attachment and new beginning', Pedder (1986) describes how a patient who had been separated from her mother for 6 months in infancy

buried her head in the pillow, extending her arms out loosely
to either side of the pillow. Her hands moved around rest-
lessly, reaching silently in my direction for some ten minutes.
Eventually I said I thought she wanted me to take her hand,
though she felt unable to say so, and then I did.

This seemed an important new beginning and she was later
able to say how she had been terrified of being too demanding
in asking me to hold a hand, fearing I might not trust her and
might have mistaken her wish to be held as sexual.

(Pedder 1986)

Secure attachment to the therapist may be part of a 'new beginning' for certain patients, and some physical expression of this
can be helpful. But – and here is the dilemma – pain and anguish
of separation also need to be re-experienced if the patient is to
feel safe enough to form new attachments, secure in the knowledge that, should things go wrong, the loss can be mourned and
that he will not be left feeling permanently bereft.

Winnicott's view that trauma needs to be brought 'within the
patient's omnipotence' is echoed by Casement (1985) in his discussion of another case in which the patient had asked to hold
her therapist's hand. This was a woman who had been badly
burned as a child and whose mother had fainted while holding
her hand when the burn was being operated on under local
anaesthetic. After initially agreeing, Casement later decided not
to accede to the patient's request. This withdrawal led to fury
and near-psychosis in the patient, but once this had been survived
she began rapidly to improve, and it seemed that the uncanny
repetition in the transference of the mother's holding and then
letting go of the patient, while remaining in a therapeutic context
that was basically secure, had contributed to this breakthrough.
Casement quotes Winnicott:

the patient used the analyst's failures, often quite small ones,
perhaps manoeuvred by the patient. . . . The patient now
hates the analyst for the failure that originally came as an
environmental factor, outside the area of omnipotent control,
but that is now staged in the transference. So in the end we
succeed by failing – failing the patient's way. This is a long
distance from the simple theory of cure by corrective experience.

(Winnicott 1965)

Bowlby the scientist was always parsimoniously trying to devise a 'simple theory' with which to explain the enormous complexity of intimate human relationships. Attachment Theory, while in general being unworried by physical contact between patient and therapist, does provide a clear rationale for exercising extreme caution in dealing with patients who have been abused in childhood, as the next example illustrates:

Safe breathing: secure base

Sarah, of the 'ums' and 'aahs' discussed above, was increasingly distressed as her elderly mother became ill. This coincided with her therapist having to change the time of her appointments. She started to sob and shake and overbreathe during the sessions. She wrote a poem in which she longed for a pure and childlike intimacy with her therapist. She wanted him inside her, breathing him in through her lungs, rather than taking him in through her mouth or genitals which she saw as sullied and contaminated. She wanted desperately to hold his hand, but he intuitively felt that this would be wrong.

When patient and therapist looked at this together they realised that this was because, as well as being the secure-base mother she so longed for, he also represented the abusive father whom she feared and loathed. Had he held her hand this would have repeated the typical abusive vicious circle in which the child clings ever more tightly to her abuser: the abuse creates a terrible anxiety which leads to attachment behaviour, which provokes more abuse and so on. By holding his hand she would have remained an *object*, albeit one in need of protection, whereas her greatest need was to become the subject of her own life, even though this meant subjecting herself to intense pain and fear. In the end she soothed herself with the idea that if she could feel that she *belonged* for a while in his consulting room, things would be all right. Like Oliver Twist (see Chapter 3), she needed first to find a place to which she could become attached, before she could begin to own her story.

4 COGNITION IN THERAPY

We have argued in the previous chapter that Bowlby's concept of internal working models acts as a bridge between psychoanalysis, which conceives of an internal world populated with objects and their relationships, and cognitive science, which acknowledges internal models of the world in the form of mental representations. Psychoanalysis is concerned with affect-laden sensations which act as a distorting prism as we confront the world; cognitive therapy, with the perceptions and constructions which we put on those sensations and erroneous assumptions which follow from them. Psychoanalysis aims to make the unconscious conscious; cognitive therapy starts from conscious thoughts but then reveals the unexamined assumptions that underlie them. Bowlby provides a bridging language between the two approaches. He sees the neurotic patient as basing his relationship to the world on outdated assumptions; for example, that he will be ignored or let down by people, or that his feelings will be dismissed or ridiculed. While these are, in his view, fairly accurate reflections of the way the person has been treated as a child, they do not necessarily bear any relation to current reality, and can lead to poor adaptation in the form of avoidant or ambivalent relationships.

Two factors are at work in maintaining these outmoded models. The first is defensive exclusion of painful emotions which can be overcome by the kind of affective processing advocated in the previous section. The second, related, phenomenon is the need to preserve meaning and to order incoming information from the environment in *some* kind of schema, however inappropriate.

Liotti (1987; Bowlby 1985) sees these schemata as 'superconscious' (rather than unconscious) organising principles 'which govern the conscious processes without appearing in them', rather as computer programmes determine what appears on the VDU screen without themselves being apparent. An important part of the task of therapy, whether cognitive or psychoanalytic, is to elicit and modify these overarching mental schemata. Given that the patient is likely to become closely attached to the therapist, it is assumed that his assumptions, preconceptions and beliefs will be brought into play in relation to the therapist, and the therapist will re-present them, as they become visible, for mutual consideration. This is Bowlby's version of the phenomenon of transference.

Always too considerate

Rose was in her fifties when she asked for help after splitting up with her second husband. She felt panicky and depressed and did not see how she could cope with being on her own. She had broken the marriage when she suddenly realised how she was compulsively deferential to her husband, and one more unreasonable request from him was the final straw.

As a child her life had changed dramatically when, at the age of seven, her father had walked out. She had been his favourite and every morning had sat on his lap while he fed her titbits. Now he had a new wife and family and she was relegated to occasional weekend visits where she slept in a cold and undecorated room, surrounded, as she saw it, by inaccessible luxury. At the same time her mother became profoundly depressed and developed an hysterical paralysis. When she recovered she had numerous boyfriends, one of whom she eventually married, and who resented Rose and her sisters' presence and insisted they went to bed at five o'clock every evening. Rose soon learned to suppress her own needs and disappointments and discovered in her teens that charm, good looks and compliance were a heady brew and she was able to attract powerful and successful men.

In her early psychotherapy sessions she announced that the last thing she wanted was any long-term commitment, merely a few sessions to 'sort her out'. She was grateful and dutifully took up any tentative suggestion from the therapist – that she might look at her dreams, or anger – with apparent enthusiasm. As the final scheduled session drew near she looked sad and tentative, but insisted that she was 'fine' and that everything was now going well. When challenged, however, she admitted that she did feel nervous about the end of therapy and really wanted to go on, but had 'assumed' that the therapist was far too busy to be bothered with her for more than a few meetings. In this example of ambivalent attachment she had reproduced with the therapist the very pattern of suppression of need, compliance and role reversal (she looking after the therapist) that characterised her relationship with her mother. She carried over into therapy the cognitive assumption 'I will only be loved if I look after others and please them'. This had served her well as an organiser of experience and a way of avoiding painful disappointment and frightening rage, but also acted as a barrier to her achieving what

she really wanted and deprived her of feelings of intimacy and
ease.

5 COMPANIONABLE INTERACTION

Attachment Theory sees exploratory and attachment behaviour
as reciprocal behavioural systems. The securely attached infant
feels safe to explore the environment; if danger threatens, exploration is abandoned in favour of proximity-seeking to an attachment figure. In adults, attachment can be differentiated from
affiliation (Weiss 1982; Sheldon and West 1989). Affiliative
relationships are typically with friends, best 'mates' (an interesting non-sexual use of the term) and comrades and are usually
based on mutual exploration of shared interests. Attachment
relationships, unlike affiliation, typically provide protection from
danger, including the dangers of painful feelings. Thus, as we
shall discuss further in the next chapter, Brown and Harris (1978)
found that women experiencing loss who had a close confiding
relationship with a spouse were protected from depression, while
single mothers, even if they had close affiliative-type friendships,
were not.

The relevance of this to psychotherapy lies in the likelihood
that Heard and Lake's (1986) companionable interaction – syn-
onymous with affiliation – is likely to be a feature of the psychotherapeutic relationship, although it is rarely considered as such
by theorists. Freud's early 'training analyses' consisted of a few
walks around the Wienerwald (Roazen 1976). A friendship bond
undoubtedly does develop in some psychotherapeutic relationships. The tension between the patient's need to see the therapist
as a friend, and the professional parameters of the relationship
may provide useful transferential material.

Contrasting opening moves

Sarah and Peter, described earlier in the chapter, provide good
examples of this point. Sarah would start each session in a bright
and breezy way, referring to the weather or to current events as
she entered the consulting room. The therapist instinctively did
not respond in kind – in a way that would, from the point of
view of affiliation, seem almost rude. It was clear from her history
that she had always managed to avoid intimacy through group

living, and by making sure she was the 'life-and-soul' in any gathering, but always keeping her real self well hidden. Her problem was with one-to-one attachments, not affiliation.

Peter similarly would start his sessions with talk about current politics or sport, but in his case the therapist was prepared to join in, in a limited way, again without this being a thought-out strategy. Eventually, when this was discussed in therapy, what emerged was his desperate need to be liked, and his fear of being an outsider, an emotional orphan whom everyone ignored.

In Sarah's case the therapist was adjusting the therapeutic space so that she could get far enough from him to look at what was going on between them; in Peter's he was encouraging him to affiliate enough for some therapeutic interaction to begin.

In most therapies there is an interplay between attachment and affiliation – which might in different terminology be seen as the interplay between transference and the working alliance. The sensitive therapist, like the good-enough parent, is always alert to the patient's need for security in the face of painful affect on the one hand, and, on the other, their wish to explore in a playful, humorous or companionable way.

The issue of affiliation is even more evident in group and family therapies. Affiliation to group members helps demoralised patients feel that they are of some value and importance, and to overcome isolation. Attachment in group therapy is to the group 'matrix' (derived from the word for mother) that holds its members securely and allows for exploration and affective processing. The family group is an affiliative as well as an attachment system, and much of the effort of systemic therapists is directed towards encouraging family members to do more things together and have more fun (while retaining their individuality and separateness). This chapter concludes, therefore, with a brief consideration of Bowlby's contribution to family therapy.

BOWLBY AND FAMILY THERAPY

In all his vast output Bowlby only published one purely clinical – as opposed to theoretical or research – paper. This was 'The study and reduction of group tensions in the family' (Bowlby 1949a). In it he describes his treatment at the Tavistock Clinic of a disturbed young adolescent boy who was destructive and difficult and failing to reach his potential at school. After two years of individual therapy Bowlby felt he had reached an impasse: there was no improvement, and the boy was becoming increasingly resistant to the therapy. In desperation he took the innovative step of arranging a joint meeting with the boy and his parents, together with a social worker. The meeting lasted two hours. The first hour consisted of a painful reiteration by the parents of their frustrations and disappointments with the boy. Bowlby countered this by suggesting that their nagging had contributed to his behaviour, but suggested that this had to be understood in the context of their own unhappy childhoods:

> After 90 minutes the atmosphere changed very greatly and all three were beginning to have sympathy for the situation of the others . . . they found themselves co-operating in an honest endeavour to find new techniques for living together, each realising that there was a common need to do so and that the ways they had set about it in the past had defeated their object. This proved the turning point in the case.
>
> (Bowlby 1949a)

One senses that here at last Bowlby was allowing himself free rein to do what he really wanted, a process which began in the 1930s when he first began to chafe at the Kleinian bit. Based on Bion's ideas about group therapy he conceptualised the processes involved in family therapy as analogous to individual therapy in which the warring parts of the personality are enabled to communicate more freely with one another and to reach compromise and accommodation. The social optimism of the period (with perhaps also a nod towards Bowlby's surgeon father) is contained within his remark that, once painful and angry feelings are openly expressed,

> the recognition of the basic fact that people really do want to live happily together and that this drive is working for us gives confidence, much as a knowledge of the miraculous healing powers of the body gives confidence to the surgeon.
>
> (Bowlby 1949a)

The paper ends with a section entitled 'Circular reactions in family and other social groups', which is thoroughly systemic in its outlook. Bowlby points out the vicious circles of neurosis in which 'insecure parents create insecure children, who grow up to create an insecure society which in its turn creates more insecure parents', and contrasts this with the virtuous circles of health and the need for 'one great therapeutic endeavour: that of reducing tensions and of fostering understanding co-operation between groups of human beings'.

Although Bowlby did not specifically return to family therapy as a topic after this, he must be credited with having introduced the technique of seeing families together at the Tavistock Clinic, and therefore, alongside Gregory Bateson's Palo Alto group (Bateson 1973), with being the originator of family and systemic therapy which was to become such an important therapeutic mode over the ensuing decades.

Bowlby's ideas have been developed in Britain particularly by John Byng-Hall (1991c), Dorothy Heard (1982) and Robin Skynner (1976). Byng-Hall has addressed the spatial aspect of attachment, which can be illustrated by Schopenhauer's porcupine metaphor as an image for 'too near-too far' dilemmas within families:

> A number of porcupines huddled together for warmth on a cold day in winter; but, as they began to prick one another with their quills, they were obliged to disperse. However the cold drove them together again, when just the same thing happened. At last, after many turns of huddling and dispersing, they discovered that they would be best off by remaining at little distance from one another.
>
> (Quoted in Melges and Swartz 1989)

Byng-Hall (1991a), from a child psychiatry perspective, sees the symptomatic patient in a dysfunctional family behaving like the buffer zone between parental porcupines: when the parents start to drift apart the child will develop symptoms which bring them together, and if they start to get dangerously close he will insinuate himself between them, thereby alleviating the imagined dangers of intimacy. Byng-Hall (1985) sees the presuppositions and assumptions which partners bring from their 'families of origin' into their 'families of procreation' in terms of 'family scripts'; namely, patterns of interaction or 'dance' (Minuchin 1974), which an individual expects of himself and those close to him. The distinction made by Minuchin et al. (1978) between enmeshed and disengaged families (the former tending to occur in anorexia, the latter in behaviour disorders), can be equated in Attachment

Theory terms with ambivalent and avoidant insecure attachment based on the parents' experiences as children and now reproduced with their own offspring.

Perhaps as a counter-balance to Bowlby and Winnicott's emphasis on mothers, Skynner (1976) highlights the role of the father in family attachment patterns. In the early stages of infancy the father's job is to protect the mother–child dyad, to allow attachment to develop and for the mother's 'primary maternal preoccupation' (Winnicott 1965) to flower. Later, he needs to intrude on the intimacy of mother and child, partly in order to make his own relationship with the child and to promote attachment to himself, but also to encourage the process of healthy separation from the mother. The child needs to be able to go off with the father, knowing that he can return to the secure base of the mother when he needs to. Without this Oedipal paternal function the mother will be more likely actively to reject the child, using threats of sending him away or even suicide, which Bowlby sees as a particularly dangerous breeding ground for insecure attachment.

The family therapy perspective shows how attachment patterns perpetuate themselves through the life cycle, event scripts being the psychological equivalent of the genome, or, in Dawkins' (1977) neologism, the 'meme'. The basic aims of psychotherapy – the need to provide a secure base, to help people express and come to terms with anger and disappointment (both of which can be seen in terms of separation protest), to achieve integration and coherence within themselves and their families – represent an attempt to intervene in this cycle, altering not so much an individual personality as a pattern of relating so that good experiences lead, by benign rather than vicious circles, to yet more good experiences, and so on. In this way a healthy social mutation will have occurred and Bowlby's vision of psychotherapy as preventive medicine will, to some degree at least, have been realised.

Chapter 9

Attachment Theory and psychiatric disorder

Many of the most intense of all human emotions arise during the formation, the maintenance, the disruption and the renewal of affectional bonds . . . in terms of subjective experience, the formation of a bond is described as falling in love, maintaining a bond as loving someone and losing a partner as grieving over someone. Similarly, threat of loss arouses anxiety and actual loss causes sorrow; whilst both situations are likely to arouse anger. Finally the unchallenged maintenance of a bond is experienced as a source of security, and the renewal of a bond as a source of joy.

(Bowlby 1979c)

Social psychiatry is concerned with the ways in which the environment influences the origin, course and outcome of psychiatric disorders. In his last, and one of his greatest papers, 'Developmental psychiatry comes of age', Bowlby (1988c) bemoans the 'kidnapping' of the label 'biological psychiatry' by those concerned with biochemical and genetic factors in mental illness. Theories of psychological development, if based on sound ethological and evolutionary principles, are no less 'biological' than is research in neurotransmitter chemistry. As the quotation above implies, a key feature of Attachment Theory is its attempt to combine the psychological and subjective with the biological and the objective. In Chapter 3 we suggested that psychotherapy could be seen as a branch of social psychiatry. The integration of psychodynamic ideas into psychiatry has always been bedevilled by the difficulty in translating the language of the inner world into the quantifiable terms of scientific psychiatry. The aim of this chapter is to explore the meeting points between social psychiatry research and the recent developments in Attachment Theory discussed in Chapter 6. Out of this encounter there is beginning to emerge the possibility of a more psychologically meaningful psychiatry, and a more scientifically based psychotherapy.

Bowlby compares the role of Attachment Theory in psychiatry with that of immunology in medicine. The comparison is apt, not just because both are concerned with the integrity and security of the individual, but also because immunology, as well as being concerned with specific disorders of the immune system, has a contribution to make to the understanding of a wide variety of medical conditions. Similarly, Attachment Theory has its 'own' disorders to which it is particularly applicable – abnormal grief, neurotic depression, agoraphobia – but can also inform many other aspects of social psychiatry.

Psychoanalytic theorising about the relationship between childhood experience and psychiatric illness – for example, Freud's linking of repressed homosexuality and paranoia – or even more recent speculations about childhood 'theories of mind' (Fonagy 1991) and borderline personality disorder have found disfavour in psychiatric circles for two main reasons. First, psychiatrists tend to use much more tightly defined categories of mental illness than do psychotherapists, for whom, for example, a term such as 'psychotic' is often used in an overinclusive and arcane way. Second, it is very difficult to specify the presence or absence of a category such as 'repressed homosexuality' in a way that lends itself to research. Bowlby's strategy for getting round these difficulties was to concentrate on external, uncontroversial events such as separations. But here too the attempt to relate adult psychological disorder to single events such as childhood separation has been found to be an oversimplification. Apart perhaps from post-traumatic stress disorders there is no one-to-one link between environmental trauma and psychiatric illness. Indeed, given the complexity of psychological development, the variety of experience, and fluidity of meanings by which experience is comprehended, it would be surprising if this were so. A more subtle, if less attractively simple, model of stress, vulnerability and buffering is required.

Attachment Theory is a theory about relationships, based on the idea that human beings evolved in kinship groups and that in the original 'environment of evolutionary adaptedness' (Bowlby

1969b) survival was increased by the maintenance of secure bonds between their members, primarily, but by no means exclusively, between parents and children. The theory, fundamental to social psychiatry, suggests that relationships and their difficulties might influence psychiatric disorder in three distinct but interrelated ways. First, the breaking or disruption of bonds is likely in itself to be a cause of disturbance. Second, the internalisation of disturbed early attachment patterns may influence subsequent relationships in a way that makes a person both more exposed and more vulnerable to stress. Third, a person's current perception of their relationships and the use they make of them may make them more or less vulnerable to breakdown in the face of adversity. We shall briefly consider each of these points, and then proceed to discuss a number of selected psychiatric disorders in the light of them.

Loss

There is strong evidence of the relationship between acute loss and increased vulnerability to psychiatric and physical disorder. Widows and widowers are more likely than non-bereaved people to die themselves from a coronary in the year following the sudden death of their partners from a heart attack. Among depressed patients 60–70 per cent have had an unpleasant loss event (usually involving the loss of or threat to an attachment relationship) in the year preceding their illness, as opposed to only 20 per cent of non-depressed controls. Schizophrenic relapse is often brought on by loss or unexpected change. People who commit suicide or attempt suicide are similarly more likely to have experienced loss than those who do not.

However, as we discussed in Chapter 3, for loss to be pathogenic it has to be in the context of other important variables. Not all those who experience bereavement succumb to depression. Those for whom the loss was sudden and untimely, who had a dependent relationship with the person they have lost, or felt ambivalent towards them, and who lack a supportive relationship and network of friends, are much more vulnerable.

A similar story appears to hold for the long-term effects of childhood loss. Early speculation suggested that childhood bereavement was an important factor in adult depression. While recent research on this point has been contradictory (Tennant

1988: Harris and Bifulco 1991), it does seem clear that the lack of good care that is so often a result of childhood bereavement is a vulnerability factor for depression, and that there are important additive effects, so that loss in adult life, in the presence of vulnerabilities in the personality, makes a person much more likely to become depressed than in their absence.

Attachment styles and vulnerability to psychiatric disorder

We presented in Chapter 6 the evidence that infant attachment patterns persist well into middle childhood, and the Adult Attachment Interview (AAI) data suggest a further continuity of these patterns into adult life. This means, in Western countries at least, that about one-third of adults are likely to have relationships which are characterised by anxious attachment, and this could constitute a major vulnerability factor for psychiatric illness when faced with stressful life events. Using postal questionnaires, Shaver and Hazan (1988; Hazan and Shaver 1987) surveyed a college freshman population and a middle-aged sample about 'romantic attachments' and found remarkable parallels with the Bowlby-Ainsworth classification of infant attachment in the Strange Situation. Of their respondents 56 per cent demonstrated a secure attachment pattern, describing themselves as finding it relatively easy to get close to others, to depend on them, and not worrying about being abandoned or about being intruded upon. Twenty-five per cent showed an avoidant pattern, with difficulty in trusting their partners, and often feeling that their partners wanted more intimacy than they felt able to provide. The remainder (19 per cent) were anxious-ambivalent, often worrying that their partners didn't really love them, and aware that their great neediness and possessiveness often drove potential partners away.

Attachment research on children has shown correlations between attachment styles and social competence. Similar connections can be demonstrated in college students (Kobak and Sceery 1988): those classified as secure on the AAI were rated by their peers as more ego-resilient, less anxious and hostile, and as having greater social support than the anxious-dismissives and anxious-preoccupieds who were less resilient, less supported and more hostile or anxious respectively.

Lake (1985) has pointed to the discrepancy between the frequent invocation of the notion of ego-strength as a mark of mental health, and the lack of a satisfactory definition and operational criteria for its presence. For him ego-strength comprises the ability to form mutually satisfying intimate relationships, the capacity to cope with change, good self-esteem, and a sense of competence. In a similar vein, Holmes and Lindley (1989) define 'emotional autonomy' as the key to mental health and a central goal of psychotherapy:

> Autonomy, in the context of psychotherapy, implies taking control of one's own life . . . emotional autonomy does *not* mean isolation or avoidance of dependency. On the contrary, the lonely schizoid individual who preserves his 'independence' at all costs may well be in a state of emotional heteronomy, unable to bear closeness with another person because of inner dread and confusion. A similar state of emotional heteronomy affects the psychopath who is unaware of the feelings of others. The emotionally autonomous individual does not suppress her feelings, including the need for dependence, but takes cognisance of them, ruling rather than being ruled by them.
>
> (Holmes and Lindley 1989)

Attachment research shows how the psychotherapeutic constructs of ego strength and emotional autonomy have their origins in early familial relationships, and how in turn they affect relationships in adult life. Social psychiatry makes the links between disordered relationships and psychiatric illness, but, as we have seen in Chapter 3, these links are not as straightforward as Bowlby's original analogy between the effects of vitamin deficiency and those of maternal deprivation would imply. Epictetus' doctrine that 'men are troubled not so much by things as by their perception of things' is a reminder that environmental difficulty is *mediated* by a person's state of mind, and that mental set may powerfully influence how a person responds to stress.

Autobiographical competence

Loss and attachment style affect vulnerability to psychiatric disorder by way of the effect on the personality of past difficulty. But a person's current relationships – the support available from family, friends, and neighbours – seem likely also to be important as a source of buffering against the impact of stress. Henderson and his colleagues (Henderson *et al.* 1981) undertook a major study of the relationship between social networks and neurotic disorder in Canberra.

Inspired by Bowlby, Henderson set out to test the 'social bond hypothesis' that deficiency in social relationships, or 'anophelia', is a causal factor in the onset of neurosis. He devised the Interview Schedule for Social Interaction (ISSI) as a way of measuring the adequacy of a person's actual and perceived social support both in the past and in their current situation. Using a General Practice community sample (that is, one with relatively low morbidity), they failed to confirm their original hypothesis, finding *no* association between morbidity and impairment of present or past social relationships. What they did find, to their surprise, was that a person's *perception* of the adequacy of their relationships did, in the face of adversity, have a big impact on whether or not they succumbed to anxiety and depression. In their epidemiological study it was not possible to tease out whether this perception was an accurate reflection of their performance, whether it was a manifestation of a 'complainant attitude' on the part of the affected individual, or whether there was a self-fulfilling pattern in which people who see their relationships as inadequate evoke unsatisfactory responses from their intimates. They conclude that 'the causes of neurosis lie much more within the person than within the social environment', and suggest, rather despairingly, that the attempt to provide good relationships for potential patients is unlikely to be an effective strategy in preventive psychiatry.

Attachment Theory suggests that this pessimistic viewpoint is unwarranted. First, we have seen that secure attachment is associated not so much with the absence of childhood disruption and trauma, as with 'autobiographical competence' – that is, the ability to give a balanced account of difficulty and the capacity for emotional processing of painful events in the past. Second, the evidence is that the 'social environment' *does* influence neurosis, but further back in the causal chain than Henderson was able to look, via the internalisation of childhood attachment patterns. Third, if perception of inadequate relationships is the crucial issue, rather than the relationships themselves, then any psychotherapeutic technique which can alter that perception, whether directly as in cognitive therapy, or indirectly as in analytic and systemic therapies, is likely to be helpful.

Armed with this optimism, let us look now at a number of different psychiatric disorders from the perspective of attachment theory.

ABNORMAL GRIEF

In his early work, Bowlby was keen to establish the reality of childhood mourning in the face of those who disputed whether children were able to experience the same full gamut of emotions as adults (Bowlby 1960d). The fact that adults *do* grieve is in itself evidence for the continuing importance of attachment throughout life. Parkes (1975; 1985; Parkes and Weiss 1983) has shown how the quality of the relationship broken by the death influences the course of mourning. Pathological grief can be divided into four distinct patterns. First is the *unexpected grief syndrome*: major losses which are unexpected or untimely, characterised by shock and disbelief and a persisting sense of the presence of the dead person. In the face of major trauma, securely attached people are as vulnerable as the less secure, and Parkes *et al.* (1991) found that 100 per cent of those referred with abnormal grief to his clinic whose capacity to trust themselves and others was good, had had sudden, unexpected or multiple bereavements. In *delayed grief*, seen typically in people with an avoidant attachment style, the patient characteristically lacks emotional response to the loss, feels numb and unable to cry, and cannot find any satisfaction in relationships or distractions. In the *ambivalent grief syndrome*, the previous relationship was stormy and difficult, often with many quarrels and much misery. Initially, the bereaved person may feel relief, and that they have 'earned their widowhood'. Later, however, intense pining and self-reproach may follow, with the sufferers blaming themselves in an omnipotent way for the death of their partners, based on the earlier unconscious or semi-conscious wishes that they would die. In *chronic grief* the sufferer becomes locked into a state of despair from which there seems no escape. These people have usually shown lifelong dependency on parents and partners. Often such dependency may mask ambivalence, and the unearthing of negative feelings can be the chink through which new life begins to appear.

MRS W: I can't bear to look

Mrs W, a fifty-year-old housewife, had been in a state of chronic grief since the death of her grandmother three years previously. She was unable to carry on looking after the house or caring for her twenty-year-old daughter, herself handicapped with agoraphobia. She was tearful and apathetic, had failed to respond to antidepressants, and her husband and GP were at their wits' end. Referred for psychotherapy, she described how she had to avert her gaze on going past her grandmother's house, tried to avoid going near it although this often meant inconvenient diversions, and could not possibly visit her uncle who still lived there.

When she was a child her father had been away in the war, but on his return when she was four, her mother promptly went off with another man, and she had had no contact with her since. She was brought up by her maternal grandmother to whom she felt close, but who ruled with a rod of iron. When she was eleven, her father remarried and she was summoned to live with him and her stepmother. She was never happy with them, and she spent her teens oscillating between her grandmother and father. At eighteen she left home, made two disastrous marriages, and eventually met her present husband, twenty years her senior, who was very 'good' and 'understanding', but, she felt, was unable to understand her grief and was intolerant of her tears.

Offered brief therapy based on 'guided mourning' (Mawson *et al.* 1981), she brought photographs of her grandmother which, initially, she could only look at with great difficulty. Mixed with her reverence and awe towards her grandmother, a new theme began to emerge – anger at the way her mother had been 'written off' and had become a forbidden subject not to be mentioned in the grandmaternal home. With therapeutic prompting, Mrs W made enquiries about her mother, found that she had died and visited her grave. Then she happened to bump into her maternal uncle at the local supermarket and was able to talk to him for the first time since her grandmother's death. She then went to the house, at first just looking at it from the outside, later going inside. When therapy came to an end after eight sessions her depressive symptoms had lifted and she felt better 'than for years' although she remained overinvolved with her daughter.

DEPRESSION

Attachment Theory has made an important contribution to current thinking about the social causes of depression. Freud's (1917) speculation about the relationship between current loss and melancholia has been repeatedly confirmed by studies showing how adverse life events can precipitate depression. His linking of depression with childhood loss has also been confirmed, although not without controversy. The balance of evidence (Brown and Harris 1978; Tennant 1988) suggests that early loss of their mother, especially if accompanied by disruption and lack of care, makes a person more vulnerable to depression when faced with adversity in adult life. Harris and Bifulco (1991) have tracked the interweaving of social and psychological variables in their Walthamstow study of a group of women who had lost their mothers in childhood. They found, as predicted, that this group of women had significantly raised rates of depression compared with non-bereaved women: one in three versus one in ten. The strand of social causation starts with early loss of mother, whether through death or separation, leading to lack of care in childhood. This is linked, in the teens of the patient-to-be, with high rates of pre-marital pregnancy. This in turn leads to poor choice of partner, so that when these women, often living in disadvantaged circumstances and therefore prone to large amounts of stress, experience loss they are more likely to have unsupportive or non-existent partners, and so to develop depression.

Harris and Bifulco's 'Strand 2', the psychological, centres on a sense of hopelessness and lack of mastery in both the childhood and current circumstances of the depressed patient. As children their depressed patients had not only lost their mothers, but also felt utterly helpless – unable to protest or grieve or retrieve or be comforted, like Bowlby's little patient who, at the age of nine, on the day when his mother died, was told to go and play in his nursery and not to make such a fuss (Bowlby 1979c). When they were adults the feeling of helplessness persisted: when they became pregnant, they coped badly with it. Their perception of their current relationships played a big part in determining whether or not they became depressed; the more helpless they felt, the greater the chance of depression, and when they felt some degree of effectiveness they were protected from it.

Harris and Bifulco (1991) distinguish between a general sense of hopelessness and lack of mastery and what they call 'vulnerable attachment styles' – that is, difficulty in interpersonal relationships. Depression was much more likely in those who showed evidence of poor relating and especially interpersonal hostility. It seems that it is the interpersonal aspect of hopelessness (as opposed to things like managing money and housework) that matters most. We have seen that it is precisely this interpersonal dimension that is formative in insecure attachments: mothers who had difficulty in attuning to their infants and who showed unpredictable hostility were more likely to have anxiously attached children.

Brown and Harris (1978) see *self-esteem* as the key psychological variable in the genesis of depression. As Pedder (1982) points out, to have good self-esteem is to have internalised a two-person relationship in which one bit of the self feels good about another. This is the good internal object of psychoanalytic theory, arising out of the responsiveness of the mother – the mother who not only feeds, but recognises one as a person, is sensitive to one's feelings and moods, whom one can influence, and with whom one can, through play, create and re-create, in the 'present moment' (Hanh 1990), the spontaneity of love.

Brown's group have also suggested a relationship between the age at which the mother is lost, the circumstances of the loss, and subsequent symptom formation. The earlier and more sudden the loss, the more likely the chance of depression, and the greater the chance that the depression will be psychotic rather than neurotic in character. Pedder relates this to the Kleinian notion of the 'depressive position' (see Chapter 5). Children who have not yet developed an internal image of a whole, good mother, safe from destruction by angry attacks, will, when depressed, be more likely to despair and feel overwhelmed with depression. Older children, who do have some sense of a whole mother, or who have had at least an inkling that loss is imminent, will react to her loss with anger and attempts to retrieve her through suicidal gestures or psychosomatic illness. Pedder (1982) relates this to

> several particular clinical situations that must be familiar to many psychotherapists which reflect this protesting state of affairs and make mourning for the lost person very difficult. One is when a parent absents themselves by suicide; another when a marital partner is left unwillingly by the other; or when

a psychotherapist abandons a patient without due warning. In all such cases there is a special problem to internalise any good version of the departing person.

(Pedder 1982)

Bowlby (1980) suggested there were three typical patterns of vulnerable personality arising out of anxious attachment: ambivalent attachment, compulsive care-giving and detachment. The Walthamstow study confirmed the importance of the first two, but found, contrary to expectation, that detachment actually protected against depression. There are two possible explanations for this. One is that their measures were not sensitive enough to distinguish between healthy autonomy (which is a form of mastery) and compulsive detachment (which is not). The second is that detachment may be connected more with borderline personality disorder than depression, a possibility we shall consider below.

Harris and Bifulco (1991) were studying only a small sub-group of depressed patients: although people who have been bereaved in childhood appear to be more vulnerable to low self-esteem and so to depression in later life, the majority of depressives come from intact homes. Parker's Parental Bonding Instrument (Parker 1983) is an attempt, via retrospective accounts, to reconstruct the family atmosphere in patients' childhoods, searching for *qualitative* features of parenting which may predispose to depression. Parker isolates a particular combination of low care and overprotection which he calls 'affectionless control' that is especially corrrelated with neurotic depression: in one study it was present in nearly 70 per cent of patients but in only 30 per cent of controls. Affectionless control conjures up a childhood in which the potential patient lacks a secure parental base, and at the same time is inhibited in exploratory behaviour, thereby reducing the two ingredients of self-esteem: good internal objects and a feeling of competence and mastery.

One of the strengths of Attachment Theory is that it brings together past and present influences, the social and the psychological, providing a comprehensive picture of the varied factors which result in the development of a psychiatric disorder. Bowlby (1988c) gives a vivid picture of this epigenetic process. There is

[a] chain of adverse happenings. For example, when a young woman has no caring home base she may become desperate

to find a boyfriend who will care for her. That, combined with her negative self-image, makes her all too likely to settle precipitately for some totally unsuitable young man. Premature pregnancy and childbirth are then likely to follow, with all the economic and emotional difficulties entailed. Moreover, in times of trouble, the effects of her previous adverse experiences are apt to lead her to make unduly intense demands on her husband and, should he fail to meet them, to treat him badly. No wonder one in three of these marriages break up.

Gloomy though these conclusions are, we must remember that a disastrous outcome is not inevitable. The more secure an attachment a woman has experienced during her early years, we can confidently predict, the greater will be her chance of escaping the slippery slope.

(Bowlby 1988c)

AGORAPHOBIA

In *Separation* (1973a), Bowlby puts forward a theory of agoraphobia based on the notion of anxious attachment. He sees agoraphobia, like school phobia, as an example of separation anxiety. He quotes evidence of the increased incidence of family discord in the childhoods of agoraphobics compared with controls, and suggests three possible patterns of interaction underlying the illness: role reversal between child and parent, so that the potential agoraphobic is recruited to alleviate parental separation anxiety (this may well have happened with Mrs W's daughter in the case described above); fears in the patient that something dreadful may happen to her mother while they are separated (often encouraged by parental threats of suicide or abandonment, Bowlby believed); and fear that something dreadful might happen to herself when away from parental protection.

Central to the theory and treatment of phobic disorders is the idea that painful feelings and frightening experiences are suppressed and avoided rather than faced and mastered. In what Bowlby first described as 'the suppression of family context' (Bowlby 1973a) and later 'on knowing what you are not supposed to know and feeling what you are not supposed to feel' (Bowlby 1988a), he hypothesised that the potentially phobic adult has first been exposed to trauma – such as witnessing parental suicide attempts, or being a victim of sexual abuse – and then subjected to intense pressure to 'forget' what has happened, either by the use of overt threats, as often happens in sexual abuse, or by denial – as, for example, when a grandmother brings up her daughter's illegitimate offspring as one of her own, and the child is led to believe that her true mother is her older sister. The use of denial means that the child does not have the experience of emotional processing of painful affect, and so cannot, as described in Chapter 6, achieve the autobiographical competence that is a hallmark of secure attachment. Liotti (1991) sees in phobic disorders a dissociation between the physiological concomitants of anxiety and the 'meaning structures' that go with them. The events which might make a child anxious cannot be linked up into mental schemata which would enable that child to face and overcome them. When, as adults, such individuals experience shock or conflict, they focus merely on the symptoms of panic, and not on the events which triggered them. He advocates an exploratory form of cognitive psychotherapy which does not merely require exposure to the feared stimulus, but also encourages self-exploration so that emotions and the relationships which evoke them can begin to be linked together in a meaningful way.

Morbid jealousy and agoraphobia

David was a fifty-year-old ex-taxi-driver who developed panic attacks whenever he was separated from his wife, even for half an hour, and could not go out of the house unaccompanied. Her life was made increasingly miserable by his possessiveness, and his ceaseless questioning of her when she returned from brief excursions to visit their daughter. During David's attacks he was convinced that he would die and frequently was rushed to hospital casualty departments with suspected heart attacks. He initially described his childhood as 'all right', that he had few childhood memories, and that 'what's past is past'. Then, in the second session, when asked again about his childhood he began to cry and talked about his terrors on being left alone by his mother who was a night-club 'hostess', about never having known his father, and his misery and confusion about the different men with whom she lived. When it was gently suggested that he must have felt very jealous of these men, and that there might be some connection between this and his present attitude towards his wife, he became extremely distressed and recounted how at the age of twelve he had attacked one of these men with a knife and was taken to a remand home as a result. In subsequent sessions he began to reveal his depression much more openly, and was gradually able to tolerate being on his own for increasing periods of time.

ATTACHMENT STYLES AND EXPRESSED EMOTION IN SCHIZOPHRENIA

It has repeatedly been stressed that Bowlby's early ideas of a simple relationship between, for example, childhood bereavement and depression, maternal deprivation and psychopathy, or anxious attachment and agoraphobia, have had to be modified into much more complex causal models in which early experience, current life situation, adverse events, personality, and mental set all contribute to outcome. It is unlikely that there is a simple relationship between particular attachment patterns in infancy and specific psychiatric diagnoses in adult life.

In considering psychoses, this multifactorial approach has to be further extended to include genetic and biochemical or even infective influences. Nevertheless, social psychiatry has firmly established the importance of the environment in determining the course of schizophrenic illness (Leff and Vaughn 1983). Patients living in families in which there is high 'Expressed Emotion' (EE) – especially high levels of hostility or overinvolvement – are much more likely to relapse than those who live with calmer, less hostile, less overinvolved relations. The effect of EE is not specific to schizophrenia, and also influences, for instance, the course of manic-depression, Alzheimer's disease and diabetes. The prevalence of high EE in the general population is unknown, but in families of schizophrenic patients about one-third are high in EE. It seems at least possible that there is a relationship between EE and anxious attachment, which also affects about one-third of the population. The two main patterns of high EE, hostility and overinvolvement, correspond with those found in anxious attachment; that is, avoidant and ambivalent attachment. The mothers of avoidant infants, it will be recalled, tend to show hostility and to brush their children aside when they approach, while the ambivalent mothers are inconsistent and intrusive. Both patterns can be understood in terms of boundaries. The avoidant mothers feel invaded by their children and tend to maintain a rigid boundary around themselves, and this may lead to hostility when confronted with a mentally ill, and therefore in some ways child-like, grown-up child or spouse. Conversely, ambivalent parents cannot separate themselves from their children, and, if one becomes mentally ill as an adult, the pattern will repeat itself. Such parents cannot draw a firm boundary between themselves and their offspring because of overwhelming feelings of guilt.

Too many telephone calls

Mr P felt intensely guilty when his son Richard developed a severe schizophrenic illness at the age of twenty-two. He blamed himself for being so heavy-handed during Richard's teens, and, as a psychiatric nurse, felt from his reading of Laing and others that he must be a 'schizophrenogenic father'. He tolerated in an almost saint-like way very difficult behaviour from Richard, who would come into his parents' bedroom throughout the night asking for constant reassurance that he was not going to die, on one occasion brandishing a knife. Occasionally Mr P would flip from excessive tolerance into furious outbursts at his son, and then feel even more guilty. When Richard was admitted to hospital and moved later to a hostel, Mr P felt even more guilty, especially as Richard insisted that he hated the hostel and his only wish was to return home to his parents and brothers and sisters (of whom he showed in fact considerable jealousy).

Mr P had himself been an anxious child and had found separations from his mother very difficult, running away from his boarding school where he was sent at the age of nine on several occasions. Therapeutic attempts to create a boundary between Richard and his family were made very difficult because every attempt to do so was immediately interpreted by Mr P as a criticism of his parenting, and as carrying the implication that he was a negative influence on his son. But when it emerged that Richard would phone home from his hostel with unfailing regularity just when the family were sitting down to tea, Mr P was asked to take the phone off the hook for that half hour each evening. With much misgiving and strong feelings that he was rejecting his son, he agreed, without disastrous results, and with a general lightening of the relationship between Richard and his parents. Through this small change the family seemed to have come to accept that a firm boundary can be a mark of loving attachment rather than rejection.

BORDERLINE PERSONALITY DISORDER

Patients with borderline personality disorder (BPD) form an increasing proportion of specialist out-patient psychotherapy practice, and comprise a significant part of the work of in-patient psychiatry, often consuming time and worry disproportionate to their numbers. Despite debate about its validity as a distinct nosological entity (Rutter 1987), BPD is, for the psychodynamically minded, an indispensable concept. It is defined in the *American Diagnostic and Statistical Manual* as comprising a constellation of symptoms and behaviours which include unstable interpersonal relationships, with violent swings between idealisation and devaluation; unstable mood states; self-injurious behaviour, including deliberate self-harm and drug abuse; angry outbursts; identity disturbance with uncertainty about goals, friends, sexual orientation; and chronic feelings of emptiness and boredom. In short, there is an atmosphere of 'stable instability' (Fonagy 1991) about these patients with which most clinicians are familiar.

Empirical studies suggest that these patients have been subjected to high levels of emotional neglect and trauma in childhood, although neither is of course confined to BPD. Bryer *et al.* (1987) found that 86 per cent of in-patients with a diagnosis of BPD reported histories of sexual abuse, compared with 21 per cent of other psychiatric in-patients, and Herman *et al.* (1989) found in out-patient BPDs that 81 per cent had been subjected to sexual abuse or physical abuse or had been witness to domestic violence, as compared with 51 per cent of other out-patients. Of those who had been traumatised in this way under the age of six, the figures were 57 per cent for BPD and 13 per cent for other diagnoses.

Psychoanalysts working with these patients (for reviews, see Fonagy 1991; Bateman 1991) have emphasised the extensive use of projective identification that arises in the transference–countertransference matrix. The therapist is, as it were, used as a receptacle for the patient's feelings and may be filled with anger, confusion, fear and disgust in a way that, for the inexperienced, is unexpected and difficult to tolerate. The patient treats therapy in a very concrete way, and may become highly dependent on the therapist, seeking comfort in fusion with a rescuing object who is, at other times, felt to be sadistic and rejecting. These latter aspects emerge especially at times of breaks, or when the therapist lets the patient down, as inevitably he will through normal human error and the pressure of counter-transference.

With an approach to these patients from the perspective of Attachment Theory two issues stand out. The first concerns the oscillations of attachment (Melges and Swartz 1989) that are so characteristic of BPD, and the related question of why they persist in relationships with their families and partners (and some-times with their 'helpers') that are so destructive. Here we are reminded of the behaviour seen in rhesus monkeys brought up on wire mothers who, when subjected to physical trauma, cling all the more tightly to the traumatising object (Harlow 1958). According to attachment theory, a frightened child will seek out their attachment figure, and if he or she is also the traumatising one a negative spiral – trauma leading to the search for security followed by more trauma – will be set up.

A second, more subtle conceptualisation of the borderline pre-dicament has been proposed by Fonagy (1991). He suggests that the borderline experience can be understood in terms of the lack in these patients of what he calls a 'mentalising capacity'. By this he means that they lack adequate internal representation of their own or others' states of mind, especially in relation to emotions. A similar idea is contained in Main's (1991) notion of deficits in 'metacognition', the ability to think about thinking. The work of Stern and the post-Bowlbian attachment researchers suggest that maternal responsiveness is internalised by the growing child so that he or she begins to build up an idea of a self that is responded to and understood, and, reciprocally, to be able to understand and take another's point of view. Where there are difficulties in responsiveness, the child is faced with levels of excitation and pain which cannot be soothed and shaped and contained by the parent (perhaps through their own depression or inability to mentalise). Also, to represent to oneself the idea that one's parent might want to hurt or exploit one would in itself be deeply painful. Deprived of the capacity for symbolic representation of their unhappiness, and therefore the opportunity for emotional processing or transcendence, the traumatised child resorts to projective identification in which the intolerable feelings of excitation and pain are 'evacuated' into those to whom he or she is attached. For the child this is the abusing parent who is clung to with 'frozen watchfulness'; for the adult patient it is their intimates, including the therapist. The patient is temporarily relieved of mental pain, at the price of a feeling of emptiness and boredom, to be followed, as the projections are returned or further trauma arises, by yet more episodes of intolerable discomfort leading to more projection.

These speculations are given some substance by a recent Attachment Theory-inspired study by Hobson and his colleagues (Patrick *et al.* 1992), in which they compared a group of twelve borderline psychotherapy patients with a similar number of depressives. They were given Parker's Parental Bonding Instrument (PBI), mentioned above, and Main's Adult Attachment Interview (AAI), described in Chapter 6. Both groups showed Parker's 'affectionless control' constellation of low parental care and overprotection, with the BPD group demonstrating this even more clearly than the depressives, a result also found by Zweig-Frank and Parris (1991). If these retrospective accounts of childhood reflect not just a person's perception of what happened but what actually took place – and there is evidence to suggest that they do (Mackinnon *et al.* 1991) – a picture emerges of parents who were anxious but unable to respond accurately to their children, and, from the child's perspective, of an attachment figure to whom one clings, but who does not assuage one's insecurity (Heard and Lake 1986), with resulting inhibition of exploration.

Even more interesting were the results of the AAI. It will be recalled that this is a psychodynamic snapshot of a person's attachments and reactions to loss in childhood. Based on the coherence and emotional tone of the transcript, the interview is scored not so much for actual trauma as for the way a person describes it – and so is a measure of autobiographical competence (Holmes 1992). There are four possible categories: secure; insecure-dismissive; insecure-preoccupied or -enmeshed; and a fourth category, recognised after the AAI was first developed, unresolved/disorganised/disoriented, which is judged when the subject is talking about past trauma and is rated in parallel to the other categories. Thus someone who can be quite coherent for most of their narrative can still receive an unresolved classification if their story becomes incoherent when they talk about trauma. The results showed that none of the BPD group was secure, and all were classified as enmeshed, while in the depressive group four were enmeshed, six dismissive and two secure. Only two of the depressives were unresolved/disorganised, but nine of the BPDs were so classified.

The combination of enmeshment with disorganisation in relation to trauma suggested that BPD patients were wrestling with an inability to find a way of describing overwhelming mental pain – implying exactly the sort of deficit in mental representation postulated by Fonagy and Main. By contrast, several of the depressives had also been traumatised, but the effect on their linguistic coherence was much less marked.

It is clear from these studies that no one diagnostic entity can be correlated with a particular childhood constellation. 'Affectionless control' occurs in both depressive and BPD; some accounts of BPD stress avoidance, others enmeshment as childhood precursors. But the evidence in general that insecure attachment is an important developmental precursor of psychopathology is increasingly strong. Herman et al. (1989) suggest that qualitative differences may relate to different diagnostic outcomes, with the most severe forms of childhood trauma and parental unresponsiveness being linked to multiple personality disorder, less severe forms with BPD, and yet milder types linked to neurotic depression and anxiety. This would be consistent with Pedder's (1982) suggestion along Kleinian lines that the greater the difficulty in integrating a parental good internal object, the greater the likelihood of severe pathology.

The Bowlbian perspective on BPD has several implications for treatment. The patient will lack a sense of a secure base. Extreme forms of avoidance or ambivalence are likely. The patient may resist any emotional involvement in therapy as a defence against the trauma that close relationships have entailed in the past, leaving the therapist with the uncomfortable feeling that he is inflicting therapy on an unwilling subject. Alternatively, the patient may cling to the therapy for dear life, leaving the therapist feeling stifled and guilty about the need to lead their own life. There may be oscillations between these two positions, so that in one session the therapist feels they are really making progress, only to be faced at the next with an indifferent patient, for whom the previous advance appeared to be an illusion. The therapist may feel paralysed, apparently of no value to the patient, and yet meeting with extreme resistance if they attempt to disengage themselves. Throughout, the overwhelming task of the therapist is, as described in the previous chapter, to remain consistent and reliable, responsive and attuned to the patient's emotional states, and to be alert to the unconscious pressure to repeat (often in subtle ways) the punitive and traumatising experiences of intimacy which the patient has come to expect.

Any evidence of mentalisation or symbolisation, however fragile and transient, should be taken as an encouraging sign. This may take varied forms – humour in the session, the bringing of a dream or poem, evidence of self- or other- awareness, an outside interest in a sport or hobby – all suggesting the beginnings of a nascent capacity for exploration that indicate the development of a secure base within the therapy and in the inner world. Although consistency is essential, it is also inevitable that mistakes *will* occur under the intense transferential pressure to which the therapist is subjected. As described in the previous chapter, if handled favourably, these can provide an opportunity for the patient to re-live earlier losses and traumata in a way that they can now be grieved and processed emotionally. This should not lead to complacency on the part of the therapist, however. Winnicott's reminder to omnipotent therapists that 'we help our patients by failing' should be balanced by Bob Dylan's dictum that 'there ain't no success like failure, and failure ain't no success at all'. Finally, therapists should never underestimate the responsibility implicit in allowing attachment to develop in these patients. As Gallwey (1985) puts it:

> Any experience of being taken on, encouraged to become deeply attached, and then terminated suddenly may be catastrophic to patients who have managed to keep themselves going by avoiding precisely that type of hazard, which no amount of interpreting in the short term can possibly alleviate.

ATTACHMENT THEORY AND COMMUNITY PSYCHIATRY

We saw in Chapter 3 how Bowlby's recognition of the traumatic effects of loss and separation led to a revolution in child care, with a move towards home-based treatments and a recognition of the potentially damaging effects of institutions which cannot cater for a child's need to form secure attachments. Although the overall effects of this perspective were undoubtedly beneficial, it was used by many local authorities and government agencies anxious to save money to close down residential homes for children without providing adequate alternatives. Winnicott was sufficiently alarmed by this trend to write to Bowlby in 1955 asking him to tone down his insistence on the dangers of residential care (Rodman 1987).

A comparable revolution has taken place over the past twenty years in the provision of care for the mentally ill. Mental hospitals have been replaced by 'community care', in which patients live with their families or in hostels and group homes, and attend day centers and community clubs. Psychiatric beds are available only for 'acute' episodes of illness or distress, to tide patients through brief periods of crisis. Although many patients have benefited from the enhanced self-respect of living independent lives, there have been losses as well as gains. The emphasis on a version of autonomy that is akin to avoidance has overlooked the continuing need for dependence, which Bowlby saw as lifelong, not confined to the young and the sick. Many patients were intensely dependent on their institutions, and, due partly to their illness, partly to the increasing isolation of modern life, are unable in the 'community' to re-create the network of emotional bonds they found in the mental hospitals.

We have seen repeatedly how there has been a movement from Bowlby's early formulations of a problem in fairly simple and concrete terms, through a series of reservations and doubts, to a much more subtle appreciation of the issues involved. For example, it was not the separation from the mother alone that was damaging when a child went to hospital, but the unfamiliarity of the ward and the punitive discouragement of protest. Similarly, anxious attachment is the result not so much of gross disruptions of care or threats of abandonment (although these are of course harmful), but more a fine-tuned failure of maternal attunement and responsiveness. The problem with institutions is not that they are intrinsically harmful, any more than the 'community' is always beneficial, but the way that care is often delivered in them. We have to look much more carefully at the actual *quality* of experience that a patient has, whether it is in hospital or in 'the community', before deciding whether or not it is bad. Winnicott's list of components of a 'primary home experience' quoted in *Child*

Care and the Growth of Maternal Love (1953b) (see page 43), is as follows. Does the patient have someone to turn to who is specifically orientated towards their needs? Are the patient's basic physiological needs and physical health adequately catered for? Are the patient's needs to hate and to love recognised, and are there clear limits against which the patient can test strengths and weaknesses, and learn to differentiate between reality and phantasy? Is the patient cared for by a team that communicate with one another and in which the 'maternal' and 'paternal' functions are differentiated and harmonious?

Continuity of care is a key issue. In the past the 'stone mother' (Rey 1975) of the institution provided a backdrop of stability for the chronically mentally ill as staff and psychiatric fashions came and went. As patients moved out into the community it was hoped that a network of hostels, day centers, day hospitals, drop-in centers and other facilities could provide a network of care where they would similarly feel at home. These places offer warmth (physical and emotional), security, stimulation and responsiveness: somewhere where one can just 'be'. But these qualities are hard to quantify – and cost money.

The move now is towards discrete 'packages' of care, often on a sessional basis, which are more 'cost-effective' and financially calculable. The Community Care Bill 1993 stipulates that each chronically mentally ill patient shall have a 'care manager' who is responsible for his or her needs and who will arrange such packages of care as are appropriate. On the basis of sound Bowlbian principles, this might be thought to offer the opportunity for a patient to develop a primary attachment bond with a principal care-giver, and to get away from the impersonality and rigidity of institutions. But it may well illustrate the difficulty of translating psychological theories into policy decisions. The reality of the new arrangements is likely to be very far from the Bowlbian ideal. Each care worker will have a large case load of patients living in the community for whom they will be responsible. Staff turnover is likely to be high and the chance of staff burn-out great. Ripped away from the concrete care of a stable if inflexible institution to which they were attached, very damaged patients will be expected to develop an internal secure base which, given the nature of their illness and its antecedents, they are likely to find impossible. The care workers are likely to be working largely alone, unsupported and unsupervised and yet expected to deliver good outcomes. Their position will be not unlike that of the unsupported mothers whom the feminists accused Bowlby of idealising in their critique of maternal deprivation (see Chapter 3). The need for support for carers, and a recognition that psychologically damaged patients who have lost their attachments will need many years of connection to a stable and secure place before that experience can be hoped to be internalised enough for them to 'move on', has not been sufficiently recognised by policy makers in search of quick and easy solutions to the problems of mental illness and personal growth.

A similar conflict between the need for stable attachments and the complexity and commercial pressures of modern life affect acute psychiatric admission wards (Holmes 1993). Two examples illustrate the point. Hospital nurses work on a shift system, which means that a patient newly admitted to hospital may be looked after by an ever-changing group of carers, thereby reinforcing that patient's difficulties in attachment and sense of isolation. Second, the introduction of market forces into health care means that there is a huge pressure for rapid turnover of patients and to increase 'throughput' in psychiatric beds. However, this is inimical precisely to the needs of patients for the gradual formation of an attachment to a ward and to a group of carers, a process which takes much time and professional skill if the many tentative advances and retreats, and the small but significant gains which underlie difficulty and destructiveness, are to be understood. Kernberg (1975) calls these divergent pressures the 'concentric' (that is, familial) and 'non-concentric' (namely, administrative) vectors within a caring environment. It would be Utopian to wish for a system of care in which all non-concentric pressures were subservient to the needs of patients and workers for a secure base within which to work. Nevertheless, for a caring environment to be 'good enough', there has at least to be the opportunity to discuss, protest and mourn the unavoidable limitations of political and social reality, an area where the psychotherapist has, through consultation and conducting sensitivity groups, a vital contribution to make to the practice of general psychiatry. It is to these wider issues and to the social implications of Attachment Theory that, in the final chapter, we shall now turn.

Chapter 10

Attachment Theory and society

> Man and woman power devoted to the production of material
> goods counts a plus in all our economic indices. Man and
> woman power devoted to the production of happy, healthy,
> and self-reliant children in their own homes does not count at
> all. We have created a topsy turvy world. . . . The society we
> live in is . . . in evolutionary terms . . . a very peculiar one.
> There is a great danger that we shall adopt mistaken norms.
> For, just as a society in which there is a chronic insufficiency
> of food may take a deplorably inadequate level of nutrition as
> its norm, so may a society in which parents of young children
> are left on their own with a chronic insufficiency of help take
> this state of affairs as its norm.
>
> (Bowlby 1988a)

Running throughout Bowlby's life and work there is a strong
moral and social vision. His credo might be summarised as follows, couched, as it so often was, in the language of preventive
medicine. The emotional deprivation of children is a social ill,
distorting and degrading the fabric of social life. It is society's
responsibility and duty to remedy this ill by appropriate social
medicine. This requires the recognition of the problem through
the acceptance of the findings of psychological science; training
cadres of child-care workers and psychotherapists who are sensitive to the emotional needs of children and their parents; helping
people to find security in their lives through the fostering of close
emotional bonds; encouragement of the expression of grief and
disappointment when they are disrupted. Devaluation of the need
for love and intimacy through the scorning of 'spoiling' and
'dependency' contribute to emotional deprivation. The celebra-

tion of mother-love and of our mutual dependency as a species should be encouraged. In these ways the vicious circles of deprivation can be broken, this generation's insecure young people no longer condemned to reproduce their own insecurities in the next.

These attitudes permeate almost every paragraph Bowlby wrote and informed his purposes in whatever sphere they were applied. In two articles written soon after the end of the war (Bowlby 1946b, 1947a) he made his social views even more explicit. In 'The therapeutic approach in sociology' he puts forward his uncompromising environmentalism:

> whether a person grows up with a strong capacity to make good personal relations – to be good – or whether he grows up with a very indifferent capacity for this depends very greatly on something which has never traditionally been regarded as part of ethics – namely on what his relation to his mother was in early life.
>
> (Bowlby 1947a)

He picks up Kurt Lewin's concept of the 'social field' and applies it to delinquency: good environments create good citizens, bad ones, bad. He contrasts three styles of social arrangements: democratic, authoritarian and *laissez-faire*. Only the democratic – one in which leaders and teachers listen and are responsive to the people – is effective:

> Any organisation, industrial, commercial, national, religious or academic, organised on authoritarian lines must therefore be regarded as inimical to the promotion of good personal relations, of goodness. And that goes for our daily lives . . . in so far as we are authoritarian in our attitude towards others we are promoting bad personal relations and evil.
>
> (Bowlby 1947a)

Poised in that statement can be felt the full weight of Bowlby's two contrary sets of experiences. On the one side are his 'town' mother with her overwhelming sense of 'rightness' inherited from 'Grampy', his remote and rather frightening father, the boarding schools, the Navy, the medical hierarchy, the narrow horizons of Psycho-Analytical Society, military authoritarianism; on the other, his intellectual curiosity, inner calm, independence and resilience, his 'country' mother with her love of nature, the 'invisible college' of Army psychiatrists, his personal optimism and that of the times. He continues:

> the drive of the organism towards achieving good personal relations is just as real and persistent as its drive towards physical health. People don't get well because doctors say they ought to get well: they get well because the living organism has a powerful biological drive to throw off noxious influences.
>
> (Bowlby 1947a)

In his celebration of democracy, Bowlby makes a link between the kind of responsiveness and attunement that good parents provide for their children, and the social arrangements which he saw as most likely to produce flourishing citizens. In 'Psychology and democracy' (1946b), with characteristic boldness and simplicity he tackles the central dilemma of political science: how to reconcile the need for social co-operation with the equally pressing but to some extent incompatible need for individual freedom. He compares the task of the political leader with that of the trusted parent who fosters collaboration among children by showing them that renouncing selfish individual pleasures will result in the ultimately greater enjoyment of shared play. Social co-operation depends on the combination of a population who, through positive childhood experiences, have learned to love and trust, with leaders who, through their democratic attitudes, are prepared to listen to the people, to show they are valued and respected.

All this may sound simplistically anodyne to our late-twentieth-century ears, attuned as we are to the ever-increasing toll of destruction and chaos man has wreaked upon himself and his environment. The Bowlbian ideal of a mother exclusively devoted to the care of her children is, in a contemporary perspective, both unrealistic and undesirable. The pattern of 'absent father – patriarchal society' (Leupnitz 1988) produces mothers who are stretched to their emotional and economic limits, barely able to provide any kind of secure base for their children. New family patterns, unimagined by Bowlby, are emerging, often with fathers who may be biologically unrelated to the children in their care, increasing the likelihood of insecurity or frank physical and sexual abuse. Bowlby's simple formulation of aggression as a response to the threat of loss seems to lack explanatory weight in the face of increasing social chaos. Yet the fundamental principles of

Attachment Theory – that parents need security themselves if they are to provide it for their children, that the threat to security is a potent cause of rage and destruction – remain valid, despite changing conditions. Bowlby may have been mistaken and simplistic in thinking that his experience with disturbed children could be translated simply from the language of psychology to that of sociology, but the challenge thrown down at them by him at the start of this chapter remains.

The Freud (1929) of *Civilization and its Discontents* came late (Pedder 1992) but decisively to the view that destructiveness and aggression were inherent features of the human psyche:

> I can no longer understand how we can have overlooked the ubiquity of non-erotic aggressivity and destructiveness and can have failed to give it its due place in our interpretation of life. . . . In consequence of this primary mutual hostility of human beings, civilized society is perpetually threatened with disintegration.
>
> (Freud 1929)

In his early work (Durbin and Bowlby 1938), Bowlby accounts for aggression in ethological terms as arising from the need for territorial defence and (what amounts to the same thing) defence of breeding and feeding rights. Later, from the perspective of Attachment Theory, he seems to abandon the notion of primary aggressivity altogether, perhaps as part of his overall project to distance himself from the Kleinian approach (Bowlby 1973a). Instead, he sees aggression as springing from insecure attachment. Anxious attachment is a defence, a compromise between the need for security in a dangerous world and the inability of the parent to provide a secure base. Similarly, despair or rage are seen as part of the grief response, frustrated attempts to recover the lost object. In the Bowlbian perspective meaning is imperative: the world must be patterned into some meaningful shape at all costs; what little security there is must be husbanded, shielded from envious eyes; loss cannot be comprehended as total and arbitrary, but construed as recoverable, however much distortion of reality this requires. The avoidant child keeps his distance, warily watching the parent whom he both needs and fears. The ambivalent child clings helplessly to his unpredictable mother. Neither feels free to explore creatively. The disorganised child is defenceless, overwhelmed by stimulus which cannot be organised into any meaningful pattern. Here, where there may have been absolute privation of care in the pre-attachment phase (that is, before six months) may be found the germs of purposeless destruction and rage.

By analogy, societies can also be seen as dealing with problems of security in many defensive ways. Insularity, suspiciousness, splitting, inability to relate generously, vengeance, chaos, internecine struggles, intolerance, exhaustion, corruption – countless examples of these phenomena can be found in social and political life just as much as in individual psychology, and each has its 'meaning', ideologies that evade, justify, excuse. Since, according to Attachment Theory, adults have attachment needs no less pressing at times of stress than those of children, the same processes which lead to insecure attachment in infants can be seen operating at a societal level. Attachment Theory offers a mechanism that connects the political with the personal. As Marris puts it:

> This is the . . . link between sociological and psychological understanding: the experience of attachment, which so profoundly influences the growth of personality, is itself both the product of a culture, and a determinant of how that culture will be reproduced in the next generation – not only the culture of attachment itself, but all our ideas of order, authority, security, and control.
>
> (Marris 1991)

Attachment Theory shows how the minutiae of interpersonal experience become internalised as personality, or attachment style. Much remains to be understood about the precise ways in which handling in the parent–infant relationship influences future character, but there is little doubt that there is a connection between them. Facing outwards as well as in, Attachment Theory also suggests an articulation between intrafamilial experience and social forces. In their personal relationships people face uncertainty or security, poverty or riches, loss or plenitude, violence or compassion, unpredictability or responsiveness, neglect or care. This will affect their capacity to care for their children, which in turn affects how secure or insecure those children will be when they become adults. The insecurity or otherwise of its citizens will affect the general cultural and economic conditions of society, and thus the cycle is complete as these factors have their impact on child care in the next generation.

Marris (1991) has used this model of cycles of security or insecurity as a metaphor for the increasing polarisation between the secure and the marginalised in modern societies (and this could be extended to international polarisation between rich and poor nations). On the basis of his work in inner cities, Marris argues that cycles of disadvantage, deriving from social factors which include poverty, poor housing, unemployment, cultural deprivation, educational disadvantage, bad health and diet, are experienced as an emptiness or evacuation of meaning, equivalent to that felt by a bereaved person whose meaning-structures are destroyed by loss. As he puts it:

> the more likely our environment is to engender unintelligible, unexpected, and disruptive events, the less support we have, and the more our confidence in attachment has been undermined or distorted by the experiences of childhood, then the more likely it is that our vital organisations or meaning will be overwhelmed, or crippled in their development. Or to put this the other way about – a society that best protected its members from grief and depression would organise its relationships so that they were as stable, predictable, understandable, and careful of attachments as is humanly possible. And the qualities of behaviour that would need to inform such relationships – sensitivity, responsiveness, mutual understanding, consistency, ability to negotiate – are very much the same as those which create secure attachment. I believe such a familial conception of social order is attractive to most of us: our need to nurture and to be nurtured, to make attachment secure, to see the meaning of our lives confirmed by the meaning of society at large, all respond to it. Yet at the same time we have powerful impulses pulling us in the opposite direction, towards an unequal, unsupportive distribution of uncertainty.
>
> (Marris 1991)

Where security is in short supply it is *contested*, whether in families (Byng-Hall 1991c) or society. For Freud, rivalry and ambivalence are inherent properties of the Oedipal situation and therefore of the human condition. For Bowlby, ambivalence is the result of maternal privation, *not* found with the 'ordinary devoted mother', who is adequately supported by her spouse, family and society. Nevertheless, suboptimal child rearing is widespread, and the ambivalently attached child clings ferociously to a mother whose attention might otherwise be diverted elsewhere – towards her other children, her partner or her own inner concerns. Between parents and children there is an inherent asymmetry. It is a parent's job to provide a secure base for children, but not vice versa. Bowlby repeatedly points to role reversal between parent and child as one of the commoner manifestations of anxious attachment, one that inevitably inhibits the exploratory capacities of the child. Sexual and physical abuse of children are extreme examples of exploitation of this asymmetry. The exploitation of women by men is another example, in which a little boy's helplessness in relation to his mother and the fear that engenders when there is no feeling of a secure base is reversed (and avenged) when he grows up and can use his physical strength to dominate a woman.

So too, Marris argues, in an unequal society, there is competition for security. Security becomes a commodity to which the rich cling, pushing insecurity to the margins of society, which then acts as a buffer zone between themselves and the vagaries of international finance and world trade which determine ultimately their economic fate (Marris 1991). And yet if we take seriously the Bowlbian vision of an essential interdependence of attachments, then this too will be seen as a defensive distortion, a variant of anxious attachment that perverts the notion of a secure base and inhibits the creative development of society. As Rustin (1991) puts it:

> The idea of development and fulfilment of the person through relationship, both internal and external . . . is a distinctively social one. . . . It goes against the widespread idea that society will be better when and if we merely give more opportunity and goods to the individual. It is the quality of relationships that individuals can generally have with others around them . . . which make for contentment and creativity, not merely gratifications of various kinds. The most beautiful house with a swimming pool is obtained at serious psychic price when there has to be an armed man at the gate to keep out intruders. Serious damage must also be done to the quality of experience of 'liberty' when its defence depends on threats to inflict total destruction.
>
> (Rustin 1991)

We are living in an era in which much that we have taken for granted is breaking down. All that is solid melts into air. It is the time of the breaking of nations. Alongside the sense of freedom, the celebration of ethnic and cultural pride and a recognition of the need to mourn past traumata, there is an increase in destructive nationalism and tribal violence. Increasingly polluted by the products of the scramble for security, the Earth itself – Mother Earth – is no longer a safe haven on which we can depend to detoxify our waste and provide a base for new growth (Lovelock 1979).

For Freud, a deep awareness of natural beauty – the oceanic feeling – was an idealisation, a projection of a pure pleasure ego uncontaminated by pain, separation and rage. He was always uncertain about the boundaries between normality and neurosis, and particularly about the distinction between aesthetic experience and pathological states (Rycroft 1985). For Freud, the basic goal of life was the search for happiness based on physical satisfaction – he saw this as inevitably doomed to disappointment. Bowlby's emphasis on security provides a more realisable aim. His vision of the harmonious reciprocity of the responsive mother and her infant offers a metaphor for a balanced relationship between man and his environment that is healthy and not based on splitting and idealisation. A secure child can cope with temporary separation and sub-optimal conditions by healthy protest and non-defensive grief. If a secure base can be achieved, exploration of possible ways out of our political and ecological crisis is possible. In a prescient statement about the dangers of nuclear weapons, Bowlby wrote:

> All our previous experience points inescapably to the conclusion that neither moral exhortation nor fear of punishment will succeed in controlling the use of this weapon. Persons bent on suicide and nations bent on war, even suicidal war, are deterred by neither. The hope for the future lies in a far more profound understanding of the nature of the emotional forces involved and the development of scientific social techniques for modifying them.
>
> (Bowlby 1947a)

A small but significant example of the kind of 'understanding' and 'technique' which Bowlby advocates can be found in Middleton's (1991) description of Sherif's Boys Camp Experiment, in which thirty teenagers were taken for a month's camping in the wilderness by a group of psychologists working as camp attendants. The boys were divided into two groups who ate, slept and played separately. Rather like in Golding's *Lord of the Flies*, two distinct cultures of behaviour, slang and group identity developed. When members of the two groups met, scuffles broke out. The experimenters then arranged for the food lorry to break down some miles from the camp, which meant that the two groups had to collaborate in bringing essential supplies to their base. The results were as follows:

> After some initial prevarication and quarrelling, the two groups coalesced into a larger and sufficiently coherent and cohesive group for this essential task. As this happened the stereotyping, antipathy and intense competition between the groups also dissolved as they worked together in pursuit of their mutual interest.
>
> (Middleton 1991)

The discovery of a superordinate goal enabled the two groups to collaborate. The leadership provided them with a secure base from which they could explore ways collectively to solve their common problem.

The ecological vicious circle the world faces is one in which, confronted with a threat to the environment and therefore to the fundaments of security, nations, and where nations break down tribal groups, fight ever more desperately to extract what resources they can from it. This is rather like the children of abusive parents who, in their fear, cling to the very object that causes their distress. The common objective of global security needs to be made real if this vicious cycle is to be put into reverse, just as the skilled therapist will see that both abusive parent and child are in search of a safety that neither can provide for the other, and, as far as possible will try to remedy this herself, or mobilise others who can do so. If we feel locally secure, with a home base which we know will be respected and protected, there will be less need to project of insecurity onto others. Secure as inhabitants of our locality, we become free to explore our citizenship of the world. As the Sicilian writer Gesualdo Bufalino puts it:

> Now I finally know this simple truth: that it is not only my right but my duty to declare myself a citizen of Everywhere

as well as of a hamlet tucked away in the Far South between the Iblei Mountains and the sea; that it is my right and duty to allow a place in my spirit for both the majestic music of the universe and that of the jet gushing from a fountain in the middle of a little village square, on the far southern bastions of the West.

(Bufalino 1992)

For Freud, our biological heritage was a shackle, creating an inevitable conflict between our selfish and drive-driven nature and the repressions of culture. In his vision of alienation we are prisoners of our paleocortex. Bowlby's more benign picture (the contrast between the two men is partly a reflection of the differing cultural heritage – one a European Jew, the other a member of the English upper middle classes) implies a need to re-establish connections with our evolutionary past. Humans survived and evolved on the basis of bonding and mutual support. Competition and the neglect of these basic ties threaten to destroy us. Nomads and agriculturalists, explorers and stay-at-homes, male and female, men and women of contemplation and of action, pursuers of the inner and outer worlds, psychologists and politicians, yogis and commissars – we all share a need for common security. We are all attached inescapably to an Earth in whose 'environment of evolutionary adaptedness' we originated, and which we now threaten with destruction as we are caught in the vortex of a negative spiral of insecurity.

Chapter 11

Epilogue

Sow a thought and you may reap an act; sow an act and you reap a habit; sow a habit and you reap a personality; sow a personality and you reap a destiny.

(Buddhist proverb; Jones 1985)

We ended the previous chapter with a rhetorical flourish which John Bowlby, however much he approved of its sentiment, would probably have considered overstated, insufficiently underpinned by close-grained scientific fact. This is perhaps excusable as we near the end of this book. As suggested in the Introduction, the biographer is both patient and therapist to his subject. At the end of therapy a patient will often yearn for a 'verdict' and ask, implicitly or explicitly, 'Well, what do you really think of me, what is your opinion?' But the therapist has already done his work, said all he can say in the course of the therapy. What more can he add? In the CAT model of brief therapy (Ryle 1990), this dilemma is met by the introduction of the 'farewell letter' which the therapist presents to the patient in the penultimate session. This attempts to summarise the patient's strengths and weaknesses, the progress that has been made in therapy, and some predictions for the future. This heterodoxy is not, it should be noted, the exclusive preserve of eclectic therapists like Ryle: Clifford Scott records that the most moving moment of his analysis with Melanie Klein in the 1930s occurred when she read out to him a long interpretation she had written over the weekend. 'This was proof that I was in her as well as she was in me' (Grosskurth 1986).

Here, then, presumptuously perhaps (but is not any therapy – or biography – an act of presumption?), is an attempt at a farewell letter for John Bowlby, with which the reader, like the patient in CAT, is also invited to disagree, add to, reject, treasure or do what they will.

Dear John,

We are nearing the end of our time together. I would like to say how much I have enjoyed working with you and how much I have learned from our collaboration. I hope you feel that justice has been done to your work and that the boundaries of privacy which, from an early age, you placed around your feelings have been handled with sensitivity.

Like many outstanding psychologists you come from a background that was not entirely easy, although it offered you many opportunities. Perhaps one of them was the fact that your family was so delightfully unpsychological. As Gwen Raverat, granddaughter of your hero, Darwin, said of her father and his brothers (all of whom were distinguished scientists):

'They had [no] idea of the complications of psychology. They found it difficult to conceive of a mixture of motives; or of a man who says one thing and means another; or of a person who is sometimes honest and sometimes dishonest; because they were so completely single-hearted themselves.

(Raverat 1952)

Perhaps it was because you were so familiar with those to whom psychology is a mystery that you were such a good populariser.

Some of your life's work at least can be understood in terms of the problems which presented themselves to you as a small child. You were the middle boy between a very bright and vigorous older brother and a younger brother who was considered backward. Your compassion for the weak and your undoubted ambition and competitiveness bear the impress of the mould you shared with them. Your father was a distant, awe-inspiring figure, whose voice you are said to have inherited and in whose footsteps you followed into the medical profession. In terms of public recognition your achievements were at least comparable with his, although as it happens, as a resilient and independent-minded person you did not appear to seek or need external approval. Your mother – or, should we say, mothers? – seems in her urban persona to have been rather neglectful and partial in her handling of the children, but was very different on those long holidays which were such an important influence on your life and work. From her you learned the importance of nature, that as creatures we are part civilised, part wild. In middle years you kept the wild side of yourself well hidden, but it was certainly there in your early independence and rebelliousness, and emerged again as you grew older.

I suspect, like many others of your generation, you were very excited when you started your training as a psychoanalyst at the prospect of being able to apply your scientific outlook not just to the external world but also to the inner landscape of feelings. Here, in your own words (Bowlby 1973a), was a continent to conquer. In those days your views were progressive and, while never a Marxist (or indeed an anything-ist), you saw an opportunity to ameliorate psychological as well as material suffering.

Your encounter with psychoanalysis did not really live up to your expectations. Your teachers did not seem particularly interested in trying to change society. They were certainly conservative in their outlook if not in their politics. They ran their society in an authoritarian way and, to succeed, you had to submit to this, even if, as I suspect, your heart was not really in it. Your analyst was Mrs Riviere, your supervisor Melanie Klein. As one of your obituarists put it, 'it is a tribute to [your] independence to point out that neither of these two formidable ladies appear to have had the slightest effect on [your] subsequent development' (Storr 1991). That is not of course quite true because you were, as you yourself later said, determined to prove them wrong. Perhaps you thought you would 'bag' them both, like a brace of pheasants (and you were never happier than after a good day's shooting), with your theory of attachment.

The way you did this was interesting. What you did, in effect, was to appeal over their heads to the higher authority of Freud, much as you might have done as a child when, with your father away at the war in France, you might have wanted some paternal authority with which to out-trump your didactic mother and dominant older brother. First, you emphasised your common scientific outlook with Freud's, in contrast to their lack of scientific understanding. Second, you insisted that they had not really grasped the importance in Freud's late work on attachment (as opposed to instinct), and the role of loss as a cause of neurosis.

You had the social and intellectual self-confidence to challenge psychoanalytic authority – and it certainly needed challenging. But perhaps you missed out on something too. So important was it for you resist what you saw as the negative influence of these wrong-headed ideas – especially the neglect of real trauma in favour of phantasy – that you did not really allow yourself to feel the full emotional impact of psychoanalysis. The imaginative leaps, the heights and depths of emotion, the understanding of how intimate experience is engendered and gendered – you seem to have avoided these. Meanwhile, you built your case, painstakingly and slowly, that psychoanalysis – or the Kleinian version of it, at least – was on a wrong course. The effort of self-control and sustained concentration that this took may have contributed to the impression you gave to some of detachment and even arrogance.

Together with your intelligence and independence you were clearly an excellent organiser and highly efficient. These qualities brought you to the top – or nearly to the top – of your professions of psychoanalysis and child psychiatry. You were Deputy Chairman of the Tavistock and Deputy President of the Psycho-Analytical Society. But something kept you from the summit. Was it your reserve, your lack of overt warmth? Or did you value most strongly the rebellious part of you which wanted to strike out on your own rather than become too identified with an institution? You mistrusted authority, although in your own way you exercised a strong hand in your research group. Running a tight ship always was your style.

Maternal deprivation made your name. What a case you built up for the mother-love which you experienced so intermittently and unpredictably in your childhood. What a devastating criticism and idealisation of motherhood that was! And how the public loved – and hated – you for it. It is a pity that you weren't able to say more about fathers, especially as they are so much more important now in child care than they were when you began your theorising. But the principles of mothering which you put forward remain valid if we speak now instead of parenting, as long as this does not gloss over the fact that the bulk of child care is still done by mothers, who are as vulnerable and unsupported now, although in different ways, as they were when you surveyed the post-war scene in the 1940s.

And loss. What a keen eye for that you had. Your understanding of it may turn out in the end to be your greatest contribution to psychology. And yet how well hidden you kept the losses in your own life that made you so sensitive to others' grief and misery. Was it your father's absence during the war? Or the loss of your younger brother's vigour? Was it your sensitivity to your parents' grief, both of whom had lost parents in their youth – your paternal grandfather's death, your maternal grandmother's preoccupation with the younger children? Or was it Durbin – your Lycidas, a close friend cut down in his prime, trying, tragically, to save another man from drowning?

I wonder what you would have made of our contemporary emphasis on stories and narrative in psychotherapy? You were suspicious of hermeneutics and tried always to stay within the confines of evolutionary science. And yet from your work has come a line of understanding which shows how the capacity for narrative, to link the past with the present and the future in a coherent way, is a continuation of that responsive handling in infancy which you (and Winnicott) saw so clearly were the foundations of security. You made the first entries in the non-verbal grammar of mother–child interaction which is slowly being written. From this has come an understanding that it is the handling of patients by their therapists that matters, not the precision of their interpretations. There is no Bowlbian school of psychotherapy because your emphasis was on the non-verbal language of care-giving. The stories – Kleinian, Freudian or what you will – come later. You were a good story-teller yourself as your books, with their logical progressions and solid factual backing for your theories, attest. You would have agreed that the ability to tell a story is the mark of psychological health. You knew that to be able to talk about pain and loss is the best way to overcome it. You would have been fascinated by the evidence – springing mostly from your work – that securely attached babies become good story-tellers in their teens, and that they in turn have securely attached babies.

I suspect you were one of those people who grow happier as they get older. Towards the end you allowed the twinkle in your eye to show more often. You could finally start to play – your way. Perhaps you hadn't really been able to do this since the thirties. Your battle with psychoanalysis was over and you could be your own man. You returned in your last years to an authority that pre-dated Freud – Darwin, to a Victorian time when progress and order and the power of science were valued, where the battle lines were clear cut, far removed from the chaos and confusion of our post-modernist world.

What of your legacy? Attachment Theory is, as you were, vigorous and independent. If anything, it is likely to come even more into prominence in the 1990s as psychoanalysis struggles with its own need for a secure base, theoretically and economically. The demand for psychological help grows ever stronger as we contemplate the emotional casualties of capitalism; the confusion of psychotherapeutic tongues grows ever louder as the different therapies compete in the marketplace. Your still – but not so small (that 'orotund' charge still rankles) – voice would have been helpful in bringing us back to earth, to the practical questions of who needs help most and with what therapy based on what theory. You would, I think, have taken much satisfaction from the cross-fertilisations stimulated by your work – by analysts like Fonagy and Hobson using the Adult Attachment Interview to study their borderline patients, developmental psychologists like Main and Bretherton beginning to look at object-relations theory.

You were never an intrusive or dependence-creating therapist, despite your insistence on the persistence of dependency needs throughout the life cycle. You have made it so that we can manage without you. You clearly saw the two poles of insecurity – avoidance and ambivalence – and, like the good navigator you once were, tried to steer a true course between them. You could see clearly the 'hardboiledness' (your word) of your affectionless psychopaths of the 1930s reminiscent of the narrow scientism of the behaviourists on the one side, and on the other the clinging adherence to unquestioned shibboleths of the psychoanalytic orthodoxy. You saw behind them to the vulnerability they were defending. You knew that the good therapist has to cultivate a state of 'non-attachment' in which people, ideas, things are neither avoided nor clung to but are seen squarely for what they are. This non-attachment can only grow in a culture of secure attachment to parents and a society that is worthy of trust. You were a good model for such trustworthiness (even if your reliability was a bit *too* much at times for us less organised types!). On the basis of this secure attachment it is possible to face the inevitable losses and failures, the essential transience of things, and to recognise that, if circumstances allow for due grief and mourning, then out of difficulty can come a new beginning.

Yours, with affection and admiration . . .

Glossary of terms relevant to Attachment Theory

ADULT ATTACHMENT INTERVIEW (AAI) A semi-structured psychodynamic interview in which the subject is encouraged to talk about their early attachments, their feelings about their parents, and to describe any significant losses and childhood traumata. The transcripts are then rated, not so much for content as for style, picking up features like coherence of the narrative and capacity to recall painful events. Subjects are classified into one of four categories: 'Free to evaluate attachment', 'dismissing of attachment', 'enmeshed in attitudes towards attachment', and 'unresolved/disorganised/disorientated'. When given to pregnant mothers the AAI has been shown to predict the attachment status of the infants at one year with 70 per cent accuracy (Fonagy *et al*. 1992).

AMBIVALENT ATTACHMENT A category of attachment status as classified in the Strange Situation (q.v.). The infant, after being separated and then re-united with its mother, reacts by clinging to her, protesting in a way that can't be pacified (for instance, by arching its back and batting away offered toys), and remains unable to return to exploratory play for the remainder of the test. Associated with mothers who are inconsistent or intrusive in their responses to their babies.

ASSUAGEMENT AND DISASSUAGEMENT Terms introduced by Heard and Lake (1986) to describe the state of satisfaction or dissatisfaction of attachment needs. The securely attached individual when re-united with an attachment figure clings to them for a few minutes and then, in a state of assuagement, can get on with exploratory activity. If the attachment figure is unable to tolerate attachment behaviour or unavailable, this produces a state of disassuagement of attachment needs associated with defensive manoeuvres such as avoidance or clinging, with consequent inhibition of exploration.

ATTACHMENT   The condition in which an individual is linked emotionally with another person, usually, but not always, someone perceived to be older, stronger and wiser than themselves. Evidence for the existence of attachment comes from proximity seeking, secure base phenomenon (q.v.) and separation protest.

ATTACHMENT BEHAVIOURAL SYSTEM This is conceived to be the basis of attachment and attachment behaviour, and comprises a reciprocal set of behaviours shown by careseeker and care-giver in which they are aware of and seek each other out whenever the care-seeker is in danger due to physical separation, illness or tiredness.

AVOIDANT ATTACHMENT Together with ambivalent attachment (q.v.), the second main category of insecure attachment delineated in the Strange Situation (q.v.). Here the child, when re-united with its mother after a brief separation, rather than going to her for assuagement (q.v.), avoids too close contact, hovering near her in a watchful way, and is unable fully to resume exploratory play. Associated with mothers who reject or ignore their babies.

BORDERLINE PERSONALITY DISORDER (BPD)   A term used rather differently by psychiatrists and psychotherapists to denote a group of difficult and disturbed patients characterised primarily by instability of mood and difficulty in sustaining close relationships. In addition, they often show self-injurious behaviour such as self-harm and drug abuse; have destructive angry outbursts; suffer from identity disturbance with uncertainty about life goals and sexual orientation; and experience chronic feelings of emptiness and boredom. Although a precise definition is difficult, the term captures the sense of an individual who often lives on the borderline of relationships, neither in nor out of them, and, psychologically, on the borderline between neurosis and psychosis.

COGNITIVE THERAPY   A form of psychotherapy associated with the work of Aaron Beck (Beck *et al.* 1979) which focuses on the patient's cognitions (i.e., thoughts) rather than emotions, based on the principle that cognitions determine feelings rather than vice versa. Thus, a depressed person may assume that everything they attempt is bound to fail, and this will lead to feelings of hopelessness and helplessness. In therapy, the patient is encouraged to monitor and challenge these automatic dysfunctional thoughts; for example, questioning whether *everything* they do really is hopeless, or only *some* things, and so begin to build up positive thoughts about themselves.

CONTROVERSIAL DISCUSSIONS (1941–44)   Series of meetings held in the aftermath of Freud's death between two factions, led by Melanie Klein and Anna Freud, in the British Psycho-Analytical Society. The two sides disagreed about theory – especially about the existence or otherwise of the death instinct, and the age at which infantile phantasies could be said to exist. Each side felt that the other had an undue influence over Training Candidates and was trying to denigrate and dismiss each other's theories. Eventually a compromise was reached in which two, and later three, streams of training were created within the society: the Kleinian, the Freudian and a third, non-aligned ('middle') group.

DEPRESSIVE   POSITION/PARANOID-SCHIZOID   POSITION   Melanie Klein's (1986) distinction between a state of mind characterised by splitting (hence the 'schizoid' aspect), in which good and bad are kept separate, and in which bad, persecutory feelings are projected onto the environment (hence the 'paranoid' aspect); and one in which good and bad are seen to be two aspects of the same thing, and which therefore leads to depressive feelings that are healthy and constructive because the sufferer is taking responsibility for their hatred and is appropriately guilty. Klein saw the infant as progressing from the paranoid-schizoid to the depressive position in the course of the early years of life. The move from one position to the other is also a feature of successful therapy. Bowlby differs from Klein in seeing splitting as a response to sub-optimal parenting, a manifestation of insecure attachment, rather than a normal phenomenon. He agrees with Klein about the importance of depression as an appropriate response to loss and separation.

EPIGENETIC   A term coined by Waddington (1977) to describe the development of a differentiated organism from a fertilised ovum. The developing embryo proceeds along a number of possible developmental pathways depending on environmental conditions. Epigenesis may be contrasted with a 'homuncular' (from 'homunculus' or 'little man') model of development in which all the stages of development are already pre-formed. Bowlby applied this distinction to psychological development, and contrasted his own approach in which there are many possible pathways which an individual may take through infancy depending on their interaction with their care-givers, with the classical Freudian approach which sees development in terms of a number of fixed 'stages' through which a person must pass, irrespective of environmental influence. He felt that his approach was more consistent with modern biological thinking, and allowed for a more subtle view of the complexity of interaction between an individual and their environment. Thus 'anxious' attachment, rather than being a 'stage', like the so-called 'oral stage' of development, becomes a possible epigenetic compromise between a child's attachment needs and a parent who is unable fully to meet them. Like Klein's 'positions', but unlike Freud's 'stages', Bowlby's attachment patterns persist throughout life, unless modified by good experiences (which would include successful therapy).

ETHOLOGY   Literally, the study of an individual's 'ethos' or character. Ethology is a biological science which studies animal behaviour in a particular way: the animal is considered as a whole; behaviour is usually studied in natural or wild conditions; there is great attention to the antecedents and consequences of behaviour patterns; the function of any behaviour is considered; and an evolutionary perspective is always taken. An attempt is made to see how the animal views the world from its own perspective and to visualise the internal 'maps' and rules which govern its activities. Ethology is contrasted with behaviourism, which usually concentrates on particular bits of behaviour and does not consider the organism as a whole and is unconcerned with evolutionary considerations. Bowlby saw the methods and theories of ethology as highly relevant to the study of human infants, and this led to a fruitful collaboration between him and the leading ethologist Robert Hinde (see Hinde 1982a and b; 1987).

EXPRESSED   EMOTION   (EE)   A   rating   scale   initially developed for the relatives of patients suffering from schizophrenia (Leff and Vaughn 1983), but applicable to other disorders including affective illness and Alzheimer's disease, measuring such dimensions as 'hostility', 'warmth' and 'overinvolvement'. Patients whose relatives score high on negative 'expressed emotions' are more likely to relapse from their illness. A link is suggested between anxious attachment and high expressed emotion (see Chapter 9).

INTERNAL WORKING MODELS   On the basis of cognitive psychology (see Craik 1943; Beck *et al.* 1979), Bowlby sees higher animals as needing a map or model of the world in the brain, if they are successfully to predict, control and manipulate their environment. In Bowlby's version humans have two such models, an 'environmental' model, telling us about the world, and an 'organismal' model, telling us about ourselves in relation to the world. We carry a map of self, and others, and the relationship between the two. Although primarily 'cognitive' in conception, the idea of internal working models is applicable to affective life. The map is built up from experiences and is influenced by the need to defend against painful feelings. Thus an anxiously attached child may have a model of others in which they are potentially dangerous, and therefore must be approached with caution, while their self-representation may be of someone who is demanding and needy and unworthy to be offered security. The relationship with a person's primary care-givers is generalised in internal working models, which leads to a distorted and incoherent picture of the world, and one that is not subject to updating and revision in the light of later experience. This, in Bowlby's eyes, is the basis for transference, and the task of therapy is help the patient develop more realistic and less rigid internal working models.

MATERNAL DEPRIVATION   A catch-phrase summarising Bowlby's early work on the effects of separating infants and young children from their mothers. He believed that maternally deprived children were likely to develop asocial or antisocial tendencies, and that juvenile delinquency was mainly a consequence of such separations. The corollary of this was his advocacy of continuous mother–child contact for at least the first five years of life, which earned him the opprobrium of feminists. Subsequent research has confirmed that lack of maternal care does lead to poor social adjustment and relationship difficulties, but suggests that disruption, conflict and poor maternal handling are more common causes of difficulties in late life than the loss of mother in itself.

METACOGNITIVE MONITORING   Concept introduced by Main (1990) and Fonagy (1991) to denote the ability to 'think about thinking'. Securely attached children and adults are able to reflect freely on their thought processes (e.g., 'I was really upset when my mum and dad split up and felt pretty hostile to all the children at school who seemed to have happy homes'), in contrast to insecure individuals, who tend either to dismiss their thought processes (e.g., 'Oh, the split-up didn't affect me at all, I just concentrated on my football'), or to be bogged down in them ('I can't really talk about it . . . it makes me too upset'). Defects in metacognitive ability are common in pathological states, such as borderline personality disorder, and one of the aims of psychotherapy is to facilitate metacognition.

MONOTROPY   An ethological (q.v.) term introduced by Bowlby to denote the exclusive attachment of a child to its principal care-giver, usually the mother. He was impressed by Lorenz's (1952) studies of geese and their young which suggested that the goslings became imprinted onto a moving object at a sensitive period in the first day or two of life. Bowlby thought that a similar process occurred in humans. In fact, imprinting seems not to be a feature of primate development, where attachments develop gradually and over a wide range from the early months to adolescence. Also, attachment in humans is not so much monotropic as hierarchical, with a list of preferred care-givers, with parents at the top, but closely followed by grandparents, siblings, aunts and so on.

OBJECT-RELATIONS THEORY (ORT)   Attachment Theory is a close relation of, and provides experimental evidence in support of, Object-Relations Theory (Greenberg and Mitchell 1983). This psychoanalytic school is particularly associated with a group of British theorists who include Klein (1986), Fairbairn (1952), Balint (1968) and Winnicott (1965), as well as Bion (1978). In contrast to Freud's early view of the organism as primarily driven by instinct and the need to discharge accumulated psychic energy ('libido'), Object-Relations Theorists see people as primarily seeking a relationship to their 'objects'. There is thus a progression in psychoanalytic thinking, starting with Freud's drive discharge theory, through Object Relations, in which a whole individual is seeking a relationship with an 'object' (i.e., not quite a person), to the reciprocity of care-giver and care-seeker implicit in Attachment Theory and recent developmental psychology.

PARENTAL BONDING INSTRUMENT (PBI)   A questionnaire test, devised by Parker (1983) to try to elicit in a systematic way an individual's perception of their parental relationships in childhood. It gives two main dimensions: 'care' and 'protection'. 'Care' ranges from warmth and empathy at one extreme to coldness and indifference at the other. 'Protection' similarly ranges from over-protection and infantilisation to promotion of autonomy. People with borderline personality disorder and depressive disorders regularly report the constellation of low care and high intrusiveness ('affectionless control'). There is some evidence that such reports of parental behaviour are an accurate reflection of their actual behaviour (Parker *et al.* 1992).

PERCEPTUAL DEFENCE   This, and the related concept of unconscious perception (Dixon and Henley 1991), refer to the apparently paradoxical phenomenon by which an individual can be shown to respond in behaviour to a stimulus without it reaching conscious awareness. Thus, for example, a subject presented with a neutral face and asked to judge whether it is 'happy' or 'sad', will be influenced by the simultaneous presentation of a subliminal word with positive or negative connotations. This provides experimental confirmation of the existence of unconscious thinking. Bowlby (1981c) uses this idea in his discussion of ungrieved loss to suggest that painful feelings are kept out of awareness but may nevertheless influence a person's state of mind and behaviour. By bringing these feelings into awareness – that is, by reducing the extent of perceptual defence – they are then available for processing (cf. 'working through'), leading to a more coherent and better adapted relationship to the world and the self.

SECURE BASE   A term introduced by Ainsworth (1982) to describe the feeling of safety provided by an attachment figure. Children will seek out their secure base at times of threat – danger, illness, exhaustion or following a separation. When the danger has passed, attachment behaviour will cease, but only if it is there to be mobilised if needed will the child feel secure. The secure base phenomenon applies equally to adults. We all feel 'at home' with those whom we know and trust, and within such a home environment are able to relax, and pursue our projects, whether they be play, pleasure-seeking or work.

STRANGE SITUATION   An experimental method devised by Ainsworth (Ainsworth *et al.* 1978) to study the ways in which one-year-old children can cope with brief separations from their care-givers. The child is left first with the experimenter and then alone while the mother goes out of the room for 3 minutes. The child's response to the separation, and more importantly to the re-union, is observed and rated from videotapes. On the basis of this rating children can be classified as secure (usually characterised by brief protest followed by return to relaxed play and interaction) or insecure, the latter being subdivided into avoidant (q.v.) and ambivalent (q.v.) patterns of insecurity. See Chapter 6, page 104, for a more detailed description.

SYSTEMIC   Adjective derived from Systems Theory, a conceptual model used by family therapists (originating with information theory), in which the family as a whole is seen as a quasi-organism, or 'system', with its own rules and ways of behaving. Certain general principles apply to systems whatever their nature, whether they are cells of the body, whole organisms, families or social groups. These include the property of having a boundary, of the need for information flow between different parts of the system, of a hierarchy of decision-making elements, and of 'homeostasis', the tendency towards inertia. Attachment Theory is systemic in that it sees care-seeker and care-giver as a mutually interacting system regulated by positive and negative feedback. Pathological states can result from the operation of such feedback – for example, when a child clings ever more tightly to an abusing parent, because the source of the attack is also the object to which the child is programmed to turn in case of danger.

Chronology

1907 Born, Edward John Mostyn Bowlby, fourth child and second son of Sir Anthony and Lady May Bowlby. Lived at Manchester Square, London.

1914–25 Preparatory school and then Royal Naval College, Dartmouth.

1925–28 Trinity College, Cambridge.

1928–29 Teacher in progressive school for maladjusted children.

1929 Started clinical medical studies at University College Hospital, London, and psychoanalytic training at the Institute of Psycho-Analysis, London. Training analyst, Mrs Joan Riviere.

1933 Medical qualification. Psychiatric training at Maudsley Hospital, London, under Aubrey Lewis.

1937 Qualified as an analyst. Starts training in child analysis, supervisor, Melanie Klein.

1938 Married Ursula Longstaff, by whom two sons and two daughters.

1940 Publication: *Personality and Mental Illness* (with F. Durbin).

1937–40 Psychiatrist, London Child Guidance Clinic.

1940–45 Specialist Psychiatrist, Royal Army Medical Corps, mainly concerned with Officer Selection Boards.

1946 Publication, 'Forty-four juvenile thieves: their characters and home life'.

1946–72 Consultant Child Psychiatrist and Deputy Director, Tavistock Clinic, London, and Director, Department for Children and Parents.

1950–72 Consultant in Mental Health, World Health Organisation.

1951 Publication of *Maternal Care and Mental Health*.

1957–58 Fellow, Centre for Advanced Study in the Behavioural Sciences, Stanford, California.

1956–61 Deputy President, British Psycho-Analytical Society.

1958–63 Consultant, US National Institute of Mental Health.

1969 Publication of *Attachment*, first volume of the *Attachment and Loss* trilogy.

— Visiting Professor in Psychiatry, Stanford University, California.

1963–72 Member, External Scientific Staff, Medical Research Council.

1972 Commander of the British Empire.

1973 Publication of *Separation*, second volume of the *Attachment and Loss* trilogy.

1973 Travelling Professor, Australian and New Zealand College of Psychiatrists.

1977 Honorary Doctor of Science, University of Cambridge.

1979 Publication of *The Making and Breaking of Affectional Bonds*.

1980 Publication of *Loss*, third volume of the *Attachment and Loss* trilogy.

1981 Freud Memorial Professor of Psychoanalysis, University College, London.

— Foreign Honorary Member, American Academy of Arts and Sciences.

1987 Celebration of Bowlby's 80th birthday with a conference at the Tavistock Clinic, bringing together researchers and clinicians, entitled 'The Effect of Relationships on Relationships'.

1988   Publication of *A Secure Base*.

1989   Fellow of the British Academy.

1990   Publication of *Charles Darwin, A New Biography*.

—— Dies while in Skye, at his holiday home where much of his writing had been done.

Bibliography

PUBLICATIONS OF JOHN BOWLBY

Personal Aggressiveness and War, (1938) (with E. P. M. Durbin) London: Kegan Paul.

'The abnormally aggressive child', (1938) *The New Era* (Sept.–Oct.).

'Hysteria in children', (1939a) in *A Survey of Child Psychiatry*, pp. 80–94, Humphrey Milford (ed.), London: Oxford University Press.

'Substitute homes', (1939) *Mother and Child* (official organ of the National Council for Maternity and Child Welfare) X (1) (April): 3–7.

'Jealous and spiteful children', (1939) *Home and School* (Home and School Council of Great Britain), IV(5): 83–5.

Bowlby, J., Miller, E. and Winnicott, D. W. (1939) 'Evacuation of small children' (letter), *British Medical Journal* (16 Dec.): 1202–3.

'The influence of early environment in the development of neurosis and neurotic character', (1940) *International Journal of Psycho-Analysis*, 21: 154–78.

'Psychological aspects', (1940) ch. 16, pp. 186–96, in *Evacuation Survey: A Report to the Fabian Society*, Richard Padley and Margaret Cole (eds), London: George Routledge & Sons Ltd.

'The problem of the young child', (1940c) *Children in War-time*, 21 (3): 19–30, London: New Education Fellowships.

'Forty-four juvenile thieves: their characters and home life', (1944) *International Journal of Psychoanalysis*, 25: 1–57 and 207–228; republished as a monograph by Baillière, Tindall & Cox, London, 1946.

'Childhood origins of recidivism', (1945–46) *The Howard Journal*, VII (1): 30–3, The Howard League for Penal Reform.

'The future role of the child guidance clinic in education and other services', (1946a) *Report of the Proceedings of a Conference on Mental Health*, (14–15 Nov.), pp. 80–89, National Association for Mental Health.

'Psychology and democracy', (1946b) *The Political Quarterly*, XVII (1): 61–76.

'The therapeutic approach in sociology', (1947a) *The Sociological Review*, 39: 39–49.

'The study of human relations in the child guidance clinic', (1947b) *Journal of Social Issues*, III (2) (Spring): 35–41.

'The study and reduction of group tensions in the family, (1949a) *Human Relations*, 2 (2) (April): 123–8.

'The relation between the therapeutic approach and the legal approach to juvenile delinquency', (1949b) *The Magistrate*, VIII (Nov.): 260–4.

Why Delinquency? The Case for Operational Research, (1949c) Report of a conference on the scientific study of juvenile delinquency held at the Royal Institution, London 1 Oct., and published by the National Association for Mental Health.

'Research into the origins of delinquent behaviour', (1950) *British Medical Journal* 1 March 11: 570).

Maternal Care and Mental Health, (1951) World Health Organisation, Monograph Series No. 2.

'Responses of young children to separation from their mothers', (with J. Robertson) (1952a) *Courier*, Centre International de l'Enfance, II (2): 66–78, and II (3): 131–42, Paris.

A two-year-old goes to hospital: a scientific film, (with J. Robertson) (1952b) *Proceedings of the Royal Society of Medicine*, 46: 425–7.

'A two-year-old goes to hospital', Bowlby, J., Robertson, J. and Rosenbluth, D. (1952) *The Psychoanalytic Study of the Child*, VII: 82–94.

'A two-year-old goes to hospital: a scientific film', (with J. Robertson) (1952b) *Proceedings of the Royal Society of Medicine*, 46: 425–7.

'The roots of parenthood', (1953) Convocation Lecture of the National Children's Home (July).

Child Care and the Growth of Maternal Love, (1953b) (abridged version of *Maternal Care and Mental Health*, 1951), London: Penguin Books; new and enlarged edition, 1965.

'Critical phases in the development of social responses in man and other animals', (1953c) *New Biology*, London: Penguin Books, pp. 25–32.

'Some pathological processes set in train by early mother–child separation', (1953d) *Journal of Mental Science*, 99: 265–72.

'Research strategy in the study of mother–child separation', (with M. G. Ainsworth) (1954) *Courier*, Centre International de l'Enfance, IV: 105–13.

'Family approach to child guidance: therapeutic techniques', (1955) Transactions of the 11th Interclinic Conference for the Staffs of Child Guidance Clinics, National Association for Mental Health (26 March).

'The growth of independence in the young child', (1956) *Royal Society of Health Journal*, 76: 587–91.

'Psychoanalytic instinct theory', (1956) in *Discussions on Child Development*, vol. 1, J. M. Tanner and B. Inhelder (eds), pp. 182–87, London: Tavistock Publications.

'The effects of mother–child separation: a follow-up study', (with M. Ainsworth, M. Boston and D. Rosenbluth) (1956) *British Journal of Medical Psychology*, XXIX, parts 3 and 4: 211–47.

'An ethological approach to research in child development', (1957) *British Journal of Medical Psychology*, XXX, part 4: 230–40.

Can I Leave my Baby?, (1958a) The National Association for Mental Health.
'A note on mother–child separation as a mental health hazard', (1958b) *British Journal of Medical Psychology*, XXXI, parts 3 and 4: 247–8.
Foreword to *Widows and their Families* by Peter Marris, (1958c) London: Routledge & Kegan Paul.
'The nature of the child's tie to his mother', (1958d) *International Journal of Psycho-Analysis*, 39, part V: 350–73.
'Psychoanalysis and child care', (1958e) in *Psychoanalysis and Contemporary Thought*, J. Sutherland (ed.), London: Hogarth Press.
'Ethology and the development of object relations', (1960a) *International Journal of Psycho-Analysis*, 41, parts IV–V: 313–17.
'Separation anxiety', (1960b) *International Journal of Psycho-Analysis*, 41, parts II–III: 89–113.
Comment on Piaget's paper: 'The general problems of the psychobiological development on the child', (1960c) in *Discussions on Child Development*, vol. 4, J. M. Tanner and B. Inhelder (eds), London: Tavistock Publications.
'Grief and mourning in infancy and early childhood', (1960d) *The Psychoanalytic Study of the Child*, XV: 9–52.
'Separation anxiety: a critical review of the literature', (1961a) *Journal of Child Psychology and Psychiatry*, 1 (16): 251–69.
Note on Dr Max Schur's comments on grief and mourning in infancy and early childhood, (1961b) *The Psychoanalytic Study of the Child*, XVI: 206–8.
'Childhood mourning and its implications for psychiatry', The Adolf Meyer Lecture, (1961c) *American Journal of Psychiatry*, 118 (6): 481–97.
'Processes of mourning', (1961d) *International Journal of Psycho-Analysis*, 42, parts IV–V: 317–40.
'Defences that follow loss: causation and function', (1962a) unpublished.
'Loss, detachment and defence', (1962b) unpublished.
'Pathological mourning and childhood mourning', (1963) *Journal of the American Psychoanalytic Association*, XI (3) (July): 500–41.
Note on Dr Lois Murphy's paper 'Some aspects of the first relationship', (1964a) *International Journal of Psycho-Analysis*, 45, part 1: 44–6.
Security and Anxiety: Old Ideas in a New Light, (1964b) Proceedings of the 15th Annual Conference of the Association of Children's Officers.
Darwin's health (letter) (1965) *British Medical Journal* (10 April), p. 999.
Foreword to *Brief Separations* (1966) by C. M. Heinicke and I. J. Westheimer, New York: International Universities Press; London: Longmans Green.
'Effects on behaviour of disruption of an affectional bond', (1968a) in *Genetic and Environmental Influences on Behaviour*, J. M. Thoday and A-S Parkes, pp. 94–108, Edinburgh: Oliver & Boyd.
'Security and anxiety', (1968b) chapter in *The Formative Years*, London: BBC Publications.
'Affectional bonds: their nature and origin', (1969a) in *Progress in Mental Health*, H. Freeman (ed.), London: J. & A. Churchill.

Attachment and Loss, (1969b) vol. 1, *Attachment*, London: Hogarth Press; New York: Basic Books; Harmondsworth: Penguin Books, 1971; 2nd edn, 1982.

'Types of hopelessness in psychopathological process', (1969c) (with F. T. Melges) *Archives of General Psychiatry*, 20: 690–9.

'Psychopathology of anxiety: the role of affectional bonds', (1969d) in *Studies of Anxiety*, M. H. Lader (ed.), *British Journal of Psychiatry*, Special Publication no. 3.

'Reasonable fear and natural fear', (1970) *International Journal of Psychiatry*, 9: 79–88.

'Separation and loss within the family', (1970) (with C. M. Parkes), in *The Child in his Family*, E. J. Anthony (ed.), New York: J. Wiley; Paris: Masson et Cie; and in *The International Yearbook for Child Psychiatry and Allied Disciplines*, vol. 1, pp. 197–216.

Attachment and Loss, vol. 2, (1973a) *Separation: Anxiety and Anger*, London: Hogarth Press; New York: Basic Books; Harmondsworth: Penguin Books, 1975.

'Self-reliance and some conditions that promote it', (1973b) in *Support, Innovation and Autonomy*, R. Gosling, (ed.), pp. 23–48, London: Tavistock Publications.

'The family for good or ill', (1973c) Report on a seminar given in the Department of Psychological Medicine, University of Otago Medical School, New Zealand Department of Psychological Medicine.

'Problems of marrying research with clinical and social needs', (1974) in *The Growth of Competence*, K. J. Connolly and J. S. Bruner (eds), pp. 303–7, London and New York: Academic Press.

'Attachment theory, separation anxiety and mourning', (1975) in *American Handbook of Psychiatry* (2nd edn), vol. VI, *New Psychiatric Frontiers*, David A. Hamburg and Keith H. Brodie (eds), ch. 14, pp. 292–309.

Bindung, translation of *Attachment*, (1975) Munich: Kindler Verlag.

'Responses to separation from parents: a clinical test for young children', (with M. Klagsbrun) (1976a) *British Journal of Projective Psychology and Personality Study*, 21 (2): 7–27.

'Human personality development in an ethological light', (1976b) in *Animal Models in Human Psychobiology*, G. Serban and A. Kling (eds), pp. 27–36, New York: Plenum Publishing Corp.

'The making and breaking of affectional bonds, (1977) I Aetiology and psychopathology in the light of attachment theory, II Some principles of psychotherapy', *British Journal of Psychiatry*, 130: 201–10 and 421–31.

'Attachment theory and its therapeutic implications', (1978) in *Adolescent Psychiatry: Developmental and Clinical Studies*, vol. 6, S. C. Feinstein and P. L. Giovacchini (eds), pp. 5–33, New York: Jason Aronson.

'On knowing what you are not supposed to know and feeling what you are not supposed to feel', (1979a) *Canadian Journal of Psychiatry*, 24 (5): 403–8.

'Psychoanalysis as art and science', (1979b) *International Review of Psycho-Analysis*, 6, part 3: 3–14.

The Making and Breaking of Affectional Bonds, (1979c) London: Tavistock Publications.

Continuing commentary on article by D. W. Rajecki, M. E. Lamb and P. Obmascher, 'Toward a general theory of infantile attachment: a comparative review of aspects of the social bond', (1979d) *The Behavioural and Brain Sciences*, 2: 637–8.

'By ethology out of psychoanalysis: an experiment in interbreeding', (1979e) (The Niko Tinbergen Lecture, *Animal Behaviour*, 28, part 3: 649–56.

Attachment and Loss, vol. 3, *Loss: Sadness and Depression*, (1980) London: Hogarth Press; New York: Basic Books; Harmondsworth: Penguin Books, 1981.

'Perspective: a contribution by John Bowlby', (1981a) *Bulletin of the Royal College of Psychiatrists*, 5 (1) (Jan.).

Contribution to symposium, 'Emanuel Peterfreund on information and systems theory', (1981b) *The Psychoanalytic Review*, 68: 187–90.

'Psychoanalysis as a natural science', (1981c) *International Review of Psycho-Analysis*, 8, part 3: 243–56.

'Attachment and loss: retrospect and prospect', (1982a) *American Journal of Orthopsychiatry*, 52 (4): 664–78.

Epilogue, (1982b) *The Place of Attachment in Human Behaviour*, Colin Murray Parkes and Joan Stevenson-Hinde (eds), pp. 310–13, New York: Basic Books; London: Tavistock Publications.

'Caring for the young: influences on development', (1984a) in *Parenthood: A Psychodynamic Perspective*, Rebecca S. Cohen, Bertram J. Cohler and Sidney H. Weissman (eds), ch. 18, pp. 269–84, The Guilford Psychiatry Series, New York: Guilford Press.

Discussion of paper, 'Aspects of transference in group analysis' (1984b) by Mario Marrone, *Group Analysis*, 17: 191–4.

'Violence in the family as a disorder of the attachment and caregiving systems', (1984c) *American Journal of Psychoanalysis*, 44: 9–27.

'Psychoanalysis as a natural science', (1984d) *Psychoanalytic Psychology*, 1 (1): 7–21.

'The role of childhood experience in cognitive disturbance' (1985) in *Cognition and Psychotherapy*, Michael J. Mahoney and Arthur Freeman (eds), ch. 6, pp. 181–200, New York and London: Plenum Publishing Corp.

'Processi difensivi alla luce della teoria dell'attaccamento', (1986a) *Psicoterapia e Scienze Umane*, 20: 3–19.

Figlio, K. and Young, R. (1986b) 'An Interview with John Bowlby', *Free Associations*, 6: 36–64.

'Defensive processes in the light of attachment theory', (1987a) in *Attachment and the Therapeutic Process*, D. P. Schwartz, J. L. Sacksteder and Y. Akabane (eds), New York: International Universities Press.

'Attachment', 'Phobias', (1987b) in *The Oxford Companion to the Mind*, R. Gregory (ed.), Oxford and New York: Oxford University Press.

A Secure Base: Clinical Applications of Attachment Theory, (1988a) London: Routledge.
'Changing theories of childhood since Freud', (1988b) in *Freud in Exile*, E. Timms and N. Segal (eds), pp. 230–40, New Haven and London: Yale University Press.
'Developmental psychiatry comes of age', (1988c) *American Journal of Psychiatry*, 145: pp. 1–10.
'The role of attachment in personality development and psychopathology', (1989) in *The Course of Life*, vol. 1, 2nd edn, S. Greenspan and G. Pollock (eds), ch. 6, pp. 229–70, Madison, WI: International Universities Press.
Charles Darwin: A New Biography, (1990) London: Hutchinson.
'The role of the psychotherapist's personal resources in the therapeutic situation', (1991) *Tavistock Gazette* (Autumn).

GENERAL WORKS

Ainsworth, M. (1969) 'Object relations, dependency and attachment: a theoretical review of the infant–mother relationship', *Child Development*, 40: 969–1025.
—— (1982) 'Attachment: retrospect and prospect', in C. M. Parkes and J. Stevenson-Hinde (eds), *The Place of Attachment in Human Behaviour*, London: Tavistock.
—— (1989) 'Attachments beyond infancy', *American Psychologist*, 44: 709–16.
Ainsworth, M., Blehar, M., Waters, E. and Wall, S. (1978) *Patterns of Attachment: Assessed in the Strange Situation and at Home*, Hillsdale, NJ: Erlbaum.
Anderson, J. (1972) 'Attachment out of doors', in N. Blurton-Jones (ed.), *Ethological Studies of Child Behaviour*, Cambridge: Cambridge University Press.
Andry, R. (1962) 'Paternal and maternal roles in delinquency', in *Deprivation of Maternal Care: A Reassessment of its Effects*, Geneva: World Health Organisation Publications.
Balint, M. (1964) *Primary Love and Psychoanalytic Technique*, London: Tavistock.
—— (1968) *The Basic Fault*, London: Tavistock.
—— (1986) 'The unobtrusive analyst', in G. Kohon (ed.), *The British School of Psychoanalysis*, London: Free Associations.
Bateman, A. (1991) 'Borderline Personality Disorder', in J. Holmes (ed.), *Textbook of Psychotherapy in Psychiatric Practice*, Edinburgh: Churchill Livingstone.
Bateson, G. (1973) *Steps Towards an Ecology of Mind*, London: Paladin.
Beck, A., Rush, A., Shaw, B. and Emery, G. (1979) *Cognitive Therapy of Depression*, New York: Guilford.
Beebe, B. and Lachmann, F. (1988) 'The contribution of mother–infant mutual influence to the origins of self–object representation', *Psychoanalytic Psychology*, 5: 305–37.

Belsky, J. and Nezworski, T. (1988) *Clinical Implications of Attachment*, Hillsdale, NJ: Erlbaum.

Bettelheim, B. (1960) *The Informed Heart*, New York: Free Press.

Bion, W. (1978) *Second Thoughts*, London: Heinemann.

Birtchnell, J. (1984) 'Dependence and its relation to depression', *British Journal of Medical Psychology*, 57: 215–25.

—— (1988) 'Defining dependence', *British Journal of Medical Psychology*, 61: 111–23.

Bowie, (1991) *Lacan*, London: Fontana.

Bowlby, U. (1991) Personal communication.

Brazelton, T. and Cramer, B. (1991) *The Earliest Relationship*, London: Karnak.

Bretherton, I. (1985) 'Attachment Theory: retrospect and prospect', in I. Bretherton and E. Waters (eds), 'Growing points of attachment theory and research', *Monographs of the Society for Research in Child Development*, 50: 3–35.

—— (1987) 'New perspectives on attachment relations: security, communication and internal working models', in J. Osofsky (ed.), *Handbook of Infant Development*, New York: Wiley.

—— (1991a) 'Pouring new wine into old bottles: the social self as Internal Working Model', in M. Gunnar and L. Sroufe (eds), *Self Processes and Development*, Hillsdale, NJ: Erlbaum.

—— (1991b) 'Roots and growing points of attachment theory', in *Attachment Across the Life Cycle*, C. M. Parkes, J. Stevenson-Hinde and P. Marris (eds), London: Routledge.

Brown, G. and Harris, T. (1978) *The Social Origins of Depression*, London: Tavistock.

Bryer, J., Nelson, B., Miller, J. and Krol, P. (1987) 'Childhood sexual and physical abuse as factors in adult psychiatric illness', *American Journal of Psychiatry*, 144: 1426–30.

Bufalino, G. (1992) 'An island between heaven and hell', *Guardian*, 21 May.

Byng-Hall, J. (1980) 'Symptom bearer as marital distance regulator', *Family Process*, 19: 335–65.

—— (1985) 'The family script: a useful bridge between theory and practice', *Journal of Family Therapy*, 7: 301–5.

—— (1991a) 'The application of attachment theory to understanding and treatment in family therapy', in *Attachment Across the Life Cycle*, C. M. Parkes, J. Stevenson-Hinde and P. Marris (eds), London: Routledge.

—— (1991b) 'Memorial service for John Bowlby: address', *Tavistock Gazette* (Autumn).

—— (1991c) 'An appreciation of John Bowlby: his significance for family therapy', *Journal of Family Therapy*, 13: 5–16.

Byng-Hall, J. and Stevenson-Hinde, J. (1991) 'Attachment relationships within a family system', *Infant Mental Health Journal*, 12: 187–200.

Casement, P. (1985) *On Learning from the Patient*, London: Tavistock.

Caspi, A. and Elder, G. (1988) 'Emergent family patterns', in *Relation-*

ships within Families: Marital Influences, R. Hinde and J. Stevenson-Hinde (eds), Oxford: Oxford University Press.

Cassidy, J. (1988) 'The self as related to child–mother attachment at 6', *Child Development*, 59: 121–34.

Chodorow, N. (1978) *The Reproduction of Motherhood*, Berkeley, CA: University of California Press.

Craik, K. (1943) *The Nature of Explanation*, Cambridge: Cambridge University Press.

Crittenden, P. (1988) 'Maternal antecedents of attachment quality', in *Clinical Implications of Attachment*, J. Belsky and T. Nezworski (eds), Hillsdale, NJ: Erlbaum.

Darwin, C. (1872) *The Expression of the Emotions in Man and Animals*, London: John Murray.

Dawkins, R. (1977) *The Selfish Gene*, Oxford: Oxford University Press.

Dixon, N. (1971) *Subliminal Perception: The Nature of a Controversy*, London: McGraw-Hill.

Dixon, N. and Henley, S. (1991) 'Unconscious perception: possible implications of data from academic research for clinical practice', *Journal of Nervous and Mental Disease*, 79: 243–51.

Eagle, M. (1988) 'Psychoanalysis and the personal', in *Mind, Psychoanalysis, and Science*, P. Clark and C. Wright (eds), Oxford: Oxford University Press.

Fairbairn, R. (1952) *Psychoanalytic Studies of the Personality*, London: Tavistock.

Ferenczi, S. (1955) *Final Contributions to the Problems and Methods of Psychoanalysis*, London: Hogarth.

Fonagy, P. (1991) 'Thinking about thinking: some clinical and theoretical considerations in the treatment of a borderline patient', *International Journal of Psycho-Analysis*, 72: 639–56.

Fonagy, P., Steele, M. and Steele, H. (1992) 'Maternal representations of attachment during pregnancy predict the organisation of infant–mother attachment at one year of age', *Child Development* (in press).

Fonagy, P., Steele, M., Steele, H., Moran, G. and Higgins, A. (1991) 'The capacity for understanding mental states: the reflective self in parent and child and its significance for security of attachment', *Infant Mental Health Journal*, 12: 201–18.

Fraiberg, P., Adelson, E. and Shapiro, V. (1975) 'Ghosts in the nursery: a psychoanalytic approach to the problem of impaired infant–mother relationships', *Journal of the American Academy of Child Psychiatry*, 14: 387–422.

Frank, J. (1986) 'Psychotherapy: the transformation of meanings', *Journal of the Royal Society of Medicine*, 79: 341–6.

Freud, S. (1910) 'Leonardo da Vinci and a memory of his childhood', *Standard Edition of the Complete Psychological Works of Sigmund Freud*, SE 9, London: Hogarth.

— (1911) 'Formulations on the two principles of mental functioning', SE 12, London: Hogarth.

— (1913) 'On beginning the treatment', SE 12, London: Hogarth.

— (1917) 'Mourning and melancholia', SE 14, London: Hogarth.

— (1926) *Inhibitions, Symptoms, and Anxiety*, SE 20, London: Hogarth.

— (1929) *Civilisation and its Discontents*, SE 21, London: Hogarth.

Frost, R. (1954) *Collected Poems*, London: Penguin.

Gabbard, G. (1992) 'Psychodynamic psychiatry in the "decade of the brain"', *American Journal of Psychiatry*, 149: 991–8.

Gallwey, P. (1985) 'The psychodynamics of borderline personality', in *Aggression and Dangerousness*, D. Farrington and J. Gunn (eds), London: Wiley.

Gardner, H. (1957) *The Metaphysical Poets*, London: Penguin.

Garland, C. (1991) 'External disasters and the internal world', in *Textbook of Psychotherapy in Psychiatric Practice*, J. Holmes (ed.), Edinburgh: Churchill Livingstone.

Gathorne-Hardy, J. (1992) *Gerald Brennan*, London: Sinclair.

Grant, S. (1991) 'Psychotherapy with people who have been sexually abused', in *A Textbook of Psychotherapy in Psychiatric Practice*, J. Holmes (ed.), Edinburgh: Churchill Livingstone.

Greenberg, J. and Mitchell, S. (1983) *Object Relations in Psychoanalytic Theory*, London: Harvard University Press.

Greenberg, M., Cummings, M. and Cicchetti, B. (1988) *Attachment in the Preschool Years: Theory, Research and Intervention*, Hillsdale, NJ: Erlbaum.

Greenson, R. (1967) *The Technique and Practice of Psychoanalysis*, New York: International Universities Press.

Grosskurth, P. (1986) *Melanie Klein: Her World and her Work*, Cambridge, MA: Harvard University Press.

Grossman, K. and Grossman, K. (1991) 'Attachment quality as an organiser of emotional and behavioural responses in a longitudinal perspective', in *Attachment across the Life Cycle*, C. M. Parkes, J. Stevenson-Hinde and P. Marris (eds), London: Routledge.

Grossman, K., Grossman, K. and Schwann, A. (1986) 'Capturing the wider view of attachment: a re-analysis of Ainsworth's Strange Situation', in C. Elzard and P. Read (eds), *Measuring Emotions in Infants and Children*, Cambridge: Cambridge University Press.

Guntrip, H. (1974) *Schizoid Phenomena, Object Relations and the Self*, London: Hogarth.

Hamilton, V. (1985) 'John Bowlby: an ethological basis for psychoanalysis', in *Beyond Freud: A Study of Modern Psychoanalytic Theorists*, J. Reppen (ed.), New York: Analytic Press.

— (1986) 'Grief and mourning in Tennyson's In Memoriam', *Free Associations*, 7: 87–110.

— (1991) 'Personal reminiscences of John Bowlby', *Tavistock Gazette* (Autumn).

Hanh, T. N. (1990) *Present Moment, Wonderful Moment*, Berkeley, CA: Parallax Press.

Harlow, H. (1958) 'The nature of love', *American Psychologist*, 13: 673–85.

Harris, T. and Bifulco, A. (1991) 'Loss of parent in childhood, attachment style and deprivation in adulthood', in *Attachment Across the*

Life Cycle, C. M. Parkes, J. Stevenson-Hinde and P. Marris (eds), London: Routledge.

Harris, T., Brown, G. and Bifulco, A. (1987) 'Loss of parent in childhood and adult psychiatric disorder: the role of social class position and premarital pregnancy', *Psychological Medicine*, 17: 163–83.

Hazan, C. and Shaver, P. (1987) 'Romantic love conceptualised as an attachment process', *Journal of Personal and Social Psychology*, 52: 511–24.

Heard, D. (1978) 'From object relations to attachment theory: a basis for family therapy', *British Journal of Medical Psychology*, 51, 67–76.

—— (1982) 'Family systems and the attachment dynamic', *Journal of Family Therapy*, 4: 99–116.

—— (1986) 'Introduction' to new edition of *The Origins of Love and Hate* by Ian Suttie, London: Free Association Books.

Heard, D. and Lake, B. (1986) 'The attachment dynamic in adult life', *British Journal of Psychiatry*, 149: 430–8.

Henderson, S., Byrne, D. and Duncan-Jones, P. (1981) *Neurosis and the Social Environment*, Sydney: Academic Press.

Herman, J., Perry, C. and Kolk, B. (1989) 'Childhood trauma in Borderline Personality Disorder', *American Journal of Psychiatry*, 146: 490–5.

Hinde, R. (1982a) 'Attachment: some conceptual and biological issues', in *The Place of Attachment in Human Behaviour*, C. M. Parkes and J. Stevenson-Hinde (eds), London: Tavistock.

—— (1982b) *Ethology*, London: Fontana.

—— (1987) *Individuals, Relationships and Culture: Links between Ethology and the Social Sciences*, Cambridge: Cambridge University Press.

Hinde, R. and McGinnis, L. (1977) 'Some factors influencing the effects of temporary infant–mother separation', *Psychological Medicine*, 7: 197–212.

Holmes, J. (1991) *A Textbook of Psychotherapy in Psychiatric Practice*, Edinburgh: Churchill Livingstone.

—— (1992) *Between Art and Science*, London: Routledge.

—— (1993) 'Psychotherapeutic aspects of the acute psychiatric admission ward', *Psychoanalytic Psychotherapy* (in press).

Holmes, J. and Lindley, R. (1989) *The Values of Psychotherapy*, Oxford: Oxford University Press.

Hopkins, J. (1990) 'The observed infant of attachment theory', *British Journal of Psychotherapy*, 6: 460–70.

Horney, K. (1924) 'On the genesis of the castration complex in women', *International Journal of Psycho-Analysis*, 5: 50–65.

—— (1932) 'The dread of women', *International Journal of Psycho-Analysis*, 13: 348–60.

Horowitz, M. (1988) *An Introduction to Psychodynamics*, London: Routledge.

Humphrey, N. (1992) *A History of the Mind*, London: Chatto & Windus.

Hunter, V. (1991) 'John Bowlby: an interview', *Psychoanalytic Review*, 78: 159–65.

Ijzendoorn, M. and Kroonenberg, P. (1988) 'Cross cultural patterns of attachment: a meta-analysis of the Strange Situation', *Child Development*, 59: 147–56.

Jones, E. (1949) *Hamlet and Oedipus*, London: Gollancz.

Jones, K. (1985) *Buddhism and the Bombs*, Preston: Buddhist Peace Fellowship (UK).

Kernberg, O. (1975) 'A systems approach to priority setting of interventions in groups', *International Journal of Group Psychotherapy*, 25: 251–75.

King, P. and Steiner, R. (1990) *The Freud–Klein Controversy 1941–5*, London: Routledge.

Klein, M. (1986) *The Selected Melanie Klein*, J. Mitchell (ed.), London: Penguin.

Kobak, R. and Sceery, A. (1988) 'Attachment in late adolescence: working models, affect regulation, and representations of self and others', *Child Development*, 59: 135–46.

Kohut, H. (1977) *The Restoration of the Self*, New York: International Universities Press.

Kraemer, S. (1991) 'Personal reminiscences of John Bowlby', *Tavistock Gazette* (Autumn).

Kuhn, T. (1962) *The Structure of Scientific Revolutions*, Chicago: University of Chicago Press.

Lake, B. (1985) 'The concept of ego-strength in psychotherapy', *British Journal of Psychiatry*, 147: 411–28.

Leff, J. and Vaughn, C. (1983) *Expressed Emotion in Families*, New York: Guilford Press.

Leupnitz, D. (1988) *The Family Interpreted*, New York: Basic Books.

Lieberman, A. and Pawl, J. (1988) 'Disorders of attachment in the second year: a clinical developmental perspective', in *Attachment in the Preschool Years: Theory, Research and Intervention*, M. Greenberg, B. Cicchetti and M. Cumming (eds), Hillsdale, NJ: Erlbaum.

Lieberman, A., Weston, D. and Paul, J. (1991) 'Preventive intervention and outcome with anxiously attached dyads', *Child Development*, 62: 199–209.

Liotti, G. (1987) 'The resistance to change of cognitive structures: a counterproposal to psychoanalytic metapsychology', *Journal of Cognitive Psychotherapy*, 1: 87–104.

—— (1991) 'Insecure attachment and agoraphobia', in *Attachment across the Life Cycle*, C. M. Parkes, J. Stevenson-Hinde and P. Marris (eds), London: Routledge.

Lorenz, K. (1952) *King Solomon's Ring*, London: Methuen.

Lovelock, J. (1979) *Gaia*, Oxford: Oxford University Press.

Mackenzie, M. (1991) 'Reminiscences of John Bowlby', *Tavistock Gazette* (Autumn).

Mackie, A. (1981) 'Attachment theory: its relevance to the therapeutic alliance', *British Journal of Medical Psychology*, 54: 203–12.

Mackinnon, A., Henderson, S. and Andrews, G. (1991) 'The Parental Bonding Instrument: a measure of perceived or actual parental behaviour', *Acta Psychiatrica Scandinavica*, 83: 153–9.

Mahler, M., Pine, F. and Bergman, A. (1975) *The Psychological Birth of the Human Infant*, London: Hutchinson.

Main, M. (1990) *A Typology of Human Attachment Organisation Assessed with Discourse, Drawings and Interviews*, New York: Cambridge University Press.

—— (1991) 'Metacognitive knowledge, metacognitive monitoring, and singular (coherent) vs multiple (incoherent) models of attachment: findings and directions for future research', in *Attachment across the Life Cycle*, C. M. Parkes, J. Stevenson-Hinde and P. Marris (eds), London: Routledge.

Main, M. and Goldwyn, R. (1984) 'Predicting rejection of her infant from mother's representation of her own experience: implications for the abused-abuser intergenerational cycle', *International Journal of Child Abuse and Neglect*, 8: 203–17.

Main, M., Kaplan, K. and Cassidy, J. (1985) 'Security in infancy, childhood and adulthood. A move to the level of representation', in 'Growing points of attachment theory and research', I. Bretherton and E. Waters (eds), *Monographs of the Society for Research in Child Development*, 50: 66–104.

Main, M. and Weston, D. (1982) 'Avoidance of the attachment figure in infancy', in *The Place of Attachment in Human Behaviour*, C. M. Parkes and J. Stevenson-Hinde (eds), London: Tavistock.

Malan, D. (1976) *Towards the Validation of Dynamic Psychotherapy*, Chichester: Plenum.

—— (1991) 'John Bowlby remembered', *Tavistock Gazette* (Autumn).

Marris, P. (1991) 'The social construction of uncertainty' in *Attachment across the Life Cycle*, C. M. Parkes, J. Stevenson-Hinde and P. Marris (eds), London: Routledge.

Masson, J. (1985) *The Assault on Truth*, London: Penguin.

Mawson, D., Marks, I., Ramm, L. and Stern, R. (1981) 'Guided mourning for morbid grief: a controlled study', *British Journal of Psychiatry*, 138: 185–93.

Mead, M. (1962) 'A cultural anthropologist's approach to maternal deprivation', in *Deprivation of Maternal Care: A Reassessment of its Effects*, Geneva: World Health Organisation Publications.

Meares, R. and Hobson, R. (1977) 'The persecutory therapist', *British Journal of Medical Psychology*, 50: 349–59.

Melges, F. and Swartz, M. (1989) 'Oscillations of attachment in Borderline Personality Disorder', *American Journal of Psychiatry*, 146: 1115–20.

Meltzer, D. and Williams, M. (1988) *The Apprehension of Beauty*, Perthshire: Clunie Press.

Menzies-Lyth, I. (1988) *Containing Anxieties in Institutions*, London: Free Association Books.

—— (1989) *The Dynamic of the Social*, London: Free Association Books.

Middleton, P. (1991) 'Some psychological bases of the institution of war' in *The Institution of War*, R. Hinde (ed.), London: Macmillan.

Minuchin, S. (1974) *Families and Family Therapy*, London: Tavistock.

Minuchin, S., Rosman, B. and Baker, L. (1978) *Psychosomatic Families*, Cambridge, MA: Harvard University Press.

Mitscherlich, A. (1962) *Societies Without the Father*, New York: Schocken.

Murray, L. and Cooper, P. (1992) 'Clinical application of attachment theory and research: change in infant attachment with brief psychotherapy', *Journal of Child Psychology and Psychiatry* (in press).

New, C. and David, M. (1985) *For the Children's Sake*, London: Penguin.

Newcombe, N. and Lerner, J. (1982) 'Britain between the wars: the historical context of Bowlby's theory of attachment', *Psychiatry*, 45: 1–12.

Oakley, A. (1981) *Subject Women*, Oxford: Martin Robertson.

Parker, G. (1983) 'Parental "Affectionless Control" as an antecedent to adult depression', *Archives of General Psychiatry*, 40: 956–60.

Parker, G., Barret, R. and Hickie, I. (1992) 'From nurture to network: examining links between perception of parenting received in childhood and social bonds in adulthood', *American Journal of Psychiatry*, 149: 877–85.

Parker, G. and Hadzi-Pavlovic, D. (1984) 'Modification of levels of depression in mother-bereaved women by parental and marriage relationships', *Psychological Medicine*, 14: 125–35.

Parkes, C. M. (1964) 'The effects of bereavement on physical and mental health', *British Medical Journal*, 2: 274–9.

—— (1971) 'Psychosocial transitions: a field for study', *Social Science and Medicine*, 5: 101–15.

—— (1975) *Bereavement: Studies of Grief in Adult Life*, London: Penguin.

—— (1985) 'Bereavement', *British Journal of Psychiatry*, 146: 11–17.

Parkes, C. M. and Stevenson-Hinde, J. (1982) *The Place of Attachment in Human Behaviour*, London: Tavistock.

Parkes, C. M., Stevenson-Hinde, J. and Marris, P. (eds) (1991) *Attachment across the Life Cycle*, London: Routledge.

Parkes, C. M. and Weiss, R. (1983) *Recovery from Bereavement*, New York: Basic Books.

Parsons, T. (1964) *Social Structure and Personality*, New York: Free Press.

Patrick, M., Hobson, P., Castle, P. *et al.* (1992) 'Personality Disorder and the mental representation of early social experience', Paper presented to the MRC Child Psychiatry Unit at the Institute of Psychiatry, London.

Pedder, J. (1982) 'Failure to mourn and melancholia', *British Journal of Psychiatry*, 141: 329–37.

—— (1986) 'Attachment and new beginning', in *The British School of Psychoanalysis*, G. Kohon (ed.), London: Free Association Books.

—— (1987) 'Some biographical contributions to psychoanalytic theories', *Free Associations*, 10: 102–16.

—— (1992) 'Psychoanalytic views of aggression: some theoretical problems', *British Journal of Medical Psychology*, 65: 95–106.

Peterfreund, E. (1983) *The Process of Psychoanalytic Therapy*, Hillsdale, NJ: Analytic Press.

Phelps-Brown, H. (1992) Personal communication.

Pines, M. (1991) 'A history of psychodynamic psychiatry in Britain', in *A Textbook of Psychotherapy in Psychiatric Practice*, J. Holmes (ed.), Edinburgh: Churchill Livingstone.

Post, R. (1992) 'Transduction of psychosocial stress into the neurobiology of recurrent affective disorder', *American Journal of Psychiatry*, 149: 999–1010.

Raverat, G. (1952) *Period Piece*, London: Faber.

Rayner, E. (1992) 'John Bowlby's contribution, a brief survey', *Bulletin of the British Psycho-Analytical Society*, 20–3.

Rey, H. (1975) Personal communication.

Riviere, J. (1955) 'The unconscious phantasy of an inner world reflected in examples from literature', in *New Directions in Psychoanalysis*, M. Klein, P. Heimann and R. Money-Kyrle (eds), London: Hogarth.

Roazen, P. (1976) *Freud and his Followers*, London: Penguin.

Roberts, G. (1992) 'The origins of delusion', *British Journal of Psychiatry*, 161: 298–308.

Robertson, J. (1952) *Film: A Two-Year-Old Goes to Hospital*, London: Tavistock.

Rodman, D. (1987) *The Spontaneous Gesture*, Cambridge, MA: Harvard University Press.

Rustin, M. (1991) *The Good Society and the Inner World*, London: Verso.

Rutter, M. (1972) 'Maternal deprivation reconsidered', *Journal of Psychosomatic Research*, 16: 241–50.

—— (1979) 'Maternal deprivation 1972–1978, new findings, new concepts, new approaches', *Child Development*, 50: 283–305.

—— (1980) 'Attachment and the development of social relations', in *The Scientific Foundations of Developmental Psychiatry*, M. Rutter (ed.), London: Heinemann.

—— (1981) *Maternal Deprivation Reassessed*, 2nd edn, London: Penguin.

—— (1985) 'Resilience in the face of adversity: protective factors and resistance to psychiatric disorder', *British Journal of Psychiatry*, 147: 598–611.

—— (1986) 'Meyerian psychobiology, personality development and the role of life experiences', *American Journal of Psychiatry*, 143: 1077–87.

—— (1987) 'Temperament, personality, and personality disorder', *British Journal of Psychiatry*, 150: 443–58.

—— (1990) *Essays in Honour of Robert Hinde*, P. Bateson (ed.), Cambridge: Cambridge University Press.

Rutter, M. and Quinton, D. (1984) 'Long-term follow-up of women institutionalised in childhood', *British Journal of Developmental Psychology*, 18: 225–34.

Rycroft, C. (1985) *Psychoanalysis and Beyond*, London: Chatto.

—— (1992) Personal communication.

Ryle, A. (1990) *Cognitive Analytic Therapy: Active Participation in Change*, Chichester: Wiley.

Schank, B. (1982) *Dynamic Memory: A Theory of Reminding and Learning in Computers and People*, Cambridge, MA: Cambridge University Press.

Shafer, R. (1976) *A New Language for Psychoanalysis*, London: Yale University Press.

Shaver, P. and Hazan, C. (1988) 'A biased overview of the study of love', *Journal of Social and Personal Relationships*, 5: 473–501.

Sheldon, A. and West, M. (1989) 'The functional discrimination of attachment and affiliation', *British Journal of Psychiatry*, 155: 18–23.

Skynner, R. (1976) *One Flesh, Separate Persons*, London: Constable.

Spence, D. (1982) *Narrative Truth and Historical Truth: Meaning and Interpretation in Psychoanalysis*, New York: Norton.

Spitz, R. (1950) 'Anxiety in infancy', *International Journal of Psycho-Analysis*, 31: 138–43.

Sroufe, A. (1979) 'The coherence of individual development', *American Psychologist*, 34: 834–41.

Steiner, R. (1985) 'Some thoughts about tradition and change arising from an examination of the British Psycho-Analytical Society's Controversial Discussions 1943–1944', *International Review of Psycho-Analysis*, 12: 27–71.

Stern, D. (1985) *The Interpersonal World of the Infant*, New York: Basic Books.

Storr, A. (1991) 'John Bowlby', *Munks Roll*, London: Royal College of Physicians.

Strachey, J. (1934) 'On the nature of the therapeutic action of psychoanalysis', *International Journal of Psycho-Analysis*, 15: 127–59.

Sutherland, J. (1991) 'Reminiscences of John Bowlby', *Tavistock Gazette* (Autumn).

Suttie, I. (1935) *The Origins of Love and Hate*, London: Kegan Paul.

Symington, N. (1986) *The Analytic Experience*, London: Free Association Books.

Tennant, C. (1988) 'Parental loss in childhood', *Archives of General Psychiatry*, 45: 1045–55.

Tinbergen, N. (1951) *The Study of Instinct*, Oxford: Clarendon Press.

Tizard, B. (1977) *Adoption: A Second Chance*, London: Open Books.

Trowell, J. (1991) 'Personal reminiscences of John Bowlby', *Tavistock Gazette* (Autumn).

Truax, C. and Carkhuff, R. (1967) *Towards Effective Counselling and Psychotherapy: Training and Practice*, Chicago: Aldine.

Van de Kolk, B. (1987) *Psychological Trauma*, Washington, DC: American Psychiatric Press.

Vaughn, B. and Egeland, B. (1979) 'Individual differences in infant–mother attachment at twelve and eighteen months', *Child Development*, 50: 971–5.

Vygotsky, L. (1962) *Thought and Language*, Cambridge, MA: MIT Press.

Waddington, C. (1977) *Tools for Thought*, London: Cape.

Webster, C. (1991) 'Psychiatry and the early National Health Service: the role of the Mental Health Standing Advisory Committee', in *150*

Years of British Psychiatry, G. Berrios and H. Freeman (eds), London: Gaskell.

Weiss, R. (1982) 'Attachment in adult life', in *The Place of Attachment in Human Behaviour*, C. M. Parkes and J. Stevenson-Hinde (eds), London: Routledge.

Westen, D. (1990) 'Towards a revised theory of borderline object relations: contributions of empirical research', *International Journal of Psycho-Analysis*, 71: 661–93.

Winnicott, D. (1965) *The Maturational Process and the Facilitating Environment*, London: Hogarth.

—— (1971) *Playing and Reality*, London: Penguin.

Wolkind, S., Hall, F. and Pawlby, S. (1977) 'Individual differences in mothering behaviour', in *Epidemiological Approaches in Child Psychiatry*, P. Graham (ed.), London: Academic Press.

Wright, K. (1991) *Vision and Separation*, London: Free Association Books.

Zetzel, E. (1956) 'Current concepts of transference', *International Journal of Psychoanalysis*, 37: 369–76.

Zweig-Frank, H. and Parris, J. (1991) 'Parents' emotional neglect and overprotection according to recollections of patients with BPD', *American Journal of Psychiatry*, 148: 648–51.

Index

abuse 123, 124
abnormal grief 183–4
Adult Attachment Interview, the 13, 113–14, 146, 162, 180, 194, 215, 217
'affectionless psychopath' 21, 22, 39, 50, 87
affective processing 162–9
affiliation 172–3
aggression 22, 88, 91, 108, 117, 132, 203
agoraphobia 188–90
Ainsworth, Mary 1, 2, 26, 27, 70, 72, 85, 103, 104–6, 114, 224
Alford, John 18
Always too considerate (case history) 171–2
Ambivalent Attachment 68, 79–81, 116, 117, 150, 163, 217
ambivalent grief syndrome 183
Anderson, J. 70
anxious attachment 141–2
assuagement and disassuagement 217–18
attachment; in adult life 81–4; anxiety, internal working models 61–7; behavioural system 68, 76; behaviour, as reciprocal relationship 75–8; and the secure base in psychotherapy 151–60
Attachment and New Beginning 167–8

Attachment, Separation and Loss 29
attachment system, development of 73–8
Attachment Theory 59–102, 132–5; and community psychiatry 196–9; and expressed emotion in schizophrenia 190–2; and language 110–12; and personality development 103, 117–18; and psychiatric disorder 177–99; and the practice of psychotherapy 149–76; and psychoanalysis 127–48; and society 200–9; spatial character of 67; theoretical and experimental background 62–7
attunement 107–8, 156–8
autobiographical competence 85–102, 158–60, 181–3
autonomy, security 113
avoidance of painful effect 116
avoidant attachment 79–81, 116–17, 150, 163, 217

Balint, M. 66, 136, 153–5, 222
Bateson, Gregory 175
Beck, Aaron 54, 218–19
bereaved wife in the casualty department, A (case history) 90
Bettelheim, B. 19, 22
Bick, Esther 26
Bion, W. 8, 9, 23, 54, 165, 174
Boston, Mary 26

borderline personality disorder
192–6, 218
Bowlby, Ben 25
Bowlby, Jim 15
Bowlby, John: biographical
background 13–36; critics 44–5;
and Darwin 34, 35; family life
24; and family therapy 173–6;
and Kohut 143; the man 30–4;
and nuclear weapons 207;
outrage 44; and the psycho-
analytical establishment 3–5, 8,
129–32; psycho-analytical
training 19–23; reservations
about psycho-analysis 128–32;
scientific method 4, 6–7; and
Winnecott 137–42
Bowlby, Lady 14, 16–17
Bowlby, Major General Sir
Anthony 14, 17
Bowlby, Tony 15, 22, 24, 29
Bowlby, Ursula 25
Brazelton, T. 8, 66, 108, 156
Bretherton 2, 120, 122, 215
Brown, G. and Harris, T. 186
Brown, Sir Henry Phelps 16
Bryer, J. 192
Bufalino, Gesualdo 208
Burlington, D. 39
Byng-Hall 2, 33–4, 175

Casement, P. 168
Caspi, A. and Elder, G. 55
Centre for Behavioural Studies,
California 28
Child Care and the Growth of
Love 27, 38–45; and psycho-
analytic principles 43–4
Child Care and the Growth of
Maternal Love 198
child care and professionalism 41
children in hospital 88
Chodorow, N. 47
chronic grief 183
Civilization and its Discontents 203
clock-watcher, The (case history)
109
cognitive analytic therapy 147,
210, 218–19

cognitive therapy 78, 146–8
cognition in therapy 169–72
Community Care Bill 1993, the
198
community psychiatry,
Attachment Theory and 196–9
companionable interaction 172–3
Contrasting Opening Moves (case
history) 172–3
controversial discussions 219
core state 149
Craik, Kenneth 62, 78
Cramer, B. 66
cross-modal attunement 107
cycles of deprivation 42–3

Darwin, Charles 13–14, 25, 30, 34,
91, 104, 162, 164, 215
Darwin and Bowlby 34–5, 162, 164
Dawkins, R. 176
defence, primary and secondary
150
democracy 201–2
delayed grief 183
depression 185–8
depressive position 186, 219
developmental pathways through
childhood 51–2
Developmental psychiatry comes
of age 177
Dickens, Charles 56–8
dismissing-detached 113
Donne, John 100–2
Durbin, Evan 19, 22–3, 25
Dylan, Bob 196

Eder, David 20
ego control, ego resiliency 110
environment as determinant of
pathology 21, 129–31, 160–2
environment mother, object
mother 140
Epictetus 181
epigenetic and homuncular
models 65, 81, 219
ethology 5, 22, 27, 61–2, 64, 124,
137, 220
expressed emotion 190, 220–1

Fairbairn, R. 66, 82, 136, 222
family care versus institutional
    care 40–1
family therapy 173–6
fathers in attachment patterns 176
feminist critique, the 45–9
Ferenczi, S. 66
*Forty-four juvenile thieves, their
    characters and their home life*
    21, 27, 50, 84, 86
Fraiberg, S. 116
Frank, J. 151
Freud, Anna 3–6, 9, 20, 23, 26,
    39, 66, 128, 219
freudian drive theory 47, 62–6,
    132–5
Freud Memorial Professor of
    Psychoanalysis 30
Freud, Sigmund 62–3, 65–6, 74,
    82, 93, 128–9, 144, 148, 152,
    172, 203, 205, 207, 209, 212
Fry, Elizabeth 38
Fonagy, P. 114, 117–18, 193, 215

Galileo 104
Gallwey, P. 196
global insecurity 206–9
Glover, Edward 9, 24, 128
Goldfarb, W. 39
Golding, W. 208
government provision 42
Guntrip, H. 28
Grossman, K. and Grossman, K.
    2, 110, 114

Hallam, Arthur 97
Hamlet 144, 156
Hamilton, Victoria 33
Harlow, H. 64, 72
Harris, T. and Bifulco, A. 185,
    187
Harris, Mrs Mattie 26
Hart, Bernard 20
Haszi-Pavlovic 54
Heard, Dorothy 2, 29, 175
Heard, D. and Lake, B. 97, 217
Heimann, Paula 9
Henderson, S. 181–2
Herman, J. 192, 195

Hinde, Robert 2, 28, 49, 62
Hobson, P. 194, 215
Holden, Hyla 30
holding environment, the 74,
    120–2, 138, 139
Holmes, J. and Lindley, R. 151,
    181
homuncular and epigenetic
    models 65, 81, 219
Horney, K. 48
Humphrey, N. 148
Hungarian school 66
Huxley, Julian 27

I hate myself (case history) 119–22
*Influence of the environment in the
    developmental of neurosis and
    neurotic character, the* 21
inhibitions, symptoms and anxiety
    62–3
In Memoriam 96–7, 99–100
insecurity, ambivalence 105
insecurity, avoidance 105, 123
insecure attachment 68
insecurity, disorganized 105
Institute of Psycho-Analysis 19
intergenerational transmission of
    attachment 112–13, 117
internal working models 78–9,
    116, 221
*International Journal of Psycho-
    Analysis* 21
Interview Schedule for Social
    Interaction (ISSI) 182
Isaacs, Susan 9

Jones, Ernest 9, 24–5, 128–9, 144

Kelly, Edward 97
Kernberg, O. 199
King, Edward 97
King Solomon's Ring 27, 62
Kleinians 4–6, 28, 58, 66, 74,
    130–1, 136, 144
Klein, Melanie 3–9, 19–20, 22–3,
    26–7, 36, 63, 69, 78, 93–4,
    128–31, 144, 160, 165, 210, 212,
    219, 222

Lacanians 144–5
Laing, R. D. 28
Lake, B. 180–1
language coherence and
    Attachment Theory 110–12
Leonardo 74
Leupnitz, S. 47
Lewis, Aubrey 19
Lieberman, A. and Paul, J. 122
line of continuity 141
Liotti, G. 189
London Child Guidance Clinic 19
lonely widow, The (case history)
    92
Longstaff, U. 24–5
Lord of the Flies 208
Lorenz, Konrad 18, 27, 62, 64
loss, anger and grief 86, 179–80
loss and psychiatric disorder
    179–80
Lycidas 96–8

Mahler, M. 136
Main, M. 2, 111, 113, 193, 194,
    215
Main, M. and Goldberg 114
Making and Breaking of
    Affectional Bonds, The 1, 30
Marris, P. 2, 204, 205, 206
Maternal Care and Mental Health
    27, 38
maternal deprivation 37–58, 221–2
Maudsley, the 19
Mayhew, H. 38
Mead, Margaret 46
Meltzer, D. 29
metacognitive monitoring 222
Middleton, P. 207–8
Milton, John 96–8, 102
Minuchin, S. 175
monotropy 68–9, 222
Morbid jealousy and Agoraphobia
    (case history) 189–90
Mostyn, May, Lady Bowlby 14,
    16–17
mourning and adult
    psychopathology 95–6
mourning, an anatomy of 89–95

Mrs W: I can't bear to look (case
    history) 184

narrative competence 9, 145–6,
    150, 214
Nature of Exploration, The 78
Nature of the child's tie to his
    mother, The 28
Neill, A. S. 18, 22
New, C. and David, M. 45–6
numbing 90

object mother–environment
    mother 140
object-relations theory 47, 63, 66,
    103, 132–6, 149, 215, 222–3
ocnophils and philobats 154
Oedipus Complex, the 66, 69, 128,
    161, 176, 205
Oliver Twist 56–8, 169
omnipotence, bringing into 165,
    168
Origins of Love and Hate 20, 62
Origin of Species, The 164

Palo Alto group 175
paranoid-schizoid position 219
Parker, G. 54, 187–94, 223
Parker's Parental Bonding
    Instrument 187, 194, 223
Parkes, Colin Murray 2, 29, 89
Parsons, T. 47
pathological grief 183
Payne, Sylvia 9, 23, 27, 128
Pedder, J. 167–8, 186–7, 195
perceptual defence 223
personal aggressiveness and war
    22
Peter, stringing a story together
    (case history) 158–60
phantasy 6
philobats and ocnophils 154
phobias 188–90
Piaget 136
Post, R. 95
post-Bowlbian research 111, 115
post-Bowlbians 1, 2, 111, 115, 155,
    193
post-Freudians 136–43

post-war period 26, 136–43
preoccupied-entangled 113
professionalism, and child care 41
protest, withdrawal, detachment
    89
psychiatric disorder and
    Attachment Theory 177–99
psychoanalysis as hermeneutics 8,
    136, 143, 145–6
psychoanalysis as science 143–4,
    146
Psycho-Analytic Society, The
    British 28, 213, 219; warring
    factions 3–6, 23–4, 128–9
psychology and democracy 202
Psychology of Insanity 20

Quinton, D. 54

Raverat, Gwen 211
reality and trauma 160–2
Rees, J. R. 24
Rivers, W. H. 20
Riviere, Joan 4, 9, 19, 27, 78, 128,
    130, 137, 212
Robertson, James 4, 26, 68, 84, 88
Rustin, M. 144, 206
Rutter, Michael 29, 38, 48–50, 54
Rycroft, C. 29, 138
Ryle, A. 54, 147

Safe-breathing: secure base (case
    history) 169
Sarah's 'ums' and 'aahs' (case
    history) 157–8
schizophrenia 190–2
Scott, Clifford 210
secure attachment 105; and
    insecure attachment, roots of 106
Secure Base, A 1, 30
secure base effect, the 70, 223–4
self-esteem 53
self-reflection 116
Separation, Attachment and Loss
    29, 188
separation 39; early studies 86–8;
    protest 72
Shaver, P. and Hazan, C. 180
Skye 30

Skynner, Robin 175–6
smiling and pattern recognition
    73–5
Social Referencing (case history)
    75
society, Attachment Theory and
    200–9
Springs of Action and of Thought
    34
Sroufe, A. 2, 106, 110
state dependent learning 166
steeplejack's wife, The (case
    history) 82
Stern, Daniel 8, 73, 107–8, 141,
    156, 193
Stevens, Adrian and Kate 25
Strachey, James 128
Strange Situation, the 72, 104–6,
    224; as a predictor of social
    adjustment 109–10
Sutherland, Jock 23, 26, 33
Suttie, Ian 20, 24, 62, 65
systemic (definition) 224

Tavistock Clinic, the 24, 26–7, 29,
    89, 173, 175, 213
Tennyson, Alfred, Lord 96–7,
    99–100
theft 139
therapeutic alliance and the 'real'
    relationship 152–5
therapist as secure base 152–5
therapists and parents 155–6
Tinbergen, N. 27, 62
Tizard, B. 51
tonsilectomy, the (case history)
    166–7
Too many telephone calls (case
    history) 191–2
touch in therapy 167–9
trauma 160–2
transgenerational transmission of
    neurosis 20
Trist, Eric 23, 33
Tulving, E. 158
Two-year-old Goes to Hospital, A
    26

unexpected grief syndrome 183

University College Hospital 19–20
'Uppie . . . uppie' (case history)
  123
unresolved-disorganized 113

*Valediction: forbidding mourning,
  A* 100–2
violence and a social facade (case
  history) 71–2

Waddington, C. 219
war years 23
Weiss, R. 97

Westen, D. 131
widower – at twenty-six, A (case
  history) 94–5
Williams 144
Winnicott 8, 9, 28, 36, 40, 57,
  73–4, 78, 84, 104, 136, 158,
  164–6, 168, 196, 197, 222; and
  Bowlby 137–42
World Health Organization 27
Wright, Kenneth 73–4, 78

York Terrace 25
yearning, searching, anger 90–1

The SOLO Librarian's Sourcebook

To my husband, Steve Bremseth, and my parents, Helen and Chester Siess—for their love, patience, and support.

The SOLO Librarian's Sourcebook

By Judith A. Siess

Information Today, Inc.
Medford, NJ
1997

Copyright© 1997 by: Information Today, Inc.
143 Old Marlton Pike
Medford, NJ 08055

Printed in the United States of America.

Library of Congress Cataloging-in-Publication Data

Siess, Judith A.
    The SOLO librarian's sourcebook / by Judith A. Siess.
        p.   cm.
    Includes bibliographical references and index.
    ISBN 1-57387-032-3 (hc)
    1. Small libraries—United States—Administration. 2. Library science—United States.   I. Title.
    Z678 S56   1997
    025.1—dc21   97-9949
                                                                        CIP

Price: $39.50

Editor: Diane Zelley
Cover Design: Jeanne Wachter

Table of Contents

Preface vii

Acknowledgments ix

Introduction 1

PART ONE: WHO WE ARE

Chapter 1. What Is a SOLO? 9

Chapter 2. Management Issues 27

Chapter 3. One More Pair of Hands—or One Less:
            Outsourcing and Downsizing 53

Chapter 4. The View from Abroad 71

Chapter 5. Education for SOLOs and Others 83

Chapter 6. The Information Superhighway:
            Technology and the SOLO Librarian 103

Chapter 7. The Future of SOLO Librarianship 117

PART TWO: RESOURCES

Chapter 8. Organizations 135

Chapter 9. A SOLO's Guide to Education 143

Chapter 10. Vendors and Suppliers 169

Chapter 11. Books and Journals 183

Chapter 12. Internet Sites and Listservs 201

Appendix I.   Library Education Questionnaire 217

Appendix II. Detailed Analysis of Questionnaire Responses . . . 219

Appendix III. SOLO Librarian Survey 223

Appendix IV. Demographics: Results of Surveys 225

Bibliography 229

Index 243

Preface

It is a privilege and an honor to have been asked to introduce Judith Siess's important contribution to the literature of information services. During the two decades that I have been involved in one-person librarianship, it has become increasingly clear that the information services professional working alone is the "wave of the future." In those two decades, I have witnessed an enormous growth of interest in the management of the single-staff information services operation, a growth that has connected quite naturally with a growth of interest in the subject within the information service field as a discipline in itself. There is no longer any question as to whether there *should* be one-person, or solo, information practitioners. The fact of the matter is, this category of information employee exists—in great numbers—and the management of the one-person, single-staff library is now an accepted and well-documented (and well-studied) branch of the information services field.

Whether we are called "solo librarians," "one-man bands," or "one-person librarians" is, in the final analysis, pretty much irrelevant, for in addition to its place in the information services discipline, the subject of solo librarianship—as a management practice—is now also a respected complementary adjunct to management in general. This is not surprising, considering the number of "sub-disciplines" (as they might be called) that make up the information services "umbrella." Those with senior management responsibility for the effective and efficient operation of various information-related activities such as records management, archives management, computer services, telecommunications operations, information brokerage, and the like—to say nothing of those to whom librarians report—have all come to look to one-person librarianship as a management model, and Siess's book, while ostensibly for solo librarians, will in fact be of value to any information delivery agency that has a single-staff unit as part of its component make-up.

What Siess has done with *The SOLO Librarian's Sourcebook* is to assemble in one place a very readable and—let it not go unnoticed—provocative introduction to solo librarianship itself, and then to follow that introduction with an amazingly complete and thorough list of resources that will come to the aid of the solo librarian. Every solo practitioner in the information services field needs to know about the resources that Siess has assembled here, and every one of them will benefit from knowing that these resources are available to help the solo practitioner when he or she needs a resource and does not have another professional information practitioner in the immediate organization.

As society changes to prepare itself for the twenty-first century and what is going to be (of this I have no doubt) a Golden Age in information services management and information delivery, the role of the solo librarian is going to become critical to the successful achievement of organization, community, and enterprise goals. In case some of our less knowledgeable colleagues fear that this critical role is to be an American trend, let me state unequivocally that the growth of one-person information services management as a distinct discipline within the information management community is an international phenomenon. Solo librarianship in various guises is being organized and promoted on a global scale, and it is only a matter of time (a very short time) before the management of the single-staff information operation will be recognized for what it is, the most efficient, direct, and customer-focused methodology for providing information to an identified user group. The time has come, it seems to me, to recognize that the single-staff information services professional is the key player in the information delivery process, and Judith Siess's important new book will do much to provide guidance, stimulation, and provocative assurance to the solo librarians who do this work.

Guy St. Clair
President
InfoManage / SMR
International New York, NY
August 1996

Acknowledgments

First of all, I want to thank Carol Bonham for starting this book and for letting me finish it. Guy St. Clair provided boundless encouragement, letting me bounce ideas off him, giving me access to his overseas contacts, and arranging the trip to South Africa. I also need to thank Guy, Andrew Berner, and Joan Williamson for the OPL books that preceded this one.

Several people helped by distributing questionnaires to SOLOs overseas: Evelin Morgenstern in Germany, Georgina Dale in Australia, Gill Owens and Kate Sherwood in South Africa. Roger Kluever of Elsag Bailey helped translate the German responses and Joanne Marshall shared the SLA competencies report with me before it was published. I appreciate the cooperation of the deans of the library schools who responded to my questionnaire. The people at my former place of employment, Elsag Bailey Process Automation, helped me in more ways than they know.

Finally, I want to thank all the members of SOLO Librarians Division of SLA for their comments and questionnaire responses. This book was written for you.

Introduction

In order to view this text as a valuable resource, the reader might need to know what my background is and whether I have the expertise to offer valuable information. As is common with librarians, I came to librarianship as a second career. I think I always wanted to be a librarian—maybe I was even destined to become one. In fact, the librarians at the Urbana (Illinois) Free Library helped pick out my name. I started reading by the time I was three and had my library card at four. I worked in my grade school and junior high libraries. After college (where, as a true child of the sixties, I received a B.A. in anthropology), I worked as research librarian for an urban planning firm, and I ran a small, SOLO library. Although I had had no formal training, years of working in and using libraries (including the great one at the University of Illinois at Urbana-Champaign), helped me to do a fairly creditable job of reclassifying the book collection and doing reference. It was here in Memphis, Tennessee, that I discovered my first special library—the Business and Technical Library of the Memphis Public Library. These wonderful folks would look up information for me and, if it was too much to give over the phone, have the books out and open for me to stop by. This was a good introduction to quality patron service.

After another few years of being sidetracked (marriage, a master's in anthropology, divorce, and several years as a secretary), I wound up in Champaign, Illinois, my hometown. There I worked as a statistical assistant to a price forecasting group in the Department of Agricultural Economics at the University of Illinois. Because I needed access to more data, I acquired the Agricultural Economics Reference Room—an unorganized collection of U.S. Department of Agriculture bulletins and statistics. About the same time I met the dean of the Graduate School of Library and Information Science, Chuck Davis (at bowling, of all places). He encouraged me to enroll in the master's program, which I did. I used the Ag Econ Reference Room as a lab for my

I

classwork, introducing online searching, an online catalog, and other innovations. I knew I wanted to work in a sci-tech library after graduation so I tailored my coursework appropriately. I took sci-tech reference, online searching, abstracting and indexing, statistical methods, government documents, special libraries, and cataloging. I also did a thesis, which was not encouraged, but I did it anyway. My research topic was "Information Needs and Information-Gathering Behavior of Research Engineers" and I had a wonderful time doing the research and learned a lot about how engineers approach (or do not approach) information and libraries. My advisor in library school was Professor Linda Smith who remains a mentor and friend.

The basis for my thesis research was an internship at the U.S. Army Corps of Engineers Construction Engineering Research Laboratory in Champaign. I went there one day a week for a summer, learning about the collection, answering reference questions, and shadowing their librarian, the late Martha Blake. I have always said that I learned 95 percent of what I know about being a librarian from Martha. She worked very closely with the engineers and they adored her; I knew then what being a librarian was all about and have always strived to make her proud of me.

After graduation in 1982, I went job hunting, and at an annual American Society for Information Science (ASIS) meeting, I found a job through ASIS's placement service. My first professional position was a SOLO library. I found I was hired to start a library for a small (fifteen employees) biotechnology company in Ashland, Ohio. As his wife was a librarian, the president understood the importance of information for research and development. Since I had never started a library before and knew absolutely nothing about enzymology, I turned to the librarians at the University of Illinois. The chemistry and biology librarians were very helpful in suggesting basic reference books to purchase, journals to subscribe to, and general guidelines for establishing a scientific library.

I was also very lucky right after I got to Ashland. Since my library consisted of a desk and a chair at that time, I went for information about stocking the office to the annual meeting of ASIS. I met a professor at the College of Wooster (twenty miles from Ashland) who was teaching his chemistry students how to search Chemical Abstracts online. I figured that if he could teach students who knew nothing about online searching how to become chemical searchers, he could teach me, who knew online searching but nothing about chemistry, the same. We contracted with him for forty hours of instruction and I became a chemical searcher. Eventually, although I was not an expert, I knew enough to do my job—proving that being open and creative is part of being a SOLO.

After three years in Ashland, the company downsized and the library was closed, and I moved on to Cleveland and worked for a friend who was establishing his own biotechnology company. I was secretary, administrative assistant, researcher, office manager, and librarian, a good experience, but not exactly what I had in mind. I got back to library work by subbing for a librarian on maternity leave from a contract chemical research facility. They had a good reference collection and I used the three months to familiarize myself with online services and reference books. I moved on to another maternity leave situation, this time at NASA Lewis Research Center where there was an even better collection, many librarians to learn from, interesting reference work, but still not what I wanted. Finally, I got a call from the Special Libraries Association (SLA) Cleveland chapter placement officer about a job at Bailey Controls Company. I had seen the ad but I figured I was overqualified since it did not require a degree. The placement officer assured me that it was just what I was looking for, so I applied. To make a long story short, I got the job and spent eight years there.

My tenure at Bailey (now Elsag Bailey Process Automation) was interesting, challenging, frustrating, rewarding, and nearly everything I could have asked for. I was the only information provider for what is now a $2 billion company with over 10,000 employees in the United States, Europe, Asia, the Middle East, and South America. The job progressed from library control technician, to technical librarian, to manager. The library changed from the Engineering Library to the Corporate Information and Research Center. For a while I had an assistant, but that did not work out, and I found I work better alone. In the beginning, it was a typical library. I had about 2,500 books, 2,500 standards, and 100 journal subscriptions and a card catalog. I purchased books and subscriptions for all 1,000 employees at Wickliffe headquarters and some field staff. Most of the time was spent on acquisitions and circulation, with some online searching and interlibrary loan.

Things had changed when I left; the CIRC had only about 600 books, the same 2,500 standards, about 25 journal subscriptions, and several CD-ROM products. The card catalog was gone, replaced by a networked online catalog, and I no longer handled company-wide subscriptions, but still ordered books and interlibrary loan for all employees. Instead of just 1,000 potential patrons, located primarily in the same building as the CIRC, there were about 12,000 potential patrons. Most of these I never met as I received and filled requests via e-mail, fax, and phone. Most of my time was spent on competitive intelligence. I produced a weekly Executive Intelligence Report and a monthly newsletter, sent via e-mail and fax to top management and marketing personnel worldwide. Both were posted on the company's World Wide Web home page so I added "Webmistress" to my duties, as I was in charge of my department's WWW pages. Circulation was down, but CIRC use was up as we headed toward a virtual library. It was certainly not the same job I started in 1988!

I left Elsag in January 1997 to pursue other opportunities, including writing, teaching, consulting, and working my own business, Information Bridges International. IBI's mission is "to arrange exchanges among librarians and other information professionals around the world." This will include, but not be limited to, internships, mentorships, and interlibrary visits. It will be my chance to give back to the profession and expand my horizons.

Throughout my library career I have been active in the profession. My proudest accomplishment is helping to give birth to the SOLO Librarians Division of the Special Libraries Association. Barbara Borrelli and I took a caucus and made it a division in just six months. They said it could not be done, but they did not reckon on the abilities of SOLOs. In 1996 the Division was the fifth largest in SLA, with over 1,000 members in just five years. I have also served as teller for the Sci-Tech Division, chaired the Meckler Award for Innovations in Technology committee, and held several positions in the Cleveland chapter. I make it a point to talk to the students at the University of Illinois Graduate School of Library and Information Science at least once a year on "Life in the Real World—What They Don't Teach You in Library School." I have also talked to the students at Kent State University in Ohio as well as contributing papers to several journals (*Journal of Agricultural Economics, Special Libraries, Searcher, The One-Person Library*) and speaking before the National Librarians Association and ASIS. The library profession has been good to me and I feel it is important to give back to it.

There are a few conventions to get out of the way before beginning. I would like to be as politically correct as possible, but the thought of using "him or her" or "he/she" every time I refer to a librarian is not only cumbersome but distracting. I plan to use "they" whenever possible, and "he" or "him" when it is not (except when the gender is obvious such as referring to a specific person). The other political football is what to call those places of higher education that confer degrees in the area of librarianship. In spite of the fact that the word "library" is disappearing from their names, for simplicity's sake I will use the term "library schools." I know that some will object to my not using "schools of library and information science" or some such, but I will stand my ground. Similarly, I will refer to the degree they confer as an "MLS." I realize that is hopelessly out-of-date (even *my* degree is an M.S. in Library and Information Science), but it has the advantage of being short and clear. I hope that these simplifications will not get in the reader's way.

Part One

Who We Are

What Is a SOLO?

A SOLO librarian . . . what's that? Is it an unmarried librarian? One who flies an airplane alone? No, a SOLO librarian is one who works in a one-person or one-professional library situation. In 1976, Guy St. Clair defined the One-Person Library as "one is which *all* the work is done by the librarian"(2). In their *Who's Who in Special Libraries* (1995-6), the SOLO Librarians Division of the Special Libraries Association (of which I had the privilege of being first Chair) defines a SOLO as "an isolated librarian or information collector/ provider who has no professional peers within the immediate organization." This definition was developed by the founder of the group, Martha Rhine, who saw "the image of featured artists with talents exceeding those of the accompanying group" (Berner and St. Clair 1990, ix). In *Managing the New One-Person Library* St. Clair and Williamson said that "the value of this definition is that it recognizes that in his or her immediate workplace this library/information professional works alone, both as a librarian and as a library manager" and called it "the best [definition] we have found" (1992, 2-3). Therefore, this is the one I will use for this book.

Other names for SOLO librarian are "One-Man Band" (in the United Kingdom), "Sole-Charge Librarian" (sometimes used in Australia and New Zealand) and "One-Person Librarian" (used almost everywhere else). I have problems with two of these terms. OMB is blatantly (though not deliberately) sexist and seems a rather frivolous term. OPL, while politically correct, seems redundant. Each librarian is just *one* person. So I prefer the term SOLO librarian. It is also the name chosen by the largest group of SOLOs in the world, the SOLO Librarians Division of the Special Libraries Association, with over 1,000 members.

A SOLO will not be found in most public libraries, nor in most college or university libraries. Where, then, does a SOLO librarian work? SOLOs work in corporate libraries, that is, libraries (or information centers) in private companies. Many are found in small public libraries, museums, schools, churches or synagogues, prisons, law firms, hospitals, etc. Most SOLOs work in special libraries. A special library is one serving a specialized or limited clientele, with specialized or limited materials and services. The emphasis is often on providing information, rather than books. The collection is often small. The librarian nearly always reports to a nonlibrarian, and the library is part of but not considered critical to the parent organization's main mission.

A WEEK IN THE LIFE OF A SOLO LIBRARIAN

The best way to illustrate just what a SOLO librarian does is to see a week in the life of one. What follows is an iteration of my activities for one week in 1992. It is *not* a composite, but an actual week.

Monday

Starting at 7:30, I read my e-mail (maybe ten messages), read my news groups (I subscribe to five listservs, with maybe fifteen messages a day each—I read maybe five each), and listen to about five phone messages. E-mail can be "to do's" from my boss, requests for engineering document numbers to be assigned, press releases, etc. Phone messages are usually follow-ups on orders placed, "can you get this?", or similar questions.

About 8:30 I go up to the mailroom for the first part of the mail. Monday is the heaviest day. I go back about 11 A.M. for the rest (and to deliver what I have gotten done) and then again after 1 P.M. for the packages. On a busy day I will go back about 3 P.M. for the rest of the afternoon mail. The mail consists of ads for new services (much of which I pitch unopened, bills to be approved, magazines to be checked in (and some read), and internal requests for information and books or magazines to be ordered.

As usual, I eat my lunch at my desk. If I am lucky I will only be only interrupted a couple of times. I do not mind, because lunch is the only time some people can get to the library so I deliberately leave my door open so I can help them. Remember, their questions do not interrupt my job, they *are* my job.

On Monday I usually check with my boss to see if he has any special projects for this week. Since he is not a librarian but an engineer, this can be anything from creating a new database, cleaning up an existing one (making abbreviations and words consistent), to locating an overhead projector for him to take on a trip.

The rest of the day consists of odds and ends. I write purchase orders for a couple of books and for new locks for the lab book files. I will pick up the locks later this week and maintenance will put install them.

Since the Open House is tomorrow, I spend about an hour getting my computer set up outside the library. It does not work right off the bat, which is normal. Nothing is ever as simple as it seems. I then leave for home about 5:30 P.M.

Tuesday

Today is my annual Library Open House. The theme this year is the Internet. I have set my computer up outside the library so that I can demo Internet, gopher, ftp, newsgroups, and our e-mail system. At 8:30 A.M. the coffee is delivered, at 9:00 the cakes arrive (one for morning, one for afternoon—if I put both out they will disappear quickly and food is a big drawing card around here). I also have lollipops, bookmarks ("When you absolutely, positively have to know . . . ask a librarian"), stickers ("I visited my library today") and notepads ("Have you tried the library?"). I have put announcements in the company weekly update, in my monthly letter, and a large sign on bulletin boards on each floor. I also reminded everyone (and vice-presidents, in particular) via e-mail. I have several in-house experts to help with the demos and questions.

As the day goes, 110 people sign in (probably more show up, since 200 pieces of cake disappear). There are lots of questions and interest in the Internet. I even do some demos of other library services. It is a very successful event.

Near the end of the open house, the president's secretary comes down. He needs me to find a press release on a new Bailey joint venture, but of course I cannot answer right away, since my modem in my office and my computer is out here. I call another special librarian whom I know has Dow Jones News Retrieval, but she is unable to locate the release. As soon as the open house is over (3 P.M.) I reassemble the computer in my office, go on Dow Jones myself, and find the article. I send it up to her via e-mail. Another satisfied customer. I go home about 5:15.

Wednesday

Yesterday was the Open House, so I did not get any "real" work done except for putting the *Wall Street Journal* out. (If I do not get the *Wall*

Street Journal first thing, the engineers get nervous.) So I do two days work in one day. This is what happens every time I am out—for a meeting, training session, SLA conference, sick, or vacation, but it is worth my time to go to the meeting or training since I have to keep up with this ever-changing profession. Besides, if I never left they would take me for granted, a piece of the woodwork. When I am gone (and no one does my work) they realize what I do for them and are somewhat more appreciative.

Three purchase orders are written today. One is for five articles that are needed rush for a manager's presentation to a potential customer. I send this order to an information broker and they come in the next day, making the patron very happy. It is also a big ILL (Interlibrary Loan) day, and my boss wants twelve articles on measuring Research and Development productivity. I locate them on OCLC, the world's largest online catalog (we are members through Ohion et), at area libraries. This takes about an hour, including looking up the ISSN's and checking the local union serials list. (By a week later, five are in, one is not available, the rest have been shipped.) I normally do about thirty ILL a month, but have done as many as sixty in one day. Occasionally I even have the opportunity to loan an item. Today I actually go home on time (more or less) at 4:30.

Thursday

I continue working with the Information Handling Services (IHS) technical rep to fix a monitor problem. This has been going on for over six months and the patrons and I are a bit peeved. The system works, but not as it should. I am trying to get IHS to make some monetary concession as well as to fix the problem. A significant part of my job is dealing with vendors who may or may not give the desired service, and IHS is not the only one I have problems with, just the one today.

The vice-president of engineering comes down with an information request; he needs information on software licensing. I do a quick search on my Computer Select CD-ROM and get about thirty articles, full-text. I send them to him via e-mail and get a nice note thanking me for my promptness and professionalism (also low cost).

A light day, only one purchase order is written. It is a rush order for four copies of a computer book. I fax it to our book vendor requesting next day delivery, the books arrive the next afternoon, and the patron is happy. The day ends at 4:45 P.M.

Friday

It is the end of the month, time for my monthly report. I put together the statistics which are the number of items circulated, number of
books or patents or standards or ILL ordered, and the questions
answered); then I write a narrative of what I did this month. This
includes direct patron service (tours of the library, special research
projects, etc.), new services added, and continuing efforts. I also include
my activities with SLA and CAMLS—the Cleveland Area
Metropolitan Library System—to remind my boss that I am a professional. This month for SLA I have worked on the local chapter directory, attended one meeting, counted ballots for the Sci-Tech Division, and
served on the nominating committee for the Engineering Division. I
also attended one CAMLS meeting this month—Special Library
Directors. We had a one-hour information sharing session which is very
helpful since we find out the resources of the other libraries. CAMLS is
invaluable for maintaining a network of local contacts from whom I can
borrow items and ask questions. This report goes to my boss, who
abridges it to his boss, who summarizes it for his boss, etc.

It is a quiet day, so I continue my project of indexing our project lab
books. On a good day I can get maybe seventy-five done. There is a total
of more than 2,800 to be done, but I have done almost 2,000 already and
am in the home stretch. This involves getting the books from the locked
files, looking through each one (these are the old ones, with no
front-of-the-book index) and deciding what the important sections are
and adding them to the dBase record. I'm not an engineer so my
indexing may not be perfect, but it is better than what we had before
which was nothing.

I printed a list of "overdue" books, but I am not sure what to do with
it. It is time-consuming to send out notices (print, address, put in mail
slots), and the return rate is under 50 percent, and it antagonizes the
patrons. I put it in the "hold" file for now.

Other accomplishments this month were that I circulated about
thirty books, journals, lab books, and standards (check-in and
check-out via our online catalog/circulation system); answered maybe
twenty-five reference questions (drop-ins, by phone, by e-mail); and
assigned ten engineering document numbers. I average over 1,000
transactions per month.

I perk up when Barbara Quint, editor of *Searcher* magazine, calls. I
had sent her an e-mail praising the timeliness and pertinence of the

latest issue, and she asked if she could print my letter. We talked about library education, SLA headquarters, vendors, and the general difficulties of our profession today. She is a fascinating speaker and really knows what is going on in the information industry. She hinted that DIALOG, the big online database vendor, is about to announce a major change in copyright that will change the way we do business. Now, did I really need to hear that? This day I leave for home about 4:45 P.M.

SOME FACTS ABOUT SOLOS

Before starting an in-depth discussion of the characteristics and skills of a SOLO librarian, it is important to give a run-down of the kinds of SOLOs, their working environment, average salary, and some of their job requirements to give an overall picture.

The average SOLO *corporate* librarian

- works alone, with no help
- has a collection of 4,000–5,000 volumes and 200–300 periodical subscriptions
- serves 3,000 patrons
- administers a budget of $90,000
- earns $37,000
- has an automated catalog and maybe automated circulation
- has one or more CD-ROMs
- became a SOLO by circumstance rather than choice

The average SOLO *law* librarian

- works alone, with no help
- has a collection of 10,000 volumes and 250 periodical subscriptions
- serves 625 patrons
- administers a budget of $220,000
- earns $43,000
- has an automated circulation system
- became a SOLO by circumstance rather than choice
- has their dues paid by their employer
- belongs to SLA and AALL (American Association of Law Librarians)
- has access to the Internet and the World Wide Web
- spends 64 percent of their budget on electronic information (Quint 1996b)

The average SOLO *medical* librarian

- works alone, with no help
- has a collection of 1,750 volumes and 125 periodical subscriptions
- serves 1,400 patrons
- administers a budget of $47,000
- earns $35,000
- has an automated circulation system
- became a SOLO by circumstance rather than choice
- has dues paid by the employer
- belongs to MLA (Medical Libraries Association) but probably not SLA

The average *museum* librarian is most likely a SOLO (Bierbaum 1996) and

- works most likely part-time (with two-thirds unstaffed)
- has a collection of 6,850 volumes
- administers a budget of $1,000 to $10,000
- is not automated, but may have online services

The average SOLO *public* librarian

- has a staff of six, all nonprofessionals or clericals
- has a collection of 40,000 books, 104 periodical subscriptions, and 1,273 audiovisual items
- serves a population of 16,000 people
- circulates 79,000 items (an average of seven per person)
- administers a budget of $199,000—divided among books, $24,000; subscriptions, $4,000; audiovisual, $4,000; plant maintenance, $28,000; and salaries: $104,000
- makes $25,000
- is not automated, but does belong to a library network

CHARACTERISTICS OF A SOLO LIBRARIAN

First, how does a SOLO librarian differ from a "regular" librarian? First of all, the SOLO is most likely in a small library, without extensive holdings or resources. Secondly, SOLOs are expected to do it all—ordering, cataloging, reference, bibliographic instruction, online searching, filing, budgeting, and so on. They may have a part-time assistant, volunteers, or if they are lucky, some full-time clerical assistance. But the SOLO is the only trained librarian on the staff. In addition, the

SOLO has no one in the organization doing the same job to go to for help, advice, or even a shoulder to cry on. SOLO librarians are probably working for a nonlibrarian—a boss who does not really understand what they do or how they do it. (It is hard to get approval to buy an automated acquisitions system if your boss does not even know what one is.)

In terms of education, does a SOLO *have* to have a library degree? For the purposes of this book, yes. I would be the first to acknowledge that there are many very competent people out there working as librarians without the benefit of graduating from library school. However, there is much to be gained by that degree and this book will use the word "librarian" to refer *only* to those with a master's or higher level degree from an accredited school of library and information science.

According to St. Clair and Williamson (1992), a library with a SOLO may be the organization's first library, newly established and unsure of how much staff it needs, destined to grow to include a larger staff. It might be a downsized library, formerly having several librarians but, due to less demand or less money or less awareness of need, is now reduced to one professional. It can also be a right-sized library, one that needs only one well-trained and efficient professional to serve the organization's information needs. This is probably the most common situation.

Why are SOLOs so important? How many SOLOs are there? Because of their singleness, there is no accurate count of SOLOs, but the following figures are available. The Special Libraries Association estimates that one-third to one-half of their over 14,000 members are in SOLO positions. That's 5,000-7,000 SOLOs in special libraries alone! The SOLO Librarians Division of SLA is only five years old, but has grown in that time from 350 to over 1,000 members. The U.S. Department of Education figures show that the vast majority of the public libraries in the United States have no more than one professional librarian. Most school libraries have only one professional (if that many), as do most hospital libraries. Small law firms are very unlikely to have more than one professional, and prison and church or synagogue libraries are lucky if they have any degreed staff.

The question might be why would anyone want to be a SOLO librarian? The three most common reasons are independence, variety, and an enhanced feeling of self-worth. SOLOs like me enjoy the ability to run their own show, set their own schedule, plan their own priorities, with a minimum of supervision (and interference). "Doing what I want to do, when I want to do it" has great appeal. We can make our own mistakes and successes. We can know exactly what is going on and the level of quality going out to customers. We value the close relationship we develop with our patrons, and the wide variety of tasks that must be done (including those pesky clerical ones) keeps us busy and not bored. We have the freedom to be creative in our solutions. We can gain the respect of our colleagues by being the sole information authority in the organization. We garner all the appreciation for library services (and all the complaints, too). As Harry Truman said, "the buck stops here." But we have the opportunity to shine and show others what a trained information professional can do. As one SOLO put it in answer to a questionnaire: "librarianship, especially solo librarianship, is a terrific career for liberal arts graduates with a passion for learning, a knack for problem solving, a touch of creativity, and a sense of humor."

The SOLO life has its drawbacks, as well. The most commonly mentioned problems are professional isolation, lack of clerical support, the need for reporting to a nonlibrarian, and low pay. Other negatives about being a SOLO include a lack of preparation for the job (in library school, on the job, and elsewhere), lack of management support, lack of job security (downsizing is always around the corner), poor physical working conditions, lack of time, frustration at not being able to "do it all," lack of status, and lack of control of policy, personnel, or budget (or all three). There never seems to be enough time to get everything done. Filing, reading, public relations, and professional development fall victim to too little time. The lack of feedback and interaction with other professionals takes its toll; there is no one to bounce ideas off of. We may feel we are underappreciated within the organization and we tire of being the only one. "Mindless" clerical work seems to get in the way of doing "real" work. (Perhaps this requires an attitude transplant; clerical work isn't mindless. It can be a welcome respite from high pressure decision making and planning, and it *has* to be done and who can do it better, faster, and more efficiently than the SOLO librarian?) Often we tire under the strain of constantly having to explain ourselves and our work to managers who do not understand us. The lack of feedback, status, and often credit for our efforts gets us down. Thus, if you are the type who needs constant reinforcement, this is not the job for you.

Since many SOLOs are SOLOs by choice, obviously the pros must outweigh (or at least equal) the cons. Most of us are very happy, as shown by these quotes from the questionnaires:

- "I love doing what I do. I cannot imagine not being involved with all aspects of running a library. It keeps me learning and constantly on the go."
- "I love flying solo! I'd do this flight again!"
- "This is an immensely satisfying business career."
- "We are a wonderful breed of human."
- "I'm overworked and underpaid, but I love what I do partly because it has so many facets . . . The frustration is in not being able to juggle everything in the available time."

Perhaps the key is in fitting the right person to the job. What kind of person should a SOLO be? Most agree that a SOLO should have flexibility and creativity; a bias toward service, sharing, coalition building, and idealism; resourcefulness, "the ability and liking for solitary endeavor . . ."(Washburne 1995). A SOLO should be able to manage time; think analytically; to see the big picture; to have curiosity, good recall, good oral and writing skills, self-confidence, a sense of humor, patience, good organizational skills; and to possess high frustration tolerance. From my questionnaire, Linda Beauchene comments that "being a SOLO requires someone who has a temperament that adjusts to working alone and being on one's own in the workplace."

Can these skills be taught? They probably cannot, but the specific tools and techniques to make the most of them can be learned, either in library school, on the job, or through continuing education. SOLOs wish they had known more about financial matters, management, corporate culture, networking, computer skills, assertiveness, time management, public relations. In short, more about the job they were to embark on.

Finally what does it take to become a SOLO librarian? I followed the SOLOLIB-L listserv for several months on the Internet, eavesdropping on discussions among SOLOs on just this subject. Their replies indicate that a SOLO must have confidence in making good decisions, an entrepreneurial attitude, comfort with networking, proficiency in gathering supporters, a lot of flexibility, good time management and balancing of priorities, a love for the profession, ability to cope with lots of bosses and patrons who think they are the only client, a readiness to take risks and learn something new every day, a passion and enthusiasm, and a willingness to dive in to do anything.

WHERE SOLOS WORK

A large number of SOLOs work in public libraries. Nearly 80 percent of public libraries serve populations of under 25,000 and are staffed by only one professional (Vavrek 1987). Times are changing in small public libraries. The days of the "shhh librarian," the library board acting on its own without interaction with the librarian, and the library not needing to justify its existence are gone. Replacing them are the outgoing librarian, willing to try new ideas; written policies; and board support of the library director (Holt 1990). But some things stay the same. The director is still the heart of the library, representing the library to the community, the board, and the staff. Collection development is a problem. You must remember that you can't please everyone, that "every book has its enemy" (Stipek 1988, 8). A written collection development policy will help, but tact and understanding will still be necessary when dealing with patrons who do not understand that you have unlimited copies of all the new bestsellers, you cannot have a complete collection of gun books (or whatever his pet subject area is), and you cannot provide all the answers right now.

As a counterpoint to my experiences as a SOLO, read about life in a more rural setting:

An Intern's Experience in a Small
Rural Public Library
by Morgan A. Tracy, now Director, Benton (IL)
Public Library District

One type of library that is home to many "solo" librarians is the rural public library, an institution that can be quite central to the social and economic viability of a small community. Recently I had the opportunity to serve an internship at such a library as part of the curriculum of study for a MLS degree from Clarion University of Pennsylvania. The library where I interned was the New Bethlehem Area Free Public Library, located in northwestern Pennsylvania, which serves a population of about 8,000 with a collection of approximately 17,000 volumes. The director of the library, who holds a MLS degree from Clarion, is responsible for every aspect of the library's operations, including the supervision of four part-time clerical staff members who assist with daily routines.

The most compelling lesson of my internship experience was that the director of a rural public library faces a multitude of challenges, and that he/she must be flexible in adjusting roles to meet those challenges. For example, a rural library director must be a competent manager, able to deal with all aspects of public and technical services within the library, as well as design the library's budget and fund-raising activities. Furthermore, a director also needs to be a skilled community developer, able to forge partnerships with local schools, businesses, and social service agencies, plus coordinate the distribution of important civic information resources. A rural library director must also meet the demand to be progressive technologically. That is to say, the well-being of a rural library, or even an entire rural community, may depend on the library director's efforts to introduce public access to networked electronic information, which is increasingly being cited as an economic and social support for small communities.

Obviously, the life of a rural library director is not an easy one, and the pressure of being the only professional librarian for miles around can add to the stress level. In combating the obvious tendency towards burnout, I observed that a rural library director is rewarded through the many personal relationships that he/she develops with patrons and other community members. I also realized that an important key to fostering these nurturing relationships is a strong desire on the part of the library director to become actively involved in a community affairs outside of the library setting. This sense of involvement, it seems to me, is a fundamental component for successful "solo" librarianship in the rural public library setting.

Public librarians face similar issues as corporate or other types of librarians: feeling a sense of intimacy with their patrons, overworking, doing it all, and dealing with nonlibrarians as supervisors (the library board). They also face some unique issues: building maintenance, raising money for new buildings, bond issues, etc. On the subject of library boards, the librarian and the board are often at odds as to the role each should play. Library directors usually feel the board's most important responsibility is to appoint the director (and then step back and let the director run things). The board may feel its responsibility is to plan for the future, although many boards feel a need to run things today, especially in the financial arena. The director usually wants more autonomy in personnel issues than the board is willing to give. One area both agree on is that the librarian should look to the board for leadership in construction and funding issues. Without the support of the board and the community, a building project is doomed to failure. Pungitore (1990) puts it simply: if you do not have the support, no matter how badly you need the space, do not build. It is seldom that the board members have had any training in how to be a board member. In fact, the library director has probably not had training in how to deal with a board.

Librarians at small public libraries face the problem of getting very little attention from their primary professional association, ALA (American Library Association), because it is dominated by the larger libraries. This is quite understandable since librarians at larger institutions have the time and administrative support to be more active professionally. This is also true of SOLOs in other fields. However, the SOLO needs more, not less, help from the association and may have to seek it out or even demand it. Another issue unique to public libraries is the relationship to the school system. Some communities may not understand the necessity to support two separate library systems. (I do not understand it myself. Why not put the public libraries in the schools? The buildings would be used more hours and the students would have a better library to use.) The public may, in fact, favor the school libraries since they are more familiar with them.

For those working in small or rural libraries, primarily public libraries, there is the Center for the Study of Rural Librarianship and the Small Library Development Center, both located at Clarion University of Pennsylvania. Founded in 1989 by Dr. Bernard Vavrek, a professor of library science at Clarion, both centers provide resources to rural and small libraries nationally and internationally through educational programs, research projects, publications, and conferences.

Law librarians serving private practice or small law bar associations are often SOLOs, as are law librarians in government institutions such as courts or agencies, and some public law libraries. Most law librarians in academia and law schools, where a library is required for accreditation, are not SOLOs. The issues facing SOLO law librarians are the need for rapid delivery of information, often with price insensitivity; the currency and accuracy of the information; the high degree of confidentiality expected, the fine line between legal research and interpretation; and the need to deal with summer interns or law clerks. These temporary employees have high expectations of librarians and add to the workload of the librarians. Also, academic law librarians are becoming increasingly responsible for teaching legal research techniques to students. Other issues not unique to law librarianship are timeliness, currency, accuracy, thoroughness, detail, rising costs, and burnout, and an emphasis on the practical uses of information. Academic law librarians get more involved in research, history, and comparative law. In a summary of several studies of how lawyers find information, researchers found that 50-60 percent of them do not go to librarians for help, even if they have trouble finding the information themselves. They do not use the librarian to learn how to search, only to provide the documents they identify from their own search. (I would wager that similar results would be found in surveying any constituency—engineers, doctors, and even the public.)

Closely related to law librarians are librarians working in the prison and jail system. Most states require the provision of access to legal materials to inmates. Most prison libraries remain SOLO positions, in spite of staffing level recommendations. In 1932 there were 133 prisons, 155 libraries, 18 librarians, and 7 library school graduates. By 1990, most of the librarians were professionals. Prison librarians have problems motivating their inmate assistants, due to turnover and lack of a strong work ethic. They are also concerned with confidentiality and the dividing line between legal reference and legal advice. Jail libraries are usually smaller and less likely to hire a professional. The emphasis is on access to legal materials and recreational reading as a form of behavior control or self-improvement, and lack of funds, censorship, and low status are major issues. Personality traits needed by the prison or jail librarians include an understanding of the political climate of the institution, survival skills, patience, a sense of humor, ability to follow the rules, and a professional demeanor.

Hospitals also must employ librarians for accreditation. Except in the large medical schools and hospitals, the librarian is often a SOLO. The needs of physicians are similar to those of lawyers—rapid delivery of current and accurate information, regardless of price and with a practical application. Many hospital SOLOs are also involved in patient service and education. They frequently have a staff of volunteers of varying degrees of training and commitment with which to work. This may or may not help the SOLO's work load. The Medical Libraries Association offers a certification program in medical librarianship. Although certification is not required for all medical librarian positions, it is strongly encouraged. Galiardi (1996) has a few suggestions for hospital libraries. Go to departments to deliver service, rather than wait for them to come to you. Create proactive reports for department, use focus groups (especially with non-M.D. personnel), serve on hospital committees, and provide information updating services to all staff, not just M.D.s. (Of course these are good ideas for any kind of library.)

Bierbaum (1996) talks about another kind of SOLO, one who works in museums. He point out that "museums and libraries have similar missions: they acquire, describe, and make accessible to us the records of our human experience . . ." Not all museums have libraries, however, and those have historically been "underfinanced, understaffed, and underutilized"(74-75). Facilities range from just a collection of books and magazines for staff use to "a fully organized and professionally directed information collection" (76). Funding is generally poor, with 45 percent of the libraries surveyed having budgets of under $1,500 and only 20 percent having budgets over $10,000. Most libraries are run by a "librarian" or "archivist," who is usually only part-time, although over 20 percent have no staff. The library is very likely to have a relatively large number of volunteers (the average is nearly seven). Collection size varies widely, from under 100 to over 300,000, with a median in the range of 1,500–5,000. Nearly all the libraries provide reference service to museum staff, members, and the general public. Few circulate items beyond the museum staff, provide online searching , document delivery, or have access to the Internet. Are museum libraries better off now than, say, twenty years ago? There has been some improvement, but not much, reports Bierbaum. They are still in need of well-trained, proactive, *professional* librarians to make the staff "aware that there is more to a museum library than keeping the doors open and the shelves neat" (85).

Many churches and synagogues have libraries, some staffed by volunteers, some with professional librarians. Nearly all of these are SOLO positions. The church library functions as a centralized place for materials for church programs (a sort of learning and resource center) with the specific aim of promoting the spiritual development of its users. A survey in 1967 showed 3,200 church and synagogue libraries; another in 1973 suggests that there are over 25,000. Most are small (less than 1,000 volumes) and run by volunteers under a nonlibrarian because "there are no specific educational requirements for the church librarian" (McMichael 1984, 32), but dedication, friendliness, a liking for working with details, neatness, patience, and sense of humor are suggested—the same criteria as for a SOLO.

School librarians and media specialists are very often SOLOs. Many of them serve two or more school libraries, with volunteers (often students) staffing the library when the librarian is not there. All professional school librarians must also have a teaching certification.

They are seen as an extension of the classroom and often assist teachers with special projects as well as running the library and teaching library skills to the students. Some even have such varied duties as holding story hours, teaching reading or English, doing computer instruction, advising student groups, running the bookstore, and supervising the lunchroom. Kramer called them "super solos" (1989, 83).

SOLO librarians also are found in nontraditional jobs or nonlibrary settings, including information brokers, sales for library-related firms, publishing, and infopreneurs. The nontraditional sector is growing rapidly. "The number of people with backgrounds as librarians or online searchers who are practicing independently has multiplied ten or twenty-fold over the past 15 years" (O'Leary 1987, 24). Horton suggests that there are more positions out there that could benefit from library skills than there are traditional library jobs (Williams 1994).

The work of information brokers falls into two main categories: information retrieval and delivery and information organization. The latter is often called "information consulting" (O'Leary 1987). An infopreneur is defined as "a person who gathers, organizes, and disseminates information as a business venture or as a value-added service" (Weitzen and Weitzen 1988, 2). The infopreneur may design and produce databases, perform primary and secondary research, obtain documents, do abstracting and indexing, evaluate libraries, manage libraries, do outreach and public relations, perform translations, act as a records manager, train librarians, write or edit books and articles, or almost anything else you can imagine. What does it take to be a successful infopreneur? It takes patience, speaking and writing and telephone skills; organizational skills; a sense of humor; ability to integrate disparate concepts; problem-solving ability; perseverance; a broad base of knowledge, dedication and hard work; an enjoyment of working alone, making decisions, and being a self-starter; the ability to prioritize; energy, intelligence; creativity; computer skills; confidence; optimism; and the ability to sell yourself and your services. In other words, the same skills as a good SOLO librarian. The newest buzzword now is "intrapreneur," a library-based information entrepreneur.

An increasing number of librarians work in the competitive intelligence field. Competitive intelligence (CI) is the gathering of information that will assist a company in maintaining its competitive edge. (It is not, as some think, only gathering information about one's competitors. It also includes information about a company's customers, keeping up with technology, and anything else that makes the company better able to compete.) Librarians are exceptionally well qualified to do CI. We are trained to search for, analyze, organize, and disseminate information. We are experienced in working in an interdisciplinary environment. We already have our own networks. Other traditional library competencies that transfer well to CI include online searching, the reference interview, current awareness, knowledge of bibliographic tools, computer skills, written presentation skills, and time management.

One last question remains: why do librarians leave the profession? Sellen (1984) found that most left because they found a better job or were just dissatisfied with their current work. A significant percentage left the library field to earn more money. She found that only about half of those she surveyed would return to library work, but over 70 percent still regard themselves as librarians or members of the library profession. Williams (1994) found that 40 percent of the librarians in a 1994 survey would like to try an alternative career. La Forte (1982) found there is a move to self-employment and charging for information. This is seen as a growth of the profession, especially in Canada, (more pride and more professional). Librarians go into brokering for several reasons: they want to deliver information rather than teach the users how to get it, they want to take a more active approach to finding out users' information needs, and they are stifled by limited resources found in some libraries. O'Leary (1987) reports that librarians may choose to go independent because of a lack of challenge in their current job or to escape the bureaucracy. Most found their alternative jobs through personal contacts, but a substantial portion (20 percent) created it themselves. But a word of caution . . . there are only about 1,000 or so *full-time* information brokers. For most, it is a part-time job. "The world is not beating a path to the information broker's door" (Rugge and Glossbrenner 1995, xviii).

CONCLUSION

There are certain defining *defining* characteristics of SOLO librarians. They must be functioning as librarians or information professionals. They must be the only information professional in their immediate organization (although it is permissible, and encouraged, that they be part of a larger network). They may have a staff, but not of other professionals. No matter where they are employed, they need to understand the corporate culture of the organization they are in; to be creative, patient, professional, able to work well with others, adaptable, and committed; and to have a sense of humor.

Some people resent the idea that SOLO libraries even exist. Herb White, former dean of the library school at Indiana University, said that "perhaps we need to postulate that 'one-person library' is an oxymoron . . . they are clerical centers for buying, lending, and recalling"(1988, 56). But the fact remains that there *are* SOLO librarians, a great many of them, and they have been largely ignored by library educators, researchers, management consultants, and even the rest of the library profession. This book hopes to change that.

Management Issues

In an article I wrote entitled, "The MLS Is Not Enough; One SOLO Librarian's View," I came to some realizations about the SOLO librarian. I called them the "Four Hard Truths":

- We have to make ourselves the information experts. No one will *give* us our place in the information society. We can make ourselves the experts by virtue of our education and our customer orientation.
- We cannot *demand* respect. We have to *earn* it, and we do this by keeping up in our field, by participating in continuing education and professional development.
- We will probably *never* be paid what we are worth.
- We are all in the marketing business—marketing our institutions, marketing our services, marketing ourselves. All the time.

It is important to realize as well that we are in the business of managing information services. SOLOs are "not just librarians ... the tasks that one-person librarians perform are not limited to information delivery any more. And it's those management tasks that really separate the serious one-person librarians from the others ..." (St. Clair 1996a, 4). In a SOLO library, all the management is done by you. What you do (or fail to do) makes the difference whether the library succeeds or not. The success of your library is almost entirely up to you. There are always factors beyond your control, such as your prime users being laid off or the company going under, but since you cannot control them, forget them and concentrate on what you *can* control. You must ensure that the library is seen as a critical part of the organization; that it is involved in *mission-critical* issues. Your mission is to make sure that the library is relevant to the lives of your users. What gives your mission value is that you know the organization and its business, know the users and their needs, and know more about how to collect, organize, and disseminate information than anyone else in the organization. You must emphasize and *exploit* this knowledge.

There are seven identified areas that SOLOs are especially concerned about: educational preparation for SOLO librarianship (see chapter 5), organizational dynamics and corporate culture, customer service, financial matters, time management, networking and public relations, and ethics and professionalism. It is impossible to tell you everything you need to know to be a better SOLO library manager in one book, let alone in one chapter, but I will try to define some issues the SOLO needs to know about and to give examples of how to go about solving them. Consult the bibliography at the end of this book and the sources in chapter 9 for more reading on the subject.

KNOW THY ORGANIZATION: ORGANIZATIONAL BEHAVIOR AND CORPORATE CULTURE

Perhaps the most important thing you can do to survive and thrive in an organization is to know the organization you're working in, whether it is a business, community, hospital, law firm, or other entity. Corporate culture is a system of shared beliefs, values and assumptions. Whether you agree with these values or not, you must accept them as part of the organization. You need to know how the organization is formally structured and how it actually works, who is in power and who is not. You need to understand what information the organization needs, who needs it, how it flows within the organization, team dynamics, communication, how to market your information product products, how to provide leadership and vision, and how to be customer-driven.

The first important need is to find out how and why the library is placed in the organization. Are you considered a professional, how does your budget compare to similar departments, is your equipment as up-to-date as others, and what is the general perception of the library (Ferguson and Mobley 1984)? You need to know what the critical issues in the company and the industry are—the "hot buttons." Don't forget to abide by the unwritten behavioral rules: work hours, work ethic, dress code, writing style, and communication style. Although you don't exactly have to follow the party line, you do need to fit in. Remember that the corporate culture operates on both the company and department level and that it may not be the same at both (St. Clair 1994b). In addition, you need a knowledge of the industry that the organization is in: who the movers and shakers are, who the competitors and partners are, what the situation is now and what is expected for the future, the trade organizations and journals.

Where do you go for this information? Talk to people, ask questions, read mission statements, annual reports, long-range plans, organizational charts, catalogs, policies and procedures, and budgets. Arrange for site visits to remote locations and don't forget a tour of your own facility. I have done all these and found that the site visits were extremely useful. People not at your facility tend to assume that you serve only the main location. Going out to the people assures them that you really are there to help them and also gives you a chance to see what their work is like and to put faces to names.

Part of being a successful SOLO is the ability to to communicate with upper management. To do this, you must be assertive, aggressive (but not too aggressive), alert, and ambitious (Merry 1994). How do you become more assertive? Williamson (1984) suggests showing your cost and time effectiveness, having a high profile, and changing your title from librarian. I reluctantly agree with the idea of removing "librarian" from your title. As much as I hate to admit it, the title "librarian" leads others to think of you as one who shelves books, not as the information leader in the organization. I would prefer it to change the image of the librarian, but until that happens—if it happens—it is best for your library's and your success to "lose" the words "library" and "librarian."

You need to learn what information management personnel need and how they need it. Then give it to them—preferably before they ask for it. The format in which you provide information is very influential in how it is received. If they want just a summary, summarize. If management wants detail, include everything. Usually, the higher up an executive is, the less information he or she wants. What management *really* wants is an answer, not information. If that is beyond your scope, try to give what information you have in as concise a manner as possible. It is important not to just talk to management when *they* want to talk. Feed them a steady stream of useful information, speak to them in the halls and say something substantial about a new trend in the industry or a big contract you've just received.

Another key to dealing with upper management is to talk in their language. They neither understand nor care about library jargon. (It took a lot of convincing for my boss to accept the work "weeding" as a real library term.) Read about management and learn to use their jargon. Sprinkling your conversation and reports with ROI, turnover, and mission-critical will enhance your professional status in their eyes. It may seem a game, but it is one in which they make all the rules.

A good relationship with your immediate supervisor is necessary. Your boss probably does not and will not ever really understand and appreciate the library as you do, but if he is cultivated properly, he can become its advocate. If you make your boss look good, you will look good and he will support you when you really need it. One form of support is to be successful; getting published inside and outside the company or winning an award enhances your (and the boss's) image. Another way is to "offer solutions, not problems" (Merry 1994, 68). Try not to go over your boss's head—except when it is absolutely necessary. It is vital that the librarian be in on the ground floor when decisions are made that affect the library. The best way is to keep in touch with your supervisor and provide him with enough information about what you are doing and what you plan to do so that he can respond to any suggested changes from above in the way that you would like. Another avenue is a library committee. Many SOLOs swear by them; some probably swear *at* them. Library committees can be quite effective if they are advisory, not administrative—remember, you are still the one responsible for the library. They should not include your boss. If there is to be a committee, three members are ideal, with a maximum of five.

To succeed or even stay alive, the SOLO library must be able to justify its existence. One way is "by aligning their services with the decision-making process of corporate management and with the company's objectives and functions" (Svoboda 1991, 240). You must become visible, indispensable, add value, take risks (St. Clair 1994b). St. Clair also feels that the annual report is "the single most important document the one-person librarian will give to management all year long" (1976, 236). He suggests it include a summary of what you have done over the past year and a plan for what you intend to do in the next. Testimonials to your excellent service are very appropriate here. Try to get your annual report to management and to your users, too.

When setting goals for yourself and your library, the most effective are in writing, done by you, challenging, attainable, with target dates, specific, flexible, and measurable (Weinsoft 1990). To perform a self-assessment, first discuss the plan with management. Then review any written mission statements, modifying them as necessary, and reviewing the changes with management. It is best to evaluate performance informally and internally, but have it evaluated or validated by outside people (within the company, but not directly in the library).

Compare the evaluations. Review areas of deficiency and prepare a memo to management with a plan for improving deficiencies and building on strength. This will provide the basis for the long-range plan (O'Donnell 1976).

It is becoming increasingly important for the library to have a written mission statement, one that defines its place in the organization. This will help avoid confusion about what the SOLO does—and does *not* do. Without one, you may find yourself in charge of all sorts of nonlibrary tasks that you have neither time nor interest to pursue. The mission statement may be a part of a larger organizational information policy or it may stand alone. In either case, it should make clear the library's relationship to the organization's mission and to its customers. If you include nontraditional library activities, be sure to state them specifically and have procedures written that limit your involvement to just what you want it to be. Although the mission statement should be written after consultation with all the stake holders (users, management, fellow workers), it is ultimately the librarian who must agree to it since he or she will be the one carrying out the mission.

How does a SOLO survive, thrive, and get promoted? O'Donnell (1976) writes that management requires the information center to demonstrate administrative competence, have adequate tools, keep them informed. A SOLO should have a mentor (as high up in the company as possible), publicize the library (open houses, brochures), get supervisory experience, and know the company's culture. You need to find friends in the organization and make them your advocates. Unfortunately, often "the person who wields the most influence over the library [vice president, dean] tends to have the lowest level of knowledge of its operations" (Drake 1990, 152). Above all, "don't ignore politics" (St. Clair 1995h). Not realizing that the organization is a political animal is dangerous at best and fatal at worst.

THE USER IS JOB 1—CUSTOMER SERVICE

In his column entitled "Adding Value—What's It Mean?", Guy St. Clair listed the "Seven Deadly Sins of Entrepreneurial Librarianship." In terms of customer service, it is important to avoid these:

1. lack of vision, resistance to change
2. lack of initiative, sticking to the old ways
3. lack of creativity
4. anti-customer attitude

5. dullness, low self-esteem, "we're just a library"
6. laziness, leading to low service standards
7. lack of interest or motivation

It cannot be stressed enough that customer service, putting the user first, is the most important factor in library success. You can have the best collection, biggest staff, biggest budget, nicest furniture, and most up-to-date computers, but if your users do not feel they are helped by the library you will not last. It would be great if all librarians graduated from library school knowing this, but it is not always so. Probably if you are a SOLO you already know this, but please, do not skip this section. A reminder of these basic issues is important.

One thing to remember is you cannot be all things to all people. You will have to be selective about services offered; which services and to whom you offer them. Choose what you can do best and what will be of the most benefit to your parent organization, then promote your services to those who can benefit most from them. It is also necessary, sometimes, to say "no." Some requests made of you may be out of the scope of your position, may be out of your range of talents, or just impossible to fit in. It often helps to have written policies to support you at a time like this.

You must become client-centered, not library-centered. By this I mean you need to understand your customers' work and vocabulary by reading their journals, talking to them, and listening to them. To be accessible, approachable, and friendly and to make sure patrons get what they came in for, do more than point to the resource and forget them. You need to encourage them to come again (Hardsog 1992). Downplay how you got the information and play up the information itself. For example, since I was not an engineer myself, I usually asked the engineers I worked with to be present for technical searches. I found that they were fascinated by the precision possible with an online search and usually appreciated the quality of the information more after watching while I searched for them, and they almost never expressed any interest in doing the searches themselves. That is how I preferred it, because it was faster for me to do it.

Presentation is very important. Segment the market, do not give the same information to everyone, customize your product to the needs of your users. Go through the information and arrange it first, summarize if appropriate, and clean up online searches. I worked for one library, however, that cleaned up the searches too much; they stripped out the search strategy so the user never knew exactly how you found the information. Now I leave the searches in. Be scrupulous about leaving copyright statements in as well, and be sure you put your name or the name of your library on every page! That way the user cannot take the information to his boss and say "look what *I* found"; he must say "look what *the librarian* found for me."

A SOLO must be proactive. You must anticipate what your patrons will need and be sure you can meet the demand, and this involves planning, thinking, anticipating, and taking the initiative. As Stephen Covey (Paul and Crabtree 1995) pointed out, you must see every "threat" as an "opportunity" and be able to turn "complaints" into new service ideas. St. Clair remarks that this proactivity is important because "the traditional library model, even the corporate library model, doesn't work in business anymore" (1995c, 1). We still need libraries, but different, more responsive ones. The keys are communication with and to customers and taking responsibility for information (evaluating it for content and quality). Since you are unlikely to get more staff for your library, plan to add services by using technology, not people.

FINANCIAL MATTERS

The relationship between the SOLO and the money people does not have to be an adversarial one as long as both understand that the library's role is to support the organization and as long as there is communication (St. Clair 1995c). Remember that "the corporate information center usually operates as a staff function which represents cost overhead and thus is particularly vulnerable in times of corporate belt-tightening" (O'Donnell 1976, 179).

The budget is a most important management tool and is too often ignored. The librarian must have input into it. Remember to allow for inflation; justify each item (in terms of time/money saved); be realistic, remembering the financial situation of your parent organization; and keep it simple. There are three types of budgets, but there is no "best" budget for all libraries; what is best is what management requires. The line-item budget is a list of items with their proposed costs. The functional budget groups related activities and most often includes expenses only, not revenues. The capital budget accounts for long-term resources. In my last position, I never got to see what was approved for the library. I had no actual budget, just part of the cost center's overall budget. This had advantages and disadvantages. The advantage was that

I did not have to make spending decisions, since I had no idea what I could spend. The disadvantage was that I never knew when I was going to be told that the money had run out. Fortunately, this is *not* the case for most SOLOs; most have a budget, however small.

A survey of spending for fifty-five corporate libraries showed that while the companies' budget increased 16 percent from 1990 to 1995, the budgets for the libraries decreased 7 percent. Most of this decrease was for materials (down 8 percent). New technology did well, with a large increase in CD-ROM (106 percent) and a 32-percent increase in online services (Corporate Library Update 3 1995). In one survey, budgets for small public libraries (in Iowa) varied from $3,000-$220,000. The mean for the smallest libraries (serving populations of less than 5,000) was only $9000–$12,000 and a mean of over $100,000 for larger (greater than 5,000 population served) libraries. In smaller libraries the director's salary can be a large percentage of budget, from 5–89 percent (with a mean of 30–40 percent), while for the larger libraries it may be only 15–16 percent (Ahlrichs and Harms 1988). My survey of SOLOs shows that in a corporate library the librarian's salary may be as much as 75 percent of the budget. Salaries are always an issue. In small public libraries, the board may want to hire volunteers rather than a professional librarian, and corporate libraries are often staffed by clerical personnel to save the expense of a professional. Public libraries also have problems with unfunded government mandates such as the Americans with Disabilities Act. The older libraries can be very difficult and expensive to upgrade (Sickles 1995).

"Fund raising is a fact of life for the small town library" (Hardsog 1992, 38), and this can be done by direct mail, Friends groups, solicitations from the business community, grants, local clubs, etc. Corporate libraries may also do fundraising, using book sales to augment their budget. At Elsag Bailey, I had a book sale every year and have made over $500 over the years. I used the money for direct patron services such as maps, atlases, and of course for goodies for the next open house. Fundraisers also can serve as a chance to promote the library and remind users of its place in their lives.

There are some easy ways to save money. Several sources suggest using formal or informal networks. You can use ILL or CD-ROM instead of purchasing many journals. Hofstetter (1991) suggests using a local discount bookstore, being a reviewer for library journals, or purchasing from government or publisher overstocks to stretch the book budget. Galiardi (1996) suggests getting sponsors for a hospital library newsletter from pharmaceutical or medical vendors (check with your board to see if this is prohibited by policy), performing online searches for doctors from outside the hospital for a fee (if you have time!), and allowing coffee in the library provided the patrons use lids *sold* by the library. I also found instances of several other libraries also selling cups or lids to allow patrons to bring beverages into the library.

One method to gain revenue is charging back. SOLO librarians are not free of the age-old issue of fee vs. free. One SOLO tells this success story: once her boss realized that chargebacks could generate revenue, he was able to justify making her position full-time and exempt, with a salary increase. He also said that "unless someone complained about my charges, I was not charging enough." (Kingsley 1995). Although I do not advocate charging what the traffic will bear, I am strongly in favor of charging back out-of-pocket expenses. Information received without cost is often perceived as being without value. Charging back connects financial value to library services (St. Clair 1995h). I prefer not to charge my time since that creates the monster of keeping track of small bits of time. No SOLO has time for that. Just make sure that management does not reduce your budget by the amount that is charged back.

Joan Gervino (1995), director of the Center for Banking Information, American Bankers Association, wrote about the concept of establishing fees for service. First, identify who your customers are, then decide what you will charge for and what will be free. Research, database searching, document delivery, prepackaged information packets, database design, and translations are usually charged for while circulation (though may charge an access fee for the collection), quick reference (under fifteen minutes) are usually free. You must focus on quality, 100 percent accuracy, timeliness, comprehensiveness, and have standards or metrics to keep track of and measure quality. "A highly pro-active marketing effort is essential to the success of a fee-based library" (Gervino 1995, 6). Be sure to evaluate the program after a while, not just on its financial success, but on its reception by your patrons.

To keep things in perspective, here are some other comments from SOLOs on charging back: "I charge back to clients and departments via a job number. This is for my time, on-line charges, ILL, and any expenses incurred for that project. When I came to this organization, the only 'rule' given to me in regards to library operation is 'Thou shalt not do an on-line search without a job number'" (Doms 1996). In an Internet post in 1996, Millie Brumbaugh said that at Household International, she works with a two-tier system. She recovers actual costs (for searches, document delivery, etc.) and gets the rest of her funding via allocation out to the other departments in the company based on total costs of the library, but this takes a lot of time. At Bailey I charged back most of my out-of-pocket costs by getting a cost center number when the patron requests an online search, book, or journal article. If the search was under $50, the library usually absorbed it, however. Books of general interest for the library collection were paid for by the library, but if the book was for the use of one department they were asked to pay for it. I did not charge for my time or overhead because that would have taken far too much time. As Herb White said in *Librarians and the Awakening from Innocence*, the library could not possibly spend enough to have any real impact on the bottom line for the company.

One of the continuing problems of libraries is that librarians have no formula to measure the effectiveness of their services. Surveys usually produce skewed results (the unhappy user does not respond, nor does the busy user, no matter how satisfied). In measuring your services, you cannot count or evaluate everything because the enormity of the task will cause you to abandon it. Do not be tempted to take the easy way out and count activities (ILL, books cataloged, circulation). Count results if a process is very complex, break it down into its component parts and analyze each of them, and all the while, keep in mind your long-term goals and those of the corporation.

Evaluating your library is critical, because, as St. Clair points out, "no one is going to value the librarian if no one knows what he is doing" (1976, 236). First you must know what you are doing, what your products are, what your strengths are, what value you add. Then you have to share this with your supervisor, your users, and upper management. "Quality information products are the measurable evidence of the library's value to a corporation" (Svoboda 1991, 240). This means this should be current, value-added, selected, sorted, classified, and analyzed information. If you are typical, your most valuable services are online searching and quick response to questions, so try to get feedback from your users on the time (translated into dollars) saved by using the library. All information transactions add some value in that the question gets answered. The real measure is when you go beyond the basics, provide more than is asked for. This is *transformational librarianship*—making a difference in the patron's life.

Remember information does not need to be free, only reasonable. "It's not information but information *gathering* that costs money" (Alsop 1995, 126). I frequently had users come to me wanting information, but only if it could be found for free (especially on the Internet). Sometimes I searched the Net for them, usually finding nothing of value. Sometimes I just said that nothing is free and they would have to pay if they want information. For one user, I spent about fifteen minutes on the Internet looking for a Microsoft book on some obscure subject. I finally asked the user "do you want it free or do you want the information?" We logged off the Internet and onto KRI/DIALOG Books in Print. In two minutes, for two dollars I had the title and price of the book he wanted. I then asked "did you learn anything from this?" We agreed that perhaps the free Internet was not always the best solution. Another example is that after an online search, patrons would sometimes complain about the cost (usually when it is only $35–50). I just asked them how long it would take them to get in the car, drive to the library, locate this information (if they could), and drive back. Then I asked their departmental charge rate (usually about $65 per hour). Almost always that is the last I hear about information costing too much.

TIME MANAGEMENT

Andrew Berner, library director and curator of collections at the University Club in New York, explains time management below. A founder of OPL Resources, Ltd., he currently serves as an editorial consultant to *The One-Person Library: A Newsletter for Librarians & Management* and writes the "Concerning Time Management" column.

The "Three Ps" of Effective Time Management

If ever there was a group for whom time management is an important concept, it's solo librarians. With so much to do and, generally, no one to whom work can be delegated, it becomes essential that the SOLO librarian be aware of the basic principles of good time management. Too often, however the librarian seeks time management "tricks," thing that will enable a job to be done more quickly. In other words, they seek efficiency, where in fact they should be seeking effectiveness. Time management is not just looking for ways to cut down on the time it takes to do specific tasks (though that certainly can be a part of it). Time management involves an overall approach to how one works, an approach that is difficult to summarize in just a few paragraphs. Still, of all the many and varied aspects of time management, there are three which stand out as the most important in any overall approach to the subject I refer to these as the "three Ps" of effective time management.

First and foremost among these is planning. Without a sense of where you want to go, how can you ever know if you are going in the right direction? Without planning you merely struggle through the day-to-day operations of the library—relieved no doubt, to get through each day—but you never bring your library any closer to realizing its ultimate goals. How can you if you have no idea what those goals are? yet is not that movement toward specified goals—for our libraries, for our parent organizations, and for ourselves—one of the things that marks us as professionals? Without it we are really nothing more than clerks.

The most often-heard cry is, "but I do not have time for planning!" I can only respond by saying you'd better find the time. Doing long-range planning will give you the direction you need for intermediate planning and for short-term planning. Before you know it, you'll have a sense of direction which may have been lacking in your work before, and suddenly you'll find that you can be making decisions about the work you do (e.g., do I *really* need to do this?) rather than simply filling your day with tasks that seem to have no purpose.

This brings to mind the second of the three Ps: priorities. Not everything you do is of equal importance and you should be able to differentiate among your various tasks and duties to set your priorities. You should also be aware of the fact that priorities are not constant. While it is helpful to list tasks and goals in writing and to assign them a priority, you cannot make the mistake of thinking that they are carved in stone. Priorities are constantly shifting as new tasks and new developments come into play. Whatever you may be working on, for example, it is likely that if your boss calls or comes in with a request, that request is going to become your number one priority (unless, of course, your boss's boss calls with a request, and then you may have to reevaluate). The important thing is to recognize that whatever criteria you may use for determining priority—and there are many—you should always be working on your highest priority items at any given time.

The last of the "Ps" is not something that you should work towards, but something that you should avoid, and that is procrastination. Accept the fact that everyone procrastinates sometimes, and understand that guilt will not help to solve the problem. It is very important, however, to keep in mind that you should not assume that because everyone procrastinates it cannot be a serious problem. It can, in fact, rob you of your effectiveness on the job. No matter what you may think and no matter what you may have convinced yourself over the years, no one works best under pressure. Procrastination only insures that you will have to rush to complete a project, and that you will have insufficient time to check your work and to create a superior product. Procrastination leaves no time for that great despoiler of work: Murphy's Law. If you leave yourself ample time for a project and something goes wrong, you'll be able to correct it and still meet your deadline. Without that sufficient time, however, your work will suffer, and no doubt your reputation will suffer along with it.

To be sure, there is much more to time management than simply being aware of the importance of planning, priorities and procrastination. Much can—and has—been written on each of them, as well as on the many other aspects of good time management. Still, these are three powerful tools (two to use and one to avoid) in any SOLO librarian's arsenal of time management weapons. A knowledge of them can be used to help the librarian function not only in a more efficient manner, but—even more important—in a more effective manner as well. And after all, that's what being a one-person librarian is all about.

Another part of time management is not to waste time. Alec Mackenzie, in *The Time Trap* (1990), lists the twenty biggest time wasters, along with their causes and solutions. I have picked out some of the most important, with the causes especially common to SOLOs. For detailed ways to solve these problems, I recommend reading the book, although many of them are addressed later in this chapter:

- Attempting too much—lack of priorities and planning, unrealistic time estimates, yielding to the urgent, perfectionism, understaffing

- Confused responsibility or authority—lack of job description, responsibility without authority, confused organization chart, other employees unwilling to accept responsibility
- Inability to say no—desire to win approval, false sense of obligation, not knowing how to refuse, no time to think of answer, lack objectives and priorities, thoughtless assumption by others that you will say yes, cannot say no to your boss
- Incomplete information—difficult to know what information is needed, providing information not requested, failure to assess priority or urgency of requested information, lack of authority to obtain information needed
- Management by crisis—lack of contingency plans, overreaction, fire fighting, procrastination, unrealistic time estimates, failure to establish controls
- Personal disorganization—lack of system, feeling of indispensability, fear of loss of control, fear of forgetting, allowing interruptions, indecision, failure to screen
- Inadequate planning—lack time to plan, crisis-oriented, lack of job description, difficulty assigning priorities to tasks, assumption that since few days are "typical" it is futile to plan
- Telephone interruptions—no plan for handling, no plans for unavailability, lack of delegation, inability to terminate conversations, ineffective screening, no one else available to answer phones, socializing to avoid dull tasks

Experts on time management agree that librarians in general need to improve their time management skills, and this may be because library managers were often promoted from within, not trained as managers. As a group, we tend to estimate time somewhat unrealistically and try to do too many things at once. Many of us feel overwhelmed by the new technology. And there is something SOLOs can really relate to, the work never seems to be done.

One problem is that librarians can misuse time and try to do too much. They tend to follow these eight common myths of time management:

1. Time can be managed. One can manage one's own activities, not time itself.
2. The longer or harder you work the more you accomplish. You can only do so much before "fatigue diminishes all returns" (Cochran 1992, 9). It is far better to work effectively.

3. If you want something done right, do it yourself. Delegating is good if done properly. Although you may not have a staff member to work to, you can often find someone else in the organization who has time or talent or whose job a task *really* is.
4. You cannot enjoy or are not supposed to enjoy work. If you do not enjoy what you are doing, you will just become frustrated and feel as if you are always behind.
5. Time management is the same as time and motion studies. Instead of just measuring how long it takes to do something, focus on effectiveness (doing the right job), not efficiency (doing the job right).
6. Other people have more time than you do. We all have the same amount of time, we just use it differently.
7. Time management requires adherence to strict rules and schedules. Any change in behavior must be personalized.
8. We should take pride in working hard. "Librarians should take pride in working smart"(Cochran 1992, 11).

One step toward effective time management is to analyze your workday to determine how much time you spend on various activities. You then decide if each activity is of high or low value (to users, management). Then prioritize what you do, keeping in mind the relative value of activities. Urgent does not equal important (Cochran 1992). Cataloging can almost always wait, a patron almost never can. In library school I participated in a time study in one of my courses. Instead of keeping a diary, which lends itself to cheating (you are not likely to put down that you spent two minutes discussing the weather from 10:00 to 10:02), we wore beepers. The beepers beeped at scientifically determined random intervals. When it beeped, we wrote down what we were doing at the time. There was no way to cheat. In fact, library patrons often would help by saying "now write down that you were just talking." After a week of doing this, I had a good idea of where my time was going. To my surprise, it was not what I had expected.

There are a number of ways to manage your time more effectively. Guy St. Clair (1995g) offers some additional time management tips especially for SOLOs:

- If possible, plan your work the day before.
- Do the least pleasant tasks first.
- Postpone unimportant tasks and do not do low priority items if it will not make a difference.

- Remember, you need not be perfect and recognize that you cannot do it all. Do not say yes, then no. Say why you cannot do it and offer alternatives.
- Avoid being over-organized.
- Do not complain—just fix the problem.
- Ask whether the trip is necessary, or could someone else do it better?
- Prioritize tasks into the essential, what must be done but not right now, and what would be nice to do but is not essential.
- Say no to inappropriate requests.
- Emphasize self-service by being proactive with bibliographic instruction and handouts.
- Do not pursue lost causes.
- Stay focused on *business* work (leave personal work for your own time).
- Understand your biorhythms and time your tasks accordingly

Everyone has tips for saving time. Here are a few I have found in the literature and from personal experience. Outsource what you can (do not do what you can buy), for example, cataloging and interlibrary loan. Use the phone, let your fingers do the walking. And while we're on the subject, here are some tips for saving time on the phone (Cochran 1992): screen calls, use cordless phones, schedule a time to make and return calls, have an agenda for the call, save amenities for last, time calls, avoid telephone tag, and avoid telemarketing calls. Most time management books say you should handle paper only once. I have found that this is almost impossible in real life. I always seem to need someone's approval, a return phone call, or some other reason causing me to have to file the paper and deal with it again (and again), but it is something to aspire to. Take advantage of found time—bring work along with you to meetings, doctor's appointments, anywhere you might have to wait for a while. I sometimes even read *The Wall Street Journal* while waiting for online searches to run. Multitasking is a way of life for the SOLO librarian. Allow time in your schedule for walking around and talking with people, but also allow for quiet time or time to work on major projects without interruptions. As for interruptions, they are a part of the job. If no one asked questions we would not have jobs. You can try to anticipate the most common questions and have answers (guides, procedures, etc.) prepared that you can quickly hand to the patron, minimizing the disruption to your work. You can also try closing your door or arranging your office to discourage drop-ins, but I think this creates an unwelcoming environment. I tried never to close my door. The only exceptions were when my boss was going over my performance review or I just had to get some task done in the next ten minutes. A closed door sends a message I do not want to send. If all else fails, hide. Go somewhere no one expects you to be and work there. Some employees use the library this way, but it obviously would not work for me. The ladies' room is an option, also the cafeteria.

Meetings can be another time-waster, and I try to avoid them because very little is ever done in them except figuring out a way to share the blame if things go wrong. If you have to hold a meeting, learn how to run it effectively. To cut down on wasting time, prepare and distribute an agenda, keep everyone on track, postpone long debates for another time, and do not plan too much. Keep the number of participants small because meeting productivity varies inversely with the number of people at the meeting. Providing food can also slow the process.

NETWORKING AND PUBLIC RELATIONS

It is safe to say that SOLOs network in some manner. Networking as used in this book is not the old boy/old girl network, not elitist, and not necessarily formal or organized. Part of networking is belonging to SLA, OCLC, or some other group or participate in informal networks at work or within our profession. I cannot imagine a SOLO who does not talk to someone! Guy St. Clair said that "interpersonal networking is the key to excellence . . . What special libraries know is important, but *what* they know must be combined with *who* they know—together, it is an unbeatable combination" (1989, 111).

Networking can be informal or formal. Informal networking involves contacts among personal friends, within the organization, former colleagues, and former co-students. Be sure not to abuse nonlibrarian sources, thank your sources, and share information. Formal networking involves use of established organizations and much of it, especially in special libraries and SOLOs, arises out of necessity. We are small, have limited resources, and have very specialized collections. Networking is a major factor not only in reducing the SOLO's feeling of professional isolation, but also in reference, document delivery, interlibrary loan, acquisitions, and continuing education. All libraries and librarians depend on the support of others. We use ILL, OCLC, consortia, vendors, temporary help, outsourcing, consultants, other departments within our institution, such as MIS, purchasing, accounting, and legal.

We rely on contacts with other professionals (through meetings, the Internet, professional reading, phone calls, whatever) to make decisions on what books to buy, which vendors to use, which meetings to attend. We call other librarians when we have a reference question that is out of our scope or need an answer in a reference book we do not own. Whether we find these other professionals formally or informally, it is still networking.

Small public libraries are very dependent on networks, but the larger libraries tend to dominate and lead the organizations (Sickles 1995). The same is often true of other SOLO libraries. My library was a member of the Cleveland Area Metropolitan Library System (CAMLS). This multitype consortium is made up of nearly seventy libraries, about half special libraries (corporate, hospital, or law) and half public and academic. The major movers and shakers are the directors of the large public and academic libraries. This is logical because they have more time to devote to network leadership activities and they have the lion's share of the resources (paper, electronic, and financial). But the network would not be as rich in information without the resources of the specialized libraries, which are often SOLOs. And these smaller institutions are able to give much faster turnaround and more personalized service than the big bureaucratic organizations. I could call another corporate library and get a faxed answer within an hour or an ILL the next day. Which may not happen in the case of the big institutional libraries (and certainly not for free). I have found that informal networking, calling a colleague, is often faster and less expensive than an online search. In larger libraries this is called "resource sharing." The resource we are sharing is ourselves and our knowledge. Remember, "libraries do not cooperate, librarians do" (Quint 1996a, 4).

Our professional organizations (ALA, SLA, AALL, MLA, etc.) are one of the best sources of networking contacts. In addition to national meetings, there are usually more frequent local meetings. Even if the topic is not of immediate interest to you, go to the meetings. First of all, you never know when you will need to know about outsourcing, or acquisitions, or whatever the topic is this month. Secondly, you need to renew your contacts with your fellow librarians, both to maintain your own sanity and to make sure they remember you when you call with a question or request. One of my colleagues referred to a consortium meeting as a "support group." By this she meant that the members could share their complaints, fears, and concerns, feeling confident that the others understood and probably had the same feelings as they did.

Talking with someone who has "been there" is frequently the only way to deal with some new frustration or challenge on the job. Being active in professional associations improves communication skills, makes us feel more connected, enhances professional awareness and personal growth, makes contacts, adds to resumes, helps us gain management skills and experience, and enhances self-esteem and self-worth. "Informal networking takes its value from relationships between people" (St. Clair 1989, 107).

Another area that library schools do not emphasize enough is publicity, public relations, PR. "If you do not promote, you're doomed to defend" (Drake 1990, 153). If no one knows what you can do and how well you can do it, you will probably not be doing it for long. The SOLO library is no place to "hide your light under a bushel." You must constantly tell management and your users exactly how you can help them. No matter how satisfied they say they are, they seem to forget you very quickly if you do not remind them.

Public librarians need to promote their libraries to their users and potential users, of course. But they also need to make sure their elected officials know about them, their services, and the economic value of the library to their communities. In an article in *Library Journal* in May 1996, Susan Goldberg Kent of the Los Angeles Public Library stressed that "politics is local, and we should be masters of local politics. Keeping your city council involved pays off in the end." She also reminds librarians to keep a positive and upbeat attitude, thus instilling confidence in potential supporters.

Some librarians are afraid to market their libraries. In an article called "Are We Mice, or Are We Marketers?", Julie Sih made the following observations. "When our livelihood [raise, budget, continued existence] is at stake, we sit up and take notice of how effectively we are marketing ourselves. However, what about the rest of the time? We need to market ourselves in a way that is consistent, all the time . . ." (1995, 1) One "particularly mousy trait" is the fear of success, that is of acquiring too many customers to handle. However, "the greater the *demand* for our services, the more *resources* we will need to meet that demand . . . and the increased business that makes [added resources] necessary also helps pay for them"(2).

You do not need lots of money or time or fancy training to do PR. There are hundreds of books and courses on how to publicize your library. ALA puts out a catalog of promotional material and many library supply vendors have ideas in their catalog. Unfortunately, many libraries tend to limit their PR activities to National Library Week (NLW). PR has to be more. It has to be year-round. It has to be focused on your users' needs. I absolutely hate the theme of NLW—"Libraries Change Lives." The buildings do nothing—it is the *librarians* within the building and the *information* they provide that change lives. And as much as I love the "READ" series of posters, I would prefer they say "LEARN" or "UNDERSTAND" or even "ASK YOUR LIBRARIAN."

To get back to the problem of PR, another good source of ideas for promoting your library is the vendors such as DIALOG, Dow-Jones, LEXIS-NEXIS, etc. They have posters and flyers and giveaways. They will even come out and do demos for you and your users—free! Do not be afraid to ask.

Many libraries have an annual Open House, invite vendors, have giveaways, raffle off books, have food (more on that later) and attract hundreds of employees. Sure, not all of them return, but they have been exposed to the library in a positive way. In the past, I have made it a practice to try to hold my Open House, not during Library Week, but during Engineers' Week (the week including George Washington's birthday). This way I took the focus off me and put it on the users, where it belonged. Most organizations have some kind of week, so this should work in any library. I put posters everywhere I could, got publicity in the weekly company announcements, sent out e-mail reminders, and I always had food. Cookies and coffee draw a crowd just as well as a fancy cake (and cost less—try one of those wholesale or discount stores). Make sure you have enough and make sure you ration it; otherwise it will all disappear in the mad rush when you open and latecomers will be disappointed. Give them something to take with them. I found stickers that said "I visited my library today" from Upstart, but other libraries have used bookmarks, notepads, post-its, or pens. Try to get them to sign a register so you have a record of how many attend, and ask for their department as well so you can follow up.

Because an open house is an important source of publicity, it is important to have an effective one. Lindy Rose of Pharmacia and Upjohn offers these additional ideas for open houses (1996):

- know your objective
- prepare ahead of time (start two months ahead)
- choose a time to maximize attendance (avoid conflicts, not Friday afternoon)

- test computers several hours before the event if you are going to use them (allowing enough time to fix/replace)
- invite the boss (the higher the better)
- have a theme
- focus on benefits, not features (services, not resources)
- provide enough food and freebies (books as a giveaway, note pads, magnets, etc.)
- promote it well
- evaluate afterwards and start planning for the next one

Another PR tactic I used is a book sale. I held my first one the year I weeded the collection for the first time, removing about one-third of the books from the shelves. I hated to see them thrown in the trash or given away, so I sold them, to the employees, for 50 cents each. (I made anyone who wants to buy a book before the 7:30 A.M. opening pay double. I always sold some that way). I made about $50 the first year. The next year, several people asked if they could bring some of their own books for the sale. The fiction sold especially well, and the last year I made $220. All the money went toward something the users want but was not in the budget (travel guides, maps, a CD-ROM encyclopedia). In addition to adding to the collection, the book sale is another opportunity to get people into the library who otherwise might not come and reminds the rest that the library is here.

Yet another tactic I use is what I call RBWA—"reference by walking around." I try to visit my patrons when I can, stopping to talk to people if they are not too busy. I ask what they are working on and offer any help I can. Just the act of walking around—being seen—reminds people that you exist and that you might be able to help them. I cannot count the number of times I have talked to someone at their desk or in the cafeteria or in the hall and had them say "Oh, yes, that reminds me, can you get . . . ?" Other PR tips include making sure you are included in any new employee orientation program or packet. What you hand out or say need not be fancy or complete, just enough to make sure they know you and the library exist. Of course if you get new employee names and follow up with a personal call or visit, that is even better. One SOLO sends out a daily news alert, making sure that the library's name is on it. This is great if you have the time.

If you can get mentioned in company publications, that is really good PR, and public libraries should use the local newspaper as a PR vehicle. Even the neighborhood throwaway is good for an article now and then. But do not stop there. Publish your own newsletter, and be sure your newsletters reach your users; also, make sure they are put where the nonusers can find them. For institutions this may be the cafeteria or smoking room; for public libraries it could be stores, doctors' offices, schools. Anything that gets your name and the name of your library out to your constituency (users and nonusers alike) is worth doing. Make sure it is professional looking, accurate, attractive, and, most importantly, frequent.

Michel Bauwens (1993), the first "cybrarian," a librarian who operates exclusively in cyberspace (with no physical facility), has some suggestions for marketing your library in cyberspace. By proactively building virtual reference areas, the cybrarian anticipates user needs and creates a one-stop shopping mall for information. He suggests a three-part system, with access to intranet (in-house) sources, access to general productivity tools (dictionaries, encyclopedias, phone books, etc.), and organization-specific resources on the Internet. Among his suggestions are: to offer something useful to attract new users and get current ones to return; provide newsgroups, listservs, and other interest groups, creating a virtual community; to use newsletters, memos, e-mail and other means to promote your virtual library; to make it easy for them to find information; and to provide means for user feedback.

PROFESSIONALISM

There are several issues involved in librarians as professionals. We have to be concerned about our image and guard our professional demeanor and ethics. We also have an obligation to continue to grow as professionals.

It is absolutely necessary that the library and the librarian have a professional image. "Our profession suffers from an identity crisis, caused in part by supervisors (and users) who do not share our professional identity" (Drake 1990, 152). Most people assume that anyone who works in a library is a "librarian"; when a member of the clerical staff cannot answer their question, or is rude, or gives them misinformation, they assume that the "librarian" was not helpful. This is especially bad in public libraries, but holds true for other types of libraries as well. As SOLOs we are not immune to this if we have clerical assistance. The other problem is that many libraries are not staffed by professionals. If they are not well-trained and do not have the customer-service ethic; their performance hurts us all.

There is controversy about whether a public library director should be a librarian. One researcher suggests that the director does not have to be a librarian, that the MBA or MPA (public administration) might be better preparation (although a combination of both is best). The important roles of the director are managing, knowing the needs and desires of community, representing the library in the community, raising money, so "library skills are less important that management skills" (Garou 1996) except for understanding of principles of intellectual freedom. Others, however, felt that the director does need to be a librarian. The keys to being a director are leadership, vision, and culture, all of which should be part of the library education (Nichols 1996). It is important to realize that "a person with a degree in the field brings with her a knowledge of the lay of the land and . . . an understanding of the special requirements made of those working under her" (Martin 1996).

Librarians are often taken for granted, and they are often patronized; it is assumed that many of their requests are well-meaning and idealistic, but not practical" (White 1984, 95). One problem is there is no accounting of a librarian's accomplishments because there are "no methods to evaluate library contributions to productivity and profits" (Prusack and Matarazzo 1990, 45-6). These statements are not unique to librarians, but that does not make them any less damaging to us.

What is more damaging to the profession is our acceptance of this image. When I was in library school I found the prevalent attitude was that our low salaries and low prestige were almost entirely due to the profession being predominantly women, which was taken as an immutable fact. I was not very popular with them as I suggested that the reason our salaries and prestige are low is that we accept them. Many library "activists" feel that we need to "demand" more respect and higher pay, but I strongly disagree. We cannot *demand* respect; we must *earn* it. How do we earn respect? Respect can be earned by a professional attitude and by producing results for our institutions and our users. We do not do ourselves any good as a profession by failing to set up explicit standards for librarians. At present, there is no consistency in the degree of preparation offered by the ALA-accredited library schools, no competency requirements, and no requirements for continuing professional development.

Besides updating standards, there are other ways to improve our image. We should be on the forefront in adopting technology, pay attention to the needs of our users, be active in the parent organization, represent our business in the community, get published outside the company, avoid the librarian stereotype, and provide information leadership in the organization. Librarians need to be more proactive and decisive. We have to promote and defend the library and get managers to see the library and the librarian as strategic resources. We must defend our turf against those who would deny our information collection, analysis, and dissemination expertise. Our title and place in the organizational structure needs to be appropriate. Even if you do not manage a staff, you manage information. Therefore, the title of manager should be yours. Several experts suggest dropping the title "librarian" from your title. As much as I hate to admit it, they are right—at least for now. Until we can update management's preconceived notion of a librarian, we are better off with some other title. Prusak and Mattarrazzo (1990) examined several state-of-the-art books on corporate information management and found no mention of libraries or librarians. What an opportunity for us! There will have to be a "mental jump" (paradigm shift) or change in professional attitude by both sides, however. SOLOs are often leading the way in redesigning the image of the librarian. Joan Williamson recently observed that "one-person librarians now have a better image of themselves" (St. Clair 1996a, 2). We tend to see ourselves not as downtrodden servants, but in terms of our value as information professionals, but there is still plenty of room for improvement.

WHAT DOES IT MEAN TO BE A PROFESSIONAL?

Herb White writes that "the smaller the professional staff, the more important it becomes to select truly excellent professionals" (1994, 53). Since a SOLO library is as small a professional staff as one can find, professionalism is especially important for us. It is a sad fact of life that, unfortunately, users will accept mediocrity and incompetence if that is what is available; it is our job to keep that from happening. As St. Clair puts it, "if you stop to worry whether you *should* be doing this or that part of the task, whether it is *appropriate* or not, you'll never get around to doing what you're supposed to be doing" (1996a, 3). Clerical tasks are just as much a part of the job as the more professional ones, and it is very important to "always think of yourself as a professional, even when performing nonprofessional tasks" (St. Clair 1976, 234). This may mean working however long it takes to get the job done, even if that exceeds forty hours.

Does definition of a professional include the need for a degree? One can act professionally without having a degree, but he or she cannot be a professional. The obtaining of a degree shows a level of commitment and a presumed minimum level of competence. But a degree is not enough because "after demonstrating that minimum standard, some soar, others crash" (MEDLIB 1996). Beyond the degrees, we, as SOLOs, are well advised to maintain grace under pressure (stay cool, lighten up, do not take ourselves too seriously), offer friendly service without playing favorites (that is, treat the janitor the same as you would the president—much easier to say than to do), stand up for ourselves, and (from Tom Peters) learn to love change. Finally, several people have suggested that we also should enjoy what we do.

Professionalism requires a continuing commitment to maintain your skills. This includes spending time and dollars on continuing education. Most employers pay all or part of the cost of your attendance at conferences, meetings, and courses. Even in public libraries about two-thirds pay for continung education, with a higher percentage in the larger libraries (Ahlricks 1988). You can make contacts at conferences and classes to fight that feeling of loneliness SOLOs often feel. Continuing education opportunities can be found within your own organization, from professional associations, from vendors, and at universities. Training opportunities vary from one type of library to another, but there is always something available. If all else fails, you can visit other libraries (both like yours and different) to get ideas. Other benefits of continuing education are that is boosts your professional esteem and demonstrates your professional attitude to yourself and to your manager (St. Clair 1987).

There is one comment that really makes me angry when I hear it from many SOLOs: "If my boss won't pay to send me to the conference, then I won't go." As far as I am concerned, if you are a professional, then you do what is necessary to keep your skills up-to-date. If this means paying your way to a conference or course, then you pay. Just because your company is not smart enough to realize the importance of contin- uing education does not mean you have to ignore it as well. There are scholarships available to many conferences or you can make it a family vacation. Remember, the information you receive will make you a better librarian, and if that does not help you on this job, it will on the next. I have never been to a conference or course that did not make me more confident of my abilities or teach me something that would come in handy down the road. Continuing education is an opportunity a profession librarian cannot afford to neglect.

One More Pair of Hands—or One Less: Outsourcing and Downsizing

This chapter is about how to grow an additional pair of hands and add hours to the clock (outsourcing) and how to cope with losing some of your staff (downsizing). Some people equate outsourcing with downsizing and are afraid of both, but they are *not* the same thing at all. Downsizing is reducing the number of people working in the library. Many SOLOs become SOLOs by being downsized from a larger staff, or a SOLO can also be downsized by losing clerical support. Of course the ultimate downsizing is cutting all staff and closing the library. On the other hand, outsourcing is the contracting out of some services, while keeping the library open; rather than being something to be feared, it can be a boon to the SOLO—if handled properly.

OUTSOURCING

It is a fact that about 86 percent of major corporations now outsource at least some services, up from 58 percent in 1992, according to A.T. Kearney; in addition, up to 25 percent of business information operations are now contracted out (St. Clair 1996f). Thus, outsourcing is a part of business life now and is often invoked in the name of re-engineering. Re-engineering, however, did not start out to be about outsourcing, but rather about changing basic problems. Outsourcing often does not change those basic problems, it just pushes them out of the company onto someone else. Perhaps outsourcing has gone too far. A *Business Week* article entitled "Has Outsourcing Gone Too Far?" reported that "the payoff from outsourcing . . . sometimes falls far short of expectations. One study found the average savings to be around 9 percent, though consultants often promise gains of 20 percent to 40 percent" (Byrne 1996, 26). In that article one consultant says that there are many failures of outsourcing contracts, sometimes costing time, money, and customers. In addition, "outsourcing could (and already has in many cases) lead to increasingly fragmented work cultures in which lower-paid employees simply get the work done, with little initiative or enthusiasm" (27). There is also little chance of change as "Few expect the trend to slow anytime soon. As long as the pressure is on to reduce costs, companies will continue to turn more of their operations to outsiders" (28).[1]

There are two kinds of outsourcing: internal and external. You can either outsource work to another department within the organization or to another organization. Both have pros and cons.

It might seem safer to outsource internally. But librarians are sometimes criticized for "collaborating with other departments in our organizations that are involved with information delivery and informa-tion transfer . . . outsourcing stuff "that 'by right' should come to us" (St. Clair 1996f, 1). But there should be is no problem with internal outsourcing as long as we make sure there is added value; we are just partnering inside the organization rather than outside. We SOLOs have been partnering with our colleagues in the organizations where we work for a long time, and "no one-person librarian would dare to think that, as a professional information services employee, he or she should stand alone. Cooperating, partnering, participating in the achievement of the corporate good, is what one-person librarians do" (St. Clair 1996f, 1).

What about external outsourcing? Some outsourcers approach senior management directly, saying that the library is not cost-effec-tive and they should outsource information services. Managers, in their ignorance, may believe it. The information customer is caught in the middle of this vendor/librarian "fight." The decision is made, not by the customer, not by the librarian, not by the vendor, but by management. "And by the time management has made the decision, it is probably too late to do much about it" (St. Clair 1996f, 6). In other words, if you have not already sold management on the value of your information expertise, it may be too late.

---

1. For more information, check out The Outsourcing Institute, founded in 1993, "an international-ly recognized professional association for objective, independent information on the strategic use of outside resources."(http: //www.outsourcing.com or 45 Rockefeller Plaza, Suite 2000, New York, NY 10111, 800-421-6767, fax: 800-421-1644)

The question arises as to when you should outsource. The general rules are you should outsource when it is to your advantage and when you can control it. In a discussion of the law library of the future (held by the American Association of Law Libraries via the Internet in May 1996), most participants did not see the library as an appropriate place for outsourcing. However, they agreed that there are some times when outsourcing does make sense: when it is economically advantageous to the firm, when there is little or no risk to the firm, when it can improve service levels at no extra cost, when a contractor would more easily be able to stay current with technology, and when you need expertise not available in-house.

Outsourcing can allow you to increase services without adding headcount, something management is always afraid of and you may not wish to supervise an employee anyway. Outsourcing can also take care of a temporary overload. We all face times where everyone wants something at the same time; outsourcing can help.

Outsourcing is also appropriate when you will be absent from the library for a relatively long period of time (for vacation, travel, illness, or professional development). This way you do not have to hire a substitute and run the risk of the organization letting you go and hiring the sub. Finally, outsourcing can be a good way to offer a new service with minimal risk. If it does not go over well, you can just drop the outsourcer.

Activities to Be Outsourced

The most common services outsourced are subscriptions, document delivery, cataloging, and online searching.

Subscriptions

The big subscription services handle thousands of journals and are set up to do it far more efficiently that you could. They can place the orders, handle address changes, and take care of claiming lost issues. Some will even add routing slips for you. This is all done through one phone number, and this can simplify your life. Of course, if you have only a few subscriptions, it probably will not be necessary or worthwhile. When negotiating with subscription services, know your collection and the needs of your patrons, establish priorities, compare prices and services, negotiate credits and service charges (almost everything is negotiable and do not be afraid to tell one vendor another offered you a smaller service charge), be open to smaller, no-name vendors, get it in writing, remember that your first loyalty is to your library, and evaluate the vendor's attitude as well as technical competence. Also, you should not be afraid to complain to the vendor and/or switch vendors if service is unsatisfactory. One caution is that switching vendors is a time-consuming and frustrating process and itself may degrade service in terms of duplicate or lost issues. It should not be done just to save a half-percentage point in service charges, but as a last resort.

Document Delivery

Document delivery, both of photocopies and books, is at best a time-consuming and mind-numbing job. Why not pay someone else to locate the items, arrange payment, and ship them to you? Most article delivery services will mail or fax the item directly to your patron, although I prefer to have it sent to me so I know it is in and can put my name on it so patrons remember who got the article for them. Renee Daulong of Information Resource Services, in an online post (1996), suggests these ways to evaluate a document delivery service: turnaround time (should be one-two days), price (around $15), quality (clean, straight, no big black margins), ability to get international documents, and payment of the royalty fees. Remember, the total cost, including royalties, is what is relevant. I would add to this whether the vendor keeps me informed. If I ask for something rush, I need to know very quickly if they can deliver in time. If they cannot, I can go elsewhere or at least tell my patron there will be a delay. Not all services do this equally well.

A good book jobber can save you not only time and aggravation, but money, and they get a discount from most publishers and will pass it on to you. On your own you are very unlikely to get such a discount from a publisher. Some jobbers also pay the shipping costs as well, an additional savings that mounts up very quickly; remember, it is the total cost that counts, not the discount alone. You do not have prepay the jobber as you do a publisher so if a book is not published for six months after you order it, you are not out the money until you receive it. Accounting departments love this. They also like the consolidated monthly bill you can get—you pay only one vendor, once a month. Do not forget to evaluate the service of the vendor, and if you are not happy, try another.

Cataloging

Many SOLOs outsource cataloging as I have. Anderson and Pawl say: "Don't waste time and money on original cataloging and processing in a one-person library . . . . Your time will be much better spent serving a user" (1979, 274). The time saved and patron satisfaction will justify the cost of commercial processing. In an 1995 Internet post, J. Hill, from a small college library in Australia, evaluated the pros and cons of outsourced cataloging. The pros are saving time and money and not hiring additional staff, and outsourcing companies maintain quality and consistency of cataloging better since they are better trained, do it more, and are almost definitely better at original cataloging, and they can even prepare the book for the shelf (pockets, call numbers, even property stamping). For her, the negative side is the need to send items away which can delay availability to customer and be expensive although you may be able to find a lower cost source. She concluded that the positives far outweigh the negatives.

Online Searching

You can use outsourcing to add expertise that you do not have. If you have a project that will require a lot of detailed chemical searching, but you are not a chemist, why not outsource those searches to an expert chemical searcher. They will be able to do it better than you could, making your patron happy and, indirectly, making you look good.

Deciding What to Outsource

Herb White (1984) suggests you try to contract out only clerical or nonprofessional tasks but I disagree. Contract out those tasks you do not do well so you can concentrate on what you do best. If you are not a cataloger, contract out cataloging to give you more time to do the online searching or database building that you do outstandingly. Dr. David Bender, executive director of SLA, suggests four questions to ask before outsourcing: "How would outsourcing this function affect the corporate memory? How would it affect the integrity of our data? What is the standing and/or reliability of this contractor? What are the cost advantages and disadvantages? If outsourcing could satisfy one's needs in some way, then there's no reason not to pursue it" (Quint 1996b, 8). But be careful to outsource only the nonstrategic because you do not want to lose control of those activities essential to the institution's mission.

Sometimes outsourcers (consultants or firms) are asked to bid on projects without the approval (or even knowledge) of the librarian or the current outsourcer. Although it is done, it is not ethical, according to Ann Davidson in an article in *Searcher* (1996). Also, it is not a good idea for outsourcers, since if they treat their current information provider this way, can you expect to be treated better? She feels that we need code of ethics for providers of outsourcing services (similar to those of the Association of Independent Information Professionals and the AALL) that protects the relationship with other information professionals.

Engineers will not review another engineer's work without their knowledge or consent, why would we?

There is often a real (or perceived) adversarial relationship between librarians and vendors. This helps no one. While we are constantly asking more of our vendors, since we are being asked more of by our patrons, librarians and vendors must understand each other's business needs. We cannot squeeze their margins so tight that they go out of business. This is not good for either party. Remember, it is in your best interest to keep the vendor in business (assuming you like his service). If he goes out of business, you get *no* service.

Besides vendors, you may find yourself working with information brokers. James Dobbs defined an information broker as "one who collects a fee for acting as an intermediary" (LaForte 1982, 84). In a sense, we are all information brokers in the strict definition of the words, since we receive a fee (a salary), but the term is more commonly used for outside vendors. Information brokers can serve the same purpose as the vendors above, giving us more expertise and time. Many librarians are afraid of information brokers because they challenge some basic library assumptions (Kinder 1988). These assumptions concern the role of the library in society, that we might become expendable; the selling of information, that information should be a free right; and the use of "free" libraries by brokers and other for-profit institutions and individuals.

However, when used judiciously and only for special projects or services, they can be valuable additions to our SOLO bag of tricks. "Working in partnership with librarians, information brokers can provide the *product*, allowing the librarian to focus attention on the *client*" (Eiblum 1995, 22). That is, after all, what we were hired to do. Information brokers can do document delivery, subject bibliographies, online searches, translations, data collection, primary and secondary market research, abstracting and indexing, writing, editing, setting up libraries, evaluating libraries, current awareness, and location of experts.

In summary, outsourcing is not the be-all and end-all of SOLO librarianship. Some of the disadvantages of contracting out are the loss of knowledge of the way the organization works and the way those in it use information, the loss of organizational memory, and the resistance a contractor may offer to changes requiring long-term or capital investments. But these can be minimized if the librarian stays in control of the outsourcing process. "Stay in close touch with your users so you know the quality of [work] done and your users know that you have access to additional and different info. Depending on the business you're in you will find one service suits you better than another" (Appel 1996, e-mail). You need to constantly reevaluate the outsourced services. What made sense to outsource last year may not make sense now. For example, I used to outsource journal subscriptions. When I handled all the subscriptions for the entire company (over 350 subscriptions) and I had the time to do it, it made sense and I had the secretaries order subscriptions directly. Cost center managers, however, objected to paying for next year's subscriptions out of this year's funds and to the service charge. At least two vice-presidents said to me what did I do besides "screw up my subscriptions," neglecting to tell me they already had a subscription at home and were getting two. I figured I had arrived at a lose-lose situation. The best I could possibly hope for was that all subscriptions would arrive on time all the time, a slight possibility. Since I was getting no glory—only grief—for doing the subscriptions, I decided to drop them.

How are our professional associations responding to the outsourcing threat? In an interview, David Bender of SLA noted that it is a complicated issue. SLA membership includes both librarians (the outsourcees) and vendors and information brokers (the outsourcers). Therefore, SLA is treading carefully. Jane Miller, president of AIIP, looks at outsourcing as a partnership with clients, not an either/or situation. She also notes that association members often "outsource" to each other, passing on assignments that they cannot handle themselves. AIIP's code of ethics does not address outsourcing directly, but does say that it will "accept only those projects which are . . . not detrimental to our profession [and] maintain a professional relationship with libraries."

DOWNSIZING

There are four common methods of downsizing: normal attrition (management just does not fill positions as they become vacant), induced attrition (offering early retirement incentives produce voluntary resignations), planned change (after an executive decision on priorities, targeting cutbacks to specific services), and the visionary approach in which the organization moves toward a new vision of the future (Khan 1987). This is more proactive than planned change and requires rethinking of traditional services and techniques.

It is a fact that 15 percent of the libraries surveyed by Prusak and Matarazzo in 1990 had closed their libraries by 1995. Why is this profession so vulnerable to downsizing and is there a way to avoid it?

"SOLO librarians are perpetually vulnerable to 'downsizing,' and ignore . . . reports of the dissatisfaction of employers at their peril" (Bryant 1995, 17). In a note of hope, St. Clair (1996e) writes that libraries in corporations, law firms, etc., might be less vulnerable to downsizing since they (presumably) meet specialized needs, although through my own research, I cannot agree.

One reason for this vulnerability is that special librarians have allowed others to fight their battles for them. This may not be limited to special librarians, for it happens in public libraries and academia, too. "We're waiting for someone else to do the work, wave the magic wand, and give us ammunition to fight the fight on our personal battlefield. We adopted the same tactics with the image issue, asking our professional associations to wage broad-based campaigns to improve the image of librarians" (DiMattia 1995, 4). It did not work, because it is our issue. We have to fight it on a library-by-library basis. DiMattia goes on to say that "special librarians continually maintain that they do not have the time nor the expertise to conduct research [on the value of the library to the organization] in addition to fighting the daily battles to stay employed" although they should make the time, and they must "be integrated in the organization and so well connected to the corporate political strength that you have a vivid understanding of the decisions being made on high. [This is much easier said than done . . .] The bottom line is to convince corporate managers that even though information may not be their core business, information is at the core of their business and their competitive advantage in the marketplace."

Reasons for Downsizing

Sometimes a new management theory can contribute to downsizing. A hot new codeword for downsizing is "disintermediation" which means doing away with the intermediary (you, the librarian) and going directly to the end users. The rise of the Internet has contributed to management's comfort level with end-user searching. I am not a fan of end-user searching. Do you want your high-priced engineers (scientists, salespeople, etc.) spending their time looking for information on systems they are not familiar with, using search logic and databases they do not fully understand? It would be better to have (relatively) low-priced information professionals who are well-versed in both sources and methods of searching doing it for them—in a better, faster, and less expensive way!

Since most organizations lack methods to evaluate and value the library, libraries are often seen only as overhead. Management does not understand how libraries can help get information (and organize and disseminate it) and therefore increase productivity and/or profitability. Other problems leading to library closings or downsizing include competition from members of other departments in the organization who think they can do the work of the library. In addition, outsourcing some library services could lead to contracting out of *all* services.

To illustrate the facts behind the phenonmenon of downsizing, St. Clair (1994b) presented two case studies. In case one, management hired a consulting firm to study the library. They found only a small core of users. The librarian declined to be involved in the study. The library was closed, no one was too upset (except the librarian). In case two the librarian heard rumors of a corporate reorganization and went to his primary users with a questionnaire on library services and satisfaction. He followed up on it, raising users' awareness of the library. The library was not downsized even though every other department was. The message is that you have to be proactive. Do not wait until they come to you. Assume there is going to be downsizing and cutbacks and have a plan.

An organization's attitude toward information is of vital importance to a library's success; if they do not value information, find a way to change their attitude; if they do, nurture it. The library must understand the organization's stated (and *un*stated) mission and its role/relationship to it—there must be a connection, the library must be *mission-critical*. The library must be perceived as supplying information in whatever form is necessary, not just in books and journals. Often those who have the authority to close or downsize a library are not library users and have no vested interest in it; since it is not valuable to them, they think that it is not valuable to anyone.

AALL has been active in its response to outsourcing and downsizing. In the spring of 1995, after a very large law firm, Baker and McKenzie, closed its library and outsourced its services, AALL formed a Task Force on the Value of Law Libraries in the Information Age. The aim was to prepare materials to assist law librarians in explaining their value to their bosses, their clients, and themselves. They also came up with a list of competencies for a law librarian at entry level, middle level, and experienced levels. Outsourcing and downsizing are not new to law librarians, since they started for them in the late 1980s. Mark Estes, a member of the Task Force, explains that since most AALL members work in small, mostly SOLO libraries, they have been especially vulnerable. "They do not have time to gather information to articulate their worth" (Quint 1996b, 14). Outsourcing is only one tool they can use, properly or improperly. Judicious use of information brokers allows the SOLO law librarian to expand service and resources. However, when outsourcing eliminates human, face-to-face connections, the firm will suffer.

Some pertinent comments came out of AALL's Law Library of the Future discussion; Chuck Stinnett, one participant, summed up the discussion with "the greater risk to job security for librarians is not from outsourcing but from their failure to become (or remain) pivotal in the central intelligence activities of the firm" (1996). He cautioned librarians not to focus on protecting their territory but to do what is best for the firm. He also reminds librarians to lead in downsizing, not to be on the defensive. Mark Estes adds that "if you, the librarian, do not know your world you're a fool. It's the responsibility of any professional librarian to pay attention to their work environment" (Quint 1996b, 16).

How to Avoid Being Outsourced or Downsized

There are several ways that might prevent your job being outsourced or downsized. While they are not guaranteed, they are worth considering:

- Write a mission statement reflecting the strategic objectives of the organization and promote the mission statement to the organization.
- Be proactive: collect statistics but be sure to give specific examples of how you saved money or solved problems. Get endorsements from your clients.
- Prepare a report showing the "unique" services which you can provide that outsourcing may not be able to (timeliness, internal control, confidentiality).
- Participate in organizational task forces to demonstrate competencies to upper management.
- Make a list of companies that used to outsource but have reversed that decision.
- Keep your skills up-to-date (both technical skills and business skills).
- Find new roles for the library to replace old ones that are obsolete, little used, or outsourceable.
- Let your patrons know that information expertise and knowledge were required to fill their request—it was not something that just anyone could have done.
- Review your procedures—are you doing your best?

There are other tactics as well. One librarian was confronted by management asking her to justify the use of commercial databases when "everything is on the Internet and is free." Another librarian's suggestion to her was to drop the commercial services, being sure to tell patrons that she cannot provide the information because management felt the service was not necessary. This is a bit dramatic and a hardship on those whose questions go unanswered, but this can be an effective way to make a point. One caution is that it will not always work. One of my managers canceled a valuable (and expensive) service for which we had no replacement. The sad part is that my patrons adjusted to this drop in service, almost without complaining.

Dealing with Downsizing

Okay, your efforts to avoid downsizing have failed. Now what? Guy St. Clair (1996e) suggests that you be proactive—offer to downsize what you can—it makes you look loyal and sacrificing. Be sure you know how downsizing will affect your customers and make the higher-ups aware of it. You may need to realign information services, make new partnerships and alliances, consolidate units, or shed responsibilities.

SOLOs cannot wait for downsizing to go away—we must be proactive. Guy St. Clair (1996e) provides a good summary in "Not Waiting For It to Happen Or, The One-Person Librarian's Outsourcing Prevention Handbook in Eight Easy Lessons":

1. "Outsourcing is not a dirty word"; outsource the tedium, the out-of-scope, the I-do not-have-time.
2. "Management's job is to control and to evaluate"; it is their job to find ways to economize (and it is yours to make sure you are not the way).
3. "External consultants are in business"; they are not the ogres.
4. "Ethics is still important"; beware the consultant that comes in and says you need to outsource the library—to them!
5. "The one-person librarian is the information expert for the organization, enterprise, institution, or community in which she is employed"; if management does not see that, it is probably YOUR fault.
6. "Advocacy is not a passive activity"; lobbying is good, library committees are good, advocates are good.
7. "The grapevine exists"; use it, know what is going one before it happens and do not let yourself be blindsided.
8. "When it's too late, it's too late . . . once the decision has been made to outsource an entire library function, it is too late for the

one-person librarian to do anything. Do not panic. And do not try to fight back"; just go quietly.

Not all closings are the librarian's fault. Some are political, some have ulterior motives, and some are just budgetary. But in some cases it *is* the librarian's fault. He or she did not promote the library and information services to the right people, the decision makers, or did not keep up with what was needed. Professional skills were not updated in terms of computer literacy, technical orientation, or business techniques. Terminology or services did not keep up. The library continued to concentrate on buying and circulating books and journals and not on information, competitive information, or the Internet.

On a precautionary note, Herb White (1984) proposes these three stages of dealing with cutback resources. They all have inherent pitfalls. The first stage is that the condition is temporary and the problem will disappear. Unfortunately this is seldom true and it usually gets worse. The second stage is that the organization can continue as it has, doing more with less. This rarely works and is counterproductive. If we *can* do more, they can say we were not working as hard as we could have been. If we can do it with less, we had too much. The last stage is that a change in resources requires a reassessment of goals, objectives, and strategies. We must decide on new priorities and how to reach them with the new level of resources.

The success of downsizing depends on how the remaining employees buy in to the changes—they must understand the reason for the change and your continued innovation and enthusiasm and challenge. You must let the patrons know of the changes and their implications and that the library will continue to help them, although maybe differently.

When downsizing, attitude is important, concentrate on the essentials, delegate what you can, use partnership and alliances. Ask "why are *we* doing this task?" Is the library the best place for this task or could someone do it better? What would the consequences be of letting someone else do it? Is this task integral (critical, strategic) to the organization's mission? to the library's? What are the costs associated with doing this task? and of outsourcing it? In other words, go down your list of tasks and ask for each, "is this trip necessary?" One tack to take is in downsizing your space—do you really need it all? Can you weed some books or journals? Can you share resources with another institution? Can you become more of a "virtual" library? "The delivery of information is not constrained by space" (St. Clair 1996b, 7).

Three Case Studies

In the course of writing this book, I have come across many examples of downsizing. The following three case studies represent the most typical.

Case Study 1: Paul Zieselman (via e-mail)

I am the solo (with an assistant and a filer/shelver/messenger) at an ninety-attorney branch of one of the top ten law firms. In 1991 we had three librarians (manager, asst. librarian and cataloger) plus mail/ILL and two filers. I then became the asst./cataloger and one filer was let go. The library manager left and I became manager/librarian/cataloger and we outsourced the filing. I then had to take on a person from another department as filer, etc. I do not know what these extra people did! Yes, sometimes I'm stretched but eventually I catch up and the attorneys are SUPER!

Case Study 2: Anonymous

We did it all. We developed our own logo and an impressive and informative brochure. We conducted well-attended open houses with demonstrations, displays and, of course, refreshments. We had a special reception for management. We presented "dog and ponies" at off-site locations and for department staff meetings and focused them to the group. We conducted seminars, handed out rolodex cards and held orientation sessions for new employees. We periodically ran surveys of users and non-users and solicited feedback from our customers. We collected and reported statistics that demonstrated growing usage across all business areas and produced an annual report with graphs and concrete examples of the research we performed. So, how did we go from a staff of eleven in 10,000 square feet to a staff of two in 2,500 square feet?

The fact is, you can do everything that the library management books and gurus recommend and still not be able to save your library. A library, like the other units in a company, is subject to all the management tools (or fads) of the moment. Today, downsizing is a way of life in the corporate world. It impacts all departments and the library is neither exempt nor singled out. Our library was formed to provide a centralized information service for all company employees. A staff of eleven (five professionals, six support) and appropriate collections were selected and placed in a 10,000-square-foot facility. The library was formed just as the company was beginning to go through a series of reorganizations and cost-cutting exercises, so from the beginning there were pressures to cut back and reduce costs.

Increased automation and more efficient procedures led to substantial savings, but every time a way was found to save money, management added charges to the library budget to be recovered from user units. These included complete cost recovery of space at premium rent charges and the cost of all support services provided (such as accounts payable, mail, etc.) and even a percentage of administrative costs from the three levels above us, i.e., our boss, his boss, and his boss's boss.

At first the changes were small. As staff left for a variety of reasons, their functions were reevaluated and work procedures were changed. Collections were weeded and library space needs were reduced. These were changes that needed to be made even without management pressure. The staff by this time consisted of eight (four librarians, four support) and the space had been reduced to 5,000 square feet. Then came the corporate mandate to all units to "decentralize." We were able to document negative cost and service implications and, thanks to some good connections, got the report into the hands of top management. The report's conclusions were accepted, but it did not matter. Decentralization was the decreed "flavor of the month" and it would happen regardless of cost, service or anything else.

The corporate library was reduced to three librarians providing reference/research services and document delivery via an outside vendor. We moved out of the library into a suite of office cubicles. The business groups made other provisions for meeting their information needs. Two years later, the pendulum swung back. Cost savings was the key corporate objective. Where we had "decentralized," now we "consolidated." We even picked up two major collections that had not been part of the original library (other departments were also "consolidating"). However, when the dust settled we were down to a staff of four (two librarians, two support).

A year later, a major business segment supported by the library moved to another site. They had accounted for 40 percent of our use. With their departure, we had to reduce staff and space by 50 percent. Figures, doesn't it! Today with one librarian and one very capable support person, we keep up with customer requests for information and documents. Just about everything else falls behind. And outsourcing still hangs heavy.

Case Study 3: Dan Trefethen, formerly of TRA Associates of Seattle

Three years ago I was faced with losing my assistant. Other overhead staff were dropping and people were starting to comment about my keeping Mark on staff. He was just finishing up a records management certificate program at the university. He needed more challenging work intellectually than what I could offer, since he was not trained for library research. I figured we could maybe engineer a win/win situation. Well, maybe not *totally* win/win, since I would lose an assistant, but maybe we could work it out all right. I discussed with Mark the possibility of a "phased out" layoff, working about three months ahead. He sounded amenable to it. He'd finish his program and be ready to job hunt with his new certificate. I could assign him some projects I wanted him to complete before I went truly SOLO.

Then it was time to talk to my boss, the financial/administrative manager of the firm. Most librarians' bosses are bottom line guys: they are presented with their numbers, and are told to hold them down or get them down further. Some bosses, like mine, are actually the numbers generators. Few of them know anything substantial about library operations, although they may be friends and allies of their library staff. The thing they hate most is for a librarian to dump a problem on them, especially one that costs money they were not counting on spending. Conversely, the thing they like most is for their people to come to them and say "we have an opportunity here to improve your bottom line, and the job situation here." Then they listen.

I told my boss we could cut my assistant, and that I'd be willing to work towards that end. We just wanted to do it in an orderly fashion. First, set a target date (which could still be a little squishy, but you need something to shoot for). Second, tell Mark what we needed to accomplish by that time. Third, without an assistant, I'd need to jettison some jobs that had fallen into my domain. This is the "office politics" part. Librarians are often stuck with duties that are tangential to our jobs. Downsizing is a *great* opportunity to dump these jobs. The story goes like this: Hey, I'm making a hell of a sacrifice here, falling on my sword for the company (most bosses—if they're guys—like military or sports metaphors). The least the company can do is help me realign my priorities and reassign some of this stuff to other units who now have more staff to deal with it. What you do is make your shopping lists: stuff I want to dump, and stuff you want to keep. If you can get away with it, you can even finesse it further: if you let me dump *more* clerical stuff, I'll take on *another* assignment (something you want to do, like marketing research, or competitor intelligence). Be prepared by knowing how much time these different chores take, so you do not end up agreeing to take more than you can dump. Try hard to get the boss to agree to everything on your "dump" list, knowing that it's more than likely he's going to get flak from others he tries to farm this out to, and come back and ask you to take back something. Then you can grudgingly say yes, and ask for something else (a computer upgrade? better software? dedicated clerical help from the department that pushed him off? whatever you thing you can get). Office politics? You betcha. Everybody's getting downsized, and others are doing it, too. How many jobs has the library picked up because of *other* departments' downsizing? You see, you can play the game, too. I'm not suggesting we all end up linking arms and go off whistling into a bright corporate future. Change is stressful. Downsizing hurts. You could lose more than you gain. You only fall on your sword when you realize (as the Roman centurions did) the alternative was even worse.

Whether we like it or not, "creative downsizing" is now a management strategy. Like any management strategy, some play it better than others. Librarians can be prepared to play it just as well or better than others. One advantage: the librarian "mystique." If they do not really know how you do what you do, they're not in a good position to micromanage you or to critique your downsizing strategy. We always say that knowledge is power. The corollary is that lack of knowledge is lack of power. Use the knowledge to your advantage.

Case Study 4: Norma Draper

When the library staff was cut in half (from two to one), I drew up a list of about ten to eleven library services I wanted to eliminate. I presented the list to the research staff who agreed to eliminate all but the routing of journals. They said that they needed to be on top of things and the fastest and easiest way was to have the journals routed to them. They believed that it was a valuable use of my time to save them time. I agreed to continue routing journals because I truly believe that my job is to provide the information the staff needs in the format that they request. I believe that the staff should have some input on the the issue. I also provide to each employee on a yearly basis a list of journals s/he no longer needs to see on a regular basis. It cuts down on the long list of people on circulation of journals to be routed. You may think that "Routing 200 is a waste of time, education, and skills" and maybe your co-workers and upper management agree, *but* if your organization values routing of journals, then you're missing out on providing what your co-workers and upper management need. *Special libraries are set up to fulfill the mission of the organization. It is important for librarians to review all the services that they provide and make sure that they are spending their time on the services that upper management and co-workers need.* [emphasis mine]

Downsizing is now a continuous process. We need to emphasize that the *real* way to save money is to have more well-trained information intermediaries and fewer expensive end users doing their own searching for information. Remember that we are not alone in being downsized. Many companies are doing away with lower-paid secretaries and having higher-paid professionals doing word processing, photocopying, time sheets, etc. This makes about as much sense to me as having us empty wastebaskets and sweep the floors.

And finally, as Elizabeth Meylor, a SOLO from Hammel, Green, and Abrahamson, e-mailed:

> Just so people do not lose hope, I've been steadily "upsizing" my library for the past seven years. Over the years I've gone from 'part-time' with administrative assistant responsibilities to "full-time" with archive responsibilities. I am finally getting Dialog and DataTimes because people understand the need for the information and the need to have it quickly. All the time I've spent giving people services they might not have thought they needed (scanning for and routing pertinent articles before they are requested, collection development, pushing for better indexes and databases, automating the catalogs) is beginning to pay off. It's a slow process and one that is by no means finished, but I think I can say that people here have come to rely on me and the library. Management always knew a library was "a good thing" or I'd have been laid off a long time ago, but they are finally seeing that having information is paying off and that's good for me.

Thus, all businesses and institutions do not downsize, but it is important for you to make yourself as essential as possible to management so they can see the value of your position.

4

The View from Abroad

SOLOs do not reside only in the United States and Canada. I was able to contact SOLOs in Australia, Germany, and South Africa. Personal contacts with librarians in the United Kingdom and Brazil provided some information. I did not find much written on SOLOs around the world, but have summarized what I did locate. I would be happy to receive additional information from SOLOs around the world.

For the most part, I found that the issues facing SOLOs in other parts of the world are about the same as in the United States. There is a greater scarcity of resources in some countries (South Africa, for example), and foreign exchange and the resultant high cost of online services and journals cause major problems. The educational systems outside the United States are structured quite differently and this has implications for SOLOs.

UNITED KINGDOM

One of the first SOLO organizations outside the United States was the One-Man Band (OMB) section of the Association of Libraries and Information Bureaux (ASLIB) in the United Kingdom. They were very active for several years, but are somewhat dormant at present (1996). Sue Bryant at the Library and Information Statistics at Loughborough University estimated in 1993 that there were 1,750 to 3,900 SOLOs in United Kingdom. This includes all the 1,070 school librarians, some SOLOs in higher education and public libraries and prisons, and many of the over 7,000 special librarians. One survey by Pitts estimated that 27 percent of United Kingdom librarians were SOLOs.

Shuter (1984) sent out 1,492 questionnaires, including the OMB group of ASLIB. Of the 241 usable, most OMBs were found in academic, business, or community (public) libraries. The "average" OMB had been on the job less than six years (63 percent), had previous library experience (72 percent), was nine to eighteen years out of school (42 percent). Only 6 percent were in their first job, but 28 percent were in their first library position. Many OMBs had some staff support: less than one FTE (10 percent), one FTE (35 percent), two or more FTE (11 percent). Sixty-one percent of OMBs belonged to a professional society (Library Association 51 percent, Institute of Information Scientists 21 percent). Most had decision making power on collection development (83 percent), personnel (60 percent), but fewer had control of their budget (38 percent). Interestingly, 5 percent refused to return the questionnaire "on grounds of sexist project title" (OMB).

SOLOs in the United Kingdom have quite a few networking resources. These include ASLIB, Institute of Information Scientists, Library Association, RSIS (Royal Society of Information Science, Women in Libraries, British Business School Librarians Group, Careers Information Officers in Local Authorities, European Business Schools Librarians, ITBs Library & Information, Management Librarians, Trade Union Librarians, Bank Librarians, British Library Information Officers, City Law Librarians, Construction Industry Information, Home Office Library & Information Science, Information Officers in Voluntary Organisations, Regional Health Authorities Librarians, UK Online User, Network of Community Resource Centers, Information Officers in Pharmaceutical Industry.

Shuter also asked OMBs what they liked best about being alone. Some of the replies were that they liked the ability to organize their own time, to be autonomous, to do interesting work, to have varied work, as well as to try out new ideas and be appreciated. On what they liked least, they felt the following were lacking: training opportunities, reliability of management support, knowledge about what's going on in organization, physical working conditions, contribution to personal development, pay job security, and a sense of being being appreciated. The most satisfying aspects of the job were researching information, serving users, achievement/involvement, autonomy, and receiving feedback and thanks. The most frustrating aspects of the job were routine work, not enough time to finish a job, isolation, low status, lack of staff, lack of authority and lack of appreciation, bureaucracy, low/no budget/resources, and inability to specialize.

The OMBs felt that the skills needed for success include self-confidence, an outgoing personality, discipline, tenacity, commitment, independence/initiative, enjoyment of hard work, patience, friendliness, ability to cope with pressure, empathy, versatility, ability to work in teams, and a sense of humor.

GERMANY

Thanks to Evelin Morgenstern, at Deutsches Bibliotheksinstitut, I was able to get thirty-one responses to my questionnaire from SOLOs in Germany. The statistics were very similar to those from the United States and are summarized in Appendix IV. Here are some of their comments:

What do you wish you'd known before you went SOLO?

- I am glad that I did not know how much work it is
- that I must know more than I learned at the library school
- that it is sometimes hard to work alone; there is nobody you can ask directly if you have questions about the job
- more about managing a library (administration)
- time management, information about business world
- how to get answers to questions I can't answer by myself
- more information on time management and general management of the library (e.g., negotiations with companies, the staff of the institute, etc.)
- accounting as it is practiced in a firm; library schools teach only about accounting practiced at governmental institutions
- that I have to take care of everything myself
- municipal budgeting practices
- budget and administration, human relations

How do you think library schools can prepare SOLOs better?

- more practical studies
- doing an internship in an OPL (one-person library); reading about problems of working in an OPL
- you should be trained to build up contacts to all sorts of librarians
- practical training in SOLO libraries
- I think they cannot prepare you better: what you must have is experience in different jobs in different libraries
- not only teach about public libraries but more about the structures in business, the role you play as an OPL, and time management
- more practice; not so much theory
- preparing them not to stick to the rules
- by offering practical studies in small libraries
- more job-oriented training which is less theoretical

What do you like most about being SOLO?

- ability to realize your own ideas, varied work
- responsibility, creativity in designing library management, and being able to see results of my work by dealing with the users directly
- working independently, variety of tasks, good contact to the users, knowing their interests
- it is interesting to do all the things yourself, not only one part of the job
- being free to make a decision what to do when and doing all that is necessary
- possibility of conceptual work, self-responsibility, complexity of work
- relatively great independence to organize things
- I can decide how I organize my time and my work; I think I can work more creatively than in a bigger library

What do you like least?

- too much work
- lack of acknowledgment, bad reputation
- lack of information network, it depends much on your own initiative whether you get the right/important information or, what is even more important, whether you find the right person to ask
- lot of work so that meetings (e.g,. with other librarians) are only possible in my free time, not enough exchange of experiences with colleagues
- being isolated, the underestimation of the library within the association
- the position is not accepted in academic circles
- I can't compare notes; there is no exchange or common planning with colleagues
- too little contact with other librarians; no communication about professional problems
- activities that belong to my work in the one-man-library but that do not have anything to do with the actual librarian's work, like administrating the material for the copy-machines, which are used by the whole institute
- you have to do your own lobbying

- lack of someone else in our staff to discuss specialist problems; I always have to phone, to write a letter
- work that is below level of qualification

Other comments?

- I think it is very important to set up a network for SOLOs, to get in contact with other SOLO librarians.
- I prefer being a SOLO than being only someone somewhere in a big library.
- I like being a SOLO librarian so much that I cannot imagine that I ever will be interested in working in a big library.

AUSTRALIA

Australia is another hotbed of SOLOship thanks to work by Guy St. Clair and Meg Paul. Australia is coming out of recession but is still dependent on the United States and Japan's economies. Their Internet access is limited but they still have the second largest Internet-user base after United States. Australian librarians have embraced the technology. The country has good special librarians, well-educated, well-read professionally, who network well. However, they have problems with downsizing, too, partly due to the lack of information to back up the need for library services.

There is now an organization just for SOLOs, OPAL (One-Person Australian Libraries), an affiliate of the Australian Library and Information Association. The first convenor is Georgina Dale (8 Powell Retreat, Westleigh NSW 2120, Australia, gdale@onaustralia.com.au.). In 1996 Meg Paul at FLIS Pty Ltd., Melbourne, started The Australasian One-Person Library, a wraparound for the One-Person Library with local content.

The survey response from Australia was small—one academic, one government, two medical, three nonprofit—but it shows a relatively high level of automation, with all respondents having access to online search services. The responses are summarized in Appendix IV.

The comments from Australian SOLOs were much the same as from other countries. Here are just a few of their responses to my questions.

What do you wish you'd known before becoming a SOLO?

- how isolated I would be, how to network better, how useful a mentor would have been, how to learn about areas I wasn't

familiar with or had no experience
- I should have been older and have had more experience under an experienced, established librarian
- better knowledge of computers/applications
- better time management and marketing skills
- the pain of managing an eight-machine network—it wasn't in the job description

How could library schools have prepared you better?

- more attention to SOLO librarianship
- concentrate more on practical work and highlight the fact that traditional systems of classification and style are not appropriate for many small special libraries
- smart ways to do things, time management, how to set priorities and limits
- much more hands-on practical work, better work experience programs
- the basics of software selection, i.e., which features to look for

What do you like most about being a SOLO?

- potential and freedom to respond to constantly changing needs and developments
- the variety of tasks involved in running the library
- being responsible for the quality of the work

What do you like least?

- isolation, frustration of juggling too much work and not enough time or staff, trying to keep up with new developments and finding a good, approachable person who is a good communicator to assist/train new technology applicants (loading software, using software or its application)
- constant interruptions
- convincing staff of keeping resources current (automating), having time to test new computer software
- high workload, the frustration of trying to convey to colleagues the nature of my work

Other comments?

- I have worked as a SOLO and as part of a team; SOLOs are much better, constantly challenged and pushed.

• While direct library work constitutes 15 percent of my work time, my library and information knowledge informs about 40 percent of my work. My skills greatly complement those of my colleagues, who are mostly social workers.

SOUTH AFRICA

For two wonderful weeks in September I had the privilege of visiting the Republic of South Africa and finding out about the SOLO scene first hand. I was one of ten librarians who made up the first People-to-People Citizen Ambassador Delegation in Special Librarianship and Information Services Management to the RSA. The trip was arranged and led by Guy St. Clair of Infomanage/SMR Inc.

Although none of the group's official visits was to a SOLO library, I had three opportunities to meet with SOLOs in a less formal setting. The first was at a meeting of the SAILIS Special Libraries Interest Section at the University of Witswatersrand in Johannesburg. SAILIS is the South Africa Institute for Librarianship and Information Science, an organization similar to our ALA. Here I met Marjorie Malan. She is retired from aircraft plant where she was downsized to SOLO. She did have an professional assistant and clerical help, but each successive manager cut more. However, the company was very generous with funding and she said she nearly always "got what I wanted." She was able to get out and network a lot. She feels it is even more important for SOLOs than others to network and not to be glued to the job.

Jenni Milward is a SOLO public librarian. She has found that public library patrons need more than just information and the librarian also serves a social function. She likes being a SOLO because she has more control and can often start her own programs without going through the bureaucracy. She is able to get a relief person so she can be active professionally, go to meetings, and present papers. She is very active in the Library and Information Workers Organization, a left-wing, nearly radical, quasi-trade union organization.

Elizabeth Robertson is the part-time (fourteen hours per week) SOLO at the Center for Health Policy—a government agency. She does not feel too alone since she has lots of contacts, made before she retired from the Medical Library at the University of Witswatersrand. The Center is a very democratic organization, with no bureaucracy, but communication is not good so she does not always know what is expected of her. She would like more time to get more done.

I also met with SOLOs at a cocktail reception sponsored by the Special Libraries Interest Group of SAILIS, Western Cape Division and at a meeting with special library leaders at Ernst & Young in Capetown. I met two new graduates, Naylah Abrahams of Investec Asset Management (a SOLO) and Marian Stuurman of E&Y. Both received their library training at the Teknikon in Capetown. It is more like a United States junior or community college, providing a very practical education. The program is three years long, with an eight-month internship. Unlike the university education, there was no theory, no professionalism, no management, no public relations or marketing, no customer service, and no subject specialization taught. Fortunately, both women had developed a professional and customer-oriented attitude on their own and further developed it during their internships at E&Y. They said most students choose librarianship because they like books.

Continuing on the subject of library education, most librarians (70 percent) attend one of the universities. There are three programs available at the universities: a four-year bachelor's degree, a fifth-year honors program, and a master's degree by research. Most graduates go to academic or national libraries. Librarians in corporate libraries are a mix of qualified and nonqualified employees. Compared to the Teknikon, the university program is more prestigious and the schools have more money to spend. The education is almost totally theoretical, although the University of South Africa (UNISA) requires two management courses. The internship is only three to four weeks long. Gill Owens, chair of SLIS, and librarian at the Cement and Concrete Institute of South Africa, said she did not even know how to stamp a book when she graduated. She had been at University and her internship had been just cataloging a collection, involving almost no interaction with the librarian.

I asked briefly about salaries for qualified librarians. They range from 3,000 rands per month for public librarians to 7,000 rands per month for special librarians. That is equivalent to $8,000–20,000 per year. The University of Witswatersrand advertised for an assistant law librarian at up to R59,000 per year (US $13,000) and had trouble filling it with an experienced person. (To put this into perspective, I looked job ads in the newspaper and found that most other positions were advertised at about 25 percent under United States salaries. The cost of housing, transportation, and food also seemed to be about 25 percent below United States levels.) They do have a serious foreign exchange problem, with the rand going from $1.25 to about $0.25 in recent years. The implication for book purchases and database and journal subscriptions is enormous.

Overall, the SOLO situation is much the same as that in the rest of the world. All the SOLOs I spoke to agreed that networking is very important and very helpful and that library school does not prepare one to be a SOLO. There is a need for more personal, people-oriented training, more interlibrary, multitype library groups. Several of the library groups in South Africa are currently working together to form one association. This presents South African librarians with a unique opportunity to merge existing groups and cooperate.

South Africa now has a SCIP (Society of Competitive Intelligence Professionals) chapter which was organized by Gareth Ochse, Chris Jordaan and Carlien Nel. Based in Johannesburg, it started with twenty-two competitive intelligence professionals. For information contact Gareth Ochse (+27-81-274-8678, fax: +27-11-462-4681, e-mail: glochse@aztec.co.za).

In 1972, Anna Louw, now a professor at the University of South Africa gave a talk to the South African Library Association. At the time she was librarian at a Johannesburg financial, mining, and industrial organization. She was the company's first professional librarian, hired to organize sixty years of material. She began with an initial staff of three, which grew to seven (two of whom were "qualified" or professional), then was downsized to a SOLO position. She found that South African libraries were not too different from those in Europe and United Kingdom, but suffered from a less reliable postal system and a weaker communications infrastructure. The responses to my questionnaire showed the South African SOLO libraries to be somewhat smaller, with smaller staffs, in smaller companies, and having a little less automation than their counterparts in Europe and the United States.

Louw noted the professionalism and difference in attitude needed by a corporate librarian. "It is not unusual for a newcomer to the staff of a company library to have to *learn* to accept [that the library staff is employed to save the valuable time of more highly paid officials] and to adapt to this approach, particularly if such a person had been working in a public library." This can be both more and less demanding on the librarian who must meet deadlines at all hours with little supervision and micromanagement. "The task of the company librarian becomes that of a source of information *about* sources of information" (not necessarily to have the information in stock, but to know where to find it). "The attitude of willingness to go to tremendous trouble, with total disregard of one's own convenience, in order to obtain the required information, is the factor that can make or break a company librarian." Of interest, also, are these comments:

> In 1996 a person who goes into a solo position almost invariable has a PC available, even in this country. Most of them are appointed specifically to help the organisations they join arrange the best access to electronically available information. The current crop of students are introduced to databases on CD and online. The South African Bibliographic and Information Network (Sabinet), which you may have visited, offers services which can be considered by even the smallest special library (Eide-Jenson, 1977).

The following are some of the comments from the questionnaires distributed by Gill Owens of SAILIS Johannesburg and Kate Sherwood of SAILIS Capetown:

What do you wish you'd known before going SOLO?

- I should have been older and have had more experience under experienced and established librarians.
- You do it all and donkey-work takes time, but must be done; also you become the victim of your own success and requests increase till it is hard to cope.
- I had gained more experience of working in a larger library

How could library schools have prepared SOLOs better?

- Grounding must be very thorough; pupils should be encouraged to experiment, i.e., a "what if" situation.
- Schools should teach time management, how to search for information with limited reference works.
- Gear the courses on a more practical level and provide more courses on information retrieval and in general more training on records management.

What do you like most about being SOLO?

- I have freedom, no sharing of personal space.
- I am responsible to myself, setting own parameters, making own rules, working alone.

• I enjoy the freedom to prioritize based on known customer needs, and the pressure of work. There is no hierarchy and the personal satisfaction of meeting customer needs.

What do you like least?

• difficulty in leaving the library to search for information, to discuss problems
• having no one to fall back on when absent or overworked
• doing all the old rubbish that an assistant should be doing
• not having a colleague to bounce "library" ideas and problems off
• constant interruptions

Other comments?

• There is a need of all the facilities possible to speed up routine tasks and data searching and a need to be part of a good network.
• The main thrust of my work, from beginning of this year, is to back up new business personnel by attempting to identify new business leads. I provide fairly in-depth research into companies identified for new business, also existing business being renegotiated. All company information research reports, file records, leads etc. will be coordinated into databases using Lotus Notes and networked from my area throughout our branches. It is challenging and seems more noted by senior management (insurance brokers).

THE REST OF THE WORLD

Eismark (1995) wrote about information brokering in Europe. These businesses were begun because of the rigid information structure, high taxes, extensive social benefit costs, "unfair" competition from subsidized public organizations, and strong university library systems. He sees nothing to indicate that lack of information brokers in Europe is due to lack of demand. The British Library markets in Germany and some other places in Europe. It competes head-to-head in Germany against Germany companies and does well, still gaining market share, mainly in document delivery. (Author's note: it does well in the United States, too, since they provide fast, cheap, and exhaustive service.) The information broker scene in Germany is smaller than in the United Kingdom, is quite invisible, and has a very small market segment, growing at maybe 10 percent per year.

Eide-Jensen found in Sweden that "the counties with a large number of one-man libraries do appear to have a worse library service than others" (1977, 15). In 1977 there were forty municipalities with only one librarian, serving 8,000-20,000 people. Professional librarians are a recent addition and the SOLO is often an administrator for "local cultural administration," helping to establish small libraries, adult education, etc. He concluded that the SOLO cannot do it all, and neglects long-range planning, personal, and professional development. There is a high turnover since "the post of one-man librarian [in Sweden] is not a particularly attractive one" (1977, 16). This is due to the low salary, long hours, lack of training for SOLOship. His solution are government intervention (salary support), better training (more administration, more continuing education), and more help from larger libraries. In Norway, Kristensen found over 1,400 libraries for over 4 million people, but most are small. There have been few changes in the past fifteen years and there are libraries serving as few as 750 people.

My last entry comes from Brazil. According to M. Cleofas F. Alencar, professor of library science at Pontificia Universidade Catolica de Campenas, Sao Paolo, Brazil, there are few corporate libraries, but most of these are SOLOs. Most of the community libraries in small towns are SOLOs as well. They have thirty undergraduate library programs and six master's level programs. All graduates find jobs, but the pay is low. If they have a MLS, they most likely will become a department head.

5

Education for
SOLOs and Others

When I started my first professional library position as a SOLO librarian, I found myself unprepared for many of the tasks confronting me. This was in spite of the fact that I had attended the number one-ranked library school in the country and had taken courses specific to my work as a science/technology librarian. Unfortunately, I had no experience in interlibrary loan or OCLC, both indispensable in a small library with very limited resources, and I knew very little about acquisitions processes, much less subscription services and book jobbers. Although I had not been taught the necessity of networking with my fellow librarians, my natural gregariousness led me to do a lot of it out of sheer necessity. Techniques for budgeting, managing a library, marketing my library and myself, and managing time were unknown to me, as well as how how to be effective in a large organization, and I had difficulty at first balancing all the demands of SOLO librarianship. This created my continuing interest in how librarians are educated for the ever-increasing SOLO librarian situation.

As I became active in the Special Libraries Association and the SOLO Librarians Division, I began asking other SOLOs if they had learned these skills in library school. Most agreed that their education had not adequately prepared them for "life in the real world" of special and/or SOLO librarianship.

Complaints about library education can be traced as far back as 1906 (Rothstein 1985). There has been an amazing consistency in their nature: too little practical training, no education for leadership, educators out of touch with the needs of the profession, instructors needing to be practitioners not just teachers, the work not really at graduate level, and courses geared too much to the public libraries.

The debate between theory and practice in library education also has been ongoing for a long time. Some writers insist that the schools emphasize or concentrate on the theoretical background for the profession. However, most realize that a mix of the theoretical and the practical is necessary. Paris and White (1986) discuss the paradox of education versus training; they believe that schools cannot do both. Employers want training; the academics want education. Various other complaints follow:

- "The sum and substance of seventy years of progress in special librarianship have had little or no impact on the direction of library science education in this country" (Cortez 1986, 198).
- "For many years, employers in academic libraries have found that newly qualified recruits have not had the level of practical experience necessary for the real-life post . . . this mismatch still exists" (Coutts 1991, 10).
- "Traditional LIS education, as embodied in the MLS degree, is perceived by many practitioners to be out of sync with the demands of the emergent market" (Cronin 1990, 262).

The statements above summarize the current situation in library education. In spite of this history of complaints, very little progress has been made. Increasing numbers of employers deem the MLS irrelevant or even a negative factor, especially in the business or industrial world (Cronin and Williamson 1988). Library schools are adding courses to the core curriculum and changing the names of others, but is there also a change in content or orientation? Cronin writes that "LIS schools will need to revise not only their curricula but also their culture if they are to become successful players in this [emerging information] market" (1988, 262) Note that he says *become*, not *stay* as players.

Obviously, the ideal library education program would be a mix of the broad, theoretical basics of information science and the specific, practical tools that will be needed on the job. Most students will not have another opportunity to learn the basics, but they will have opportunities to learn more techniques and technologies. But a purely theoretical education will not produce graduate librarians who are ready to face the real world. Perhaps the solution is to teach the basics, some of the technologies and tools, and then enough learning and reasoning skills so that the student knows how to find out the answers to situations that develop once they are on the job. Students cannot be sure what kind of library they will be working in later, so the school needs to educate very broadly, emphasizing the relevance of concepts to the preferred type of library. Graduates need knowledge not only of theory and skills but also of what questions to ask and how to find the answers.

Another problem with library education is how students select a library school. By a margin of two to one, most students select a library school because of geography, according to a survey of students and alumni from twelve library schools (White and Mort 1990). This is *not* the best criterion to use in selecting something as important as education for your future career. However, library students are older (with an average age of about thirty-five) and are established, with a job and/or family holding them to a specific area. Since library schools are not evenly distributed geographically, this becomes a more difficult problem. In the United States, there are some Eastern cities that have more than one school, while many Western states have none. Outside the United States there are fewer library schools and they are concentrated in a few countries. Students must travel long distances or relocate to attend library school. Many schools have some type of distance education opportunities, usually within their own state; however, they are usually offered in limited areas and at limited times.

There are some new trends. At least two schools, Syracuse University and the University of Illinois at Urbana-Champaign, have begun offering a MLS over the Internet. I had an opportunity to visit the UIUC and find out more about the program and meet members of the first LEEP class. The program begins and ends with a two-week on-campus experience in which the students get to know each other and the faculty. They are a self-selected, highly motivated, and self-directed group of adults, most already working in the field. Classes are to be held both via Internet postings and question-and-answer/discussion sessions and via traditional audio- or videoconferencing. Faculty have the option of requiring an on-campus weekend for a particular course. All regular courses will be offered via the LEEP option. It will be interesting to watch this program and see how it develops. I think that this is a very good direction for library education to take and hope that other schools develop such programs.

Also presenting a difficulty for library education is that the type of library that students think or plan that they will work in changes from enrollment to graduation and throughout their careers. In addition, there is very little other information (such as listings or comparisons of specialties, courses, etc.) available on which to base a decision. On their first job, less than half of the respondents were working in the type of library they expected when they enrolled in library school. After nine years on the job, nearly 30 percent were working in yet a different type of library (White and Mort 1990). The implication is that library schools need to concentrate more on basic, transferable skills *and* on introducing students to *all* types of libraries and giving them a general idea of what they need to know for each type.

WHAT IS BEING TAUGHT NOW?

In August of 1993, questionnaires were sent out to deans of the fifty-nine ALA accredited library schools listed in the ALA brochure. Forty-nine were returned (83 percent). The responses are summarized below and a detailed analysis is provided in Appendix II.

The average library school is small, with less than a dozen full-time faculty and a like number of adjunct faculty. Just over half the schools offer a concentration in special librarianship, and many of these are in the medical or legal areas rather than special librarianship in general. The majority of the schools require the ALA minimum thirty-six hours for the master's level degree. Of those with a different requirement, the tendency is to move toward more rather than fewer hours. A thesis is required by only 14 percent of the schools, but another 37 percent make it optional. The primary requirement for entrance into the degree program is a specified grade point or test score, and only 29 percent of the schools required computer skills. A few also looked for quantitative skills, experience, subject specialization, management skills, written communication skills, or a foreign language.

Library management was required by twelve of the forty-nine schools. Other applicable required courses include special libraries, online searching, automation, computers or telecommunications, system analysis or research methods, abstracting and indexing, fieldwork, database management or information storage and retrieval, and information mediation.

Special libraries, health and biomedical information, business information, and science-technology were offered by over 50 percent of the respondents. At least one-quarter of the schools offered one of the following: archives or records management, management or administration, government documents, legal information, online searching, automation or networks or the Internet, humanities information, or computers or telecommunications. The courses most often taught by adjunct faculty were health or biomedical information, business information, legal information, and humanities information.

SPECIAL LIBRARIES—ARE THEY DIFFERENT?

Are special libraries different? Do those librarians who run them have special educational needs? Are SOLO librarians even more different? Special libraries do have several distinct characteristics. They are often *the* library of an organization and, as such, serve all the organization's information needs. The object of the organization is not primarily a library objective. They have the risk of being closed if their costs are too high or their parent organization does not find enough benefits in their existence.

While the total number of librarians is increasing at a very slow rate (from 1–5 percent, approximately the same rate as that of their clientele), the number of special librarians is increasing at a much faster rate. From 1978 to 1990, the number of librarians increased from 126,400 to 137,500, under 9 percent, while the number of special librarians grew 47 percent from 15,600 to 22,900 (Lynch 1991). The *U.S. Occupational Outlook Handbook of 1994-1995* predicts that employment in special libraries is expected to grow faster than average. These figures probably do not include librarians working in nonlibrary settings such as sales, independent consulting, and information brokering.

There are over 14,000 members of the Special Libraries Association. Not all work in special libraries (some are educators or former special librarians or students) and not all those who work in special libraries are members of SLA. According the SLA figures, 52 percent of the membership work in corporate libraries. About 60 percent are employed in small libraries (six or fewer employees), with the most common library size being one employee (30–50 percent of the members) The SOLO Librarians Division of SLA has over 1,000 members, making it the fifth largest division in SLA, after only five years of existence.

In the SLA report of the PREPS Commission, it is pointed out that "special librarianship is different from the other branches of the profession, and as such requires knowledge, skills, and attitudes that are different from those needed in the other branches of the profession . . ." and that "the standards for [ALA] accreditation, however, are too general to insure adequate preparation for the special library environment." Also, although they may be aware of special librarianship as a career option, many students do not really know what a special library is. A small library or SOLO may have very different needs from a large one. Tees (1986b) points out that most studies of special library needs have been made of larger libraries and are not necessarily relevant for the more common small libraries. In addition, many management courses assume management of a large library and not SOLO situations. Since special librarianship in not emphasized in most library schools, it is more probable that the special librarian did not anticipate being in this situation and may not have chosen to take courses emphasizing skills needed in special libraries. In their SOLO position, they are now responsible for all areas of librarianship and may not be prepared adequately. As Bierbaum comments ". . . in graduate school you may have taken courses in reference, cataloging, serials, conservation, administration and the like, but it probably never occurred to you that you'd be responsible for *all* of those aspects of library work" (1986, 2).

SOLOs assume a managerial role earlier in their careers or even at the beginning. SOLO librarians are much more likely to need entrepreneurial and business skills, for they are running their own little businesses. These problems may take on added importance since SOLO librarians are often the only information professionals in an organization and thus represent the library profession to their constituency and management.

In a survey of SOLOs, they were asked "What do you wish you had known before you became a SOLO?" Frequent responses were time management, general management skills, office politics, negotiation skills, technical processing, a practicum or internship, and less theory and more practical courses. Williamson's study of One-Man Band (1984) produced similar answers. Members of the LIBREF-L listserv, when asked what librarians need to know, produced the following comments in *Footnotes*, the online newsletter of the University of Arizona's Library Student Organization:

- "Librarians should know the ethical bases for our profession."
- "You have to remember that you're there for your union card."
- "Do not believe a word anyone says!"(on the reliability of patron information on a reference source)
- "For accurate and prompt reference assistance, the thorough reference interview is vital."
- "Major skills I am not seeing in candidates or new hires are true public service and a tolerance for the varying needs and skills of the population served. No, the customer is not always right, but we should be tolerant of their circumstances and be empathetic."
- ". . . as much about teaching and communication as possible . . . the need to stay polite, even under pressure; there is no one perfect set of reference books [so] master the ones that are available on your new job."

- "Never be afraid to ask for help or advice."
- "Grades are important, but what is even more important is getting some practical experience so that you will have some good references when you graduate, and you can show that you are able to perform a reference interview, do original cataloging, use computer databases, and basically work with others in a library setting."
- "Learn as much as you can about as many online services and CD-ROMs as you can find. Jobs are scarce and technology, whether or not you approve, is here to stay. Get comfy with the click-click of keyboards."
- "Prepare yourself to move around" (from job to job)
- "I'd advise anyone, whether interested in being a director or not, to learn as much as you can about library financing and the budget process. Also, if you do not have a spreadsheet, get one and *learn how to use it*, especially the graphing capabilities."

Although library schools are doing a much better job of preparing graduates for positions in special and SOLO libraries now than they have in the past, there are still some issues of concern. Are the right people being recruited or admitted into library schools? Are we looking for bright, creative, flexible, computer-literate, user-friendly individuals who will become the information leaders of tomorrow? If we admit anyone less, we run the risk of dragging everyone in the profession down, including those already out there in the trenches. It may be true that it is "unfair to suggest that perhaps library schools are somewhat at fault for producing the wrong type of graduate for SOLO libraries" but "a good three-quarters of what is taught in library school either doesn't work or doesn't *quite* work in a small library" (Sipek 1988, 3).

LIBRARIAN COMPETENCIES

Competencies have been defined as sets of knowledge, the characteristics of a high achiever, the acquisition of a set of skills, or the ability to function in a job. From my readings, I have developed the following fourteen clusters of skills and proficiencies that I call competencies—what we need to be good librarians. To determine the relative importance of these competencies, I counted each time a category or member of a category was mentioned in the literature that I read and in the comments on the questionnaires, then ranked the categories according to the frequency of occurrence (see Table 5.1).

In 1996 Joanne Marshall and the SLA Special Committee on Competencies for Special Librarians (Bill Fisher, Lynda Moulton and Roberta Piccoli) developed a list of competencies for special librarianship, divided into professional and personal competencies. They are listed on the next page with my comments in parentheses.

Table 5.1 Rankings of Competencies

Summary

	overall rank	readings rank	comments rank	
general management	1	1	4	management theory and anything not mentioned elsewhere
public relations	2	5	2	publicity, marketing, presenting to management
organizational dynamics	3	3	7	organizational behavior, corporate politics
analytical thinking	4	3	11	systems analysis, problem solving, evaluation, resource management, decision-making, ability to integrate concepts
human resources	5	5	7	interpersonal relations, personnel issues, hiring and firing, discipline, supervision
communications skills	6	5	10	public speaking, writing, presentation skills
financial skills	6	8	4	financial management, budgeting, financial reporting
time management	8	11	3	prioritization
customer service	9	8	13	customer needs, user orientation
technology skills	10	2	1	including online searching, computer skills, cataloging
networking	11	13	6	interpersonal networking cooperation among libraries
library experience	12	14	7	
professionalism	12	10	12	including ethics
research skills	14	11	13	including information theory

Professional Competencies
A competent librarian who is a professional

- Has expert knowledge of the content of information resources, including the ability to critically evaluate and filter them
- Has specialized subject knowledge appropriate to the business of the organization or client (Much of this is learned on the job.)
- Develops and manages convenient, accessible and cost-effective information services that are aligned with the strategic directions of the organization
- Provides instruction and support for library and information service users (This will not be done effectively without the proper mind set.)
- Assesses information needs and designs and markets value-added information services and products to meet identified needs
- Understands and uses appropriate information technology to acquire, organize, and disseminate information
- Understands and uses appropriate business and management approaches to communicate the importance of information services to senior management
- Develops specialized information products for use inside or outside the organization or by individual clients (This is not really a competency, but an outcome of other competencies.)
- Evaluates the outcomes of information use and conducts research related to the solution of information management problems
- Continually improves information services in response to the changing needs (This is also probably an outcome.)
- Is an effective member of the senior management team and a consultant to the organization on information issues (This is *definitely* an outcome.)

Personal Competencies
- Commits to service excellence
- Seeks out challenges and sees new opportunities both inside and outside the library
- Sees the big picture (This is a professional skill, that of analytical thinking.)
- Looks for partnerships and alliances
- Creates an environment of mutual respect and trust

- Develops effective communications skills (As phrased, this is not a skill. If stated as "communicates effectively," it is a professional competency.)
- Develops the ability to work well with others in a team. (This may be at odds with the next competency.)
- Provides leadership
- Plans, prioritizes, and focuses on what is critical (This is a combination of time management and analytical thinking, both professional skills.)
- Commits to lifelong learning and personal career planning
- Develops personal business skills and creates new opportunities
- Recognizes the value of professional networking and solidarity
- Is flexible and positive in a time of continuing change

Skill Set or Mind Set?

I have combined the above lists into a paradigm based on two types of competencies—a skill set and a mind set. Unfortunately, most employers, librarians, and educators have concentrated on the skill set. We do a poor job of selecting librarians based on the mind-set competencies. This is exactly backwards. One can take a person with the correct mind-set and teach him or her the appropriate skills to become a good librarian. It is much less likely that a person who has mastered the skill set but lacks the librarian mind set will become a successful professional. Most of the competencies in the skill set can be taught and learned. Many, but not all, are already covered in most library school curricula. Most of the competencies in the mind set cannot be taught. They must already be present in the future librarian's personality. However, they can *and should* be encouraged and developed both in library school and on the job.

The Skill Set

- knowledge of information sources
- subject knowledge
- ability to develop and manage information services
- ability to provide instruction and user support
- ability to assess information needs, to provide and market value-added services
- understanding and mastery of technology
- ability to communicate, especially with senior management
- research and evaluation skills
- knowledge of management and financial tools

The Mind Set

- commitment to service excellence
- entrepreneurial attitude, including seeking challenges and having flexibility, leadership, and a positive attitude
- team player, including seeking partnerships and alliances and working well with others
- commitment to lifelong learning
- behavior in a professional and ethical manner

It is clear that special and SOLO librarianship are different. Is what is being taught now in library schools what is needed by specials and SOLOs? If not, there are changes that need to be made.

WHAT SHOULD BE TAUGHT

Library students need to be taught a variety of skills and subjects. They need a good grounding in management, the role of the library in the parent organization, time management, budgeting, planning for and implementing automation and the Internet, networking, public relations and publicity, networking and library cooperation, interlibrary loan (hands-on, not just a mention), funding, some familiarity with the clerical tasks they surely will be called upon to do, grantsmanship, and working with upper management. Public librarians call for teaching about construction, building maintenance, dealing with boards and volunteers, and running political (bond issue) campaigns.

Another area that needs to be emphasized is practical experience in a library. "Do library school graduates possess the actual skills needed to function in the real world?" (Ferguson and Mobley 1984, 177) Many students hold assistantships or work in the campus library while they are in school; this is fine, but it only gives them experience in one type of library—the academic institution. Internships need to be available in a variety of library types: public, corporate, not-for-profit, large, small, and SOLO. If possible, students should be encouraged to intern in a library type in which they have no experience or a type different from the one they plan to work in after graduation. I have found that graduates do not always get the type of position for which they prepared.

All special librarians would like to see a required exposure to libraries other than public and academic, whether in a separate course or as part of other courses. For instance, a cataloging course could include sections on "quick and dirty" cataloging, outsourcing, and alternatives to Dewey and Library of Congress. It is *very* important that special library courses be taught by practitioners rather than by academic types. Even if professors *used* to work in a special library, they do not do so now and therefore may not be aware of the current issues in the field. At a minimum, there should be many guest lecturers in a special library course. Most SLA chapters can provide speakers and few special librarians would turn down the chance to talk to students. Many responses to the questionnaires showed that the possibility of SOLO librarianship was not even mentioned in library school. SOLOs would like to see this changed, since it is quite possible graduates will eventually wind up in SOLO positions, and some of them may even start out in a SOLO library, as I did.

Another need I see is for some integration of library coursework. Cataloging is an extension of reference; customer service is part of library building; abstracting and indexing is related to acquisitions. We need well-rounded librarians, entrepreneurs, who are capable of handling all parts of librarianship. This is not just a SOLO issue. How can a library director who has never been a cataloger (or on the reference desk or in acquisitions or whatever) be expected to supervise those areas? As a rule, students take a series of discrete courses and then graduate. We need a thesis, senior project, final course, or something that requires the students to look at the totality of what they learned and determine how it all interrelates. Most other disciplines require such a summing up for their master's degrees—how can we ask to be considered their equal if we do not? For example for my M.A. in anthropology, I was required to write a thesis and defend it to a committee of professors, pass comprehensive examinations in all four subfields of anthropology—physical, archaeology, cultural, and linguistics—and pass a language proficiency exam. Library schools should ask the same of their students.

This is not to say that library school is a waste of time. The general grounding in library principles, theory, and practice is necessary for the beginning librarian. "What library school did do was make me a knowledgeable user of information and provide the mechanism on which to build information management and theory" (Acton 1986, 387). This is a start, but it just does not go far enough.

The question remains: what are the most-desired changes in library education? From my own experience and research, I have come up with eight important points:

1. We need to produce more well-rounded librarians. Many schools train primarily for public and academic libraries. Granted, that is

still where most librarians will work, but the mix is changing. Also, the role of the public and academic librarian is changing, moving closer to that of the traditional special librarian (and of course, special librarianship is changing as well).

2. We need to devote more time to the study of management, budgeting, personnel issues, time management.

3. We need to produce librarians who are more customer-focused. The customer is and always has been king, but with the advent of CompuServe, the Internet, and other information providers, he or she no longer has to go to the library for information. There are other sources. If we do not provide the service that is required, the customer *will* go elsewhere and then where will we be?

4. We need to produce librarians who are more computer-literate than ever. We need to know not just *how* to use computers, but *when* and *why*. Our customers are increasingly knowledgeable about computer and information sources and we have to improve our skills just to keep up, let alone be the information leaders and teachers.

5. To be sure of attracting the best potential librarians and teachers, we need access to library education, especially geographically. We need to get away from the current practice of students considering only the school closest to them. Another source of geographic diversity should be the availability of distance learning (correspondence courses, courses via television, or courses over the Internet).

6. Library schools may need to specialize in public, academic, or special librarianship, or information studies, or whatever. And they certainly need to advertise in which areas they are strong. We also need more courses in corporate and special librarianship.

7. One is not a librarian on the day he or she graduates with an MLS. Experience is vital. Our schools need to require or very strongly encourage some type of work experience or internship.

8. Most important, educators need to have input from the field, from practitioners, from *us* (input into courses, internships, mentoring, lecturing, advisory boards).

SUGGESTIONS FOR IMPLEMENTATION

The above list details what would be good changes in our professional education, but we need ways to achieve these goals. The following discussion details ways to achieve these changes by building on what exists now.

The master's level degree is the primary library degree. Since there are very few undergraduate library programs, this can be seen as a first degree rather than a terminal degree. Advanced certificates are not a major force so I would like to see more post-master's offerings. Most special librarians do not need a Ph.D., but they and the profession would benefit by a more structured advanced degree program.

The majority of schools require only the minimum number of hours, no thesis, no internship, and few competencies for admission other than grades or test scores. To increase the competence of graduating librarians, we need to increase the quality of entering library students. We should require computer skills, quantitative (mathematical) skills, proven written and oral communication skills, and proven dedication to the needs of the user before entrance to library school. Increasingly, a scientific or technical background is needed, and a basic knowledge of how a library works is a must. This could be obtained through paid or unpaid library experience and a demonstrated knowledge of "The Foundations of Librarianship" obtained from required readings assigned after admission but before enrollment.

A concentration in special libraries is not available in every school. There are many courses offered that are of interest to special librarians, but most are taught by educators, not practitioners. In one school, according to my research, twenty-nine of thirty-three courses in special libraries are taught by regular faculty. It would seem to me that this, of all courses, should be taught by a practitioner. Of course it is possible that heavy use of guest lecturers does not show up in these statistics. Unfortunately, the smallness of library schools is likely a factor in the limited offerings. Increased use of adjunct faculty, i.e., those actually practicing the profession who are familiar with real-world problems, would enable new graduates to be more effective on their first day on the job. Courses in management and related skills should be required, along with courses in specific technologies, such as cataloging, interlibrary loan, acquisitions, online searching, database management, subject specialties.

The rigor of the library school program should be increased to more closely match those of other master's level programs. A subject master's often requires a thesis or research paper, an oral defense, proficiency exams, demonstrated competence in a foreign language, in addition to coursework. A MLS may require none of these, yet we often ask society to consider these degrees as equal. Thus, a thesis or research paper should be required, in part to show written communication skills and in part to serve as a summing up and integration of the courses taken. Proficiency exams in various areas of librarianship should be considered in order to assure prospective employers that the student is at least familiar with all aspects of librarianship. Students might choose to learn these skills outside of formal classes but would be required to prove their knowledge.

An internship or fieldwork program (paid or unpaid) should be required of all students who are not working in libraries or do not have extensive library work experience. This internship might be set up like student teaching rather than merely shadowing a librarian for a couple of weeks. A graduate assistantship in an academic library produces a different experience than work experience in a special library outside of academia.

I am well aware that these changes might necessitate a longer program. We need to consider whether teaching the students only the minimum is still satisfactory. Students cannot learn everything about everything. But they *have* to learn the questions to ask and how to go about finding out the answers. According to Murphy (1988), the thirty-six-hour program is obsolete. If we had a two-year program, the first year could concentrate on the fundamentals and the second on specific tools and technologies, with the last semester emphasizing the integration of the two. I realize that employers might not pay more for a two-year degree (at first), but a higher quality and more focused degree might keep us in the information game, instead of being passed over in favor of MBAs, computer professionals, and others seen as more relevant by employers.

Special librarians must also get more actively involved in library education. This can involve teaching a course, being a guest speaker, serving on a curriculum advisory committee, planning a field trip, hosting a faculty sabbatical, or supervising an internship. A 1994 study by the Special Libraries Association found that less than 10 percent of the chapters and 20 percent of the divisions were actively involved in the graduate library education in any meaningful way (Bender 1994).

The profession should emphasize, encourage, support, even require continuing education. Griffiths and King (1986) believe that those involved in library education must make sure that information professionals acquire the necessary competencies to perform their work. This includes professionals, their employers, professional societies, and educators.

With the current rapid changes in information theory and technology, no matter how recent or how good our education is it becomes out-of-date very quickly. Weingand estimates the shelf life of an MLS at less than five years unless updated. "The librarian who relies on the preservice degree to carry through the working lifetime cannot hope to negotiate the perpetual whitewater of today's changing society" (1994, 174). Yet that is what many of our colleagues do. Why? There is no requirement to do otherwise. There is often no economic incentive to get added training. Good or relevant courses may not be available in an appropriate location or form. SOLOs have even stronger needs for continuing education. They are isolated, without other professionals to draw from. Educational needs most often cited by SOLOs are for new technologies, communication skills, information retrieval, and organizational dynamics.

CONTINUING EDUCATION

Where is this continuing education to come from? Berry states that library schools neglect continuing education "even for their own alumni" (1993, 102). Companies are doing most of the management training now (Murphy, 1988). "The professions themselves must take responsibility for satisfying this need, if for no other reason than to survive as a profession" (Allen 1974, 1). A recent SLA survey showed that 62 percent of SOLOs did not attend the most recent Annual Conference and 70 percent did not attend SLA education courses. However, 63 percent said they had gone to non-SLA courses in the past year (Bender 1994). SLA offers courses covering topics requested by SOLOs in the Middle Management Institute. If this program were retitled and expanded, perhaps more SOLOs would take advantage of it. Another source of continuing education, often forgotten, is training courses offered by vendors. These are often in locations near the students, low cost, short, and very relevant. Continuing education can also take the form of conference calls, computer-based training (such as SLA is beginning to offer), and even courses on the Internet. Special librarians may keep up-to-date by reading professional journals and newsletters, networking, in-house training, attendance at professional conference workshops, online user groups, and formal classwork. Murphy (1988) also found that all of these were at company expense. I fear that this was a very atypical example. Many special librarians, and most SOLOs, do not enjoy such generous corporate support of their continuing education needs.

There are many advantages in continuing education (CE). It enhances our professional competencies, helps avert burnout, reduces technostress, fends off technical obsolescence, increases self-confidence, provides personal renewal, increases enthusiasm for the job or profession, increases productivity, improves general morale by acknowledging the importance of the individual, and provides coping skills to deal with change. Field (1996) adds that you should make sure you get sent to the same training as others at your level in the organizations (management, technology, etc.) and the importance of paying for CE yourself if necessary. Library schools do offer continuing education courses, but often they are only or primarily for their own graduates. They are usually only on campus or in a few locations—not exactly ideal for a working professional. Do not forget other training opportunities such as Toastmasters, courses offered by other professional organizations like MLA, ARMA, and regional library organizations. What is the end result of continuing education? You have empowered yourself, you have increased your sense of self-worth, you have improved your productivity and the value of your services, and you have provided the structure for lifelong success.

In a study in the United Kingdom, Sue Bryant (1995) found that SOLOs are motivated to pursue professional development by ambition, a desire for recognition learning, change or fulfillment, fear of obsolescence, commitment to high standards of service, and as a path to career advancement. The United Kingdom's Library Association has a "Code of Professional Ethics" (1995) that requires continuing education, specifying that "members must be competent in their professional activities . . . [and] keep abreast of developments in librarianship." It also recommends four to six working days per year be devoted to continuing education. "Ironically, the difficulties which SOLO librarians and information workers commonly experience in attending formal events may encourage them to become more adept at exploiting a wider range of informal and work-based opportunities" (Bryant 1995, 3). Bryant finds that professionals must be self-motivated to pursue CE, which should be based on their personal values and goals. Some get their CE from experience in the workplace, but this is not enough. She offers several nontraditional professional development ideas which may be especially beneficial to SOLOs, including shadowing another librarian, staff exchanges, mentors, research and writing, committees and activity in professional organizations, visits to other libraries, reading, and exhibits at conferences.

One avenue to encourage continuing education is certification. Boaz commented that "some people are predicting that certification will become more important than academic degrees" (1981, 767). The library profession considered certification years ago, but opted in favor of accreditation of degree programs. Certification is already required or encouraged in many fields, including environmental engineers, geographical information systems analysts, meeting professionals, turnaround professionals, secretaries, computer professionals, sales and meeting executives, association executives, internal auditors, accountants, travel agents, life insurance agents, crop advisers, and small business owners. In the information area, the Medical Libraries Association, Society of American Archivists, Institute of Certified Records Managers, and American Association of Law Librarians already have certification programs, as do most states for school and media librarians. The National Librarians Association has been calling for certification for librarians for ten years.

PROPOSAL FOR CERTIFICATION

My proposal for certification has the following elements. Graduation from an ALA-accredited library school with an MLS or equivalent gives immediate certification, good for two to three years. Certification is renewable only through continued learning, by one or more of the following:

- additional academic coursework (not only in library science, but in related areas such as computer science, management, etc.)
- formal classes from associations, vendors, or consortia
- in-house training (such as on the company network, if such training is offered)
- attendance at national, regional, or local professional society meetings (and it is important to include such nonlibrary associations as the Society of Competitive Intelligence Professionals, the Association of Records Managers and Administrators, etc.)
- reading of professional journals (the Institute of Internal Auditors, for example, does this by printing a quiz in the association's magazine which must be taken and sent in for continuing education credit—you really have to *read* the articles to pass the quiz!)
- participation in collegial activities such as association committees or offices, Internet listservs, etc.

Certification should be administered by a joint commission of library associations (ALA, SLA, MLA, AALL, ARMA, etc.) and involve a minimum of paperwork.

Certification has the following advantages: it may enhance the stature of the profession, may increase rewards (e.g., salaries), protect the public from incompetents, and encourage continuing education and professional activity. On the negative side, a certificate is no guarantee of competency; it is hard to develop an objective measurement tool due to the variety of organizations and positions; librarians produce an intangible and nonmeasurable product (the time and expense may not be warranted by the market); and it could lead to fewer professional positions. There is also the issue of when to certify—after the MLS, after a certain number of years of experience, or after passing a test. Certification may not be the answer, but it could be a step in the right direction.

CONCLUSION

The most important action we can take is to begin to take the problem of library education seriously. We all need to become involved in identifying the competencies to be taught, innovative methods for delivering library education, and making sure librarians stay on top of the information explosion. To quote Hillel the Elder, the Jewish sage, "if I am not for myself, who will be for me; if I am for myself alone, what am I, if not now, when?" It is our profession and we have an obligation to do *something*. Each of us needs to examine what we are doing to help those who will come after us and to ask ourselves: is there more that we can do?

6

Along the Information Superhighway: Technology and the SOLO Librarian

T echnology is one of the biggest aids to the SOLO—and one of the biggest threats. This chapter explores the history, present, and future of technology in general and the Internet in particular. It will also look at how the Internet does and will affect us as SOLOs and how best to exploit it to our advantage.

Technology has been part of libraries for decades. In the 1960s large mainframes first appeared in large institutions. In the 1970s personal computers were developed. Large, mostly academic libraries started automating their card catalogs and circulation. OCLC started production of cataloging and catalog cards. In the 1980s, networking (LANs) began to link computers within libraries. Later in the decade networking and modems allowed libraries to start reaching out of their buildings. E-mail became more common. The 1990s are the decade of personalized information at the users' desktops or in their homes, and, most importantly, the 1990s have seen the Internet become a part of everyday life for many people.

When asked to identify the milestones of the last 100 years in medical information, many of those nominated by subscribers to MEDLIB-L were technology oriented: online databases like Index Medicus, and MEDLARS, photocopy and fax machines, computers, and the growth of library networks.

When CD-ROM first came along it was predicted that it would revolutionize home entertainment (it has), eliminate low-density media (it has supplanted, but not replaced, floppies), and revolutionize publishing (there has been some change, but definitely not a revolution). Why has CD-ROM not been more successful? There have been problems with distributed networking, requiring much programming time, and problems with intellectual property rights and permissions; their capacity, while great, is being exceeded by demands of software and data. CD-ROM is still a slow technology compared to online, but not compared to the Internet. The media are now touting the Internet as the be-all and end-all and CD-ROM is out of favor. Some publishers, however, also feel that CD-ROM is on its way out (Thompson 1996). Philip Kerr of Teton Data Systems expects CD-ROMs to be the best distribution method for the next five years, but then they will fade away. Another publisher, Dr. Clifford Butler, Delmar Publishers, sees the Internet as the depository of information for the future, with CD-ROM dropping out.

In a presentation at Betty Burrows Memorial Seminar in Cleveland, Jose-Marie Griffiths, formerly dean of the Library School and now vice president for information at the University of Tennessee, commented on the future of computing and communications. She described the key trends as the convergence of hardware and software, the convergence of computer and communications, and the convergence of networks and systems. The world is toward "anywhere-anytime" computing and special purpose workstations, preconfigured with pointers to resources. Information overload is a concern, but there is a concern with *mis*information. We librarians need to teach users when to search for themselves and when they need to come to us. Griffiths also warns that "technology can be a black hole for money." We need to partner with other groups within our organization, focusing on the problems technology can solve, not on the technology itself. Finally, "the only thing we really have to look forward to is more change." We must get comfortable with it; learn to take risks, identify opportunities, take action; and realize and accept that anything new will be obsolete within a couple of years.

THE INFORMATION FUTURE AND LIBRARIANS

Information Today has rated librarianship as one of the ten "coldest" professions for the future, but online content providers as one of the ten hottest—we need to tell them that we *are* content providers (or if we are not, we had better start doing it).

What is the meaning of this information future for us? We must go back to basics, our core functions: our ability to manage knowledge resources, in all forms; our ability to focus on the users (which differentiates us from IS professionals); and our facility with using tools and technologies, as Dr. Griffiths says, to *mediate* the interface and *provide access* to information.

What does Dr. Griffiths mean by "mediate and provide access"? It includes using tools and technologies to do the following:

- create secondary sources (including electronic publishing and the WWW)
- capture information and convert it to another (digital) form
- collect data on a just-in-time rather than just-in-case basis
- organize physical items, intellectual content, and collections
- store and retrieve information in multiple formats
- analyze, interpret, synthesize, and repackage information
- deliver information in the form the user wants
- preserve information

We also must help build tools and systems and interfaces and, increasingly, primary resources themselves. The tools we use may change, but the mediator role will not. We must use both the new and the old tools.

As Smock (1995) points out, there are some other issues of consequence as well. What is the life expectancy of electronic documents? How well do electronic media preserve information? If we assume that preservation of our cultural and intellectual history is one of the responsibilities of libraries, we must be concerned if the hardware and software to access the information will be there tomorrow in five, ten, fifty, one hundred years? We also must ascertain what do people *really* need online?

Dr. Griffiths expects some librarian functions to become *more* important in the future. These include the intellectual organization of information, including resources outside the organization; information analysis, synthesis, packaging; design of user interfaces; user education and training, especially on the resources available; access and search skills; limitations of the tools; and knowing when it is not appropriate for end users to search for themselves. Functions that will grow to become *less* important are the building of physical collections; provisions for physical proximity (although users will still need a physical place to go to—delivery to the desktop is not enough); and circulation. In addition, as information professionals of the future, we will need to be user-oriented (we are already good at this, but we can improve); proactive; and a team player with users and vendors.

THE VIRTUAL LIBRARY

One current focus on the use of technology in the future has been on the virtual library. One of the first such efforts was by Michel Bauwens, who coined the phrase "cybrarian" to describe his role in the virtual library. At BP Nutrition in Belgium, faced with declining financial and personnel support, Bauwens first identified the information needs of those in senior management. They needed current, fast, accurate, selective information on competitors, markets, and regulations in an attractive, readable, and usable form (Matarazzo and Drake 1994). To provide this, he abolished his paper library, freeing up the time and money it had taken to manage it. He did not try to compete with analysts within the company (insufficient time and expertise), but worked with them. Information was seen as the property of the whole corporation, not just the person using or paying for it. Another example of a virtual library is at Lotus Inc. (Rich 1994). As a result of downsizing they needed to focus on their most valued services. Using Lotus Notes, they provided access to news wires, market research, library catalogs, and electronic newspapers; supported electronic document requests and an electronic mailbox for questions. This required some new skills and the redeploying or refocusing of old skills. For instance, book acquisition becomes choosing online sources.

THE INTERNET

One of the most visible forms of information technology now is the Internet. Started in the 1950s as a network for information exchange among defense researchers, it is now found in nearly every corporation and school, and most libraries. The Internet has grown very rapidly, doubling in size every twelve to fifteen months. This is expected to continue for next three years or so, then taper off. Everyone agrees that there is a lot of information available on the Internet. Sometimes it is useful and someday it may become one of a librarian's most important resource. BUT that is not today's reality. What is true is that in many cases, our patrons are ahead of us in use of the Internet. Robert Hertzberg, editor of the *Internet Business Report*, called the Internet "the single most over hyped communications medium to come along in a long time" (*Corporate Library Update*, March 11, 1995, 2–3). This will get worse before it gets better.

Internet is opening up information to the individual. There are "no more gates to keep" said Searfossas (1995, 51). The importance of the Internet according to Doran (1996) is that it frees us from the bonds of time, money, and space, it adds unpublished sources such as news groups to our information bank, it provides connectivity, and it encourages open-ended, lateral thinking. The librarian's role is to integrate the Net with printed, traditional sources, organize it, and teach it to our users.

Another concern is what will be the effect of the Internet on the producers of traditional online services. In a speech at the SLA Midwest

Regional Conference in 1995, Barbara Quint warned that their interfaces must catch up with the flash and ease of the Internet if they expect
to continue to attract end users. There is also the danger that even intermediaries will abandon the majors (DIALOG, LEXIS-NEXIS, Dow
Jones, etc.) for the cheaper full-text services on the Internet. Fletcher
(1996) writes that the costs of going online are dropping rapidly and that
many companies are getting into the business (MAID, Infoseek, etc.)
because making such services available is easier than ever. No more do
they need to distribute software and manuals to the desktop—it is all on
the Net. With overhead costs lessened, the online provider can focus on
marketing and content. And even marketing costs are diminished by
using the Internet itself. Other advantages are a large customer base, user
perceptions of low or free Internet costs, increased user mobility among
services (a two-edged sword at best), and more information provided by
companies themselves via Web home pages.

All is not roses on the Internet, however. Fletcher points out such
disadvantages as wasted user time, unreliable searching and navigating, user
overload (too much information), and system overload with its attendant
delays and frustrations. Added value and completeness may also suffer.
"Most people are not willing to pay for the added value of thoroughness
unless there's a mission critical situation. Ease of search is more important"
(1996, 44). I would add that the simplicity of the search engines on the
Internet passes some costs from the provider to the user. If it takes longer
to find information, then the user is "paying" in extra time spent searching.
And how do you measure the cost of incomplete or incorrect information?
What will be the effect on the published forms of information, such as
directories? Will these be forced out of print by the economics of direct
publishing on the Internet? If they are, how will those who cannot afford
the Internet access this information? Fletcher, however, sees great opportunities for information intermediaries. "Knowing how to get information
economically, how to synthesize material, how to distill facts to answer
questions, and how to extract the right question from the client" (44) are
our core competencies and there exist—at present—no online search
engines that can do what we do.

HOW DO LIBRARIANS USE THE INTERNET NOW?

Librarians use e-mail for collection management activities such as
questions about vendors, and library management issues (salaries, etc.)
Many would prefer to use the Internet more for e-mail. They use

listservs to stay informed, to stay connected, and to follow library issues, instead of or in addition to professional meetings, as well as using them for reference, and for interlibrary loan and duplicates exchange (Ladner and Tillman 1993). The Internet has implications for team building and collaboration (with users and with other librarians). Madden and Gilman in posts on LIBREF-L and PACS-L mentioned other professional uses of the Internet by librarians. They include searching online catalogs around the world, searching one's own catalog from home, accessing commercial databases such as LEXIS-NEXIS and DIALOG, finding and downloading documents, answering consumer health questions (but one must screen sources—the American Heart Association and the Diabetes Association are good sources), finding government statistics or publications, locating information about companies, obtaining country-specific travelers' information and CDC health advisories, locating working papers and conference announcements, and downloading maps and other geographic information. One deaf librarian uses it the way other librarians use the phone, and one satisfied user, Mike Scully at the Swedish Medical Center in Seattle, wrote this testimonial on the usefulness of a listserv: "Inside of an hour seven of the nine messages in our in-box were regarding my query. I have several good sources to check . . . The speed of the Net and the helpfulness of the MEDLIB-L people never ceases to amaze me!"

Bob Berkman, editor of *The Information Advisor*, did a survey of how people use the World Wide Web for business research (1996). The top fifteen responses follow:

1. to locate obscure information not found anywhere else, by using search engines such as Alta Vista or Savvy Search
2. to find government information, especially from the Census Bureau and the SEC
3. to find information on a company that is posted on its home page
4. to get alternative views found in nonmainstream journals published on the WWW
5. to peruse primary sources such as court options, press releases, white papers
6. to find out information about communities or other entities, from the Web sites of their chambers of commerce or own home page
7. to find news and information from professional societies and universities, not before available online

8. for inexpensive, albeit incomplete, access to newspapers and magazines
9. to find experts on an unfamiliar topic (via newsgroups)
10. for economical access to reference materials you do not have access to in print
11. for access to graphical materials not available online
12. to access sources formerly available in print now only available on the Web
13. for one final check on a research project
14. to find out who else might be interested in the same project you are
15. to search a Web version of a traditional database when it is less expensive

Technology (online, CD-ROM, Internet) widens the range of services available to law librarians. The information is more current and there are more search entry points. "A sophisticated research strategy employs a variety of tools, exploiting the best aspects of each of them" (O'Toole, Knuth, and Selden-Althouse 1995, B10). Technology can also put small law firms "more on a par" with larger firms. Law firms still need someone to manage and support the automated research tools—a librarian. But technology may allow the firms to reallocate space from the library, it being historically the largest office, centrally located, and expensive to build (Stathis 1995). Another concern is whether the Internet is "helping or harming law librarians . . . Right now it is doing both" (Baker 1975, B13). It distracts from other activities, not all information there is valuable, not all valuable information is there, some rely on newsgroups instead of themselves or users for ideas, and librarians become too accessible (to users) due to e-mail. "Librarians . . . must take steps to ensure that they are masters of the Internet, not its slaves" (B14).

The Information Advisor comments that "the current state of the Internet is still *not* well-suited for serious market research. However, there are some exceptional sites . . ." (1996, 1). The problems are inefficient/time-consuming searching, good sounding Web pages which may not be reliable or worthwhile, and lack of information about the context or background of the information. There are positives as well; newsgroups and listservs are good sources of information or advice, broad market statistics may be available from major market research publishers for little or no cost, a great deal of information is available on company Web pages, and data can be collected via surveys. The

Internet can be used to gather competitive intelligence. Collecting information, monitoring listservs, checking on competitors, providing cheaper access to commercial databases, locating and sharing sales leads, external and internal communication via e-mail, networking, and easier and cheaper information dissemination are all possible on the Internet (Cronin et al. 1990).

Of course there is a downside to the Internet as well. Proliferation of messages, lack of time, its "addictive potential," lack of relevant listservs for some, lack of in-house experts or training, the primitive searching capabilities, and unfriendly interfaces are some of them. There is also a threat to our profession. One newspaper librarian commented on the trend of users (and management) to try to get information themselves, without using the librarian. We have all heard comments like "I could get it myself if I had access to the Internet" and "Surely you can teach me to do what you do in five minutes." This shows a lack of respect for and understanding of our profession. The response should be along the lines of "shoemaker stick to your last"—that is, everyone should do what they do best or I will not do engineering (bookkeeping, whatever) if you will not do librarianship.

THE NET AS LIBRARY SERVICE AND RESOURCE

A library marketer, Chris Olson and Associates, offers these tips for promoting the Net as a library service: plan what you will offer, then decide how to package and promote it. Promote yourself as the Internet guru, promote training, and offer home pages. Collins in his "WebWatch" column (1996) details the following guidelines in creating homepages. For content, be concerned with substance, depth, uniqueness, accuracy, and currency. To judge authority, check institutional affiliation and developer credentials. The organization should be easily grasped, logical, and be clearly divided. The search engine should have clear instructions on usage, Boolean capabilities, keyword searching, frequent index updates, speed, and well-formatted output. Be sure that the page is consistently accessible and provides text-based alternative pages. A minimum of graphics helps with speed of download and minimizes confusion.

How does the Internet compare with traditional reference sources? It can be very current, it has information like company press releases, work in progress (like committee reports, working papers, draft standards), local resources not available elsewhere, and government documents and statistics. For instance, many of the series from the United States Bureau of Labor Statistics are no longer available in print form, but they are on the Internet. Nancy Garman, editor of *Online User*, cautions that the librarian needs to be careful in how and what is looked for on the Internet (and online, for that matter). Be sure to look in the right place. Sometimes, however, online (or print) is a better choice. Think about and question the source of Internet information. Who is behind it and is it reliable? Construct the question properly. Start with the answer you want and work backward, taking advantage of advanced search capabilities on many of the WWW search engines. Analyze the results. Do they make sense? Are they corroborated elsewhere?

WHAT THE INTERNET IS AND IS NOT

The best way to evaluate whether to use the Internet for information or another source is to know what it can do and what it cannot. The following lists will give you a guideline.

What It Is

- a great communications tool
- a great leveler (if made available to all, in public libraries or other locations)
- a giant "mail order" catalog
- a great information dissemination tool for business (technical manuals, product literature, catalogs, technical support, software)
- a great information dissemination tool for government (bills, position papers, feedback from people to government)—but not a substitute for print
- an ephemeral storage medium
- cheap

What It Is Not

- a good reference tool (except for posting questions on listservs among professionals)
- secure
- the answer to all information needs (you still need verified sources)
- a substitute for libraries (books are more user-friendly and better for most reference)
- a substitute for librarians (we need them as information guides and consultants and evaluators and indexers)
- an archival medium
- fast

One of the biggest issues in electronic information and the Internet is how to evaluate the information on it. Hope Tillman (1995) has developed some criteria for evaluating Internet resources. Who are the authors? how does it compare to other sources? how stable is the information? how appropriate is the format? what is the cost? how easy is it to use? how convenient? how fast? In the Information Strategies course at Purdue, students compare finding and evaluating information in print sources with same process online to teach new strategies (Brandt 1996). There is a difference in how the information is "published." Print sources are usually internally and then externally peer-reviewed and are indexed for public access. Internet sources are put up directly on the Net via newsgroups, listservs, and the Web. Indexing is done by computers, not human indexers and additional or controlled vocabulary is not used and sources are not evaluated. Not all search engines are inclusive (Yahoo, for example) so sources may be missed. Some guidelines for evaluating the sources are to check the author's credentials and affiliation, to check to see if there is reason to assume a bias in the information or its source, and to make sure the information is appropriate for your purpose by checking its scope, coverage, and level. There is also the question as to whether these sources should be cataloged. Craig Summerhill of the Coalition for Networked Information argues that the cataloging of URLs is a waste of time and "insane." He also maintains that "librarians can assist in dissemination of and access to information by lending organization to the knowledge universe," but he objects to the methods used (Internet post, June 6, 1996).

THE FUTURE OF THE INTERNET

"We have been spoiled by the computer on *Star Trek* which instantly answers Captain Kirk's requests" (Smock 1995, B1). Our patrons expect this kind of service from the Internet and from us. Unfortunately this this is not possible—yet. What then do the experts say about the future of the Internet?

Writing in *InfoWorld*, Bob Metcalfe predicted the imminent collapse of the Internet. This will come to pass due to lack of money and lack of support. The Internet is proving not to be the cash cow some expected. He expects phone monopolies will raise prices, making access economically infeasible. Users will get bored with the Internet and its hype and lose interest. The security, privacy, and censorship issues and capacity problems will overwhelm the system. Already some of the Internet pioneers are fleeing the system. Newsgroups are flooded with "nonexperts" and "irrelevancies," naive or silly questions, inaccurate information, and flaming; the impending collapse will be good, Metcalfe adds later. It will dispel the myth of the Internet as a "wonderfully chaotic and brilliantly biological and homeopathically self-healing" system and lead to the realization that "it needs to managed, engineered, and financed as a network of computers . . ." (1995, 61).

In rebuttal, George Gilder (1996) replied in "Will the Internet Collapse? No Way!" He says that as it expands, each new user adds resources as well as using them. This process of growth pushes the ISPs (Internet service providers) to add more capacity and the backbone providers to follow suit, keeping the Net from collapsing. He expects communications power to grow at least ten times faster than computing power over the next decade. One remaining obstacle to the fulfillment of the promise of the Internet is government regulation, which Gilder sees as being resolved by business's increasing need for the Net and its lobbying of the regulators.

The question remains how the Internet will affect librarians in the future. Ladner and Tillman feel that the Internet "has the potential to make or break the profession of special librarianship" (1993, 1) Sharyn Ladner goes on to make this "fearless prediction":

> The Internet is not an end-all and be-all, but a catalyst, because it affects the rate of change. It will either make or break the small special library. If you don't grasp the technology, you will die. If you do run with it, especially if you implement the Internet, you will be viewed as more than a librarian, you will be viewed as a valued member of the company team (personal communication, January 27, 1996).

PROBLEMS TO COME

With the growing use and versatility of the Internet, performance and bandwidth problems are increasing as are problems due to multimedia, graphics, and number of users. More bandwidth comes at a cost. "Just as software programs expand to take advantage of each advance in microprocessor technology, so too will media types expand to fill the available capacity on the Internet" (Gurley 1996, 181–182). One solution could be allocation of bandwidth by application (e-mail taking precedence over video, for instance). But this is hard to police. Gurley sees three trends for future.

- Proliferation of "middle-nets"—virtual communities, private networks
- Commodity content increasing—less multimedia, video, etc., more stock prices, news, weather, etc.
- Pricing by priority—limit demand by billing by bit, hour, surcharges on heavy users instead of unlimited usage for a flat fee

He is still optimistic about the importance of the Internet as a "global communications infrastructure" although the "future may not be the Utopia some people imagine" (186).

The future should bring a meshing of cable and telephone services in regard to information. Unfortunately, "the ballyhooed combination of television, cable, and phone empires, should it come about, will give the average consumer more access to information—but absolutely no more understanding of what to do with it" (Everett and Crowe 1994, 8). Librarians need to participate with cable and telephone utilities, government, publishers, and the public in decisions about how information will be disseminated. Young (1994) feels that there are opportunities for public/private cooperation and partnerships with libraries taking the lead in defending the public's interest (or the patron's interest in the case of corporate libraries).

WHAT IS A LIBRARIAN TO DO?

Nearly all librarians have heard, "Everything's electronic now, isn't it?" from someone (a boss or a patron) and it is often used as a reason for closing libraries or limiting our resources. There is a definite need to educate our bosses as to why we are needed still—or maybe even more—in this new Internet age. We need to emphasize that end users cannot do as thorough a search as librarians can. They may not find the best sources, just the easiest. We must build relationships with our customers based on trust, confidence, and added value. Since we have limited time and resources, we can let them do the easy searches, leaving the more complex ones for us. We can expect to see more job descriptions like these:

- Electronic-Oriented Librarian: extensive computer background required, orients new students to Internet access [and] the dynamics of electronic information search and retrieval, serves as both knowledgeable technical source and liaison to area library consortia (The Open University, November 16, 1995).

- Collegiate Librarian Information Officer (a new position): "on-site, intradepartmental, discipline-related consulting to expand their awareness and use of information and technological resources, both internal and external to the university. must have technical competencies and experience in the use of networked information resources, be resourceful, demonstrate effective instructional and communications skills, and have a strong client ethic" (Virginia Tech, June 21, 1996).

PERSONAL PREDICTIONS

What do *I* see as the future of the Internet? Copyright issues will be addressed, but not necessarily settled. Security issues will be addressed, but hackers can crack security faster than it can be developed so security will always be an issue. Censorship issues (both pornography and personal use in the workplace) will be addressed, but, again, not necessarily settled. Bandwidth problems may improve, but technology will find ways to exceed the improvements and the problems will reappear. In late 1995 I predicted that if too many nonresearch/personal users take over the Net, a parallel, fee-based, research/serious user network may develop, similar to where the Net was a few years ago. In August 1996, the National Science Foundation announced grants to thirteen universities to develop a very high-speed Backbone Network Service to connect 100 universities, national laboratories, and other research organizations (*InfoWorld* 1996)—the alternative Internet I predicted. (It is so nice to be right!)

Jose-Marie Griffiths has created a great metaphor about the "Information Highway." The roads are built by the communications companies. The vehicles are built by the computer manufacturers. The services are built by the content providers. What is the role of the information professional? We provide the signage, the travel guides, the maps and most importantly—the drivers' education.

The Future of SOLO
Librarianship

This chapter will first look at what people are saying about the future of librarianship in general, then about the specific future of the one-person or one-professional library. Part of the chapter will also be some of my own observations and expectations.

Before speculating about the future of librarians, there is a basic question which Raitt stated well: "Will librarians still be around in 2024, and if so, what are they likely to be doing?" (1994, 275) Why do we ask this question and do teachers, doctors, or lawyers ask this about their profession? Is it the fact that information is becoming more available or that librarians are becoming more insecure? It is probably more the latter (insecurity) than the former (the threat of technology). As discussed earlier in this book, librarians have a historically poor self-image, which leads to more introspective questioning of the future than is probably either necessary or healthy. But, since the question has been asked, this chapter will perhaps provide some answers.

TECHNOLOGY

We librarians cannot overestimate the impact technology will have on our future. The greatest impact may come from client/server technology providing information at the desktop, with graphics, sound, video; in full text with copyright taken care of; databases of internal documents; personalized news updates—all available from anywhere in the world to anywhere else. There is the ever-present danger of technolust that new is always better than old, the future is always better than the present. There is a tendency to assume that any and all improvements are worthwhile. In addition, there is always the nerd's cry of "gotta have it now."

The library must add value with the technology, not just add the technology, lest "the new technologies empower the end user" (Giles,

Internet post, February, 16, 1996). Prusak (1995) points out four steps to bringing new value to the organization:

1. Decide whom you want to help and choose them with care; find those with a clear need for information and who value information, and abandon universal service.
2. Get to know those in the group well and use their vocabulary; people are not aware of what they do not know and may also be reluctant to admit it, especially to junior staff.
3. Figure out what information would add value for them.
4. Learn their concerns and mission critical projects and build core services and products to serve them; read what they read.

Beyond these points, other authorities have remarked on technology. Suzi Hayes states that "access to information technology tools gives us more opportunity for collaboration and creating value with the information we produce. Such technologies as the Internet are enablers" (1994, 4). Crawford and Gorman also feel "the most important element of enhanced library service is cooperation [among libraries]" (1995, 177). Foster (1994) predicts that management will be leaner, flatter, and more informal. Upper management will understand IT better, leading to more integration between information services and IT. There will be more emphasis on cost and performance measures and more emphasis on quality service.

What happened to the paperless society, widely predicted a decade ago? With the advent of CD-ROM and the Internet and World Wide Web, is it still on the horizon? Howard Besser, University of Michigan, predicts that "future librarians will be working in environments that are half physical and half virtual" (1996, 21). On the other hand, Crawford and Gorman point up that "people prefer the printed page to the screen for all but the shortest text passages, for sound ergonomic reasons that will not be eliminated in the near future" (1995, 34). At the National Online Meeting in May 1995, Vance Opperman, president of West Publishing, said that paper will continue in the future and that there is also a niche for CD-ROMs, especially if they can be updated via satellite. There is no doubt that some print publications *should* disappear: those which are used primarily on a paragraph-by-paragraph basis (ready reference, dictionaries, statistics), those whose probable use is less than 10 percent of the whole over their lives (back runs of little used serials, government documents, conference proceedings), and those for which delays in publication outdate the information (consumer and price guides, financial information). All these are probably best done electronically.

It is obvious that "technology offers more opportunity than obstacle for future generations" (Hayes 1994, 5). The issue is how we will use it. In *Future Libraries*, Crawford and Gorman (1995) see room for a revision or new view of Ranganathan's Five Laws of Library Science: (1) books are for use, (2) every reader has his book, (3) every book its reader, (4) the library should save the time of the reader, and (5) the library is a growing organism. The move will be to libraries that serve humanity, respect all forms by which knowledge is communicated, use technology intelligently to enhance service, protect free access to knowledge, and honor the past and create the future, in other words, those which use technology intelligently.

Technology must be a tool to solve problems, not an end in itself, leading us only to find new ways to use new technology. We must weigh the costs, benefits, and impact on users of any proposed innovation. We should rethink the entire service, not just automate it (and only automate what is improved with automation). Crawford and Gorman also identify a potential problem with an all-electronic library: the danger of losing perspective. If we only look at preselected topics (the ones in our computerized profile or online newspaper or custom alert), we may not get a well-rounded view of the world. (For example, who would choose Bosnia as a keyword? Very few, but most of us will at least glance at the headlines about it.) The researcher runs the risk of only finding the material available online. If it has not been indexed, it becomes invisible, and he or she may make document retrieval decisions based on what is available online in full-text rather than what will present a well-balanced view of the issues. There is also the danger of "The Young Scholar's Peril." The Young Scholar will define a field so narrowly and search so restrictively that he will miss important research *and* that he will spend so much time keeping up with new postings in this area that there will be no time to organize, analyze, synthesize, all that constitutes original research.

In the 1960s, Guy Lyle interviewed college and university librarians and concluded that in terms of shaping librarianship "technology is one of the compelling forces" and "specialization proliferates." The library becomes "one element in a complex communication system and the pressure is on librarians to produce faster and better ways of acquiring, organizing and retrieving information . . . When [we catch up] library aims and services will probably be altered to a degree which will make them unrecognizable . . ." (Riggs and Sabine, vi).

In 1988, Riggs and Sabine asked library leaders to predict what libraries would be like in 1998. It is not quite 1998 yet, but many of their predictions have come true already. In answer to what new library services these leaders anticipated in the next ten years, the following were their responses. My comments follow in parentheses.

- school librarians more involved in teaching (this has come true)
- more in-house databases (true)
- more networking (true)
- more full-text periodicals (more, but probably not as many as they expected)
- more access of the library from home (true, thanks to the Internet and the World Wide Web)
- fax connecting libraries (true as of about five years ago, being supplanted by the Internet)
- more multimedia (boy, is this true!)
- artificial intelligence for searching (not here yet)
- basic reference answered by technology, reference more of readers' advisory (we are working on it, but definitely not here yet)
- librarians as advisors, more like special librarians (also coming, but not here yet)
- more online delivery (some available, but not as much as everyone wants)
- more emphasis on small children (true)
- more active research, for a fee (true in many public and academic libraries—seen in corporate libraries as more chargebacks)

Another question asked concerned library users. What would they be like in 1998? The responses are as follows:

- expect materials from anywhere in the world available instantly (increasingly true, but service is not quite available yet)
- more library education in public schools (there is more, but not nearly enough)
- raised expectations (thanks to the Internet)
- more adept at using technology (depends on the age of the user)
- more visual (especially true of younger users)
- non-White (increasingly true, especially in the United States Southwest)

Finally the question was posed as to what the impact of technology would be. A summation of the answers follows:

- increased productivity (we can do things faster, but we are also asked to do more things, overall—a wash)
- new job responsibilities/positions (increasingly true, especially in corporate libraries)
- not reduce staff, but create more (not true for the majority of us—decreasing staffs)
- too much emphasis on technology, not enough on results (unfortunately, true)
- less contact with people (except for online/Internet catalogs, this has not come true)

THE LIBRARY OF THE FUTURE

Michael Gorman (1996) focused on three aspects of the library of the future, that is, the madness—a network of human and electronic resources, available in only one form (electronic); the reality—the library as a place with or without walls, influenced by money or the lack of it, requiring us to do more with less; and the dream—a library freely available to all, staffed by skilled professionals, marked by local and national cooperation, intelligently using technologies old and new, with free access to remote resources. In their book *Future Libraries: Dreams, Madness, and Reality* in the section on "Deconstructing Dreams of the All-Electronic Future," Crawford and Gorman question the vision of all data/information/knowledge being online and universally available, of everyone making effective use of this data and being happy to pay, and of solving copyright problems; they called this vision "irresponsible, illogical, and unworkable" (87). Libraries as physical entities will not cease to exist, nor will print. They also point out the dangers of the "Enemies of the Library" which include enemies within, such as the suicidal librarian (those who call themselves information specialists and library managers without library educations); and doomsayers among library school faculty (predicting the death of print and removing the word "library" from the name of the school). "Librarianship will die if librarians and library educators kill it off" (107). Also on the enemies' list are those who deny or minimalize the professionalism of reference librarianship, those who encourage users to the research skills needed to replace the librarian (that is, assuming that they even *want* to do so), and the new barbarians who believe that facts are all that is important, not knowledge or organization or preservation.

In an article in *Library Journal,* Schement sees the threat coming from another direction. According to him "in the long run, the decline of community threatens librarians most severely. However, the information society is evolving away from the traditional notion of community" (1996, 35). The library of the future must first teach "mediacy" skills (coined by Toni Carbo Bearman, who defines them as literacy plus knowing where to find information plus knowing what to do with it). Next, the library should be put in every household (via television, the Internet, reference resources, mediacy services). Finally, new communities of the twenty-first century should be built, that is, virtual communities. Thus the library turns from a territorial institution to a functional institution. Libraries must act decisively; talk with other libraries, museums, schools, media; develop alliances because "not only do librarians have a great stake in the information society, but all of us as citizens have a great stake in the success of libraries" (36).

Much of what is predicted is based on false assumptions. Libraries never were the primary source for up-to-date information—there have always been newspapers and television for this. In the past, people used to buy more books but recent trends show that bookstores are booming, and more books are sold than ever before. If information becomes totally electronic, public libraries may or may not be obsolete because people will still need a *place* to go, and electronic data will not replace the library role in preservation of information and culture for future generations. Remember also that there is no *ultimate* library or patron— "different libraries and different library users have different needs and problems" (Crawford and Gorman 1995, 130). Finally, the importance of "and" not "or" is stressed. Adopt the new, but keep the old: print *and* electronic communication; linear *and* hypertext; mediation *and* end-user access; collections *and* access; and library as edifice *and* interface.

FUTURE ROLES OF THE LIBRARIAN

To survive, librarians will need to carve out a specific niche based on their own unique competencies, and they will need to demonstrate the value of these competencies who employ them. *Working Woman* magazine predicted that the career of corporate librarian is one of the twenty-five hottest careers. The magazine expects "the explosion of on-line research is sure to sustain demand for well-trained information specialists" (July, 1995, 40). This niche may be to help those who will need to cope with all this information. As librarians have organized all kinds of information throughout the history of the profession, they can take this capability outside the library. "However, the service will evolve outside of the library . . . [and] this effort cannot take place without a paradigm shift in the library professions, with librarians reimaging themselves in the context of the new information society" (Schement 1996, 34-35).

Job descriptions, such as these from the University of Houston and the University of the Pacific sent over the Internet, may become more common in the future:

- plan and evaluate electronic services (databases, fulltext, online searching, CD-ROM, Internet)
- bibliographic instruction
- collection development, print and electronic
- innovation required
- liaison with other departments and vendors
- user-oriented

The definition of what librarians are is evolving. A client panel at the April 1995 meeting of the AIIP agreed that what is needed are information consultants, not brokers. Librarians of the future will need to provide training for end users and will have to be more technologically savvy. Customers will require faster turnaround or response time and will be willing to pay higher prices if service is better. Merry fears that "those librarians who continue to focus primarily on acquisition and distribution of information . . . will likely be absorbed into other functions . . . or be increasingly relegated to the sidelines of an exciting business environment" (*Corporate Library Update*, August 1, 1995).

In the corporate world, Tice encourages librarians to partner with other areas of the company, especially IS, establish "intellectual capital repositories"—in-house expert networks (*Corporate Library Update*, October, 15, 1995). Lou Parris of Exxon believes that "the integration of internal information assets (archives and more) and access to external information resources (libraries) [are] the evolving province of librarians. It's here that we will utilize our skills and education to maximize our organization's information assets and increase our contribution to its success" (post on SLA listserv, May 10, 1996).

In this new electronic setting, the librarian's scope becomes broader. "For librarians hoping to preserve their function's distinctive value in the new, wired-up world, much internal marketing and business case development will need to be done" (*Corporate Library Update*, August 1, 1995). We cannot aim low. Merry (1994) noted that in the organization of today the CIO (Chief Information Officer) is usually an IS/MIS/IT [computer] person. This position should actually be called the CTO, Chief Technology Officer. The CIO should be librarian or information professional. This will be a hard sell, but it is how we should envision our role in the future.

We must not resist change. The only thing that is constant is change. If we keep doing what we did yesterday, we, as librarians, will be passed over, made obsolete. "Librarians, like libraries, should exist for function, not form. Librarians serve clients' information needs by gathering and preserving information, by locating and delivering information, and by building information systems that increase access and guarantee quality of information. The good librarian defines performance by a service ethic to clients" (Quint 1991, 59). St. Clair adds further comments on the need for change:

> I love librarianship and all it stands for, and I am quick to say to any young person who comes to me for career advice that librarianship is the best of all careers because it *can* engage you intellectually while you are being of service—*truly* of service— to others. But I also tell them that it is a career in which everything changes. It always has and it always will, and they must be willing to deal with change throughout their careers. That, in a nutshell, is what is exciting about librarianship. (1996f, 3).

There are those who also see positive changes coming, as well as a positive need for librarians. Ferguson urges "librarians [to] take off your black arm bands, stop the funeral dirge, cease the endless wringing of hands, stop sounding the death knell of collection development, stop moaning about the end of librarianship as we know it today. We are all going to be busier in the future than in the past" (1996, 10). Users will need even more guidance through the "chaos" of the Internet since it is continually changing. Collection development will take more time because digital materials need more evaluation than books. The safeguarding of intellectual property will be more complicated and require more technical competence. "Our shelves may be digital, but the work of filling them and keeping them filled continues to be complicated and important. Job security for the information professional is assured" (89).

LIBRARY SCHOOLS AND THE CURRICULUM OF THE FUTURE

Just as the focus of librarians may change in the future, so should their preparation. Referring back to the survey of Riggs and Sabine that was already discussed, another question that was posed to their experts was how should library school curricula change by 1998? A summation of the responses follow with the addition of my comments:

- more interaction of practitioners and educators (we are still asking for this)
- expand faculty (this is happening at some schools, but overall there are less)
- problem of updating faculty—keeping current (an increasing problem)
- more innovation, especially in children's programs
- student must be computer and online literate from the start (increasingly an entrance requirement or at least required by graduation)
- attract more science and math students (very slowly coming true)
- mandatory management, administration, public speaking courses (not yet)
- emphasize indexing (not being done—and I am not sure it is necessary)
- library directors coming from technical service, not reference
- not sure if cataloging and reference will be taught (still being taught, but is beginning to be more integrated into other courses)
- need to prepare librarians to be better managers (still a burning need)
- more user education courses, financial management, statistics (still on our want list)

The survey went on to address what the experts considered the number one challenge for library schools during the decade ending in 1998. The experts felt that there are three challenges facing library schools: the recruitment of bright students, credibility and the need for increased research production, and quality. Although there has been some progress, they remain challenges still to be met.

There was also the question of what would be new entry-level qualifications for librarians? Of the following list, I wish all those listed below were required, but progress is slow in recruiting the right kind of students:

- communication skills
- analytical skills
- technological synthesis

- more organizational political skills
- high-technology and people-orientation
- more backgrounds in science
- more aggressive, more entrepreneurial
- more manager-type people
- skills in cultural differences

As far as continuing education, there is a question as to whether it has fallen behind. Unfortunately, in my view it has. Although it is definitely getting better, and the leaders' predictions that vendors would provide some continuing education (CE) and that much of the fundamentals are now in MLS programs, CE still suffers from logistical problems (cost of equipment, lack of teachers), and lack of support from the institution. Alternate methods of delivery are needed as well.

THE FUTURE FOR SPECIFIC TYPES OF LIBRARIANS

Holt (1990) sees a good future for small public libraries and their staff. Patrons will present a different set of needs (such as requesting more audiovisual and multimedia materials), and libraries will bring in new patrons with new services. Networking will continue to be important, as will better community public relations and better service.

The special librarian is also predicted to survive. Ferguson and Mobley wrote that "we believe there *will* be librarians operating in the future [and] we firmly believe that the special librarian can make a more successful transition to the future than any other type of practitioner in the profession" (1984, 177-78). They feel that the librarian of the future may be more of an intermediary, packager, or interpreter of information, than he or she is now.

The law librarian of the future, according to Stathis (1995), must be computer-literate, more of an administrator than a data gatherer, and an essential presence. Shaffer predicts that law librarians may have law degrees although she feels the knowledge and skills the librarian brings to a firm are more important than a law degree. With online services growing and with time being money, "law librarians will play an increasingly vital role in helping their firms get the information they need . . . Law librarians will increasingly play an added-value role in law firms, finding and condensing information that attorneys don't have time to find and learn" (1996, 37). The AALL Renaissance Committee, whose charter is to "redefine law librarianship in light of radical changes in systems of information delivery and to recommend measures AALL might take to facilitate the transformation of the profession in accord with that definition," is exploring standards for law librarians and CE program (Shaffer 1996).

Finally all of these issues, new methods of working, and new skills coalesce into a new term, cybrarian, as coined by Michel Bauwens in the "Cybrarian's Guide to Cyber-Marketing." He describes the role of the cybrarian as follows:

> The function of information intermediaries will be essential as it is precisely those people who intercede between the exponential information overload, and the constricted human bandwidth, which will be important "attention," and thus ultimately "power" brokers.
>
> In the physical world of books, librarians needed to be together. In the immaterial world of electronic information, this expertise can be distributed. Hence, I see a great future for solo librarians, which I consider to be the "third way" of information retrieval. The first way is the universal "human-produced" knowledge indexes á la Yahoo, which are ever running behind reality and will be able to catalog an increasingly smaller share of knowledge production; the second way are the universal search tools á la Hotbot and AltaVista, who are tireless and never sleep, but will never match human contextual intelligence. Both these options will collapse under their own weight, making place for a myriad of specialized indexing services. Thus the third way is the distributed way of human expertise, who will develop increasingly specialised and contextual knowledge maps within their domains of experience. Technology exists today, to do remote updating of knowledge centers from all over the world, for the benefit of the whole world, and this will be the job of the solo librarians or cybrarians.
>
> From the point of view of the cybrarians, these knowledge centers will act as externalisations of their own mind, like the "Memory Palaces" which helped medieval scholars organize their knowledge, only now, these are "physical" and can be accessed by third parties. This then is the role of solo librarians in the future: to create real-time knowledge maps of their expertise, accessible through the Web. In other words, what is needed is a direct link from their brain to the Web,

and the other way around. I look forward to the day of these "cyborg librarians," and invite readers to look at my own current attempt of achieving this, the "Cyrarian's Guide to Cyber-Marketing," available at http://www.iocom.be/.

THE FUTURE OF SOLO LIBRARIANSHIP

Back in 1986, Guy St. Clair, predicted that there would be more interaction among SOLOs, more literature written about them. He was confident that SOLOs would continue to exist and increase. This has all come to pass. What he says now about our future is that "managements will find that they get more value for their money by employing one highly skilled and effective librarian/information specialist instead of a team—however small—of generalists who are not as skilled" and "there is also recognition in the profession that one-person librarianship just might become a standard for library staffing in the future" (1987, 267).

Other thoughts from St. Clair from the same source round out the picture of the SOLO librarian. He believes the number of SOLO operations will get larger because management will realize that "one excellent, efficient, and enthusiastic librarian or information specialist is preferable to two or more who do not provide the same level of service for users" (267). There have been drastic changes in the information services discipline since then, but the desire for good library service or good information delivery has not changed. The difference is that this is increasingly being done by one person rather than a larger staff. These changes have taken place because of the following:

- advances in technology which allow the SOLO to provide good service
- avoidance or elimination of processes of deliverables that are not mission-critical
- increasing focus on the customer or organization rather than on the library
- better training for SOLOs
- greater sense of self-worth by SOLOs

Berner and St Clair (1996) say that this new information specialist must perform many functions to manage and to deliver information for a particular unit of an organization. This is what St. Clair and Berner are now calling *insourcing*. Insourcing emphasizes the relationship between the information professional and the narrowly defined customer base.

The librarian is no longer a "support" function, but a critical member of the team. (Another term for insourcing might be partnering, or even just good SOLO librarianship, since what we try to do is bond with our users and tailor our services to their needs.)

On the occasion of its tenth anniversary, *The One-Person Library* (1994) saw the following as important issues to the future of SOLO librarianship. What's important is "value added"; one of our strengths is our closeness to the customer; and an entrepreneurial spirit will take us far. We will become increasingly technology driven, especially regarding electronic document delivery and remote access to "library" collections. Our role will evolve into facilitators or information advisors.

Rhea Austin, 1996-97 Chair of the SOLO Librarians Division of SLA, sees a number of issues in our future. The idea that "everything, for free" is on the Internet is an obstacle we all have to face. We must show our patrons that they have only found the tip of the iceberg and the rest is in "professional databases" that we can help them navigate. "A real, live librarian can provide more information than they already have." A second major challenge is downsizing. "We need to show our management how invaluable we are so we will not be downsized right out the door." We have a responsibility to those who follow us—to help newcomers find out how great it is to be SOLO. "If we do our best, we can have a very rewarding future!"

Mary Ellen Bates, a consultant in Washington D.C., believes "that the future of solo librarians is very positive. SOLOs are in the front line of the battle for the hearts and minds of information consumers—they can run lean and mean operations within their organizations to educate, consult with, and provide in-depth research for the professionals within their organizations." She goes on to say:

> Clearly, the role of solo librarians has changed. In the past, they had to do all the library functions—manage the library budget, catalog materials, provide research services, reshelve books, do inter-library loans, and, oh yes, try to keep updated on new information industry developments as well. I see solo librarians as evolving dramatically. There will be less ILL as more information is either available online or can be ordered online through document delivery services. There may be a lessening of the simple reference requests as solos train the information users within their organizations to use the tools available to do some of their own basic searching. Products

such as HeadsUp and the Electric Library, user-friendly front-end software like KR BusinessBase and Dow Jones GUI software, and consumer online services such as CompuServe and America Online all provide enough basic tools to enable many non-professional searchers to conduct their own simple searches.

She also explains just what this can mean for us, the SOLOs:

Solo librarians can move up a notch—their roles will be to teach consumers how to shop around and select the most appropriate information resources, train them in the most cost-effective search techniques, and support them when they need more complex research done that goes beyond the capabilities of the end-user search tools. Sometimes it's difficult to give up some of the online searching—this is the part that many solos enjoy the most. But in handing over the basic tools to library patrons, solo librarians can build their jobs into that of information consultant and guru instead of information go-fer. And remember, patrons will still come back when they find that they're not finding what they want . . . and they have a much higher appreciation of the information gathering and analysis skills of librarians as a result.

Linda Appel, former Chair, SOLO Librarians Division, reiterates an important point that change is "the major issue" facing SOLOs. It should be something that is recognized and planned for it will "test us, nurture us, and stretch us and, perhaps, lead each of us in exciting path we would never have foreseen . . . In my twenty-five year career we've been swept into an electronic environment. The organizations we work for are finally discovering that success in an increasingly competitive international marketplace depends on information, and their reactions are thrusting additional change upon us."

Guy St. Clair (1995) has noted that in the future the librarian may perform as purchasing agent, gatekeeper, network manager, internal trainer, information specialists, or chief information officer. In fact, individual librarians in specific organizations are performing each of these roles now, mainly in response to circumstances. A little brainstorming will undoubtedly suggest additional roles we could fill. Unfortunately, there has been no general planning and preparation for these possibilities among librarians or library educators. However, one of the great joys of SOLO librarianship is the freedom it confers on each of us to shape our jobs to our own specifications. None of us can fill all the possible roles of an information guru within our organization. Nevertheless, each of us can examine the needs of our organization, discern some possibilities that its culture would support, know our own strengths, talents, and sources of satisfaction, and fit this information together into a broad plan of development for ourselves and our information services that will enable us to foresee and welcome change. So stay alert and stay loose. If we bring energy, enthusiasm, and experimentation to our jobs we will find fun and fulfillment in them.

Robert Berkman, editor of *The Information Advisor*, addressed fears of downsizing and this can be "an exciting and dynamic time to be your organization's information expert" (1995, 20), if the possibilities of the job can be demonstrated to senior management. How can this be accomplished? Berkman stresses the importance the of library getting into the Competitive Intelligence business. Librarians will have to work on transforming libraries because a love of books will not be enough anymore; it will need leadership. They will need to have a vision, a new vision, to work with and inspire others, to think long-range, to be enthusiastic, and to take action. Partnering with the computer people, with vendors, and with other information professionals and librarians will be required. Librarians may want to start new services such as creating an in-house database of expertise, like Teltech (people are an organization's most valuable asset). Berkman emphasizes the future in the chapter entitled "Training and Consulting: Your New Role?" With end-user searching, interest often wanes after the first rush—when users find that it is harder than they thought. That is where we can step in. If users embrace end-user searching, we can still act as a filter, checking out quality, recommending sources, training, and doing the really hard searches.

MY OWN OBSERVATIONS

The future of librarianship will increasingly depend on technology. We must be sure we become the masters of it, rather than letting it use us. We must ensure we do not let it co-opt our role in the transfer of knowledge. Since it is unlikely that our current or prospective employers will jump to train us in the new technology, it remains our responsibility to obtain this training ourselves.

In order to remain part of the information mainstream, we must change our roles and become information and knowledge leaders, facilitators, mediators, advisors. No longer will it be enough to be passive question-answerers; we must take a proactive role in promoting information services and the importance of our role in the process. A major first step is to change our education and our image. We must be prepared for the future. We will gain respect not by demanding it, but by earning it.

It is almost certain that in the future there will be more SOLOs in corporate and other institutional settings, and probably even in public and academic settings. While some may see this as a bad thing, I see it as an opportunity for those of us who enjoy working alone. However, to succeed we need to have more contact and interchange among SOLOs. This is especially true for those of us working outside the United States where there are fewer opportunities to meet with peers. We also must establish and maintain mentoring relationships with students and new librarians so that they will no longer feel unprepared and alone.

Note that I use "we" throughout these thoughts. None of us can sit back and wait for the future to happen—for "them" to make changes. We all have to take an active part in making the future happen the way we envision it. We need to have the right education, the right attitude, and the right image. We need to make sure that we are experts, but in the right things. We need to have the knowledge that is needed by our employers, customers, competitors, and colleagues, and they need to know what we have to offer. We have to convince them that we are the *best* (maybe the *only*) ones to help them meet their goals. We must position ourselves to become an indispensable part of their business plan. Then—and only then—we will be paid what we are worth. Because we will be worth what we are paid. We will be able to be full partners in the worldwide information process.

Part *Two*

Resources

8

Organizations

Some of the most important sources of information, guidance, and help for SOLOs are organizations, both library and otherwise. They are almost always happy to answer your questions or send you information, whether or not you are a member. (Of course, they will be more helpful to members.) So, here are lists of useful organizations in the United States, Canada, and other countries, along with their addresses, phone numbers, and e-mail addresses, if available. They are arranged alphabetically within the following categories:

- General Library Organizations
- Specialized Library Organizations
- Alternative Careers
- Church and Synagogue Library Organizations
- Law Library Organizations
- Medical Library Organizations
- Records Management Organizations

At the end of the chapter are listed some library joblines, both national and regional. Some of the numbers will most certainly have changed by publication date, so check with your local library organization.

GENERAL LIBRARY ORGANIZATIONS

American Library Association (ALA), 50 E. Huron St., Chicago, IL 60611-2795, 800-545-2433

American Society for Information Science (ASIS), 8720 Georgia Ave., Suite 501, Silver Spring, MD 20910-3602, 301-495-0900, e-mail: asis@cni.org, Internet: http://www.asis.org

Association of Libraries & Information Bureaux (ASLIB), Information House, 20-24 Old St., London EC1V 9AP, England, 071-253-4488,

fax: 071-430-0514; One Man Bands Special Interest Group, c/p Chris
Wilson, Chair, CIPFA, 3 Robert Street, London WC2N 6BH, 0171-
895-8823; Newsletter Editor: Geraint Hughes, Policy Research
Institute, Leeds Metropolitan University, 16 Queen Square, Leeds LS2
8AJ, 0113-283-3225, fax: 0113-283-3224, e-mail: g.hughes@lmu.ac.uk

Canadian Library Association, 200 Elgin St., Suite 602, Ottawa, Ontario
K2P 1L5, Canada, 613-232-9625, e-mail: ai077@freenet.carleton.ca

Institute of Information Scientists, 44-45 Museum St., London WC1A
1LY, England, 0171-831-8003, fax: 0171-430-1270, e-mail: iis@dial.
pipex.com, Internet: http://www.dcs.gla.ac.uk/IIS/

The Library Association, 7 Ridgmount St., London, England WC1E
7AE, 071-636-7543 (including Industrial & Commercial Libraries
Group, Health Libraries Group, Special Libraries Committee, School
Libraries Group)

Library Association of Ireland, 53 Upper Mount St., Dublin 2, Ireland
1-619000

National Federation of Abstracting and Information Services (NFAIS),
1429 Walnut St., 13th Floor, Philadelphia, PA 19102, 215-564-2406

National Librarians Association, P.O. Box 486, Alma, MI 48801,
517-463-7227

New Zealand Library Association, Level 8, Petecorp House, 86 Lambton
Quay, Wellington North, New Zealand, 04-473-5834

Public Library Association (PLA), a Division of ALA, includes Small &
Medium Sized Libraries Division

Scottish Library Association, Motherwell Business Centre, Coursington
Road, Motherwell, Strathcyde, Scotland ML1 1PW, 698-252526

Sociedad de Bibliotecarios de Puerto Rico, University of Puerto Rico
Station, P.O. Box 22898, Rio Piedras, PR 00931, 809-758-1125

Special Libraries Association (SLA), 1700 18th St., NW, Washington, DC
20009, 202-234-4700, includes SOLO Librarians Division, Library
Management Division

SPECIALIZED LIBRARY ORGANIZATIONS
(see separate entries for Church and Synagogue, Law, Medical, and Records Management)

African Library Association of South Africa, Library, University of the
North, Private Bag X1106, Sovenga 0727, South Africa 01522-4310

American Association of Museums (AAM), 1225 Eye St., NW,
Washington, DC 20005, 202-289-1818

American Association of School Librarians (AASL). 50 Huron St., Chicago, IL 60611, 312-944-6780

American Association for State & Local History (AASLH), 530 Church St., #600, Nashville, TN 37219

American Indian Library Association, c/o Lisa Mitten, 207 Hillman Library, University of Pittsburgh, Pittsburgh, PA 15260, 412-648-7723, e-mail: lmitten@vms.cis.pitt.edu

American Society of Indexers (ASI), P.O. Box 386, 503 S. 12th St., Port Aransas, TX 78373, 512-749- 4052

American Society of Interpreters (ASI), P.O. Box 9603, Washington, DC 20016, 703-998-8636

American Translators Association (ATA), 109 Croton Ave., Ossining, NY 10562, 914-941-1500

American Zoo and Aquarium Association Librarians Special Interest Group, 7970-D Old Georgetown Road, Bethesda, MD 20814, 301-907-7777

Art Libraries Society, North America (ARLIS/NA), 3900 E. Tinrod St., Tucson, AZ 85711; or 4101 Lake Boone Trail, Suite 201, Raleigh, NC 27607, 919-787-5181

Art Libraries Society, (ARLIS)/UK and Ireland, 18 College Rd., Bromsgrove, Worcestershire, B60 2NE, England

Asociacion Mexicana de Bibliotecarios, Apartado Postal 27-651, Adminstracion de Correos 27, 06760 Mexico DF, Mexico, 05-575-1135

Association of Architectural Librarians, 1735 New York Ave., NW, Washington, DC 20005, 202-347-7490

Association of Assistant Librarians, British Library Science Reference and Information Service, 25 Southampton Buildings, London WC2A 1AW, England, 71-323-7959.

Association of Canadian Map Libraries and Archives, National Archives of Canada, 344 Wellington, Room 1016, Ottawa, Canada K1A0N3, 613-992-8188

Association of Mental Health Librarians, c/o Lenore W. Freehling, Research Library, Reiss-Davis Child Study Center, 3200 Motor Ave., Los Angeles, CA 90034, 310-204-1666

Australian Library and Information Association, Box E441, Queen Victoria Terrace, Canberra ACT, Australia 2600, 062-285-1877

Australian Society of Indexers, GPO Box 1251, Melbourne VIC, Australia 3001, 61-3-9571-6341

Council on Botanical and Horticultural Libraries, c/o John F. Reed, New York Botanical Garden, 200th St. and Southern Blvd., Bronx, NY 10458, 718-817-8705, ext. 8729, e-mail: jfreed@nybg.org

Council of Planning Librarians, 1313 E. 60th St., Chicago IL 60637, 312-947-2163

International Association of Music Libraries, City College, Music Library, Convent Ave. at 138th St., New York, NY 10031, 212-650-7631

International Association of School Librarianship, P.O. Box 1486, Kalamazoo, MI 49005, 616-343-5728

Music Library Association, P.O. Box 487, Canton, MA 02021-0487, 617-828-8450

One-Person Australian Librarians (OPAL), Convenor: Georgina Dale, Librarian, Janssen Cilag Pty. Ltd., 706 Mowbray Road, Locked Bag, Post Office Lane Cove, New South Wales 2066, Australia, +61-2-779-2364, fax: +61-2-772-2399, e-mail: gdale@ilanet.slnsw.gov.au

Society of School Librarians International, 620 W. Roosevelt Rd., Suite B2, Wheaton, IL 60187, 708-665-7977

Theatre Library Association, 111 Amsterdam Ave., Room 513, New York, NY 10023, 212-870-1670

Welsh Library Association, c/o Publications Office, Public Library, Dew St., Haverford West, Dyfed, Wales SA62 1SU, 0437-764591, ext. 5245

Western Association of Map Libraries, c/o Herb Fox, 1883 Ashcroft, Clovis, CA 93611, 209-294-0177

ALTERNATIVE CAREERS

ALA Discussion Group for Alternative Careers, Independent Librarians Exchange Round Table

Association of Independent Information Professionals (AIIP), 245 5th Ave., #2103, New York, NY 1–16, 212-779-1855, full membership $160, associate $85, members must own or rent their own facilities, not for library fee-based services

SLA Caucus on Professional Librarians in Alternative Non-Traditional Careers (PLIANT, Consultants Section of Library Management Division)

CHURCH AND SYNAGOGUE LIBRARY ORGANIZATIONS

American Theological Library Association (ATLA), 820 Church St., Suite 300, Evanston, IL 60201-5613, 708-869-7788, fax: 708-869-

8513, e-mail: atla@atla.com, monographs and serials in religion on microform

Association of Christian Librarians, P.O. Box 4, Cedarville, OH 45314, 513-766-7842

Association of Jewish Libraries, 15 E. 26th St., Room 1034, New York, NY 10010, 212-678-8092, Internet: http://aleph.lib.ohio-state.edu/www/ajl.html

Catholic Library Association, c/o Jean R. Bostley, SSJ, St. Joseph Central High School, 22 Maplewood Ave., Pittsfield, MA 01201, 413 447-9121

Church & Synagogue Library Association (CSLA), P.O. Box 19357, Portland, OR 97280, 503-244-6919, annual conference, publications, local chapters

CSLA affiliates: Church Library Council (Washington, DC), Church & Synagogue Librarians Fellowship (Baltimore), Pacific Northwest Association of Church Librarians, Congregational Librarians Association of British Columbia, Church Library Association (Toronto), Lutheran Church Library Association, Catholic Library Association

LAW LIBRARY ORGANIZATIONS

American Association of Law Librarians (AALL), 53 W. Jackson Blvd, Suite 940, Chicago, IL 60604, 312-939-4764, e-mail: lawchq@orion.depaul.edu

British-Irish Association of Law Libraries, University of Wales Law Library, College of Cardiff, Box 430, Cardiff, Wales CF1 3XT, 021-200-1050

International Association of Law Libraries, c/o Roberta Shaffer, Library Director, Covington & Burling, 1201 Pennsylvania Ave., NW, P.O. Box 7566, Washington, DC 20044, 202-662-6152

MEDICAL LIBRARY ORGANIZATIONS

Association of Academic Health Sciences Library Directors (AAHSLD), c/o Joyce Welch, HAM-TMC Library, 1133 M.D. Anderson Blvd., Houston, TX 77030, 713-790-7060

Association of American Medical Colleges (AAMC). 1 Dupont Circle, NW, Washington, DC 20036, 202-828-0400

Canadian Health Libraries Association, P.O. Box 94038, 3332 Yonge St., Toronto, Ontario M4N 3R1, Canada, 416-485-0377

Library Services to Hospital Patients and Handicapped Readers, (formerly Hospital Libraries Section), IFLA

Medical Libraries Association (MLA), 6 N. Michigan Ave., Suite 300, Chicago, IL 60602, 312-419-9094, e-mail: cfunk@life.jsc.nasa.gov

National Institutes of Health (NIH), Bethesda, MD 20892, http://www.nih.gov/

National Library of Medicine (NLM), 8600 Rockfille Pike, Bethesda, MD 20894, 800-272-4787, 301-496-6308, Internet: http://www.nlm.nih.gov/

RECORDS MANAGEMENT ORGANIZATIONS

Association for Federal Information Resources Management (AFFIRM), P.O. Box 11967, Alexandria, VA 22312, 202-376-4200

Association for Information and Image Management (AIIM), 1100 Wayne Ave., Suite 1100, Silver Spring, MD 20910-5603, 301-587-8202

Association for Information Management (AIM), 2026-C Opitz Blvd., Woodbridge, VA 22191, 703-490-4246

ARMA International (Association of Records Managers and Administrators), 4200 Somerset Dr., Suite 215, Prairie Village, KS 66208, 800-422-2762, 913-341-3808

Information Industry Association (IIA), 555 New Jersey Ave., NW, Suite 800, Washington, DC 20001, 202-639-8262

National Association of Government Archives and Records Administators (NAGRA), c/o Executive Secretariat, New York State Archives, Room 10A46, Cultural Education Center, Albany, NY 12230, 518-473-8037

Society for Information Management (SIM), 401 N. Michigan Ave., Chicago, IL 60611-4267, 312-644-6610

Society of American Archivists (SAA), 600 S. Federal St., Suite 504, Chicago IL 60605, 312-922-0140

JOB HOTLINES (from *1996 Librarian's Yellow Pages*, page 217)

National

ALA, 312-280-2464
SLA, 202-234-3632
AALL, 312-939-7877
ASIS, 301-495-0900
MLA, 312-419-9094

State and Regional

AZ, 602-275-2325
BC, 604-430-6411
CO, 303-866-6741
CA/SLA/San Andreas/SF, 415-528-7766
CA/SLA/SoCal, 818-795-2145
CA/CLA/North, 916-443-1222
CA/CLA/South, 818-797-4602
CT, 203-889-1200
DC, 202-962-3712
DE/DLA, 302-739-4748
DE/Division of Libraries/In-state, 800-282-8696
DE/Division of Libraries/NJ & PA listings, 302-739-4748
FL, 904-488-5232
IL, 312-828-0930
IN/Central, 317-924-9584
IA, 515-281-6788
KS, 913-296-3296
KY, 502-564-3008
MD, 410-685-5760
MI, 517-694-7440
MO, 314-442-6590
Mountain Plains Library Association, 605-677-5757
NE, 402-471-2045
New England, 617-738-3148
NJ, 609-695-2121
NY/SLA, 212-679-9100
NY/NYLA, 518-432-6952
NC, 919-733-6410
OK, 405-521-4202
OR, 503-585-2232
PA, 717-234-4646
Pacific Northwest Library Association, 206-543-2890
SC, 803-777-8443
TX, 512-463-5470
VA, 703-519-8027

A SOLO's Guide to Education

This chapter is for those contemplating library school, those interested in preparing for SOLO librarianship, and those concerned about the future of library education. The first section lists schools offering ALA-accredited master's degree programs in the United States and Canada. The listings are arranged alphabetically by state. Each of the entries has the address, phone and fax numbers, e-mail and/or World Wide Web addresses, the name of the dean, other degrees offered, and any distance education programs. From my 1993 survey, I also include the number of faculty, whether they have a special libraries track, what hours are required, whether a thesis is required, what competencies are required for admission or graduation, and what courses are identified by the school as relevant to special libraries. Although some details may change, this should give the prospective student some basis for comparison among schools. (Note that the adjunct faculty are usually practicing librarians, and SL stands for Special Libraries. If there is no survey information, the school did not respond.)

The second list is an incomplete list of academic programs in library and information science in other countries, arranged alphabetically by country and institution. A list of other information related programs in the United States and library programs not accredited by the ALA follows. Since not everyone is located near a library school, I have made a list of distance education resources, including books, listservs, and institutions specializing in distance learning.

Continuing education is very important in maintaining a librarian's skills. Opportunities can be found in offerings of associations, private firms, and from vendors. Samples of the kinds of training that can be found are presented next. Finally, there is a list of further readings on the subject of education for librarianship and especially SOLO librarianship.

SOME FACTS AND FIGURES

The number of library schools in the United States rose from fifty-three in 1973 to a high of sixty-nine in 1980–81 and back down to fifty-six in 1994. The average faculty size is ten to eleven, but ranges from five to thirty-four. The faculty training level is improving, with 87 percent of them with earned Ph.D.s, up from 62 percent in 1977. Twenty-three schools have 100 percent earned doctorates. In 1994 there were 3,914 full-time students at ALA-accredited library schools and 3,471 full-time equivalent part-time students, for a total FTE of 7,385 students. Total FTE in both accredited and nonaccredited schools totaled 10,217. For the same year, ALA-accredited schools graduated 4,805 students with the MLS degree. Another 563 graduated from nonaccredited schools, for a total of 5,368 new graduates, and nearly 80 percent were female. Tuition and fees ranged from zero to $21,000, with a mean in-state of $5,800 and out-of-state of $12,000. Scholarship money was available at all schools, in amounts ranging from $3,000 to $225,000 per school. Assistantships accounted for another $4.8 million in available aid.

ALA ACCREDITED MASTER'S PROGRAMS IN THE UNITED STATES

AL: University of Alabama, School of Library and Information Studies, Box 870252, Tuscaloosa , AL 35487-2052, 205-348-4610, fax: 205-348-3746

MLS, Ph.D., MFA in Book Arts, Educational Specialist in Librarianship; courses offered in Birmingham, Huntsville, Mobile; faculty: 10 full-time, 5 adjunct; SL track; 36 hours; SL courses: SL, Business Information, Music, Legal

AZ: University of Arizona, School of Library Science, 151 E. First St., Tucson, AX 85719, 520-621-3566, fax: 520-621-3279, e-mail: ualibsci@ccit.arizona.edu; Internet: http://www.sir.arizona.edu

M.A., Ph.D.; faculty: 6 full-time, 2 adjunct; 36 hours; thesis optional; Competencies: computer skills; SL courses: SL, Corporate Libraries

CA: San Jose State University, School of Library and Information Science, 1 Washington Square, San Jose, CA 95192-0029, 408-924-2490, fax: 408-924-2476, e-mail: office@wahoo.sjsu.edu

MLS, courses offered in San Diego, Pasadena and by interactive video; faculty: 10 full-time, 8-10 adjuncts; SL track; 42 units; thesis or comprehensive exam required; SL courses: SL, Online, Abstracting & Indexing, Systems Analysis, Research Methods, Government

Information, Information Brokering, Competitive Information Services, Library Management, Marketing Information Products and Services, Planned Organizational Change, Management of Conflict and Competition, Organizational Communication

CA: University of California, Los Angeles, Department of Library and Information Science, Graduate School of Education and Information Studies, 2320 Moore Hall, Mailbox 951521, Los Angeles, CA 90095-1521, 310-825-8799, fax: 310-206-3076, e-mail: cborgman@ucla.ed; Internet: http://www.gslis.ucla.edu/LIS

MLIS, Ph.D., MLIS/MA in History or Latin American Studies, MLIS/MBA, post-MLIS

CT: Southern Connecticut State University, School of Communication, Information and Library Science, 501 Crescent St., New Haven, CT 06515, 203-392-5781, fax: 203-392-5780, e-mail: libscienceit@scsu.ctstateu.edu

MLS, MLS/JD, MLS/MS in Chemistry, English, Foreign Languages, History or Instructional Technology, Sixth Year Diploma, School Media Specialist

DC: The Catholic University of America, School of Library and Information Science, Washington, DC 20064, 202-319-5085, 202-319-5574

MSLS, MSLS/JD, MSLS/MA in English, Greek and Latin, History, Musicology, Religious Studies, Biology, Post-Masters Certificate; faculty: 8 full-time, 40 adjunct; SL track; 36 hours; SL courses: Government Documents, SL, Business, Management, SciTech, Online, Systems Analysis, Automation, Management, Health Literature, Health Librarianship

FL: Florida State University, School of Library and Information Studies, Tallahassee, FL 32306-2048, 904-644-5775, fax: 904-644-9763

MS, MA, Ph.D., B.A., Information Studies school media certification; courses offered at Gainesville, Jacksonville, Panama City, Pensacola; faculty: 14 full-time; SL track; 38 hours; SL courses: SL, Management, Business Information

FL: University of South Florida, School of Library and Information Science, 4202 E. Fowler Ave., CIS 1040, Tampa, FL 33260-7800, 813-974-3520, fax: 813-974-6840, e-mail: epate@cis01.cis.usf.edu, Internet: http://www.cas.usf.edu/lis/index.html

MA, educational media certification, courses offered in Ft. Lauderdale, Ft. Myers, Gainesville, Lakeland, Miami, Orlando, Palm Beach and by Internet; faculty: 9 full-time, 7 adjunct; SL track planned; 36 hours; SL courses: SL, Law Librarianship, Health Sciences, Business Reference, Microcomputers, SciTech

GA: Clark Atlanta University, School of Library and Information Studies, 300 Trevor Arnett Hall, James P. Brawley Drive at Fair St., Atlanta, GA 30314, 404-880-8695, fax: 404-880-8395

MSLS, specialist in library service; faculty: 8 full-time; 36 hours; thesis optional; competencies: foreign language; SL courses: Management (required), SL, Research Methods, Automation (required), Government Publications

HI: University of Hawaii, School of Library and Information Studies, 2550 The Mall, Honolulu, HI 96822, 808-956-7321, fax: 808-956-5835

MLIS, Ph.D., certificate in advanced LIS, some distance education via Hawaii Interactive TV; faculty: 8 full-time, 3 part-time, 5 adjunct; SL track; 42 hours; thesis optional; competencies: computer and quantitative skills; SL courses: Information Industry, Abstracting and Indexing, Records Management, Database Design, Advanced Online, Media Technology

IA: University of Iowa, School of Library and Information Science, 3087 Library, Iowa City, IA 52242-1420, 319-335-5707, 319-335-5374, Internet:wwwuiowa.edu/departments/libsci/index.html

MA, MA/JD, MA/MBA; faculty: 7 full-time, 5 adjunct; SL track; 36 hours; thesis optional; SL courses: Management (required), Research Methods (required); SL, Bibliography, Information Storage & Retrieval, Advanced Reference, Government Publications

IL: Rosary College, Graduate School of Library and Information Science, 7900 W. Division St., River Forest, IL 60305, 708-524-6845, fax: 708-524-6657

MLIS, MLIS/MA public history, MLIS/MBA, MLIS/M. Divinity, MLIS/M. Music, MLIS/MS MIS, certificate of special studies in law librarianship, library administration or technical services, IL standard special certificate in media specialist, courses offered in Chicago, St. Paul, MN; SL track; 36 hours; SL courses: Science Reference; SL; Indexing and Abstracting, Health Sciences, Medical Librarianship (both administration and reference); practicum

IL: University of Illinois at Urbana-Champaign, Graduate School of Library and Information Science, 501 E. Daniel St., Champaign IL 61820, 217-333-3280, fax: 217-244-3302, Internet: http://alexia. lis.uiuc.edu

MS, Ph.D., certificate of advanced study, courses offered in Fairview Heights, Oak Brook, Peoria, Rockford, Springfield, LEEP program

(MS via the Internet with two-week residency); faculty: 15 full-time, 3 adjunct, 14 part-time; 40 hours; thesis optional; competencies: computer; SL courses: Medical Literature, Reference Service in the Sciences, Library Administration, Online, Automation, Telecommunications

IN: Indiana University, School of Library and Information Science, Library 011, Bloomington, IN 47405-1801, 812-855-2018, fax: 812-855-6166, e-mail: iuslis@indiana.edu, Internet: http://www-slis.lib.indiana.edu

MLS, Ph.D., M. Information Science, MLS/JD, MLS/MA in comparative literature, history, history and philosophy of science, journalism, music, MLS/MPA in Information Systems Management, specialist in LIS, courses offered in Indianapolis, South Bend; faculty: 18 full-time, 30 adjunct; 36 hours; competencies: computers; SL courses: SL, Legal Bibliography; Health Sciences Librarianship, Art Librarianship, Music Librarianship, Government Publications, SciTech, Automation, Management

KS: Emporia State University, School of Library and Information Management, P.O. Box 4025, Emporia, KS 66801, 316-341-5203, fax: 316-341-5233, Internet: http://www.emporia.edu/S/www/slim.htm

MLS, Ph.D., MLS with History, English, Music and Business, School library media specialist, courses offered in Denver, CO; Kansas City; Wichita; Grand Forks, ND; Portland, or Salt Lake City, UT; and via videotape interactive video

KY: University of Kentucky, School of Library and Information Science, 502 King Library Building S, Lexington, KY 40506-0039, 606-257-8876, fax: 606-257-4250, Internet: http://www.uky.edu/CommInfo Studies/SLSIS

MSLS, courses offered in Ashland, Covington, Elizabethtown, Highland Heights, Paducah, and Cincinnati, OH; faculty: 10 full-time, 20 adjunct; 36 hours; SL courses: see catalog

LA: Louisiana State University, School of Library and Information Science, 267 Coates Hall, Baton Rouge, LA 70803, 504-388-3158, fax: 504-388-4581, e-mail: lsslis@lsuvm.sncc.lus.edu

MLIS, MLIS/systems science, certificate of advanced study in LIS, LA certification in school librarianship, courses offered in New Orleans and Shreveport and via compressed video; faculty: 10 full-time, 10 adjunct; SL track; 36 hours; thesis optional; SL courses: SL, Health Information Center, Business Resources, Field Experience, SciTech, Government Information, Business Information, Automation

MA: Simmons College, Graduate School of Library and Information Science, 300 The Fenway, Boston, MA 02115-5898, 617-521-2800, fax: 617-521-3192, e-mail: sknowles@vmsvax.simmonsedu

MS, MA, MS/MA History, MS/MS Education; faculty: 13 full-time, 1 part-time, 18 adjunct; SL track; 36 hours; competencies: technology; SL courses: Corporate Libraries, Information Retrieval, Business Literature, Medical Librarianship, Music Librarianship, Legal Bibliography, Art Documentation, Records Management, Organizational Ethics, SciTech, Management Theory

MD: University of Maryland, College of Library and Information Services, 4105 Hornbake Library Building, College Park, MD 20742-4345, 301-405-2033, fax: 301-314-9145, e-mail: ap57@umail.umd.edu

MLS, MLS with Geography or History; faculty: 15 full-time, 20 adjunct; 36 hours; thesis optional; SL courses: Health Sciences, Archives, Geographic Information Systems, Management, Business Information, Legal Literature, Government Information, SciTech, Social Sciences Literature

MI: University of Michigan, School of Information and Library Studies, West Engineering, 550 E. University Ave., Ann Arbor, MI 48109-1092, 313-763-2285, fax: 313-764-2475, e-mail: sils.admissions@umich.edu, Internet: http://www.sils.umich.edu

MLIS, Ph.D.

MI: Wayne State University, Library and Information Science program, 106 Kresge Library, Detroit, MI 48202, 313-577-1825, fax: 313-577-7563, e-mail: info@lisp.purdy.wayne.edu, Internet: http://www.wayne.edu

MLIS, specialist certificate, archival administration certificate, courses offered in Farmington, Grand Rapids, Lansing, and Saginaw; faculty: 12 full-time, 42 part-time; SL track; 36 hours; thesis optional; computer and word processing skills required; SL courses: Special Libraries, Business and Industry Information Resources

MO: University of Missouri-Columbia, School of Library and Informational Science, 104 Stewart Hall, Columbia, MO 65211, 314-882-4546, fax: 314-884-4944, Internet: http://www.phlab.missouri.edu/~slis

MA, courses offered in Kansas City and St. Louis (distance education course for health sciences librarians, see http://www.hsc.missouri.edu/library/is410 for details); faculty: 11 part-time; SL track; 36 hours; competencies: computer skills; SL courses: SL, SciTech, Medical Subject Analysis, Biomedical Community

MS: University of Southern Mississippi, School of Library and Information Science, Box 5146, Hattiesburg, MS 39406-5146, 601-266-4228, fax: 601-266-5774

MLIS, MLIS/MA History, courses offered in Cleveland and Oxford and via interactive video; faculty: 6 full-time, 4 adjunct; 38 hours; thesis required; SL courses: SL, Special Collections/Archives; SciTech

NC: North Carolina Central University, School of Library and Information Sciences, P.O. Box 19586, Durham, NC 27707, 919-560-6485, fax: 919-560-6402

MLS, MLS/JD, MIS, courses offered at Fayetteville, Pemboke, and Wilmington

NC: University of North Carolina at Chapel Hill, School of Information and Library Science, CB #3360, 100 Manning Hall, Chapel Hill, NC 27599-3360, 919-962-8366, fax: 919-962-8071, e-mail: info@ils. unc.edu, Internet: http://ils.unc.edu/ilshome.html

MSIS, MSLS, Ph.D., certificate of advanced studies, media coordinator certificate, media supervisor certificate, instructional technology specialist, courses offered at Asheville and Charlotte; faculty: 16 full-time, 1 part-time, 15 adjunct; 48 hours; thesis required; SL courses: Records Management, Science Information, Health Sciences, Business Information, Law Libraries, SL/Information Brokering, Music Librarianship, Field Experience

NC: University of North Carolina at Greensboro, Department of Library and Information Studies, Greensboro, NC 27412

faculty: 7 full-time, 5-7 part-time; SL track; 36 hours; Master's project required; competencies: computer skills; SL courses: SL, SciTech, Public Documents, Business Reference

NJ: Rutgers University, School of Communication, Information and Library Studies, 4 Huntington St., New Brunswick, NJ 08901-1071, 908-932-7500, fax: 908-932-6916

MLS, Ph.D., sixth-year specialist program; faculty: 16 full-time, 10 adjunct; SL track; 36 hours; SL courses: Information Mediation/ Searching (required), Technology (required), MIS, Database Management, Records Management

NY: Long Island University, Palmer School of Library and Information Science, C.W. Post Campus. 720 Northern Blvd., Brookville, NY 11548-1300, 516-299-2866, fax: 516-299-4168, e-mail: palmer@ aurora.liunet.edu

MSLS, certificates in archives or records management, courses offered in Manhattan, Westchester County and via two-way interactive audio and video; faculty: 12 full-time, 5 adjunct; 36 hours; thesis optional; competencies: computer literacy by graduation; SL courses: SciTech, Social Science, Health Sciences, Legal, Business & Economics

NY: Pratt Institute, School of Information and Library Science, 200 Willoughby Ave., Brooklyn, NY 11205, 718-636-3702, fax: 718-636-3733, e-mail: sils@acnet.pratt.edu

MSLIS, JS/JD, MSLIS/MS art history, advanced certificate; faculty: 7 full-time, 19 adjunct; SL track; 36 hours; thesis optional; competencies: computer skills (preferred); SL courses: Management (required), Health Sciences, Business Reference, Management of Special Collections

NY: Queens College, City University of New York, Graduate School of Library and Information Studies, 65-30 Kissena Blvd., Flushing, NY 11367, 718-997-3790, fax: 718-997-3797

MLS, post-master's certificate; faculty: 6 full-time, 5-8 adjunct; SL track; 36 hours; thesis/project required; SL courses: Business Reference Sources, Law Librarianship, SciTech Information, Systems Analysis, Database Searching, Microcomputer Applications, Special Libraries, Health Sciences Librarianship

NY: St. John's University, Division of Library and Information Science, 8000 Utopia Parkway, Jamaica, NY 11439, 718-990-6200, fax: 718-380-0353, e-mail: libis@sjumusic.stjohns.edu

MLS, MLS/MA Government and Politics, MLS/MS pharmaceutical sciences, advanced certificate in LIS; faculty: 7 full-time, 10 adjunct; SL track; 36 hours; SL courses: Indexing and Abstracting, Law Library Administration, Records Management, Business and Economics Sources; Health Sciences, Business Databases Online, Legal Bibliography, Legal Databases Online, Information Sources in Religion

NY: Syracuse University, School of Information Studies, 4-206 Center for Science & Technology, Syracuse, NY 13244-4100, 315-443-2911, fax: 315-43-5806, Internet: http://istweb.syr.edu

MLS, courses also available via the Internet with 1-week residencies for core courses; faculty: 18 full-time, 1 part-time, 10 adjunct; 36 hours, SL courses: Biomedical Information Services, Business Information and Strategic Intelligence

NY: State University of New York at Albany, School of Information Science and Policy, 135 Western Ave., Draper 113, Albany, NY 12222, 518-442-5110, fax: 518-442-5232, e-mail: infosci@cnsvax.albany.edu

MLS, Ph.D., MSIS, MLS/MA in English or History, certificate of advanced study, courses offered in Binghamton, New Paltz; faculty: 12 full-time, 4 adjunct; SL track; 36 hours; thesis optional; SL courses: Health Sciences, Information Services in the Sciences; SL; Economics of Information Management, Online

NY: State University of New York at Buffalo, School of Information and Library Studies, 381 Baldy Hall, Buffalo, NY 14260-1020, 716-645-2412, fax: 716-645-3775, e-mail: sils@ubvms.cc.buffalo.edu

MLS, Ph.D., MLS/MA in Music History or Music Librarianship, advanced studies certificate, courses offered in Rochester; faculty: 9 full-time, 2 part-time, 4 adjunct; SL track; 36 hours; thesis optional; SL courses: Health Science Librarianship, Records Management, Business Information Sources, Nontraditional Sources of Business Information

OH: Kent State University, School of Library and Information Science, Room 314 KSU Library, P.O. Box 5190, Kent, OH 44242-0001, 216-672-2782, fax: 216-672-7965, Internet: http://www.kent. eduslis

MLS, 6th year advanced certificate program; SL track; 36 hours; research paper required; SL courses: Special Libraries, practicum

OK: University of Oklahoma, School of Library and Information Studies, 401 W. Brooks, Rm. 120, Norman, OK 73019-0528, 405-325-3921, fax: 405-325-7648, e-mail: slisinfo@uoknor.edu, Internet: http://hoek.uoknor.edu

MLIS, MLIS/MA in history of science, MLIS/MBA, MLIS/M.Ed., certificate of advanced studies, courses offered at Tulsa; faculty: 7 full-time, 4 adjunct; SL track; 36 hours; thesis optional; SL courses: SciTech, Development of Special Collections, Biomedical Bibliography and Reference, Library Administration (required), Biomedical Databases

PA: Clarion University of Pennsylvania, College of Communication, Computer Information Science and Library Science, 109 Becker Hall, Clarion, PA 16214, 814-226-2328, fax: 814-2262186

MSLS, certificate of advanced studies, courses offered at Harrisburg; faculty: 8 full-time; 36 hours; SL courses: Business Reference, Rural Librarianship (various courses)

PA: Drexel University, College of Information Science & Technology, 3141 Chestnut St., Philadelphia, PA 19104, 215-895-2474, fax: 215-895-2494, Internet: http://www.cis.drexel.edu

MS, Ph.D., MS/MSIS, graduate certificate of advanced study, courses offered at Wilmington, DE; Horsham; King of Prussia; Philadelphia; Willow Grove; and via asynchronous learning network;

faculty: 17 full-time, 20 adjunct; 60 quarter hours; SL courses: Quantitative methods (required), Data Communications, Law, Medical Libraries, Automation, Online, SciTech, Medical Bibliography, Biomedical Online, Business Sources, Government Publications, Legal Bibliography

PA: University of Pittsburgh, School of Library and Information Science, 505 SLIS Building, Pittsburgh, PA 15260, 412-624-5230, fax: 412-624-5231, Internet: http://www.lis.pitt.edu

MLS, Ph.D. (Library Science or Information Science), MLS/M. Div., MSIS, MS Telecommunications, certificates of advanced study (automation and technology, health information management, information science, information services, archives and preservation, library systems management, services to children and youth), some distance education opportunities; faculty: 17 full-time, 10 adjunct; SL track; 36 hours; competencies: word processing; SL courses: Government Documents, SciTech, Business Resources, SL, Health Sciences, Management

PR: University of Puerto Rico, Graduate School of Library and Information Science, P.O. Box 21906, San Juan, PR 00931-1906, 809-763-6199, fax: 809-764-2311

MLS; faculty: 9 full-time, 4 adjunct; 42 hours; thesis required; Competencies: Spanish; SL courses: Indexing, Science Resources, Government Publications, Latin American Bibliography, Law Materials, System Analysis, Online

RI: University of Rhode Island, Graduate School of Library and Information Studies, Rodman Hall, Kingston, RI 02881, 401-792-2947, fax: 401-792-4395

MLIS, MLIS/MA in history, MLIS/MPA, courses offered in Amherst, MA; Boston; Durham, NH; faculty: 9 full-time, 15 adjunct; 42 hours; SL courses: Health Sciences, Law; SL

SC: University of South Carolina, College of Library and Information Science, Davis College, Columbia, SC 29208, 803-777-3858, fax: 803-777-7938, Internet: http://www.libsci.scarolina.edu

MLIS, MLIS/Applied History, MLIS/English, certificate of graduate study, specialist in LIS, courses offered in Maine; faculty: 12 full-time, 1 part-time, 5 adjunct; SL track; 36 hours; SL courses: SL, Database Design, Online, Business Information, Records Management, SciTech, Government Information, Networks

TN: University of Tennessee, School of Information Sciences, 804 Volunteer Blvd., Knoxville, TN 38996-4330, 423-974-2148, fax: 423-974-4967, Internet: http://pepper.lis.utk.edu

MS; faculty: 10 full-time, 6-8 adjunct; 39 hours; thesis optional; SL tracks in SciTech, Corporate, and Health Informatics; SL courses: SciTech, Government Publications, Management, Special Libraries, Records Management

TX: Texas Woman's University, School of Library and Information Studies, P.O. Box 425438, Denton, TX 76204-3438, 817-898-2602, fax: 817-898-2611

MLS, MALS, Ph.D., learning resources endorsement, courses offered at Canyon, Dallas, Mount Pleasant; faculty: 10 full-time, 8 adjunct; SL track; 42-48 hours; thesis required; SL courses: SL, Health Sciences (2 courses), Business Information, Fiscal Management, Online, Information Audits

TX: University of North Texas, School of Library and Information Sciences, P.O. Box 13796, NT Station, Denton, TX 76203, 817-565-2445, fax: 817-565-3101, e-mail: slis@unt.edu, Internet: http://www-lan/slis/

MS, Ph.D., MS/MS in History, certificate of advanced study, school librarianship/learning resources endorsement, courses offered in Houston and Lubbock

TX: The University of Texas at Austin, Graduate School of Library and Information Science, Austin, TX 78712-1276, 512-471-3821, fax: 512-471-3971, e-mail: gslis@uts.cc.utexas.edu, Internet: http://fiat.gslis.utexas.edu

MLIS, Ph.D., certificate of advanced study, learning resource endorsement, endorsement of specialization, courses offered in El Paso and San Antonio and via interactive TV; faculty: 18 full-time, 10 adjunct; SL track; 36 hours; SL courses: Online, Records Management, SciTech, Government Information, Health Sciences, Law Resources, Business Resources, SL, Law Libraries, Medical Libraries, Automation, Management, Information Marketing

WA: University of Washington, Graduate School of Library and Information Science, 133 Suzzallo Library, Box 352930, Seattle, WA 98195-2930, 206-543-1794, fax: 206-616-3152, Internet: http://www.grad.washington.edu/htdocs/gslishome.html

Master's in Librarianship, learning resources endorsement/school library, media specialists, some distance education opportunities; faculty: 10 full-time; 63 quarter hours; thesis optional; SL courses: Services for Special Groups, Special Librarianship, Health Sciences

WI: University of Wisconsin-Madison, School of Library and Information Studies, Helen C. White Hall, 600 N. Park St., Madison,

WI 53706, 608-263-2900, fax: 608-263-4849, e-mail: uw.slis@
doit.wisc.edu

MA, Ph.D., specialist degree, courses offered at various sites in WI;
faculty: 13 full-time, 6 adjunct; SL track; 42 hours; SL courses:
Research Methods (required); Field Project, Special Library,
Reference, Online, Government Publications, SciTech

WI: University of Wisconsin-Milwaukee, School of Library and
Information Science, Enderis Hall 1110, 2400 E. Hartford Ave.,
Milwaukee, WI 53211, 414-229-4707, fax: 414-229-4848, Internet:
http://www.uwm,edu/dept/slis

MLIS, Ph.D., MLIS/MA (geography, history, English, languages,
literature), MLIS/M.Music, MLIS/MS Urban Studies, certificate
of advanced study, undergraduate certificate, courses offered in Eau
Claire, Fox Valley, Menasha, Oshkosh and various sites in WI via
satellite; faculty: 8 full-time, 10 adjunct; SL track; 36 hours; thesis
not required; SL courses: Management (required), Special Libraries,
Online, Business Sources, SciTech

ALA ACCREDITED MASTER'S PROGRAMS IN CANADA

AB: University of Alberta, School of Library and Information Studies,
3-20 Rutherford South, Edmonton AB T6G 2J4, 403-492-4578, fax:
403-492-2430, e-mail: office@slis.ualberta.ca

MLIS; faculty: 8 full-time, 1 part-time, 5 adjunct; 48 hours; thesis
optional; SL courses: SL, Legal Bibliography, Science Literature,
Archives, Records Management

BC: The University of British Columbia, School of Library, Archival and
Information Studies, 1956 Main Mall, Rm. 831, Vancouver BC V6T
1Z1, 604-822-2404, fax: 604-822-6006, e-mail: slais@unixg. ubc.ca,
Internet: http://fdziza.arts.ubc.ca/slais/slaisa.html

MLIS, M. Archival Studies; SL track; 60 hours; thesis optional;
competencies: computer skills, experience preferred; SL courses:
Electronic Information Services, Automation, Networking/Internet,
Management, Human Resource Management, Financial Management,
SL, Legal Bibliography, Medical Libraries

ON: University of Toronto, faculty of Information Studies, 140 St.
George St., Toronto, ON M5S 1A1, 416-978-8589, fax: 416-978-5762,
e-mail: muia@fis.utoronto.ca

MIS, Ph.D., courses available via videoconferencing, Internet;
faculty: 16 full-time, 1 part-time, 9 adjunct; competencies: word

processing, statistics; SL courses: Legal Literature; Business Information Resources; SciTech; Health Sciences; Online; Records Management; SL

ON: The University of Western Ontario, Graduate School of Library and Information Science, Elborn College, London, ON N6G 1H1, 519-661-3542, fax: 519-661-3506

MLIS, Ph.D.; faculty: 16 full-time, 7 adjunct; 45 hours; SL courses: SL

QP: McGill University, Graduate School of Library and Information Studies, 349 McTavish St., Montreal, QB H3A 1Y1, 514-398-4204, fax: 514-398-7193, e-mail: ad27@musica.mcgill.ca, Internet: http://www.gslis.mcgill.ca

MLIS, Ph.D., post master's graduate diploma; faculty: 8 full-time, 6 adjunct; SL track; 48 credits; thesis optional; SL courses: SL

PQ: Universite de Montreal, Ecole de bilbiotheconomic ct des sciences de l'information, C.P. 6128, Succursale Centre-Ville, Montreal, QB, H3C 3J7, 514-343-6044, fax: 514-343-5753, Internet: http://tornade.ere.umontreal.ca/~carmellu/ebsi

MLIS, certificate in archives

A PARTIAL LIST OF ACADEMIC PROGRAMS IN LIBRARY AND INFORMATION SCIENCE IN OTHER COUNTRIES[2]

ASIA, AUSTRALIA, AND NEW ZEALAND

Australia
ACT
   University of Canberra, faculty of Communication, Library and
      Information Studies
NSW
   Charles Sturt University
   University of New South Wales, School of Information, Library and
      Archive Studies
NT
   Northern Territory University
QLD
   Queensland University of Technology (Gardens point), School of
      Information Systems
   Queensland University of Technology (Kelvin Grove), School of
      Language and Literacy Education)

---

2. not reviewed or accredited by ALA

SA
  University of South Australia, School of Communication and
    Information Studies
VIC
  Deakin University (Rusden), Department of Information Management
  Monash   University   (Clayton),   Graduate   Department   of
    Librarianship, Archives and Records
  Monash University (Gippsland), School of Education
  Royal Melbourne Institute of Technology, Information Management
    and Library Studies Department
  University of Ballarat, School of Management
WA
  Curtin University, School of Information and Library Studies
  Edith Cowan University (Mt. Lawley and Perth), Department of
    Library and Information Science
Asia
Hong Kong
  Chinese University of Hong Kong, Department of Information
    Engineering
Japan
  University of Library and Information Science (Ibaraki)

  University of Tokyo, Department of Information Science
New Zealand
  Victoria University of Wellington, Department of Library and
    Information Studies

EUROPE

Austria
  Johannes Kepler University of Linz, Department of Information
    Systems
Belgium
  Free University of Brussels, Principia Cybernetica
Czech Republic
  Charles University (Prague), Institute of Information Studies and
    Librarianship
Denmark
  Danmarks Biliotekssk, Aalborg, Royal School of Librarianship
Finland
  Oulu University, Department of Information Studies and Sociology

Tampere University of Technology, Graduate School in Information Science and Engineering, a joint program with University of Tampere

France

Ecole Nationale Superieure des Sciences de l'Information et des Biblioteques (Billeurbanne)

Germany

Fachhochschole Hannover, Fachbereich Informations und Kommunikationswesen

Freie Universitat Berlin, Arbeitsbereich Informationswissenschaft

Heinrich Heine Universitat, Dusseldorf, Philosophische Fakultat, Abteilung Informationswissenschaft

Universitat des Saarlandes (Saarbrucken), Philsophische Fakultat, Fachrichtung

Universitat Konstanz, Fachgruppe Informationswissenschaft

Holland

The Hague Polytechnic, Department of Library and Information Science

Ireland

University College (Dublin), Department of Library and Information Studies

Italy

University of Parma, Institute of Library Science and Paleography

Norway

Oslo College, Department of Journalism, Library, and Information Science

Poland

University of Wroclaw, Institute of Library Science

Sweden

Goteborg University, Research Centre for Library and Information Studies

Lund University, Biblioteks- & informationsvetenskap

Umea University, INFORSK Research Center

University College of Boras, Swedish School of Library and Information Science

Switzerland

University of St. Gallen, Institute for Information Management

United Kingdom

Brunel University, Computer Centre/Brunel Library and Information Science

City University, Department of Information Science

Loughborough University of Technology, Centre for Library and Information Studies at Computers in Teaching Initiative, and Department of Information and Library Studies

Manchester Metropolitan University, Department of Library and Information Studies

Queen Margaret College (Edinburgh), Department of Communication and Information Studies

Robert Gordon University (Aberdeen), School of Information and Media

Sheffield University, Department of Information Studies

University College (London), School of Library, Archive and Information Studies

University of North London, library and information management courses

University of Northumbria (Newcastle), Department of Information and Library Management

University of Portsmouth, School of Information Science

University of Strathclyde, Department of Information Science

University of Sunderland, School of Computing and Information Systems

University of Wales (Aberystwyth), Department of Information and Library Studies

NORTH AMERICA

Canada

Dalhousie University, School of Library and Information Science

United States

CA

Stanford University (Palo Alto), Center for Information Technology, Center for the Study of Language and Information

University of California at Irvine, Information and Computer Science Department

University of California at San Francisco, Center for Knowledge Management

University of California at Santa Cruz, Computer Engineering and Computer and Information Sciences Department

University of Southern California (Los Angeles), Information Sciences Institute

GA

Georgia State University (Atlanta), Computer Information Systems Department

IN

Indiana University Purdue University at Indianapolis, Department of Computer and Information Science

KS

Kansas State University (Manhattan), Computing and Information Sciences

University of Kansas (Lawrence), Telecommunications and Information Sciences Laboratory

MA

Boston University, Multimedia Communications Laboratory

University of Massachusetts (Amherst), Center for Intelligent Information Retrieval

NV

University of Nevada, Las Vegas, Information Science Research Institute

OH

Ohio State University (Columbus), Department of Computer and Information Science

OK

University of Oklahoma (Norman), Management Information Systems Program

OR

University of Oregon (Eugene), Department of Computer and Information Science

PA

University of Pennsylvania (Philadelphia), Computer and Information Science Department

Temple University (Philadelphia), Computer and Information Science Department

TX

Baylor University (Waco), Department of Information Systems

SOUTH AMERICA

Brazil
    30 undergraduate programs
    6 MLS programs
    Pontifica Universidade Catolica de Campenas (PUCCAMP), Sao
    Paolo
        Universidade de Sao Paolo
        Universidade Federale de Minas Gerais
        Universidade de Brasilia
        Universidade Federale de Rio de Janeiro/Brazilian Institute of
        Information Science & Technology (specializing in community
            libraries)
        Universidade Federale de Paraiba

DISTANCE EDUCATION RESOURCES

American Center for the Study of Distance Education, The Pennsylvania State University, College of Education, 403 S. Allen St., Suite 206, University Park, PA 16801, DEOSNEWS (an online journal, to subscribe: LISTSERV@PSUVM.PSU.EDU, listserv DEOS-L: same address)

Canadian Adult Education Network, ADLTED-L (listserv, to subscribe: LISTSERV@UREGINAL1.BITNET)

Distance Education: An Annotated Bibliography, by Terry Ann Mood, Englewood, CO: Libraries Unlimited, Inc., 1995. ISBN 1-56308-160-1

Distance Education Clearinghouse: gopher://gopher.uwex.edu/70/11/distanceed

Diversity University, telnet://moo.du.org 8888, offers online courses, including Online Instructional Strategies, Librarian's Online Strategies Course, and HTML Publishing

Electronic University Network, 1977 Colestin Rd., Hombrook, CA 96044, 800-22LEARN or 503-482-5871, e-mail: EUNLearn @aol.com, Dr. Steve Eskow, Director, courses about $350 each, US/Canadian contact for Heriot-Watt University (UK), offering MBA online, approximately $700-900 per course, 9 courses required

External Studies in Librarianship: An Investigation into the Potential Efficacy of External Studies in Librarianship in Australia, by Margaret Trask and Mairead Browne, Lindfield, Australia: School of Library and

Information Studies, Kuring-gai College of Advanced Education, 1979, 2 vol. ISBN 0-9091777163-1 (v. 1), 0-90917717-1 (v. 2)

External Studies in Library and Information Science, Edward R. Reid-Smith, editor, Wagga Wagga, Australia: Office of Research in Librarianship, 1980, 1986. ISBN 0-86184165-4.

International School of Information Management, University Business Center, P.O. Box 1999, Santa Barbara CA 93116, online study

Open Polytechnic of New Zealand, Private Bag 31-914, Lower Hutt, New Zealand, e-mail: boykat@mhs.topnz.ac.nz

New York Institute of Technology, Old Westbury, NY 11568, 800-222-6948; online study

Nova Southeastern University, Center for Computer and Information Sciences, 3100 SW 9th Ave., Ft. Lauderdale, FL 33315, 800-987-2247 or 305-475-7352, fax: 305-476-4865, e-mail: ccisinfo@alpha. acast.nova.edu, MS in computer information systems, Ph.D. in CIS, IS, Information Science, some residence required, about $900 per course

Peterson's Electronic University: A Guide to Distance Learning Programs, ISBN 1-56079-664-2, $24.95 ($19.96 for nonprofits), 800-338-3282, fax: 609-243-9150, e-mail: custsvc@pgi.petersons. com

Spectrum Virtual University, Internet: http://horizons.org/campus/, sample courses (1995): exploring the Internet (8-weeks), exploring the World Wide Web (8-weeks), macro/micro Internet economics, all taught via e-mail

University Distance Program, University of Santiago, Chile, listserv EDISTA, to subscribe: LISTSERV@USACHVM1.BITNET)

University of Phoenix Online Campus, 100 Spear St., 2nd floor, San Francisco, CA 94105, 415-541-0141, fax: 415-541-0761, degrees in business and management including an MBA in Technology Management, sample courses: introduction to technology systems, information technology and decisions science, intellectual property management, human relations and organizational behavior, technology transfer, each course 6 weeks

University of Wales, Aberystwyth, offers a M. Librarianship by distance learning

Victoria University of Wellington, Department of Library & Information Science, P.O. Box 3438, Wellington, New Zealand, e-mail: asmith@vuw.ac.nz

The Virtual College, Information Technologies Institute, New York University, 48 Cooper Square, New York, NY 10003-7154, 212-998-7190, fax: 212-995-4131, e-mail: vigilante@acfcluster.nyu.edu, offers teleprogram in information technology using Lotus Notes, $2,000 per course, $8,000 for entire course

SAMPLE OF CONTINUING EDUCATION OPPORTUNITIES

National Associations

Association of Independent Information Professionals (AIIP), annual conference, cost about $300, exhibits, seminars, workshops

Special Libraries Association, annual conference, Winter Education Conference, Middle Management Institute, 5 subject units: technology and applications, management skills, human resources, analytical tools, and marketing and public relations, "participants should be familiar with the basics of management and have a working knowledge of current office and information technologies," $495 members, $535 nonmembers for each unit, offered over a year in various locations in the U.S. (including annual conference and winter meeting)

Regional and Local Associations

CAPCON Library Network (DC), http://www.capcon.net, 202-331-4368, fax: 202-331-5771, CE program in spring; 1996 offerings included CD-ROM: Access via LAN, WAN, and the Internet; Redesigning Work in a Changing Library Environment, Positive Politics: Communication Strategies for Results, Managing Electronic Serials in the Library; Making Presentations Work; Client/Server: Options for Small and Large Libraries; Strategically Planning Reference Services in an Electronic Environment; Cataloging Internet Resources; and Making Your Information Resources Accessible via Internet Technologies

DC/Baltimore/Northern VA SOLO group, c/o Anne Marie Hules, NAHB Research Center, 400 Prince Georges Blvd., Upper Marlboro, MD 20774-8731, 301-249-4000, ext. 614, fax: 301-249-0305, e-mail: ahules@capcon.net, very informal group, brown bag lunches, etc., sample meeting: keeping up with new technology, how to cope with wearing so many hats

Ohionet and other library networks offer training on OCLC and computer hardware and software

Sheridan Park Association, Mississauga, Ontario, Canada, an association of cooperate information specialists in an R&D research park, offers programs, networking, resource sharing (ILL and union list of journals), sample programs (1995-96): tour of *Toronto Globe & Mail* (newspaper), copyright update, evaluation of CD-ROM products, cultural sources of misunderstanding, the virtual library, benchmarking, DIALOG update

SAMPLE OF CE OFFERINGS FROM PRIVATE FIRMS

British and Irish Legal Education Technology Association, annual conference, 1996 was on "Electronic Publishing," cost £120 academic, £180 nonacademic

Computers in Libraries, Information Today, Inc., February, $295 for conference, $110 per half-day pre- or post-conference workshops, several tracks: Internet, digital libraries, library systems, Web for libraries, information delivery, education and technology, CD-ROM and multimedia, the electrifying environment, special and virtual libraries, sample workshops: technology planning, market research on the Net, LAN security, evaluating quality on the Net, Web basics, tips and tricks for searching the Net, automated systems procurement, effective multimedia presentations, surviving in the cyberspace-oriented environment

German One-Person Library Round Table, first held 1995, Berlin, organized by Evelin Morgenstern, Deutsches Bibliothekinstitut, Berlin, made five recommendations about establishment of commission on OPL, specific curriculum on OPL, handbook for OPLs in German, newsletter for OPLs in German, and working group to meet once a year

The Information Professionals Institute, 3724 FM 1960 West, Suite 214, Houston, TX 77068, 713-537-8344, Information Brokers Seminar, Public Records Seminar, Comparative Online Searching, Internet Seminars, $225 each

Howard McQueen & Associates, Inc., experts in CD-ROM and Internet

The Montague Institute, 55 Main Street, P.O. Box 8, Montague, MA 01351, 413-367-0245, workshops on Internet marketing, Internet business research, run by Jean Graef, editor of the SCIP Web Journal, $200 per half-day session

InfoManage/SMR International, Hill Station, P.O. Box 948, New York, NY 10156, 212-683-6285, fax: 212-683-2987, e-mail: 73042.67

@compuserve.com, Guy St. Clair and associates, sample offerings: Delighting in the Challenges: Librarianship and Information Services in the 21st Century; Entrepreneurial Librarianship: The Key to Effective Information Services Management; The One-Person Library: Management Tools for Success in a SOLO Information Unit; Creating an Information Audit: How to Identify Information-Seeking Behavior and Determine the Role of the Information Services Unit Within the Organization; Performance Evaluation and Effectiveness Measures; On Your Own But Not Alone: Management Strategies for the One-Person Library; The Strategic Planning Process

Snowbird Leadership Institute, recommended by Laura Olsen Dugan in Corporate Library Update 4(19):1-2, 12/15/95; six-day intensive institute on leaderships, risk-taking, role of technology

TFPL Ltd., 17-18 Britton St., London EC1M 5NQ, UK, 44-171-251-5522, fax: 44-171-490-4984, e-mail: 100067.1560@compuserve.com, central @tfpl.demon.co.uk, Internet: http://www.tag.co.uk/tfpl/tfpl home.htm, U.S. office: 345 Park Ave. South, 10th Floor, New York NY 10010, 212-213-5990, fax: 212-213-6887, e-mail: 74044.3166@ compuserve.com, sponsor of European Business Information Conference, held in March in various European countries, sample programs from 1996 (Milan): Corporate Change and Corporate Restructuring, Information as an Asset, Information Is at the Heart of Business Re-engineering, The Market for Business Information, The Future of Business Information Services and Their Markets, New Online Services, Product Reviews, and workshops: Gap Analysis, Using Information Audits, Quality Skills, Beyond the End User, Competitor Intelligence, Value of Information, cost $975 or £650

TRAINING FROM VENDORS

KRI offers the Quantum program for corporate librarians, with assistance in online searching, finance, and marketing. Lexis-Nexis' similar service is called The Information Partnership and focuses on marketing. They have produced several videos to present to management on your behalf. In addition, many vendors offer training and product updates at national conferences (almost always without charge).

ADDITIONAL READINGS ON LIBRARY EDUCATION FOR THE INFORMATION PROFESSIONAL

Abram, Stephen. 1993. Sydney Claire: SLA professional award winner 2005: Transformational librarianship in action. *Special Libraries* 84(4): 213-215.

Anderson, A.J. 1985. They never taught me how to do this in library school: Some reflections on the theory/practice nexus. *Journal of Library Administration* 6 (no. 2):1-6.

Auld, Lawrence W.S. April 4, 1987. The King Report: New directions in library and information science education. *College & Research Libraries News*:174-179.

Auld, Lawrence W.S. May 1, 1990. Seven imperatives for library education. *Library Journal* 55-59.

Campbell, Jerry D. 1986. Changes in library education: The deans reply. *Special Libraries* 77 (4):217-225.

Campbell, Jerry D. June 1993. Choosing to have a future. *American Libraries* 560-566.

Clough, M. Evalyn, and Thomas J. Galvin. January 1984. Educating special librarians: Toward a meaningful practitioner-educator dialogue. *Special Libraries* 75 (1):1-8.

Courrier, Yves. 1992. Information for research: Keynote presentation. *Conference on Curriculum Design for the Information Market Place, University of Tromso, Norway, 1992*: 1-13.

Culnan, Mary J. 1986. What corporate librarians will need to know in the future. *Special Libraries* 77 (4):213-216.

Dosa, M. 1985. Education for new professional roles in the information society. *Education for Information* 3:203-217.

Evans, G. Edward. 1992. Elements for consideration in curriculum design for information management. In *Conference on Curriculum Design for the Information Market Place, University of Tromso, Norway, 1992*: 57-72.

Faries, Cindy. 1994. Reference librarians in the information age: Learning from the past to control the future. *The Reference Librarian* (43): 9-28.

Fisher, William, and James M. Matarazzo. 1993. Professional development for special librarians: Formal education and continuing education for excellence. *Library Trends* 42 (2):290-303.

Garrison, Guy. 1974. Changes in the structure and content of the core. *Drexel Library Quarterly* 10 (3):3-18.

Hale, Martha L. 1991. Getting ready for tomorrow—or today. *RSR: Reference Services Review* 19 (1):77-80.

Hazelton, Penny A. 1993. Law libraries as special libraries: An educational model. *Library Trends* 42 (2):319-341.

Holt, Glen E. 1993. Alternative futures for the development of library science education: A view from inside the library. in *Education for the Library/Information Profession: Strategies for the Mid-1990s.* Rutgers School of Communication, Information and Library Studies, Jefferson NC: McFarland 41-62.

Kaatrude, Peter B. 1992. Librarian certification and licensing: A brief accounting. *Public Libraries* (5-6):156+.

Koenig, Michael E.D. 1993. Educational requirements for a library-oriented career in information management. *Library Trends* 42 (2):277-289.

Lancour, Harold. The new training pattern looks good. *Library Journal* December 12, 1993:S8. (Originally printed May 1, 1948)

Lucas, Linda. 1990. Educating prison librarians. *Journal of Education for Library and Information Science* 30 (3):218-22.

Macfarlane, Judy, and Miriam Tees. 1993. Special library education and continuing education in Canada. *Library Trends* 42 (2):304-418.

Malinconico, S. Michael. 1992. The implications for curriculum design in the age of technology. *Conference on Curriculum Design for the Information Market Place, University of Tromso, Norway, 1992* 15-38.

Malinconico, S. Michael. 1992. What librarians need to know to survive in an age of technology. *Journal of Education for Library and Information Science* 33:226-240.

Massey-Burzio, Virginia. 1991. Education and experience: Or, the MLS is not enough. *RSR: Reference Services Review* 19 (1):72-74.

Nelson, Milo. November 1993. The lights in library schools are going out one by one (Viewpoint). *Information Today* 48-49.

Ojala, Marydee. 1993. Core competencies for special library managers of the future. *Special Libraries* 84 (4): 230-233.

Powell, Ronald R., and Douglas Raber. 1994. Education for reference information service: A qualitative and quantitative analysis of basic reference courses. *The Reference Librarian* (43):145-217.

Quint, Barbara. 1994. Write if you get work (Searcher's Voice, editorial) *Searcher* 2 (1):4,6.

Robbins, Jane. February 1, 1990. Yes, Virginia, you can require an accredited master's degree for that job! *Library Journal* 40-44.

Rohde, Nancy Freeman, and Nancy Herther. 1993. Staffing an integrated information center and its implications for the education of information professionals. *Proceedings of ASIS Annual Meeting, Columbus, OH.* White Plains NY: Knowledge Industry Press, Inc. for American Society of Information Science: 231-234.

St. Clair, Guy. 1991. The one-person/one-professional librarian in the future. *Future Competencies of the Information Professional.* Washington DC: Special Libraries Association, 1991. (SLA Occasional Papers Series Number One.)

St. Clair, Guy, and Joan Williamson. *Managing the New One-Person Library.* London: Bowker-Saur, 1992.

Siess, Judith. 1994. If I ruled the world: Library schools would . . . *Searcher* 2 (7):14-16.

Siess, Judith. 1995. The M.L.S. is not enough: One solo librarian's view. *The One-Person Library* 12 (5):4-7. (Also presented at Annual Meeting, National Librarians Association, Chicago IL, June 1995.)

Tchobanoff, James B., and Jack A. Price. 1993. Industrial information service managers: Expectations of, and support of, the education process. *Library Trends* 42 (2):249-256.

Usher, Elizabeth R. October 1973. The challenge for library schools: An employment view. *Special Libraries,* 64(4):439-44.

White, Herbert S. October 15, 1993. Your half of the boat is sinking (The White Papers, column). *Library Journal:*45-46.

White, Herbert S. April 15, 1994. Small public libraries—challenges, opportunities, and irrelevancies (The White Papers column). *Library Journal:*53-54.

Yocum, Patricia, and Maurita Peterson Holland. May 1993. Yes! You can! Your future in library service. *Wilson Library Bulletin:*47-49.

Zink, Steven D. 1991. Will librarians have a place in the information society? *RSR: Reference Services Review* 19 (1):76-77.

10

Vendors and Suppliers

All libraries need to purchase supplies or services. The dilemma is how to get the best product at the best price. I have several suggestions to solve this dilemma.

Talk to vendors at library conferences. Spend as much time as you can at the exhibits. If possible, do this at a time when there are fewer people at the exhibits—you will have more time to talk with the vendors. I usually try to make one pass through the exhibits to see what is there, then return to talk to the vendors who interest me the most. Leave your business card and ask them to send their literature to your office.

Talk to *selected* vendors in your office. You do not need to talk to every vendor who calls you on the phone or sends you literature, but you should talk to any that sell services you need now or are likely to need in the future. Set aside an hour or so and listen to what they have to say. Use salespeople as a resource—ask questions, ask for samples of their work, ask for references. I always ask for a free sample of their services, a demo search, a month of free service, etc. The worst they can do is say no, and if they say yes you get a real chance to evaluate their service. (In fact, I will not buy a service *without* a sample of their work up front.) It is very important that you do not create an adversarial relationship. Be open and honest and, if possible, share information with them.

Ask other librarians for their opinions of a potential vendor. Listservs on the Internet are excellent places to do this. I have seen many questions and discussions on LIBREF-L, BUSLIB-L, SOLOLIB-L, and MEDLIB regarding vendors, with many varied but always useful responses. There is even a listserv dedicated to discussions of document delivery issues which has many discussions on quality of service.

Remember that the vendors cannot succeed without customers. It is to their advantage to make us happy. If they do not, tell them—then tell others. To be fair, if they do a good job, tell them and others as well. The customer is, or *should be*, always right. Sometimes you will have to remind the vendor of this. If they do not get it, if they will not work the way you want to work, change vendors! You always have alternatives.

An asterisk (*) after a vendor's name indicates that they have recommended by *at least* one SOLO, sometimes the author. The others were chosen by reputation or because they often appear at SLA conference exhibits. Not all vendors are represented, but this should give you a place to start looking. If there is a vendor that you recommend that is not listed, please let me know. Also, if you have had a bad experience with a listed vendor, let me know so I can consider removing their name from future editions of this book.

Resources included in this chapter are as follows:

- guides to products and services
- print resources (book jobbers, subscription services, CI/market research, document delivery, patents, standards)
- electronic resources (library automation, CD-ROM, databases, Internet, online)
- other (supplies/furniture, library consultants, movers, translation services, etc.)

For information about services available on the Internet, see chapter 12.

GUIDES TO PRODUCTS AND SERVICES

Library Journal Sourcebook: The Reference for Library Products & Services, supplement to December issue, 249 West 17th Street, New York, NY 10011, 212-463-6819, fax: 212-463-6734, directory of products, services, suppliers, showcase of products

The Librarian's Yellow Pages, P.O. Box 79 Larchmont, NY 10538, 800-235-9723, e-mail: libnyellopg@delphi.com, Internet: telnet:// database.carl.org, includes 800 numbers, fax numbers, e-mail and WWW home pages

BOOK JOBBERS

Amazon Bookstore, 2250 First Avenue South, Seattle, WA 98134, 206-622-0761, fax: 206-622-2405, Internet: http://www.amazon.com (over 1 million titles listed)

Baker & Taylor Books, 2709 Water Ridge Parkway, Charlotte, NC 28217, 704-357-3500, fax: 704-329-8989, e-mail: BTinfo@baker-taylor.

e-mail.com, Internet: http://www.baker-taylor.com, books, AV, software, electronic ordering, cataloging and processing

Barton Business Services*, 216 U.S. Route 206, Suite 18, P.O. Box 1268, Somerville, NJ 08876-1268, 800-244-5707, 908-281-1411, fax: 800-244-5698, any book in print, shipping included

Bernan/UNIPUB, 4611-F Assembly Dr., Lanham, MD 20706, 800-274-4888, 301-459-7666, fax: 800-865-3450, e-mail: query@ kruas.com, exclusive distributor for the U.S. government, U.N. and other agencies (including UNESCO, FAO, IAEA, HMSO, EC)

Book Clearing House*, 46 Purdy St., Harrison, NY 10528, 800-431-1579, 914-835-0015, fax: 914-835-039

The Book House, Inc.*, 208 W. Chicago St., Jonesville, MI 49250, 800-248-1146, 517-849-2117, fax: 800-858-9716, e-mail: bookhous@ mlc.lib.mi.us, any book in print, CD-ROM, software

Computer Literacy Bookshop, stores in San Jose, Sunnyvale, and Cupertino, California and Tysons Corner, Virginia, 408-435-1118, 703-734-7771, fax: 408-435-1823, 703-734-7773, Internet: http:// www. clbooks.com

Corporate Book Resources*, 305 Main Street, Sutton, WV 26601, 800-222-7787, fax: 800-932-0033, e-mail: cbrbk@aol.com, http://www. cbrbk.com, any book in print, shipping included, a founding sponsor of the SOLO Librarians Division

Emery-Pratt Company, 1966 W. Main St., Owosso, MI 48867-1372, 800-248-3887, 517-723-5291, fax: 517-723-4677, for all libraries, including medical

Ingram Library Services Inc., One Ingram Blvd, La Vergne, TN 37086-1986, 800-937-5300, fax: 615-793-3810, books, AV, multimedia

The Lawbook Exchange, Ltd., 965 Jefferson Ave., Union, NJ 07083-8605, 800-422-6686, 908-686-1998, fax: 908-686-3098, e-mail: lawbkexc@superlink.net, Internet: http://www.abaa-booknet.com/ usa/lbe/

Libros Sin Fronteras (Books Without Borders), P.O. Box 2085, Olympia, WA 98507-2085, 800-464-2767, 206-357-4332, fax: 206-357-4332, distributor of Spanish-language books, CDs and AV, specializing in schools and public libraries

Login Brothers Book Company*, 1436 W. Randolph St., Chicago, IL 60607-1414, 800-621-4249, 312-733-6424, fax: 800-339-1077, e-mail: sales@lb.com, Internet: http://www.lb.com, health sciences books and media, specializing in consumer health

Majors Scientific Books*, P.O. Box 819074, Dallas, TX 75381-9074, 800-633-1851, 214-247-2929, fax: 214-888-4800, distributor of health, science, scientific books and media

Matthews Medical and Scientific Books, Inc., 11559 Rock Island Ct., Maryland Heights, MO 63043, 800-633-2665, 314-432-1400, fax: 800-421-8816, e-mail: ask@mattmccoy.com, health sciences, medical nursing, dental, bioscience books and electronic media

Midwest Library Service, 11443 St. Charles Rock Rd., Bridgeton, MO 63044-2789, 800-325-8833, 314-739-3100, fax: 800-952-1009, all titles, technical processing

Powell's Technical Bookstore, 33 NW Park Avenue, Portland, OR 87209, 800-225-6911, 503-228-3906, fax: 503-228-0505, Internet: http://technical.powells.portland.or.us

Research Books, Inc.*, 38 Academy Street, P.O. Box 1507, Madison, CT 06443, 203-245-3279, fax: 203-245-1830

Rittenhouse Book Distributors*, 511 Feheley Drive, King of Prussia, PA 19406, 800-345-6425, 610-277-1414, fax: 800-223-7488, Internet: http://www.rittenhouse.com, specializes in health science, print and electronic media

Schoenhof's Foreign Books, Inc., 76A Mt. Auburn St., Cambridge, MA 02138, 617-547-8855, fax: 617-547-8551, importer of foreign-language books

Total Information, Inc.*, 844 Dewey Avenue, Rochester, NY 14613, 800-786-4636, 716-254-0621, fax: 716-254-0153, President: John Smith

SUBSCRIPTION SERVICES

Basch Subscriptions, Inc., 26 Perley St., Concord, NH 03301-3653, 603-25-5109, fax: 603-226-9443, e-mail: subs@basch.com ("Buzzy" Basch was instrumental in the creation of the SOLO Librarians Division of SLA)

EBSCO Subscription Services*, P.O. Box 1943, Birmingham, AL 35201-1943, 205-991-6600, fax: 205-995-1636

Faxon Canada, P.O. Box 2382, London, ON N6A 5A7, 800-263-2966, 519-472-1003, fax: 519-472-1072

The Faxon Company* (A Dawson Company) 15 Southwest Park, Westwood, MA 02090, 800-93766-0039, 617-329-3350, fax: 617-329-9875

Readmore, Inc., 22 Cortland St., New York, NY 10007, 800-221-3306, 212-349-5540, fax: 212-385-2350

Readmore Canada Ltd., P.O. Box 119, Millbrook, ON L0A 1G0, Canada, 705-932-3620, fax: 705-932-3621

Swets Subscription Service, 440 Creamery Way, Suite A, Exton, PA 19341, 610-524-5355, fax: 610-624-5366, specializing in foreign subscriptions, current awareness, and document delivery services

Turner Subscription Service (A Dawson Company), 1005 W. Pines Rd., Oregon IL 61061, 800-847-4201, 815-732-4476, fax: 815-732-4489, specializing in public libraries, schools, and community colleges

COMPETITIVE INTELLIGENCE, MARKET RESEARCH

Find/SVP, Inc., 625 Avenue of the Americas, New York, NY 10011, 800-346-3787, 212-807-2635, fax: 212-807-2676, also has a subscription custom research service

The Freedonia Group, Inc., 20600 Chagrin Blvd., Cleveland, OH 44122, 216-921-6800, market reports

The Information Specialists*, 2490 Lee Blvd., Cleveland, OH 44118, 216-321-7500, fax: 216-321-7683, e-mail: infospec@wariat.org (also document delivery, consulting)

Lexis-Nexis (Reed-Elsevier), P.O. Box 933, Dayton, OH 45401, 800-227-9597

MIRC/Frost & Sullivan, 2525 Charleston Road, Mountain View, CA 94043, 415-961-9000, fax: 415-961-5042

Technical Insights, Inc., P.O. Box 1304, Ft. Lee, NJ 07024-9967, 201-568-4744, fax: 201-568-8247, e-mail: tiinfo@insights.com, technical intelligences for executives, via print, Internet, disk, fax

Teltech Resource Network Corp.*, 2850 Metro Dr., Minneapolis, MN 55425, 612-851-7500, fax: 612-851-7799, technical and business intelligence, consulting, location of technical experts and vendors, document delivery

DOCUMENT DELIVERY

Advanced Information Consultants, 1200 Broad St., Suite 202, Durham, NC 27705, 919-296-3715, e-mail: hullp@nando.net (home office: P.O. Box 87127, Canton, MI 48187-0127, 800-929-3789)

Ark Information Services (part of Disclosure), New York, NY, 212-397-6232, hard-copy of annual reports.

Bay Tact Corporation*, 440 Route 198, Woodstock Valley, CT 06282, 800-4-annual, annual reports on demand

Biggers Research Service, 819 Kings Avenue, Brandon, FL 33511-5926, 813-654-6806, e-mail: biggerj@scfn.thpl.lib.fl.us, flat fee, 1-2 day delivery, copyright included, extra charge for fax service

British Library, Boston Spa, Wetherby, West Yorkshire LS23 7BQ, UK, 44-937-546060, fax: 44-937-546333, extensive coverage, but fax service is expensive and photocopy service can be slow

Canada Institute for Scientific and Technical Information (CISTI)*, 800-668-1222, fax: 613-952-9112, e-mail: cisi.info@nrc.ca, guarantees same day on orders placed by noon central time, over 20K current titles

Chemical Abstracts Service, 2540 Olentangy River Rd., P.O. Box 3012, Columbus, OH 43210, 800-848-6538, 614-447-3670

EBSCODoc, P.O. Box 1943, Birmingham, AL 35201-1943, 205-991-6600, fax: 205-995-1636

InFocus Research Services, 1335 Rockville Pike, Rockville, MD 20852, 301-217-9311, e-mail: infocus@access.digex.net, technical reports and U.S. government publications

The InfoStore, 500 Sansome St., Suite 400, San Francisco, CA 94111-3219, 800-248-0360, fax: 415-433-0100, e-mail: orders@infostore. com, Internet: http://www.umi.com

Infotrieve* (IMED), 10966 Le Conte, Los Angeles, CA 90024, 800-422-4633, 310-208-1903, fax: 310-208-5971

ISI, Genuine Article* (Thomson Corp.), 3501 Market St., Philadelphia, PA 19104, 800-336-4474, 215-386-0100, fax: 215-386-2911, Internet: tga@isinet.com, 5-years of full-text coverage of over 7,000 journal titles, 24-hour service

KRI/Article Express/Source One, 2440 El Camino Real, Mountain View, CA 94040, 800-4DIALOG

Library of The Royal Netherlands Academy of Sciences (Library KNAW)*, P.O. Box 41950, 1009, DD Amsterdam, The Netherlands, 31-20-668-5511, fax: 31-20-668-5079, can order online on DIMDI, Datastar, STN, e-mail: docdel@library.knaw.nl, Internet: http:// library.knaw.nl, 24-hour delivery by fax, same day if placed by noon (Dutch time), over 6K current medical journals, price depends on location (starts at about $25 per article)

Linda Hall Library*, 5109 Cherry St., Kansas City, MO 64110, 816-363-4600, extensive technical collection, took over Engineering Societies Library collection

The Medical Library Center of New York (MLCNY)*, 212-427-1630, fax: 212-876-6697, e-mail: mlcny@metgate.metro.org, medical library consortium, $10 per article or NN/LM members, $14 for nonmembers, fax surcharge of $4-5 plus 25 cents per page

Moody's Docutronics Information Group, 99 Church St., New York, NY 10007, 800-227-5595, 212-553-0546, fax: 212-553-4700, e-mail: fbavent@radix.net, annual reports (originals)

The Research Investment, Inc.*, 20600 Chagrin Blvd., Suite 450, Cleveland, OH 44122, 216-247-8945, fax: 216-247-5015 (staff formerly of The Information Specialists)

TDI & Co.*, 2218 Wilshire Blvd., Suite 787, Santa Monica, CA 90403-5784, 310-820-3651, fax: 310-826-3932

UMI: ProquestDirect, 300 North Zeeb Road, P.O. Box 1346, Ann Arbor, MI 48106-1346, 800-521-0600, ext. 2705, (313) 761-4700, ext. 2705, fax: 800-864-0019

The UnCover Co. (KRI), 3801 E. Florida, #200, Denver, CO 80210, 303-758-3030, fax: 303-758-5946, e-mail: uncover@carl.org, online access to articles from over 15K journals, can be ordered online and delivered via fax

University Book Services, P.O. Box 728, Dublin, OH 3107, publisher overstocks

PATENTS

Airmail Patent Service*, P.O. Box 1732, Rockville, MD 20849, 301-424-7692, fax: 301-424-8211, patents, trademarks, U.S. and foreign, 1-week delivery, $6 for U.S. patents

Derwent North America/Rapid Patent, 1921 Jefferson Davis Highway, Suite 1921D, P.O. Box 2527, Eads Station, Arlington, VA 22202, 800-336-5010, 703-413-5050, fax: 703-413-0127

KRI/Source One*, 2440 El Camino Real, Mountain View, CA 94040, 800-4DIALOG

STANDARDS

American National Standards Institute (ANSI), 11 E. 42nd St., New York, NY 1036, 212-642-4900, fax: 212-302-1286, all ANSI approved standards, must be prepaid, shipping 7 percent additional

ASTM (American Society of Testing and Materials), 1916 Race St., Philadelphia, PA 19103, 215-299-5400, prepay or add 7 percent for shipping

Canadian Standards Association (CSA), 178 Rexdale Blvd., Rexdale, Ontario M9W 1R3, Canada, 416-747-4000

Defense Printing Service, Building 4D, 700 Robbins Ave., Philadelphia, PA 19111-5094. 215-697-2179, fax: 215-697-2978, MIL-STDS only

Document Center*, 1504 Industrial Way, Unit 9, Belmont, CA 94002, 415-591-7600, fax: 415-591-7617, e-mail: doc@netcom.com, Internet: http://doccenter.com/doccenter/home.html, can supply all standards, IEC in stock, strong supporter of SOLO Division

Global Engineering Documents, (part of Information Handling Services), 15 Inverness Way East, Englewood, CO 80112-5704, 800-854-7179, can supply almost any document (expensive)

National Center for Standards and Certification Information (NIST), Building 411, Room A163, Gaithersburg, MD 20899, 301-975-4040, fax: 301-926-1559, Joanne Overman can help with standards information, no standards supplied (NIST Publications Office: 301-975-3058, Reference Desk: 301-975-3052)

National Technical Information Service (NTIS), 5295 Port Royal Rd., Springfield, VA 22161, 703-487-4650, fax: 703-321-8547, deposit account or prepayment, relatively slow but rush service available at extra cost, government publications of all types

Underwriters' Laboratories Inc. (UL), 333 Pfingsten Rd., Northbrook, IL 60062, 708-272-8800, must prepay

LIBRARY AUTOMATION

Ameritech Library Services, 400 Dynix Dr., Provo, UT 84604-5640, 801-223-5200, fax: 801-223-5202, Internet: http://schunxl.us.dynix. com/als/als.html

Best-Seller Inc., 3300 Cote-Vertu, Suite 303, Saint-Laurent, Quebec, Canada H4R 2B8, 514-337-3000, fax: 514-337-7629, Internet: http://www.bestseller.com

Brodart Authomation, 500 Arch St., Williamsport, PA 17705, 800-233-8467, ext. 640, fax: 717-327-9237, Internet: http://www.brodart. com

CASPR, Inc., 635 Vaqueros Ave., Sunnyvale, CA 94086-3524, 800-852-2777, 408-522-9800, fax: 408-522-9806, LibraryWorld (groupware)

COMPanion Corp., 1831 Fort Union Blvd., Salt Lake City, UT 84121, 800-347-6493, 801-943-7277, fax: 801-943-7752

Comstow Information Services, Inc., 249 Ayer Rd., P.O. Box 277, Harvard, MA 01451-0277, 508-772-2001, fax: 508-772-9573, e-mail: comstow@delphi.com, BiblioTech and BiblioTix software for UNIX

Data Trek, Inc., 5838 Edison Place, Carlsbad, CA 92008-6596, 800-876-5484, 619-431-8400, fax: 619-431-8448, e-mail: marketing@datatrek.com, Internet: http://www.datatrek.com, cataloging, serials, acquisitions, AV, OPAC, integrated automation software

DRA, 1276 N. Warson Rd., St. Louis, MO 63132, 800-325-0888, 314-432-1100, fax: 314-993-8927, e-mail: sales@dra.com, Internet: http://www.dra.com, client-server library automation, network design

Eloquent Systems Inc., 25-1501 Lonsdale Ave., N. Vancouver VC V7M 2J2, Canada, 800-663-8172, 604-980-8358, fax: 604-980-9537, Internet: http://www.eloquent-systems.com/gencat, Eloquent Librarian software OPAC

Follett Software Company*, 1391 Corporate Dr., McHenry, IL 60050-7041, 800-323-3397, 815-344-8700, fax: 815-344-8774, e-mail: marketing@fsc.follett.com, Internet: http://www.follett.com, Follett of Canada 800-323-3397 ext. 7932, UNISON Catalog Plus/Circulation Plus MARC library microcomputer management (DOS and Mac), used extensively in public schools

Gateway Software Corp., P.O. Box 367, Fromberg, MT 59029-0367, 800-735-3637, 406-668-7661, fax: 406-668-7665, Internet: http://www.imt.net/~gateway/index.html

ILS International Library Systems, 1135-13560 Maycrest Way, Richmond BC, Canada V6V 2J7, 604-761-8083, fax: 604-278-9161

Information Dimensions, Inc. (a subsidiary of OCLC), 5080 Tuttle Crossing Blvd., Dublin, OH 43016-3569, 800-DATAMGT, 614-761-8083, fax: 614-761-7290, Internet: http://www.idi.oclc.org, TECHLIBplus integrated library system, OPAC, cataloging, circulation, serials, acquisitions, WWW access on VAX/UNIX

IME, 140-142 St. John St., London EC1V 4JT, England, 44-171-253-1177, fax: 44-171-608-3599

Inmagic, Inc.*, 800 W. Cummings Park, Woburn, MA 01801, 800-229-TEXT, 617-938-4442, fax: 617-938-6393, automation software for Windows-based PCs, strong supporter of SOLO Division.

Library Associates, 8845 W. Olympic, #201A, Beverly Hills, CA 90211, 310-289-1067, fax: 310-289-9635, e-mail: fastcat@primenet.com, cataloging, foreign languages, retrospective conversion

The Library Corp., Research Park, Inwood, WV 25428, 800-325-7759, 304-229-0100, fax: 304-229-0296, e-mail: info@bibfile.com, Internet: http://www.bibfile.com, BiblioFile for Windows, Z39.50-compliant

Marcive, Inc., P.O. Box 47508, San Antonio, TX 78265-7508, 800-531-7678, 210-646-6161, fax: 210-646-0167, e-mail: custserv@ marcive. com, Internet: http://www.marcive.com, PAC, GPO catalog database, technical processing

Nutshell/Ultraplus*, Judy Barnes, Lansing, MI, cataloging, acquisitions, journal check-in, ILL, circulation, AV (designed for small hospital libraries)

On Point, Inc. /TLC Total Library Computerization, 2606 36th St., NW, Washington, DC 20007, 202-338-8914, fax: 202-337-7107, e-mail: onpointinc@aol.com, text-based integrated library management system for smaller libraries, cataloging, circulation, ILL, serials, acquisitions

Personal Bilbliographic Software, Inc., P.O. Box 4250, Ann Arbor, MI 48106, 313-996-1580, fax: 313-996-4672, e-mail: sales@pbsinc. com, ProCite reference management database and bibliography maker, Biblio-Link to transfer records from online into ProCite

Professional Software*, Glen Ridge, NJ, low prices cataloging, serials, holdings

Right On Programs, 775 New York Ave., Suite 210, Huntington, NY 11743, 516-424-7777, fax: 516-424-7207, e-mail: riteonsoft@aol. com, inexpensive circulation, online catalog, periodical manager, inventory, etc.

Special Libraries Cataloguing, 4493 Lindholm Rd., Victoria BC V9B 5T7, Canada, 604-474-3361, fax: 604-474-3362, e-mail: jelrod@ islandnet.com, photocopies of title pages, labels, cards, MARC records

VTLS, Inc., 1800 Kraft Dr., Blacksburg, VA 24060, 540-231-3605, fax: 540-231-3648, Internet: http://www.vtls.com

Winnebago Software Co., 457 E. South, Caledonia, MN 55921, 800-533-5430, 507-724-5411, fax: 507-724-2301, e-mail: sales@ winnebago.com, Internet: http://www.winebago.com, circulation, catalog, acquisitions, card programs, retrospective conversion services

ONLINE, CD-ROM, AND OTHER ELECTRONIC MEDIA

Bowker Electronic Publishing (Division of Reed Reference Publishing), 121 Chanlon Rd., New Providence, NJ 07974, 800-323-3288, 908-665-2865, fax: 908-665-3528, Books in Print, Ulrich's, Directory of Corporate Affiliations, Marquis Who's Who on CD-ROM and tape

CD Systems, 3201 Temple Ave., Pomona, CA 91768, 800-CD
TOWER, 909-595-5736, fax: 909-595-3506, CD towers for mutiple
disc installations

Chadwyck-Healey Inc., 1101 King St., Suite 380, Alexandria, VA
22314, 800-752-0515, 703-683-4890, fax: 703-683-7589, e-mail:
mktg@chadwyck.com, reference products on CD-ROM, microform
and print

CINAHL Information Systems, 1509 Wilson Terrace, Glendale, CA
91206, 800-959-7167, 818-409-8005, fax: 818-546-5679, nursing
and allied health literature, print, CD-ROM, online

Context Ltd*., London, JUSTIS, CD-ROM, EU documents

Counterpoint, Box 928, Cambridge, MA 02140, 800-998-4515, 617-
547-4515, fax: 617-547-9064, e-mail: info@counterpoint.com,
Internet: http://www.counterpoint.com, products: environmental,
health and safety, regulations on CD-ROM, Federal Register and
Archives, via Internet and CD-ROM; Full-text CFR, via Internet
and CD-ROM; Nuclear Information Service, via Internet and CD-
ROM; Hawley's Condensed Chemical Dictionary, Sax's Dangerous
Properties of Industrial Materials; Commerce Business Daily, via
Internet and CD-ROM

Dow Jones News Retrieval*, P.O. Box 300, Princeton, NJ 08543-0300

Dun's Direct Access (DDA), Dun & Bradstreet Information Services, 3
Sylvan Way, Parsippany, NJ 07054-8396, 800-526-0651, 201-605-
6714, fax: 201-605-6911

Information Access Co., 362 Lakeside Dr., Foster City, CA 94404, 800-
227-8431, 415-378-5200, fax: 415-378-5369, InfoTrac FaxLine:800-
700-1890, Europe: 44-071-930-3933, fax: 44-071-930-9190, Internet:
http://www.iacnet.com, full-text and bibliographic databases on CD-
ROM, Internet, online

Information Handling Services, 15 Inverness Way East, P.O. Box 1154,
Englewood, CO 80112, 800-525-7052

iSCAN Intelligent Scanning Inc., 2255 St. Laurent Blvd., Suite 304,
Ottawa, ON K1G 4K3, Canada, 800-668-SCAN, 613-526-7226,
fax: 613-526-1496, backfile conversion to CD-ROM or microform

Knight-Ridder Information, Inc., 2440 El Camino Real, Mountain
View, CA 94040, 800-334-2564, 415-254-8800, fax: 415-254-8350,
Europe: 44-01-865-326226, fax: 44-01-865-326282, DIALOG, KR
Information OnDisc CD-ROMs, SourceOne Document Delivery

Legi-Slate, Inc., 777 N. Capital St., NE, Suite 900, Washington, DC
20002, 800-733-1131, 202-898-2300, fax: 202-898-3030, e-mail:

legislate@legislate.com, online and Internet news service covering Congress and U.S. regulations

LEXIS/NEXIS*, P.O. Box 933, Dayton, OH 45401, 800-227-9597, CELEX, "Legis" subfile, EU Official Journal regulations, directives, some treaties

Moody's Investors Service (Dun & Bradstreet), 99 Church St., New York, NY 1007, 800-342-5647, ext. 0546, 212-553-0437, fax: 212-553-4700, business and financial information in print, online, or CD-ROM

OCLC, Inc., 6565 Frantz Rd., Dublin, OH 43017, 800-848-5878, Internet: http://www.oclc.org

OVID Techologies (formerly BRS), 333 Seventh Ave., New York, NY 10001, 800-950-2035, 212-563-3006, Internet: http://www.ovid.com

Questel-Orbit, Inc., 8000 Westpark Dr., McLean, VA 22102, 800-456-7248, 703-442-0900, fax: 703-893-4632, specializing in intellectual property, chemistry, business, and news

SilverPlatter Information, Inc., 100 River Ridge Dr., Norwood, MA 02062-5043, 800-343-0064, 617-769-2599, fax: 617-769-8763, e-mail: info@silverplatter.com, medical, academic, and professional databases on CD-ROM or Internet

Statistics Canada, Holland Avenue, Ottawa, ON K1A 0T6, Canada, 800-263-1136, fax: 613-951-0581, Internet: http://www.statcan.ca, print and electronic socioeconomic data

Thomson & Thomson, 500 Victory Rd., North Quincy, MA 02171-1545, 800-692-8833, 617-479-1600, fax: 617-786-8273, trademark and copyright research services, online and CD-ROM

UMI (Bell & Howell), 300 N. Zeeb Rd., Ann Arbor, MI 48106, 800-521-0600, 313-761-4700, fax: 313-761-6686, information products in print, CD-ROM, online, microform, books on demand, document delivery

WLN (Washington Library Network), 4424 6th Ave., Building 3, P.O. Box 3888, Lacey, WA 98509-3888, 800-DIALWLN, 360-923-4000, fax: 360-923-4009, e-mail: info@wln.com, bibliographic information service, online databases, CD-ROM catalogs, database preparation

SUPPLIES

ALA Graphics* (American Library Association), 50 E. Huron St., Chicago, IL 60611, 800-545-2433, 312-280- 3252, fax: 312-280-2422, posters, bookmarks, t-shirts, etc. (includes NLW and "READ" series)

Brodart Co., 1609 Memorial Ave., Williamsport, PA 17705, 800-233-8959, 717-326-2461, fax: 800-283-6087, all kinds of supplies, furniture, AV and computer equipment

Demco, Inc., 4810 Forest Run Rd., P.O. Box 7488, Madison, WI 53707, 800-356-1200, 608-241-1201, fax: 800-245-1329, library supplies and equipment

Gaylord Bros., P.O. Box 4901, Syracuse, NY 13090, 800-448-6160, 315-457-5070, fax: 800-272-3412, Internet: http://www.gaylord.com, full line of supplies, equipment, furniture, automation products

Highsmith Inc.*, W5527 Highway 106, P.O. Box 800, Fort Atkinson, WI 53538, 800-558-2110, 414-563-9571, fax: 800-835-2329, full line of furniture, supplies, equipment

The Library Store, Inc., 112 E. South St., P.O. Box 964, Tremont, IL 61568, 800-548-7204, 309-925-5571, fax: 800-320-7706, supplies and furniture

Russ Bassett Co., 8189 Byron Rd., Whittier, CA 90606, 800-350-2445, 310-945-2445, fax: 310-698-8972, AV and microform storage systems

Spacesaver Corporation, 1450 Janesville Ave., Fort Atkinson, WI 53538, 800-492-3434, 414-563-6362, fax: 414-563-2702, compact shelving

Upstart* (A Division of Highsmith, Inc.), W5527 Highway 106, P.O. Box 800, Fort Atkinson, WI 53538, 800-448-4887, fax: 800-448-5828, supplies and incentives especially appropriate for school and public libraries

Vernon Library Supplies, Inc., 2851 Cole Court, Norcross, GA 30071, 800-878-0253, fax: 800-466-1165, e-mail: vernon@vernlib.com, full line of supplies and furniture

The Worden Co., 199 E. 17th St., Holland, MI 49423, 800-748-0561, 616-392-1848, fax: 616-392-2542, furniture and shelving

LIBRARY CONSULTANTS

C Berger and Company, 327 E. Gundersen Dr., Carol Stream, IL 60188, 800-382-4CBC, 708-653-1115, fax: 708-653-1691, e-mail: c-berg@dupagels.lib.il.us, temporary help in IL area, outsourcing, records management, planning, needs assessment, cataloging and indexing

Aaron Cohen Associates Ltd., 159 Teatown Rd., Croton-on-Hudson, NY 10520, 914-271-8170, fax: 914-271-2434, consulting, architectural and interior design

Chris Olson & Associates*, 857 Twin Harbor Dr., Arnold, MD 21012-1027, 410-647-6708, fax: 410-647-0415, e-mail: olson@access.digex.net, graphics for libraries, consultation on library promotion

Gossage Reagan Associates, Inc., 25 W. 43rd St., #812, New York, NY 10036, 212-869-3348, fax: 212-997-1127, executive search, placement, consulting, temporary staff in NY area, records management

InfoManage/SMR International* (St. Clair Management Resources), P.O. Box 948, Murray Hill Station, New York, NY 10156, 212-683-6285, fax: 212-683-2987, e-mail:73042.67@compuserve.com, training and management consulting for SOLOs, Guy St. Clair, President

J.P. Jay Associates*, 1313 Roth Ave., Allentown, PA, 18102-1140, 215-435-9666, fax: 610-435-9216

Thomas Rode*, independent information professionals, Meunzstrasse 10, D53332, Bornheim, Germany, 49-2227-1580, fax: 49-2227-1575, e-mail: rode@info.su.edunet.de

TFPL Inc., 345 Park Avenue South, 10th Floor, New York, NY 10010, 212-213-5990, fax: 212-213-6887, headquartered in London, U.S., and European business information

MISCELLANEOUS

CanCOPY, Canadian Copyright Licensing Agency, 6 Adelaide St. E., Suite 900, Toronto, ON M5C 1H6, Canada, 800-893-5777, 416-868-1620, fax: 416-868-1621

Copyright Clearance Center, 222 Rosewood Dr., Danvers, MA 01923, 508-750-8400, fax: 508-750-4470, e-mail: info@copyright.com, Internet: http://www.copyright.com

Information Bridges International, 477 Harris Rd., Richmond Heights, OH 44143, voice/fax: 216-486-7443, e-mail: jsiess@en.com; "arranging exchanges among libraries and librarians around the world"

Hallett Movers, 7535 W. 59th St., Summit, IL 60501, 800-645-MOVE, 708-458-8600, fax: 708-458-7116

Polyglot International, 340 Brannan St., 5th Floor, San Francisco, CA 94107, 800-829-7700, 415-512-8800, fax: 415-512-8982, e-mail: polyinfo@polyglotint.com, translation for technical, legal, and promotional materials, any language, some document retrieval and consulting

Ralph McElroy Translation Company, 910 West Ave., Austin, TX 78701, 800-531-9977, 512-472-6753, fax: 512-472-4591, technical translations

University Bindery, Inc., 4238 Utah St., St. Louis, MO 63116, 314-772-5095

William B. Meyer, Inc.*, P.O. Box 4206, Bridgeport, CT 06607, 800-873-6393, 203-375-5801, fax: 203-377-3838, library moving specialist

Books and Journals

In addition to the sources listed in the bibliography, which were quoted in or used in the research and writing of this book, I have compiled a list of other resources. I have not read *all* of these books, just most of them. They were chosen for their relevance to the issues presented earlier in this book. When a relatively old book is included, it is either a classic or the latest I could find on a subject. The addresses for many of the publishers are listed at the end.

The listings below are in alphabetical order, by title, in the following categories:

books of special interest to SOLOs
- management
- small public libraries
- jail and prison libraries
- museum libraries
- church and synagogue libraries

other books not specific to SOLOs
- about the profession
- management
- Internet and online searching
- outsourcing
- alternative careers/information brokers
- law
- public and school libraries
- health sciences
- miscellaneous

journals of special interest to SOLOs

other journals of interest

- records management, law librarianship, law book jobbers and publishers, church librarianship, religious publishers (and their denominations)—names only

publisher names and addresses

An asterisk (*) after titles indicates that they have been recommended by at least one SOLO, sometimes by the author.

BOOKS OF SPECIAL INTEREST TO SOLOS

Management

Automating Small Libraries, by James Swan, Summer 1996, Highsmith, ISBN 0-917846-78-8, $15.00.

The Best of OPL: Five Years of The One-Person Library, Andrew Berner and Guy St. Clair, 1990, SLA, ISBN 0-87111-357-0; especially great if you are new to being SOLO, a history of the profession in very readable form (general considerations, management strategies, advocacy, marketing, profiles, helpful tips, bibliography).

The Best of OPL, II: Selected Readings from The One-Person Library: A Newsletter for Librarians and Management, 1990-1994, Andrew Berner and Guy St. Clair, 1996, SLA, $34.50 members, $43.50 non-members, ISBN 087111-438-0; the latest summary of OPL, worth a re-read if you are a subscriber.

Cataloging and the Small Special Library, Joseph Palmer, 1992, SLA, $22.50 members, $28 nonmembers, ISBN 0-87111-370-8.

The Cybrarian's Guide to Cyber-Marketing, http://www.iocom.be/pilot/cybermarketing/; published by Michel Bauwens, Internet Consultant/Cyber-marketeer, IO Communications, ch. De Charleroi, 182 B-1060 Brussels, Belgium, Tel:+32-2-534.07.37; fax: 07.57; e-mail: mbauwens@iocom.be.

Financial Management for Small and Medium-sized Libraries, Madeline J. Daubert, 1993, ALA, $34.20 members, $38 nonmembers, ISBN 0-8389-0618-4.

Managing Small Special Libraries, 1992, SLA, $15 members, $20 nonmembers, ISBN 0-87111-382-1; a classic.

Managing the One-Person Library, Guy St. Clair and Joan Williamson, Butterworth, 1986. ISBN 0-408-01511-X; no SOLO should be without this and the next one.

Managing the New One-Person Library, Guy St. Clair and Joan Williamson, Bowker Saur, 1992; profiles, isolation, education and CE, advocacy, managing, time management, collection development, finances, technology, marketing.

Reference Sources for Small and Medium-size Libraries, 5th ed., Jovian P. Lang, ed., 1992, ALA, $36 members, $40 nonmembers, ISBN 0-8389-3406-4.

SMR Special Reports, SMR International, 1995:

1) Paul, Meg and Sandra Crabtree, Strategies for special libraries
2) St. Clair, Guy, The one-person library in the organization
3) St. Clair, Guy, One-person librarianship: The authority of the customer
4) St. Clair, Guy, What the one-person library does
5) St. Clair, Guy, Finances and value: How the one-person library is paid for
6) St. Clair, Guy, Dealing with downsizing: A guide for the information services practitioner, (1996).
7) St. Clair, Guy, The OPL casebook; 30 studies from *The One-Person Library*

Small Libraries: Organization and Operation, 2nd ed., by Donald J. Sager, Highsmith, May 1996, ISBN 0-917846-79-6, $12.00; includes chapters on public, school, church and synagogue, law, business, medical, museum and other libraries.

Winning Marketing Techniques: An Introduction to Marketing for Information Professionals, (self-study), Sharon Dean, 1990, SLA. $60 members, $75 nonmembers, ISBN 0-87111-390-2.

The Value of Corporate Libraries: Findings From a 1995 Survey of Senior Management*, Laurence Prusak and James Matarazzo, 1995, SLA, $5.00 members, $75.00 nonmembers, ISBN 0-87111-449-6.

Small Public Libraries

Administration of the Small Public Library, 3rd ed., Darlene E. Weingand, 1992, ALA, $27 members, $30 nonmembers, ISBN 0-8389-0583-8.

Behind the Scenes at the Dynamic Community Library: Simplifying Technical Services in the Small Library, Beth Wheeler Fox, 1990, ALA, $31.50 members, $35 nonmembers, ISBN 0-8389-0531-5.

A Bookkeeping System for Small Public Libraries, William D. Campbell, Center for the Study of Rural Librarianship, $7.95.

A Budgeting Manual for Small Public Libraries, William D. Campbell, Center for the Study of Rural Librarianship, $6.95.

Budgeting Techniques for Libraries and Information Centers, Michael E.D. Koenig, Special Libraries Association Professional Development Series 1, 1980; written while he was VP at Swets; detailed examples.

LAMA Small Libraries Publications Series, ALA, $4.50 members, $5 non-members: publications on trustees, budgeting, PR, administration, cooperation, buildings, reference, AV, collection development, automation, personnel, and volunteer management.

Technology or Tradition: Uncharted Waters: Managing Change in Small and Medium-sized Public Libraries, (audiotape), 1994, Teach 'em, $24, ALA443.

This Old Library: The Small Public Library Makeover, (audiotape), 1994, Teach 'em, $12, PLA467.

Jail and Prison Libraries

Correctional Facility Law Libraries: An A to Z Resource Guide, AALL Standing Committee on Law Library Service to Institution Residents and American Correctional Association, 1991, ISBN 0-929310-55-1

Jail Library Service: A Guide for Librarians and Jail Administrators, Linda Bayley, et al., 1981, ALA, ISBN 0-8389-3258-4.

Manual for Prison Law Libraries, Oliver James Werner, 1976, FB Rothman for AALL.

Museum Libraries

Libraries for Small Museums, 3rd ed., 1977, Linda M. Anderson, Museum Brief 7, Museum of Anthropology, University of Missouri, Columbia, MO.

Museum Librarianship: A Guide to the Provision and Management of Information Services, 1994, Esther Green Bierbaum, McFarland, ISBN 0-89950-971-1.

Church and Synagogue Libraries

Church Library Promotion: A Handbook of How-Tos, Ginger Caughman, 1990, McFarland, ISBN 0-899502-881.

Church and Synagogue Library Association Guide Series, CSLA P.O. Box 19357, Portland, OR 97219; how to set up a library, cataloging, policy manuals, reference, etc.

Church and Synagogue Library Resources, 5th ed., Dorothy Rodda, 1992, CSLA, ISBN 0-915324334.

121 Ways Toward a More Effective Church Library, Arthur K. Saul, 1980, Victor Books, ISBN 0-88207-171-8.

OTHER BOOKS, NOT SPECIFIC TO SOLOS

About the Profession

Continuing Professionalism: Education and IFLA: Past, Present and a Vision for the Future, 1994, Bowker-Saur, $110, ISBN 3-598-21794-3.

Information Ethics: Concerns for Librarianship and the Information Industry, Anne P. Mintz, 1990, McFarland, ISBN 0-89950-514-7.

*Librarians and the Awakening from Innocence: A Collection of Papers**, Herbert S. White, 1989, G.K. Hall, ISBN 0-8161-1892-2; the first collection of Herb's writings, should be read, memorized, and followed by all librarians.

Management

Accounting for Librarians and Other Not-for-Profit Managers, G. Stevenson Smith, American Library Association, 1983. ISBN 0-8389-0385-1; very detailed instructions for fund accounting and financial analysis, with exercises.

Against All Odds: Case Studies on Library Financial Management, Linda Crismond, ed., 1994, Highsmith Press, ISBN 0-917846-28-1.

At the Crossroads: Libraries on the Information Superhighway, Herbert S. White, Libraries Unlimited, 1995. ISBN 1-56308-165-2; a collection of his writings from 1980-1994: librarians and their roles as defined by themselves and others, librarians and their self-image and the perceptions that define their preparation, and librarians in the cruel world of politics and money; excellent introduction.

CD-ROM in Libraries: Management Issues, 1994, Bowker-Saur, $60, ISBN 1-85739-086-5.

*Competitive Advantage: Creating and Sustaining Superior Performance**, Michael E. Porter, Free Press, 1985, ISBN 0-02-925090-0, one of the best introductions to how business works.

Control of Administrative and Financial Operations in Special Libraries, Madeline J. Daubert, 1996, SLA, $60 members, $75 nonmembers.

Corporate Library Excellence, James M. Matarazzo, Special Libraries Association, 1990. ISBN 0-87111-367-8 (profiles of 13 corporate libraries voted outstanding by the boards of 6 Special Libraries Association chapters).

Divorcing a Corporation: How to Know When—and If—a Job Change is Right for You, Jacqueline H. Plumez and Karla Dougherty, Villard Books, 1986, ISBN 0-394-54457-9; I did not look at this, but from the title it sounds fascinating.

Document Delivery Services: Issues and Answers, Eleanor Mitchell and Sheila Walters, 1995, Information Today, ISBN 1-57387-003-X, $42.50.

The Evolving Virtual Library: Visions and Case Studies, Laverna M. Saunders, editor, 1996, Information Today, Inc., ISBN 1-57387-013-7, $39.50.

The Information Audit: An SLA Information Kit*, 1995, SLA, $16 members, $21 nonmembers, ISBN 0-87111-452-6, with input from Guy St. Clair; how to find out how your organization uses information.

Information for Management: A Handbook*, James M. Matarazzo and Miriam A. Drake, 1994, SLA, $32 members, $40 nonmembers, ISBN 0-87111-427-5; how to present information to upper management, information needs assessment, organizational dynamics, communication with management, records management, TQM, virtual library, nonprofits, information technology.

Information for Management: A Handbook, James M. Matarazzo and Miriam A. Drake, Special Libraries Association, 1994.

The Information Services Management Series, Guy St. Clair, Bowker-Saur:

- *Customer Service in the Information Environment,* ISBN 1-85739-004-0, 1994, $34.95.
- *Entrepreneurial Librarianship: The Key to Effective Information Services Management,* ISBN 1-85739-014-8, 1996, $45.00.
- *Power and Influence: Enhancing Information Services Within the Organization,* ISBN 0 85739 098-9, 1994, $34.95.
- *Total Quality Management in Information Services,* ISBN 0-85739-039-3, 1996, $45.00.
- *Human Resources in Information Services Management* (with Meg Paul), ISBN 1-85739-118-7, August 1997.
- *Corporate Memory: Information Management in the Electronic Age,* ISBN 1-85739-158-6, May 1997.

Knowledge for Europe: Librarians and Publishers Working Together, 1993 Bowker-Saur, $65, ISBN 3-598-11164-9.

Librarians and the Awakening from Innocence: A Collection of Papers, Herbert S, White, G.K. Hall, 1989; education, the political process, users, economic issues.

Libraries and Copyright: A Guide to Copyright Law in the 1990s*, Laura N. Gasaway and Sarah K. Winant, 1994, SLA, $40 members, $50 nonmembers, ISBN 0-87111-407-0; written by the SLA expert on copyright, has all you need to know and more.

The Library Manager's Deskbook: 102 Expert Solutions to 101 Common Dilemmas, Paula Phillips Carson, et al., 1995, ALA, $27 members, $30 nonmembers, ISBN 0-8389-0655-9.

Managing Change: A How-to-do-it Manual for Planning, Implementing, and Evaluating Change in Libraries, Susan C. Curzon, Neal-Schuman, 1989, ISBN 1-55570-032-2.

Managing the Economics of Owning, Leasing and Contracting Out Information Services, Woodsworth, Anne and James F. Williams II, Ashgate Publishing, 1993; good review in *InfoManage* 1(1):8, 12/93

Moving Your Library, A. McDonald, London: ASLIB, 1994, ISBN 0-85142-328-0.

Owning Your Numbers: An Introduction to Budgeting for Special Libraries, (self-study) Alice Sizer Warner, 1992, SLA, $60 members, $75 nonmembers, ISBN 0-87111-387-2.

Part-Time Public Relations With Full-Time Results, Rashelle S. Karp, ed., ALA, LAMA PR Section.

Practical Help for New Supervisors, 2nd ed., Joan Giesecke, ed., 1992, ALA, $18 members, $20 nonmembers, ISBN 0-8389-3408-0.

Rethinking the Corporate Information Center: A Blueprint for the 21st Century, Berkman, Robert I., Find/SVP Inc., 1995, ISBN 1-56241-214-0.

Special Libraries: A Guide for Management, 3rd ed., Elin B. Christianson, SLA, ISBN 0-87111-380-5; a classic.

Stress and Burnout in Library Service, Janette S. Caputo, 1991, Oryx, ISBN 0-897746023.

Time Management Handbook for Librarians, J. Wesley Cochran, Greenwood Press, 1992, ISBN 0-313-27842-3.

The Virtual Library: An SLA Information Kit*, 1994, SLA, $15 members, $20 nonmembers, ISBN 0-87111-428-3; a compilation of articles on how to go virtual.

Internet and Online Searching

The Canadian Internet Handbook, John A. Carroll, Prentice Hall Canada, 1994, $16.95, ISBN 0-13-304-395-9.

The Complete Internet Companion for Librarians*, Allen C. Benson, 1995, Neal-Schuman, $49.95, ISBN 1-55570-178-7; many lists of useful places to find information on the Net.

Directory of Directories on the Internet: A Guide to Information Sources, Gregory B. Newby, Mecklermedia, 1993, $29.50, ISBN 0-88736-786-2.

An Internet Guide for the Health Professional, 2nd ed., Michael Hogarth, MD, David Hutchinson RN, e-mail: medguide@midtown.net.

The Internet and Special Librarians; Use, Training and the Future*, Sharyn J. Ladner and Hope N. Tillman, 1993, SLA, $26.50 members, $33 nonmembers, ISBN 0-87111-413-5; results of a survey.

Internet Slick Tricks, Alfred and Emily Glossbrenner, Random House, 1994, $16, ISBN 0-679-75611-6.

Internet Tools of the Profession: A Guide for Special Librarians*, Hope Tillman, ed., 1995, SLA, $30.00 members, $37.50 nonmembers, ISBN 0-87111-430-5.

Key Guide to Electronic Resources Series, Pat Ensor, Series Editor, Information Today, Inc., all $39.50: *Art and Art History*, 1996 (ISBN 1-57387-020-X), *Engineering*, 1995 (ISBN 1-57837-008-0), *Health Sciences*, 1995 (ISBN 1-57387-001-3), and *Agriculture* (ISBN 1-57837-000-5).

Leveraging Know-how: The Internet's Role in the Corporate Knowledgebase, Jean Graef, 1996, The Montague Institute, 18 Main St., P.O. Box 8, Montague, MA 01351-0008, 413-367-0245, email: jgraef@montague.com, Internet: http://www.montague.com, $30.

Secrets of the Super Searchers: The Accumulated Wisdom of 23 of the World's Top Online Searchers,* Reva Basch, 1994. Eight Bit Books, 462 Danbury Rd., Wilton, CT 06897-2126, ISBN 0-910965-12-9, a combination of tips and tricks and confirmation that you have been doing it right.

UKOLUG Quick Guide to the Internet, 4th ed., Phil Bradley, UK Online User Group, c/o Christine Baker, The Old Chapel, Walden, West Burton, Leyburn DL8 4LE, UK, e-mail: CABaker@UKOLUG.demo.co.uk, £16 nonmember in UK, £20 nonmember in Europe, £24 nonmember rest of world, ISBN 1-870254-08-2.

Using the World Wide Web and Creating Home Pages: A How-To-Do-It Manual for Librarians, Ray E. Metz and Gail Junion-Metz, 1995, Neal-Schuman Publishers, $39.95, ISBN 1-55570-241-4.

The Whole Internet User's Guide and Catalog,* 2nd ed., Ed Krol, 1994, O'Reilly, ISBN 1-56592-063-5, the first and still one of the best guides to the Internet.

Outsourcing

Managing Information Technology Investments with Outsourcing, Mchdil Khoerowpour, 1995, Idea Group Publishing, $60, ISBN 1-878289-20-9.

Outsourcing Cataloging, Authority Work, and Physical Processing: A Checklist of Considerations, Marie A. Kascus and Dawn Hale, eds., 1995, ALA, $13.50 members, $15 nonmembers, ISBN 0-8389-3449-8.

Outsourcing Library Technical Services: A How-to-Do-It Manual for Librarians, by Arnold Hirson and Barbara Winters, New York: Neal-Schuman, 1996, ISBN 1-55570-221-X, $45, accompanying disk of ready to import RFP specifications, ISBN 1-55570-272-4, $20.

Alternative Careers/Information Brokers

The Burwell World Directory of Information Brokers, 1995-96*, Burwell Enterprises, $99.50 (ISBN 0-938519-11-5).

Careers in Other Fields for Librarians, Rhoda Garoogian, 1985, ALA, ISBN 0-8389-0431-9.

The EIRENE Directory (European Information Researchers' Network), £55, First Contact Ltd., UK, 44-71- 490-5519, fax: 44-71-490-4610.

Extending the Librarian's Domain: A Survey of Emerging Occupation Opportunities for Librarians and Information Professionals, Forest Woody Horton Jr., 1994, SLA Occasional Papers Series 4, $23 members, $29 nonmembers, ISBN 0-87111-419-4.

The FISCAL Directory of Fee-Based Research and Document Supply Services, 4th ed., 1993, Steve Coffman and Pat Weidensohler, County of Los Angeles Public Library, $65, ISBN 0-8389-2161-2, ISSN 1067-7674.

Making It on Your Own: Surviving and Thriving the Ups and Downs of Being Self-Employed, Paul and Sarah Edwards, 1992, Jeremy P. Tarcher, ISBN 0-87477-636-8.

Mind Your Own Business: A Guide for the Information Entrepreneur, Alice Sizer Warner, Neal-Schuman, 1987, ISBN 1-555-70014-4; business plans, money, sales and marketing, pitfalls to avoid, management issues

Opening New Doors: Alternative Careers for Librarians, Ellis Mount, editor, Special Libraries Association, 1993, ISBN 0-87111-408-9; profiles of 12 entrepreneurs and 16 workers in nontraditional positions.

Health Science

Current Practice in Health Sciences Librarianship, 1994-, MLA, v. 1: Reference and Information Services in Health Sciences Libraries, M. Sandra Wood, ed., ISBN 0-8108-2765-4. Future volumes include educational services, information access and delivery, collection development, acquisitions, bibliographic management, health sciences environment and librarianship, administration and management.

Handbook of Medical Library Practice, 4th ed., Louise Darling, ed., 1982, MLA, ISBN 0-912176-11-3, 3 volumes: technical services, public services, health sciences librarianship and administration.

Health Industry QuickSource, QuickSource Press, 415-851-2556, fax: 415-851-9347; descriptions and contact information for periodicals, CD-ROM, online databases, updated annually, 1,000 pages; $225 $180 public libraries and nonprofit organizations.

Information Sources in the Medical Sciences, 4th ed., Leslie Morton and Shane Godbolt, eds., 1992, Bowker-Saur, $100, ISBN 0-86291-596-1.

Law

Basics of Law Librarianship (Haworth Series in Special Librarianship, v. 2), Deborah S. Panella, 1991, Haworth Press, ISBN 0-86656-9898.

Building Your Law Library: A Step-by-Step Guide, Voges, Mickie A., Chicago: American Bar Association, 1988, ISBN 0-89707-361-4; (videotape also available).

The Legal Researcher's Internet Directory, Josh Blackman, 718-399-6136, $49.95.

Managing the Private Law Library 1993: Managing in a Changing Economy, Practicing Law Institute.

Manual of Law Librarianship: The Use and Organization of Legal Literature, Elizabeth M. Moys, ed., GK Hall for the British and Irish Association of Law Librarians.

Reflections on Law Librarianship: A Collection of Interviews, Marjorie Garson, et al., 1988, FB Rothman.

Public and School Libraries

Neal-Schuman How-To-Do-It Manuals for Librarians: trustees, boards, managing time.
The School Librarian's Sourcebook, Claire Rudin, 1990, RR Bowker, ISBN 0-835227111.

Miscellaneous

Business Information, How to Find It, How to Use It, 2nd ed., Michael R. Lavin, Oryx Press, 1992, $38.50, ISBN 8-89774-643-0.
Competitor Intelligence: How to Get It, How to Use It*, 2nd ed., Leonard M. Fuld, 1994, Wiley, $24.95, ISBN 0-471-585-09-2.
Directory of Library Automation Software, Systems, and Services, Pamela Cibbarelli, editor, Information Today, Inc., 1996, $79, ISBN 1-57387-021-8.
Find It Fast: How to Uncover Expert Information on Any Subject, 3rd ed., Robert I. Berkman, Harper Collins, 1994, $12, ISBN 0-06-0964863
How to Find Information About Companies, Washington Researchers, 202-333-3499, 3 volumes, $395 per volume; sources, techniques, case studies.
International Business Information: How to Find It, How to Use It, Ruth Pagell and Michael Halperin, Oryx Press, 1994, $74.50, ISBN 0-89774-736-4.
New York Public Library Book of How and Where to Look it Up, Sherwood Harris, McMillan, 1991, $30, ISBN 0-13-614728-3.
Patent, Copyright and Trademark: A Desk Reference to Intellectual Property Law, Stephen Elias, 1996, Nolo Press, $24.95, ISBN 0-87337-236-0
The Whole Library Handbook 2*, George M. Eberhart, ed., 1995, ALA, ISBN 0-8389-0646-X.

JOURNALS OF SPECIAL INTEREST TO SOLOS

The One-Person Library*, SMR International; if you subscribe to just one journal, this is the one it should be.
Flying Solo*, SOLO Librarians Division, SLA, quarterly, free with membership.
Corporate Library Update*, Library Journal, P.O. Box 1983, Danbury, CT 06813, 800-722-2346, 2/month, $69.
InfoManage: The International Management Newsletter for the Information Services Executive*, SMR International, monthly, $77.50/year for new subscribers, $87.50 Canada, $97.50 rest of world; although not

written just for SOLOs, this has some excellent management techniques and ways to approach upper managers.

Rural Library Services Newsletter, NORWELD, 251 N. Main St., Bowling Green, OH 43402, 419-352-2903, email: shill@ohionet.org, $20/year

Rural Libraries, semi-annual, $10/year, Center for the Study of Rural Librarianship.

OTHER JOURNALS OF INTEREST

Against the Grain, Katina Strauch, Citadel Station, Charleston, SC 29409, 803-723-3536; about libraries, publishers, jobbers, subscription services, 5/year, $30 U.S., $40 foreign, ISSN 1043-2094.

American Libraries (ALA) 0002-9769.

ASLIB Proceedings (UK), 0001-253X.

Bottom Line: A Financial Magazine for Librarians, Neal-Schuman Publishers, quarterly, ISSN 0888-045X.

Bulletin of the MLA 0025-7338.

Business Information Alert: Sources, Strategies, and Signposts for Information Professionals, Alert Publications, 1042-0746, 10/year, $152 U.S., $99 for public and academic libraries.

Canadian Library Journal, 0008-4352.

Computers in Libraries, Information Today, Inc., 1041-7915, 10/year, $87.95 U.S., $97.95 Canada and Mexico, $105.95 rest of world, includes Internet Librarian and CD-ROM Librarian, Libraries of the Future, Current Cites.

Database, 6/year, Online, Inc., $49.50, http://www.onlineinc.com/database

The Electronic Library, Learned Information Ltd., 0264-0473, 6/year, $120 U.S.

Emergency Librarian, Rockland Press, Box C34069, Dept. 284, Seattle WA 98124-1069, 604-825-0266, fax: 604-925-0566, 284-810 W. Broadway, Vancouver BC V5Z 4C9, Canada, library services for children and young adults, 5/year, $49 billed, $44 prepaid.

Health Care on the Internet, The Haworth Press, Inc., quarterly, $38 individual, $85 libraries.

Infomediary, Pergamon, quarterly, Canadian

Information Advisor, R. Berkman, editor, FIND/SVP, Inc., 625 Avenue of the Americas, New York, NY 10011, 212-645-4500, monthly, $130/year, 1050-1576.

Information Broker, Burwell Enterprises, 6/year (formerly *Journal of Fee-Based Information Services*).

The Information Report, Washington Researchers, Ltd.

Information Technology Newsletter, Idea Group Publishing, 4811 Jonestown Road, Suite 230, Harrisburg, PA 17109-1751, 717-541-9150, fax: 717-541-9159, e-mail: 75364.3150@compuserve.com, semi-annually, free.

Information Today*, Information Today, Inc., 11/year, $47.95, U.S., $59.95 Canada and Mexico, $65 rest of world, 8755-6286, news about the library and information world, book reviews.

Information World Review, Information Today, Inc., 11/year, 0950-9879, $62.95 U.S., $72.95 Canada and Mexico, European information industry, reports in French, Dutch, and German.

Internet Reference Services Quarterly, The Haworth Press, Inc., $36 individual, $48 libraries.

Journal of Business and Finance Librarianship, The Haworth Press, Inc., quarterly, $36 individual, $75 libraries.

Journal of Interlibrary Loan, Document Delivery and Information Supply, The Haworth Press, Inc., quarterly, $36 individual, $60 libraries.

Journal of Library Administration, The Haworth Press, Inc., quarterly, $40 individual, $105 libraries, 0193-0826.

Journal of Religious and Theological Information, The Haworth Press, Inc., biannual, $24 individual, $48 libraries.

Kirkus Reviews, 200 Park Ave. Co., New York, NY 10003, fax: 212-979-1352, 24/yr., adult and children's prepublication book reviews.

Legal Information Alert: What's New in Legal Publications, Databases, and Research Techniques, 0883-1297, 10/year, Alert Publications, $159/year.

Legal Information Management Reports, Library Specialists, Inc., Marietta, GA, 770-578-6200, fax: 770-578- 6263, quarterly.

legal.online, Legal Communications Ltd., Philadelphia, 800-722-7670, e-mail: lawline@ix.netcom.com, monthly, $149/year; "first newsletter dedicated to guiding lawyers through the maze of legal resources and information on the Internet."

Legal Reference Services Quarterly, The Haworth Press, Inc., $40 individual, $115 libraries.

Library Journal, this is the other publication you should get to stay abreast of the non-SOLO library world, worth the price just for the reviews and columns.

Library Management 0143-5124, MCB University Press, Ltd., UK, expensive.

*Library Management Quarterly**, SLA LM Division, free with membership.

Library Trends 0024-2594, University of Illinois at Urbana-Champaign, Graduate School of Library and Information Science, $67/year quarterly, scholarly, but very readable.

Link-Up: The Newsmagazine for Users of Online Services, CD-ROM, and the Internet, 0739-988X, Information Today, Inc., 6/year, $28.95 US, $35 Canada and Mexico.

Marketing Library Services (MLS), Information Today, Inc., 8/year, $65

Marketing Treasures, Chris Olson and Associates, bimonthly, 0895-1799, $54 US, $59 Canada, $66 rest of world, $24 extra for computer disk with clip art or disk available alone for $36, marketing hints and 25-30 clip art graphics per year.

Medical Reference Services Quarterly, The Haworth Press, Inc., $32 individual, $105 libraries.

Online, 6/mo., Online, Inc., $49.50, http://www.onlineinc.onlinemag.

Online User: A Practical Magazine for Knowledge Workers, 0896-4149, Online Inc., 6/year, $24 U.S. and Canada, $42 Mexico and Central America, $50 rest of world.

Publishers Weekly Religion Bookline, PO Box 6457, Torrance, CA 90504-0457, 800-278-2991 or 310-978- 6916, fax: 310-978-6901, 2/month, $79 U.S., higher rest of world.

Research Advisor: Information Solutions for Today's Legal Professionals, Alert Publications, Inc., 6/year, $49 U.S., $59 Canada and Mexico, $20 elsewhere.

*Searcher: The Magazine for Database Professionals**, Information Today, Inc., 1070-4795, 10/year, $55.95 U.S., $67 Canada and Mexico, $78 rest of world, invaluable for what's new in online and for Barbara Quint's unique point of view.

Supervisory Management, American Management Association, monthly, 0039-5919, very helpful tips for supervising—and for dealing with your supervisor.

It is also a good idea for librarians to read the journals of the area they are working in and some of the most important business journals, such as *Forbes, Fortune, Business Week*, and *Harvard Business Review*. Another must is *The Wall Street Journal*. If you cannot take time to read the articles, at least scan the headlines to see what is being talked about. You can then mention to someone that you saw it in the *Journal*, making you sound more informed than you are. At Bailey, I tried to scan a number of the journals we receive, such as *Hydrocarbon Processing*, *Control*, *Control Engineering*, *InTech*, etc. This gave me an idea of the issues that are important in the field as well as providing input to my weekly news for management.

Here are some specialized titles recommended in various books. I have not looked at them so cannot recommend them myself, but if you are involved in these areas, you should take a look at them.

Records Management

IMC Journal, *Inform*, *International Journal of Information Management*, *Record Facts Update*, *Records and Retrieval Report*, *Records Management Quarterly*, *American Archivist*, *Archives*, *Information Processing and Management*, *International Journal of Micrographics and Optical Technology*, *Journal of Management Information Systems*, *Microcomputers for Information Management*

Law Librarianship

AALL Directory and Handbook, *AALL Newsletter*, *Law Library Journal*, *Legal Information Alert*, *Legal Information Management Index*, *Legal Information Management Report*, *PLL Perspectives* (Private Law Libraries special interest section, AALL), *State, Court and County Law Libraries Newsletter* (special interest section, AALL), *Technical Services Law Librarian* (Technical Services special interest section, AALL), *Trends in Law Library Management and Technology* (FB Rothman), *Current Publications in Legal and Related Fields*, *Advance Bibliography of Law and Related Fields*, *Bowker's Legal Publishing Preview*, *Practical Law Books Review*

Law Book Jobbers and Publishers

Ballen, Blackwell North America, Booklink (Austin TX), William W. Gaunt and Sons Inc., William S. Hein and Co., Fred B. Rothman and Co., Claitor's Used Books (Baton Rouge), Lawbook Exchange Ltd. (New York), John R. Mara Law Books (Dallas), Oceana

Church Librarianship

Christian Bookseller and Librarian, *Christian Librarian*, *Christian Periodical Index*, *Christian Review*

Religious Publishers (and Their Denominations)

Augsburg Publishing House (Lutheran), The Bethany Press (Disciples of Christ), Abingdon Press (United Methodist), The Brethren Press (Church of the Brethren), Broadman Press (Southern Baptist), Concordia Publishing House (Lutheran), Gospel Publishing House (Assembly of God), Fortress Press (Lutheran), Judson Press (American Baptist), John Knox Press (Presbyterian), Seabury Press (Episcopal), Sweet Publishing Co., (Church of Christ), Westminster Press (Presbyterian)

PUBLISHERS

Alert Publications, Inc., 401 W. Fullerton Parkway, Suite 1403E, Chicago, IL 60614-2805, 312-525-7594, fax: 312-525-7015, e-mail: 72164.507@compuserve.com.

American Library Association, 50 E. Huron St., Chicago, IL 60611, 800-545-2433, Canada: order through CLA, 613-232-9625, ext. 310, primarily for public libraries, but some publications are of interest to all.

Books on Tape, Inc., P.O. Box 7900, Newport Beach, CA 92658, 800-541-5525, 310-799-0796, fax: 714-548-6574, unabridged audio-books.

R.R. Bowker (Reed Reference), 121 Chanlon Rd., New Providence, NJ 07974, 800-521-8110, fax: 908-665-6688, e-mail: info@reedref.com, Internet: http://www.reedref.com, wide range of reference books, especially in library/book area.

Bowker-Saur (Reed Reference), 121 Chanlon Rd., New Providence, NJ 07974, 800-521-8110, 908-464-6800, fax: 908-665-6688, e-mail: info@reedref.com, Internet: http://www.reedref.com; German-speaking Europe: K.G. Saur Verlag, 49-89-76802-0. fax: 49-89-76902-250; rest of world: 441-342-330-100, fax: 441-342-330-198, library/ information science books, IFLA proceedings (European focus).

Center for the Study of Rural Librarianship, The Small Library Development Center, Clarion University of Pennsylvania, Clarion, PA 16214, a mix of scholarly and very useful publications, including bibliographies on subjects such as rural library service, public relations, administration, technical service, etc., $2 each.

The Haworth Press, Inc., 10 Alice St., Binghamton, NY 13904-1580, 800-342-9678, fax: 800-895-0582, 607-722-6362, e-mail: getinfo@ haworth.com, books and serials on reference and technical services.

InfoManage/SMR International, Murray Hill Station, P.O. Box 948, New York, NY 10156, 212-683-6285, fax: 212-683-2987, e-mail: 73042.67@compuserve.com, publications especially for SOLOs and library managers.

Information Today, Inc., 143 Old Marlton Pike, Medford, NJ 08055, 800-300-9868, 609-654-6266, fax: 609-654-4309.

Libraries Unlimited, P.O. Box 6633, Englewood, CO 80155-6633, 800-237-6124, 303-770-1220, fax: 303-220-8843, library textbooks and reference works, much for educators and school librarians.

Marquis Who's Who (Reed Reference), 121 Chanlon Rd., New Providence, NJ 07974, 800-521-8110, 908-464-6800, fax: 908-665-6688, e-mail: info@reedref.com, Internet: http://www.reedref.com, biographical reference books.

Neal-Schuman Publishers, Inc., 100 Varick St., New York, NY 1–13, 212-925-8650, fax: 800-584-2414, e-mail: neal-schuman@icm.com, mostly library and information science books.

Online, Inc., 462 Danbury Rd., Wilton, CT 06897-2126, 800-248-8466, 203-761-1466, fax: 203-761-1444, e-mail: ngarman@well.com, Internet: http://www.onlineinc.com.

O'Reilly and Associates, Inc., 103 Morris St., Suite A, Sebastopol, CA 95472, 800-998-9938, 707-829-0515, e-mail: nuts@ora.com, Internet and computer books.

Public Library Association, a division of the American Library Association, 50 E. Huron St., Chicago, IL 60611, 800-545-2433

Special Libraries Association, 1700 18th St., NW, Washington, DC 20009-2508, 202-234-4700. fax 202-265-9317, e-mail: sla1@capcon.net.

Teach 'em, 160 E. Illinois St., Chicago, IL 60611, 800-225-3775, 312-467-0424, fax: 312-467-9271, audiotapes from ALA and elsewhere

HW Wilson Co., 950 University Ave., Bronx, NY 10452, 800-367-6770, 718-588-8400, fax: 718-590-Gale Research Inc., P.O. Box 33477, Detroit, MI 48232-5477, 800-877-GALE, 313-961-2242, fax: 800-414-5043, Internet: http://www.thomson.com/gale.html, mostly reference books.

Internet and Listservs

Here are many useful Internet sites that I have found, both in my surfing and from monitoring listservs and getting suggestions from other librarians. They should give you a sampling and flavor of what is out there and encourage you to surf for others. I have looked at many of the sites to make sure they are what they say they are, but those that I have not seen personally were recommended by reliable sources. There is no guarantee that they will still be available when you read this, but something similar probably will be.

They are arranged as follows:

- finding aids
- library-related information
  library listservs
  SLA addresses
  SLA chapters
  SLA divisions
  SOLOLIB-L
  SLA home pages
- business information
- church and synagogue library information
- legal information
- medical information
- world information
- reference
- community networks and free-nets

FINDING AIDS

These are search engines that allow you to find out where to look for specific information. New ones appear every day, but these are some that I like.

Alta Vista (http://altavista.digital.com): allows you to search either Web sites or Usenet newsgroups—and you can look at the news items even if you don't subscribe to the newsgroup—probably the best as of this writing

DejaNews (http://dejanews2.dejanews.com): use for searching Usenet newsgroups

Electric Library (http://www.elibrary.com): search newspapers, magazines, etc., $10/mo. for unlimited searching after free trial

GTE SuperPages (http://yp.gte.net): yellow pages

HotBot (http://www.hot.bot.com): allows limiting of searches by date, type of file extension, and terms that "must not" appear

LISZT, Directory of e-mail discussion groups (listservs) (http://www.liszt.com/): covers over 50,000 lists from nearly 2,000 sites (I entered "librarian or librarians" and got 86 lists)

MetaCrawler (http://www.cs.washington.edu/research/projects/ai/meta crawler/www/home.html): a brand-new summer 1996 meta-search engine

Savvy Search (http://www.cs.colostate.edu/~dreiling/smartform.html): neat meta-search engine, accesses up to 19 search engines at once

Search.com (http://www.search.com): from C|Net, organizes over 250 of the biggest and best search engines, by category, with evaluative comments and Top Picks, customizable

Switchboard (http://www.switchboard.com): white and yellow pages, fast

Webcrawler (http://www.webcrawler.com): indexes all sites on the Web, less comprehensive than Alta Vista, but sometimes that is good

WebFerret (http://www.muskrat.com): worldwide search engine, heavy on non-U.S. sources

Yahoo (http://www.yahoo.com): widely cited, but it only indexes sites that have been submitted to it

LIBRARY-RELATED INFORMATION

Surfing the Internet, an introduction for librarians, by Jean Armour Polly, ftp://nysernet.org,cd/pub/resources/guides/surfing or gopher://nyser net.org, special collections: Internet help, surfing

British Library, http://portico.bl.uk

BUBL's LIS Page (Bulletin Board for Library Information Services, U.K.), http://www.bubl.bath.aca.uk/BUBL/Library.html

Linda Hall Library (very large private science library in Kansas City, new home of the Engineering Societies Library collection), http://www.lhl.lib.mo.us

ICONnect, from American Association of School Librarians, a division of ALA, gopher://ericir.syr.edu:7070

Library Humor, gopher://snymorva.cs.snymor.edu—/library services/ library humor

Library Computer Accessories on the Internet, http://www.auburn.edu/~fostecd/docs/accessories.html

Library Listservs

To subscribe, send a message to the e-mail address, no subject, put "subscribe LISTNAME first name last name" as the message for complete list; see Library-Oriented Lists and Electronic Serials, http://info.lib. uh.edu/liblists/home.htm

AIB-CUR (Italian librarians), listserv@icineca

ACQLIBS (Australian acquisitions librarians), mailserv@ qut.edu.au

ANZ-LAW-LIBRARIANS (academic law librarians in Australia and New Zealand), ANZ-LAW-LIBRARIANS@uow.edu.

APLA LIST (Atlantic Provinces Library Association, Canada), mailserve@ac.dal.ca

ARCLIB-L (Irish and U.K. architectural librarians), listserv@irlearn. ucd.ie

ARLIS-L (Art Libraries Association of North America), listserv @ukcc.uky.edu

ARLISANZ (Arts Libraries Society of Australia and New Zealand), majordomo@info.anu.edu.au

ASIALIB (Asian librarianship in Australia), majordomo@info. anu.edu.au

ASIS-L, listserv@vmd.cso.uiuc.edu

ATLANTIS (church and synagogue libraries): listserv@harvada. harvard.edu

ATLAS-L (American Theological Library Association), listserv@ harvarda.harvard.edu

BACKSERV (serials back issues and duplicate exchange), listserv@ sun.readmore.com

BUSLIB-L (business librarians), listserv@idbsu.idbsu.edu

CANMEDLIB (Canadian Health Sciences Libraries), listserv@ morgan.ucs.mun.ca

CDLAN (CD-ROM on LANs), maiser@zb.ub.uni-dortmund.de

CHINF-L (chemical information sources), listserv@iubvm.ucs. indiana.edu

DENTALIB (Dental Librarians List), listproc@usc.edu

FEDREF-L (Federal Reference Librarians Discussion List), listserv @loc.gov

FLIN-L (Australian Federal Libraries Information network), listproc@ nla.gov.au

GOVDOC-L (government documents), listserv@psuvm.psu.edu

ILL-L, listserv@uvmvm.uvm.edu

INETBIB (Internet usage in German or German-speaking libraries), maiser@zb.ub.uni-dortmund.de

INT-LAW (foreign and international law librarians), listserv@ uminn1.edu

IWETEL (Spanish electronic forum for libraries), iwetel-request@ gorbea.spritel.es

LAW-LIB, listserv@ucdavis.edu

LAWLIBREF-L, listserv@acc.wuacc.edu

LIBREF-L, listerv@listserv.kent.edu

LIS-LAW, mailbase@mailbase.ac.uk

LIS-MEDICAL (U.K. Health Sciences Libraries), mailbase@maibase. ac.uk

LIS-SCITECH (U.K. Science and Technology Libraries), mailbase @mailbase.ac.uk

LIB-L (German and German-speaking libraries), maiser@zb.ub.uni-dortmund.de

LIBJOBS (from IFLA), listserv@infoserv.nlc-bnc-ca, archives at: http://www.nlc-bnc.ca/cgi-bin/ifla-lwgate/LIBJOBS/

LIBPER-L (library personnel and organizational development), listserv@ksuvm.ksu.edu

LIBSUP-L (library support staff), listproc@washington.edu

LITA-L (Library and Information Technology Associations), listserv@uicvm.uic.edu

MEDIBIB-L (German medical libraries discussion, in German), med bib-l-request@uni-muenster.de

MEDLIB-L, listserv@ubvm.cc.buffalo.edu

MLA-L (Music Library Association), listserv@iubvm.ucs.indiana.edu

OZBIZ (Australian business librarians), listproc@gu.edu.au

PUBLIB, listserv@nysernet.org

PUBLIB-NET (Internet use in public libraries), listserv@nysernet.org

PUBYAC (library services to children and young adults in public libraries), listserv@nysernet.org

REFLIBS (Australian reference librarians), reflibs-request@newcastle. edu.au

TECH (technical services in special libraries), listserv@ukcc.uky.edu

STUMPERS (difficult reference questions—lots of traffic), mailserv@ crf.cuis.edu

SWALL-L (Southwest Association of Law Libraries), mailserv@ post-office.uh.edu

SYSLIBS (Australian systems librarians), syslibs-request@library. adelaide.edu.au

TQMLIB, listserv@cms.cc.wayne.edu

WAIN (library and information profession in Western Australia), listproc@info.curtin.edu.au

SLA Addresses

http://www.sla.org—information about divisions, chapters, services, conferences, continuing education, etc.

e-mail: sla1@capcon.net

jobline, SLAJOB, listserv@iubvm.ucs.indiana.edu

SLAJOB home page:http//www.indiana.edu/~slajob/

SLA Chapters

Boston Chapter, SLA-BOSTON, listserv@babson.edu

Central Pennsylvania Chapter, SLA-L, listserv@psuvm.psu.edu

Cleveland Chapter, telnet: freenet-in-a.cwru.edu, login as guest, choose Library, Special Libraries Association

Connecticut Valley Chapter, SLACVC-L, listserve@yalevm.cis.yale.edu

Fairfield County Chapter, FCCSLA, majordome@estnet.com

Heart of America Chapter, SLAHOA-L, listserv@ukanvm.cc.ukans.edu

Illinois Chapter, SLA-ILLINOIS, listproc@prairienet.org

Indiana Chapter, INSLA, listserv@indycms.iupui.edu

International Information Exchange Caucus, European Chapter, International Relations Committee, EURSLA-L, listserv@psuvm.psu.edu

Kentucky Chapter, KYSLA, listserv@ukcc.uky.edu

New Jersey Chapter, SLA-NJ, listserv@hslc.org

New York Chapter, SLANY-L listproc@metro.org

North California Chapter, NCLA-LIB, listproc@ucdavis.edu

North Carolina Chapter, NCSLA, listserv@gibbs.oit.unc.edu, http:// ils.unc.edu/ncsla/nchome.html

Philadelphia Chapter, SLA-PHIL, listserv@hslc.org

Princeton-Trenton Chapter, SLA-PT, listserv@hslc.org

Rocky Mountain Chapter, RMSLA, rmsla-request@tali.ushsc.edu

San Diego Chapter, SLA-SD, listproc@qualcomm.com

St. Louis Metropolitan Area Chapter. SLA-ARCH, listproc@mail.wustl.
edu

South Carolina Chapter, SCLIBN-L, listserv@univscvm.csd.scarolina.edu

Toronto Chapter, SLA-TORONTO, majordomo@worl.mmltd.com

Western Canada Chapter, SLA-WCC, listproc@ppc.ubc.ca

Western Michigan Chapter, WMICHSLA, listserv@msu.edu

Virginia Chapter, SLA-VIRGINIA, obenhaus@vt.edu, send name,
address, phone, e-mail address

SLA Divisions and Caucuses

Aerospace Division, SLA-AERO, listserv@sti.nasa.gov

Association Information Services Caucus, listserver@abanet.org

Biological Sciences Division, BSDNET-L, listserv@listserv.ncsu.edu

Business and Finance Division, SLABF-L, listsev@psuvm.psu.edu

Education Division, SLAEDD-L, listserv@nervm.nerdc.ufl.edu

Engineering Division, SLA-ENG, majordomo@iee.org.uk

Environment and Resource Management Division, ERMD, listproc
@mail.auburn.edu

Food, Agriculture and Nutrition, SLA-FAN, listserv@ukcc.uky.edu

Information Technology Division, SLAITE-L, listserv@babson.edu

Technical Services Section, Information Technology Division, SLA-
TECH, listserv@ukcc.uky.edu

Legal Division, SLA-LAW, majordomo@albertus.lawlib.uh.edu

Library Management Division, LDSLA-L, listserv@psuvm.psu.edu

Museums, Arts and Humanities Division, MAHD, listserv@gibbs.oit.
unc.edu

Natural History Caucus, NHC-SLA, aschiff2cas.calacademy.org

News Division, NEWSLIB, listserv@gibbs.oit.unc.edu, http://www.
nando.net/prof/poynter/nd/ndmenu.html

Nuclear Science Division, NUCSCI-L, listserv@bnl.gov

Petroleum and Energy Resources Division, PER_FORU, PER-req
@TUred.pa.utulsa.edu, put "register me" in subject line, include name,
address (Internet and mailing), phone, fax

Physics-Astronomy-Mathematics Division, SLA-PAM, david.e.stern@
yale.edu

Science-Technology Division, SLA-ST,listproc@indigo.lib.lsu.edu

Social Science Division, SOCSCI-L, majordomo@indiana.edu

SOLO Librarians Division, SOLOLIB-L, listserv@silverplatter. com

Telecommunications Division, SLA-TEL, swhite@qualcomm.com

SOLOLIB-L details, as of 5/19/96

601 subscribers; 513 U.S., 83 Canada, 22 rest of world (Australia, Canada, Denmark, Finland, France, Germany, Iceland, India, Netherlands, Norway, South Africa, Spain, Sweden, U.K.); .com 261, .edu 85, gov 15, .mil 7, .net 69, .org 60, .us 24

SLA Home Pages

Arizona Chapter: http://www.medlib.arizona.edu/SLA/

Florida and Caribbean Chapter: http://amelia.db.erau.edu/sla/index.html

Information Technology Division: http//www.library.miami.edu/ITE/home.htm

Legal Division: http://www.law.uh.edu/sla/

Michigan Chapter: http://www.umd.umich.edu/lin/sla

New Jersey Chapter: http://www.hslc.org/slanj.html

News Division: http://www.nando.net/prof/poynter/ndndmenu. html

North Carolina Chapter: http://ils.unc.edu/ncsla/nchome.html

Oklahoma Chapter: http://www.ikstate.edu/cis_home/lgp/okslahome.html

Physics-Astronomy-Mathematics Division: http://galileo.ifa.hawaii.edu/pamnet/quik.html

San Andreas Chapter: http://www.san-andreas-sla.org/

San Diego Chapter: http://ww.qualcomm.com/~sla/sla-sd/

San Francisco Bay Region Chapter: http://witloof.sjsu.edu/proj/sfsla/main.html

Southern California Chapter: http://outworld.compuserve.com:80/homepage/rayhewitt/

Telecommunications Division: http://www.qualcomm.com/~sla/sal-tel/indextel.html

Texas Chapter: http://www.eden.com/~texassla/

Toronto Chapter: http://www.infomart.ca/sla/

BUSINESS INFORMATION

Addresses for U.S. public companies, http://networth.galt.com/www/home/info/insider/publicco.htm

ASI's Market Research Center, http://www.asiresearch.com

Big Yellow, Web access to yellow pages from throughout the U.S., http://www.bigyellow.com

Business Researcher's Interests, from Yogesh Malhotra at University of Pittsburgh, Katz Graduate School of Business, http://www.pitt.edu/~malhotra/interest.html

Dun and Bradstreet Information Services, http://www.dbisna.com

EDGAR, U.S. Securities and Exchange Commission (electronic copies of most filings), http://www.sec.gov/edaux/searches.htm

Find/SVP, market research, http://www.findsvp.com

Gartner Group and Dataquest, market research and information, http://www.gartner.com or http://www.dataquest.com

Hoover's Online, http://www.hoovers.com, company profiles, stock quotes, SEC documents, directory of 10,000 companies, IPO documents, links to corporate Web sites; some services available free, the rest by subscription ($9.95/month)

Japan Corporate Information Bank (information on Japanese corporations), http://www.dir.co.jp

Japan External Trade Organization (JETRO), http://www. jetro.go.jp/

Layperson's guide to Online Market Research, http://www.vivamus.com

Open Market's Commercial Sites Index, http://www.directory.net

Price Waterhouse's Doing Business In . . . guides, http://www.tpusa.com/pw/mmenu.html

Society of Competitive Intelligence Professionals (SCIP), http://www.scip.org

World Bank, gopher://gopher.worldbank.org

CHURCH AND SYNAGOGUE LIBRARY INFORMATION

ATLANTIS (church and synagogue libraries): listserv@harvarda.harvard.edu

Catholic Information Center, http://www.catholic.net

HASAFRAN (Association of Jewish Libraries), listserv@lists.acs.ohio-state.edu

Jewish Communications Network, http://www.jcn18.com

LEGAL INFORMATION

AALLNET, American Association of Law Libraries, http://lawlib.wuacc.edu/aallnet/aallnet.html

ARCLIB-L (Irish and U.K. architectural librarians), listserv@irlearn.ucd.ie

AIB-CUR (Italian librarians), listserv@icineca

ANZ-LAW-LIBRARIANS (Academic law librarians in Australia and New Zealand), ANZ-LAW-

Cindy Chick's Law-Related Internet Resources, http://www.well.com/user/cchick/sources.html

Cornell University's Legal Information Institute, http://www.law.cornell. edu/lii.table.html

FLIN-L (Australian Federal Libraries Information network), listproc @nla.gov.au

Index of legal sites, http://starbase.ingress.com/tsw/road.html

INT-LAW (foreign and international law librarians), listserv@uminn1.edu

LAW-LIB, listserv@ucdavis.edu

LAWLIBREF-L, listserv@acc.wuacc.edu

LIBRARIANS@uow.edu.au

LIS-LAW, mailbase@mailbase.ac.uk

OZBIZ (Australian business librarians), listproc@gu.edu.au

Seamless Website, Law and Legal Resources, http://seamless.com/

Villanova Center for Information Law and Policy's Federal Web Locator, http://ming.lwa.vill.edu

WAIN (library and information profession in Western Australia), listproc @info.curtin.edu.au

Washlaw (full-text law journals, case law), http://lawlib.wuacc.edu/wash law/washlaw.html

West's Legal Dictionary, http://www.westpub.com/ or gopher: //wld. westlaw.com

MEDICAL INFORMATION

Listservs

BACKMED, Back Issues and Duplicate Exchange Service, listserv@ sun.readmore.com

BIB-MED, Medical libraries, in Spanish, listserv@listserv.rediris.es

MEDIBIB-L (German medical libraries discussion, in German), medbib-l-request@uni-muenster.de

MEDLIB-L, Medical libraries listserv, listserv@ubvm.cc. buffalo.edu

Medical Information by Disease Name

http://www.kumc.edu:80/mmatrix/DISEASE.HTML

gopher://info.med.yeal.edu:70/11/Disciplines/Disease

http://www.scl.ncal.kaiperm.org/medadvice/index.html

Alzheimer's research: http://werple.mira.net.au/~dhs/ad.html

American College of Cardiology, http://www.acc.org

Cardiology general info, http://avnode.wustl.edu

CDC, http://www.cdc.gov

CINAHL, Embase, Psychinfo, etc.

Clinical alerts, gopher://gopher.uic.edu/11/library/clinaler

Diagnostic Test info, http://dgim-www.ucsf.edu/TestSearch.html

Emergency Room info, http://herbst7.his.ucsf.edu

FDA: http://www.fda.gov

Good medical gopher, gopher://gopher.austin.unimelb.edu.au

A Guide to the Internet for Medical Practitioners, http://www.tecc.co. uk/bmj/archive/7017ed2.htm

Hardin meta directory of Internet Health Sources: http://www.arcade. uiowa.edu/hardin-www/md.html

Harvard University Biopages: http://golgi.harvard.edu/ biopages/medi cine.html (a good starting point)

HealthGate, http://www.healthgate.com, $15/mo+25 cents per cite: includes Medline, Cancerlit, AIDSline,

Healthcare Internet Server (HI-NETS): http://www.virtueli.ca/ HI-NETS (in French, http://www.virtueli.ca/NETS)

Health Education Program (patient education materials), http:// research.med.umkc.edu/aafp/pt_edmhtml

Health Services Research Journal, http://www.xnet.com/~hret/ hsr.htm

Hospital Web: http:/demonmac.mgh.harvard.edu/hospitalweb.html

Internet Guide for the Health Professional, first ed., http://www.mid town.net/~medguide/

Japan Cancer Center, gopher://gopher.gopher.ncc.go.jp

Journal of the American Medical Association, http://www.ama-assn.org

Martindale's Health Science Guide: http://www-sci.lib.uci.edu/ HSG/HSGuide.html (includes multimedia)

MD Anderson information, http://.utmdacc.uth.tmc.edu/MDA/mdain fo.html or telnet TXCANCER.MDA.UTH.TMC.EDU

Medical Matrix: Guide to Internet Clinical Medical Resources: http:// wwwkumc.edu/mmatrix/ (from University of Kansas Medical School)

NetWellness, from UC Medical Center Libraries, drug, health, directo-ry information for the public, http://www.netwellness.uc.edu

NLM clincal alerts: http://www.swmed.edu/hom_pages/library/alerts.htm

NLM, gopher://gopher.nlm.nih.gov

Nursing, http://www.csv.warwick.ac.uk:8000/nurse-internet.html

Patient Health Info, gopher://gopher.vixen.cso.uiuc.edu/11/UI/CSF/ health/heainfo

Pathology atlas, http://www.med.uiuc.edu/titlepage.html

Pediatric Critical Care, http://.amber.medlib.arizona.edu/homepage.html

Pharmacy info, http://pharminfo.com

Physicians Assistant site, http://www.halcyon.com

Primary Care Handbook, http://www.med.ufl.edu/medinfo/baseline/hn1.html

Article: The internet: a valuable resource for the hospital librarian, Janet Ohles, *Bulletin of the Medical Library Association* 84(1):110-111, 1/96

Article: Finding medical information (Column: The Internet Express), Aggi Raeder, *Searcher* 4(4):40-43, 4/96

WORLD INFORMATION

Listservs

ACQLIBS (Australian acquisitions librarians), mailserv@ qut.edu.au

ANZ-LAW-LIBRARIANS (Academic law librarians in Australia and New Zealand), ANZ-LAW-LIBRARIANS@uow.edu.au

APLA LIST (Atlantic Provinces Library Association, Canada), mailserve@ac.dal.ca

ARLISANZ (Arts Libraries Society of Australia and New Zealand), majordomo@info.anu.edu.au

ASIALIB (Asian librarianship in Australia), majordomo@info.anu.edu.au

AW4LIB-L (Australian Web Librarians List), listproc@scu.edu.au

CANMEDLIB (Canadian Health Sciences Libraries), listserv@morgan.ucs.mun.ca

CDLAN (CD-ROM on LANs), maiser@zb.ub.uni-dortmund.de

CYBRARIAN (New Zealand Librarians Accessing Resources on the Internet), majordomo@massey.ac.nz

EURSLA-L, International Information Exchange Caucus, European Chapter, International Relations Committee, listserv@ psuvm.psu.edu

FLIN-L (Australian Federal Libraries Information network), listproc@nla.gov.au

INETBIB (Internet usage in German or German-speaking libraries), maiser@zb.ub.uni-dortmund.de

IWETEL (Spanish electronic forum for libraries), iwetel-request@gorbea.spritel.es

LIB-L (German and German-speaking libraries), maiser@zb.ub.uni-dortmund.de

LIS-MEDICAL (U.K. Health Sciences Libraries), mailbase@mailbase.ac.uk

LIS-SCITECH (U.K. Science and Technology Libraries), mailbase@mailbase.ac.uk

MEDIBIB-L (German medical libraries discussion, in German), med
bib-l-request@uni-muenster.de
MELANET-L (Middle East Librarians Association), listproc@cornell.edu
REFLIBS (Australian reference librarians), reflibs-request@newcastle.
edu.au
SYSLIBS (Australian systems librarians), syslibsrequest@ library.adelaide.
edu.au

General Information

Electronic Embassy, http://wwwembassy.org
Embassy Page, http://www.globescope.com/web/gsis
Penn World Tables, University of Toronto, demographics, economic and
social statistics, http://cansim.epas.utoronto.ca:5680/pst
Political Leaders of the World (names, birth and death dates, by
country), http://130.89.41.97/~lanzing/politica/00index.htm
Rulers of the World (names, birth and death dates, by country), http://
www.geopages.com/Athens1058/rulers.html

Area or Country information

Asia-Pacific

Asia-Pacific Information, http://asiabiz.com, http://wwwaisa-directory.
com/~bruno
Australia, http://www.nla.gov.au/oz/gov
China on the Web, http://www.hk.net/~drummond/milesj/ china.html
Chinascape: http://harmony.wit.com/chinascape
Hong Kong Government, http://wwwinfo.gov.hk
Japanese Information http://www.ntt.jp/japan/index.html
New Zealand, http://www.gov.nz
Other New Zealand and Australia sites are available at http://www.
vuw.ac.nz/~agsmith/, home page of Alastair Smith, Department of
Library and Information Studies, Victoria University of Wellington
Taiwan: http://peacock.tnjc.edu.tw/roc_sites.html, http://gio.gov.tw

The Americas

Canada's Parliament, http://www.parl.gc.ca or gopher://gopher.parl.gc.
ca (tours, transcripts, not email)
Latin America and Caribbean Information Center (from Florida
International University), gopher://gopher.fiu.edu:70/acadinfo/lacci
Latin American Network (from University of Texas), http://lanic.
utexas.edu

Mexico and Central America, http://www.mexonline.com/grupoam1.htm
Micromedia Limited (Canada's Information People), http://www.mmltd.com
Peruvian Web site (introduction in English or Spanish, articles in
  Spanish), http://www.rcp.net.pe
Western Canada Chapter, SLA-WCC, listproc@ppc.ubc.ca

Europe

Belgium, http://www.cais.net/usa
British Library, http://portico.bl.uk
Central and Eastern Europe Business Information Center, http://www.
  itaiep.doc.gov/eebic/ceebic.html
Denmark, http://www.info.denet.ck/dk-infoservers.html
Der Spiegel (in German), http://news.hamburg.pop.de/bda/int/spiegel/
  spiegel
European Commission: http://www.cec.lu/en/comm.html
European Union: http://www.cec.lu/en/index.html
Finland, http://www.kaapeli.fi/tiedontalo/english-20
France (maps and information), http://web.urec.france/france.htm
General information, Yellow Web, http://www.yweb.com
Ireland On-Line, http://ireland.iol.ie/resource
Italian Zip Codes, http://www.crs4.it/~france/CAP/cap.html
Northern Ireland, http://www.nics.gov.uk
Spain (from Embassy in Spain), http://www.docuweb.ca/sispain
Statistics Netherlands, http://www.cbs.nl
Statistics Norway, http://www-open.ssb.no/www-open
Statistics Sweden, http://www.scb.se
Statistisches Bundesamt (Germany), http://www.statistik-bund.de
Switzerland, http://swissinfo.ch/main/oben_r.htm
U.K.: HMSO, http://www.hmso.gov.uk, Commonwealth information,
  http://www.fco.gov.uk

Other

Middle East Business Review, http://fs1.ms.rhbnc.ac.uk/mbr.html
Palestinan Liberation Organization, http://www.cs.tu-berlin.de/~ishaq/
  pla/palestine
Russia, http://www.hibo.no/stud/sh4/russia/bsns.html
Saudi Arabia, http://imedl.saudi.net
South Africa, http://wwwtmn.com/safrica/index.html, http://wwwsacs.
  org.za/level5/yearb95.htm
Tunisia, http://www.idsonline.com/tunisia
Yugoslavia, http://www.umiacs.umd.edu/users/lpv/yu/html/yu.htm

REFERENCE

Everything you want to know is *not* on the Internet, but a great deal is. Here are some interesting and useful sites I have found and used:

News

CNN News Interactive (today's news), http://www.cnn.com

The Electronic Newsstand (Business Week, Economist, Scientist), http://www.enews.com, gopher://enews.com

GrayFire Information Services (custom news), http://www.grayfire. com

Electronic Newspaper Archives

The Boston Globe, http://www.globe.com

Der Spiegel (in German), http://news.hamburg.pop.de/bda/int/spiegel/spiegel

New York Times, http://www.nytimes.com

Philadelphia Inquirer and Daily News, http://www.phillynews.com

SF Chronicle and Examiner, http://www.sfgate.com/

San Jose Mercury news, http://www.sjmercury.com/

Other Reference Materials

800 number index (from AT&T): http://att.net/dir800

Bartlett's Familiar Quotations: http://www.columbia.edu/~svl2/bartlett/ (that's "s v ell," not the number one)

Beginner's Guide to HTML, http://www.ncsa.uiuc.edu/demoweb/html-primer.html

Bureau of Labor Statistics, U.S. Dept. of Commerce, http:///stats.bls.gov/

Canada's Parliament, http://www.parl.gc.ca or gopher://gopher.parl.gc.ca (tours, transcripts, not e-mail)

CARL Uncover (tables of contents and document delivery), http://www.carl.org/carl.html

Chemical Abstracts Service, http://www.cas.org

China on the Web, http://www.hk.net/~drummond/milesj/china.html

CIA World Factbook (lots of information on countries of the world), http://www.odci.gov/ or gopher://hoshi.cic.sfu.ca:70/0/dlam/cia

Create a Calendar, http://hoohoo.ncsa.uiuc.edu/cgi-bin/calendar

Currency conversions, http://gnn.com/cgi-bin/gnn/currency

Distance between almost any 2 cities in the U.S., http://gs213.sp.cs.cum.edu/prog/disc

FedWorld (gateway to U.S. government sites and information), http://www.fedworld.gov

Financial Aid on the Web (including fastWEB, a forms-based search tool to locate scholarships), http://www.cs.cmu.edu/afs/cs/usr/mkant/Public/FinAid/finaid.htm

France (maps and information), http://web.urec.france/france.htm

How to use the Freedom of Information Act, gopher://gopher.wiretap. spies.com, government docs, citizens guide

Information Infrastructure Task Force, http://iitf.doc.gov or gopher://iitf.doc.gov

Internet Search Engine "Cheat Sheet," http://www.intersurf.com/~powerdan/duz/search/boolean.htmlItalian Zip Codes, http://www.crs4.it/~france/CAP/cap.html

Jumbo Shareware, http://www.jumbo.com/index.htmlLatin American Network (form University of Texas), http://lanic.utexas.edu

KRI/DIALOG (with bluesheets), http://www.dialog.com

Latin America and Caribbean Information Center (from Florida International University), gopher://gopher. fiu.edu:70/acadinfo/lacci

List of Internet Service Providers, http://www.thelist.com

MACintosh resources, http://rever.nmsu.edu/~elharo/faq/Macintosh.html

NASA (U.S. aerospace agency), http://www.gsfc.nasa.govOLC Searchable Catalog of Internet Resources (InterCAT), http:// www.oclc.org:6990

Online English Grammar Helper, http://www.edunet.com/english/grammar/index.html

Peruvian web site (introduction in English or Spanish, articles in Spanish), http://www.rcp.net.pe

Peterson's Education Center, http://www.petersons.com

Rulers of the World (names, birth and death dates, by country), http://www.geopages.com/Athens1058/rulers.html

Searchable database of listservs, http://scwww.ucs.indiana.edu/mlarchive

Statistical Abstract of the U.S., http://www.census.gov:80/stat_abstract

Telephone area codes and country codes, http://www.xmission. com/~americom/aclookup.html

Time Zone converter, http://hibp.ecse.rpi.edu/cgi-bin/tzconvert

Top 10 things not to do on a Web page, http://ee.standord. edu/eecns/www/donts.html

ULTIMATE Mac site, http://www.freepress.com/myee/ultimate_mac.html

U.S. Census information, http://www.census.gov:80/

U.S. Congress (full text of bills, etc.), http://thomas.loc.gov

U.S. Occupational Safety and Health Administration (OSHA), http://www.osha.gov

U.S. Public Broadcasting Service, http://www.pbs.com

U.S. Zip Code server (input a name and address and get the zip code), http://www.cedar.buffalo.edu/adserv.html

Virtual Computer Library (listing of computer resources), http://www.utexas.edu/computer/vcl

Web site ratings from Point Communications, http://www.pointcom. com

COMMUNITY NETWORKS AND FREE-NETS

Big Sky Telegraph, MT, telnet: bigsky.bigsky.dillon.mt.us

Blacksburg Electronic Village, VA, http://www.bev.net/BEV/ home. html or gopher://gopher.bev.net

Boulder Community Network, CO, http://bcn.boulder.co.us

Buffalo Free-Net, NY, telnet: freenet.buffalo.edu (login as freeport)

CapAccess, DC, http://www.capaccess.org

Charlotte's Web, NC, http://www.charweb.org, gopher://gopher. charweb.org, telnet wilbur.charweb.org

Chebucto Free-Net, Halifax NS Canada, http://cfn.cs.dal.ca./cfn/

Cleveland Free-Net, OH (the grandaddy of them all), telnet: freenet-in-a.cwru.edu

Heartland Free-Net, IL, telnet: heartland.bradley.edu (login as bbguest)

La Plaza Telecommunity, NM, http://laplaza.taos.nm.us

LibertyNet, PA, http://libertynet.org

National Capital Free-Net, Ontario, Canada, telnet: freenet.carleton.ca (login as guest)

Plugged In, CA, http://www.pluggedin.org

PrairieNet, IL, telnet: firefly.prairienet.org

Seattle Community Network, WA, http://www.scn.org or telnet: scn.org (login as visitor)

Tallahassee Free-Net, FL, telnet: freenet.fsu.edu (login as visitor)

Victoria Free-Net, BC Canada, telnet: freenet.victoria.bc.ca (login as guest)

Appendix I

Library Education Questionnaire

Degrees granted: ___ B.A./B.S. ___ M.A./M.S./M.L.S ___ Ph.D ___Other

Number of faculty: _____ full-time _____ part-time

_____ adjunct (e.g., practitioners)

Do you have a specialization/track for special/corporate/hospital librarianship?

_____ yes _____ no _____ no, but one is planned

How many credit hours are required for the MA/MS/MLS? _____

Is a thesis required for the MA/MS/MLS? ____ yes ____ no ____ optional

What competencies do you require for entrance into the degree program? (e.g., computer skills, math skills, foreign language, library experience, etc.)

_____

_____

_____

Please list the courses you offer that you consider relevant to special/corporate/hospital librarianship. Also, list the name of the faculty member who

217

usually teaches the course, whether they are regular or adjunct faculty, how long they have been teaching (not just this course), and if the course is required.

Course title	faculty	reg/adj	experience	required?

Thank you very much for your cooperation.

Appendix II

Detailed Analysis of Library School Questionnaire Responses

	degree	number	percent
Degrees granted:	BA/BS	5	(10.2%)
	MA/MS/MLS	48	(98.0%)
	Ph.D	22	(44.9%)
	Other	9	(18.4%)

	status	mean	high	median
Number of faculty:	full-time	10.9	18	10
	part-time*	3.5	14	1
	adjunct	11.5	68	8

• only 14 schools reported having part-time faculty

Do you have a specialization/track for special/corporate/hospital librarianship?

	yes	27	(55.1%)
	no	19	(38.8%)
	no, but one is planned	3	(6.1%)

How many credit hours are required for the MA/MS/MLS?

	36 hours (ALA minimum)	28	(57.1%)

overall mean = 38.8 hours, high was 60, low was 30

Is a thesis required for the MA/MS/MLS?

yes	7	(14.3%)
no	24	(49.0%)
optional	18	(36.7%)

What competencies do you require for entrance into the degree program?

computer skills	14	(28.6%)
quantitative skills	3	
experience	2	
other	8	

(subject specialization, management skills, written communications skills, foreign language)

Courses listed as relevant to special/corporate/hospital librarianship:
(* indicates courses of special relevance to SOLO librarians)

	number	regular faculty	adjunct faculty	required
Special libraries*	33	29	4	2
Health/biomedical info*	39	15	24	
Business info*	30	14	16	
Science-technology*	28	21	7	
Archives/records management	20	11	9	
Management/administration*	20	19	1	12
Government documents/info*	20	15	5	
Legal info*	18	4	14	
Online info/searching*	15	13	2	2
Automation/networks/internet	14	9	5	1*
Humanities info*	12	3	9	
Computers/telecommunications*	12	11	1	2
Systems analysis/research methods*	9	7	2	1
Abstracting/indexing	8	7	1	1

	number	regular faculty	adjunct faculty	required
Fieldwork/internship*	8	6	2	1
Database management/info storage & retrieval*	7	6	1	1
Management of a special library*	6	3	3	
Organizational behavior*	6	6		
Social sciences info*	6	4	2	
Information structure	5	5		
Advanced online/Medline*	5	3	2	
Alternate careers*	3	3		
Publicity/marketing*	3	2	1	
Planning/design of libraries*	2	2		
Budgeting*	2	2		
Serials management*	1	1		
Media technology	1	1		
Multilingual info	1	1		
Competitive intelligence*	1	1		
Info mediation	1	1		1
Rural librarianship	1	1		
Online catalogs*	1	1		

Appendix III

SOLO Librarian Survey

First, a bit about you and your library:

Type of library?

___corporate	___law	___medical
___ academic	___government	___not-for-profit
___ self-employed	___other (explain)_____	

Size of collection?

book volumes _____

serial titles _____

other (what?_____

Size of staff? (full-time equivalents)

professionals? _____

non-professionals/clerical? _____

How many people in your company? _____

How many people do you serve? (active users) _____

How much money to do you control or influence? $_____

(please include all library-related information products and/or services, whether for the library or not)

What is your budget?
(not including your salary & benefits) $_____

What is your annual compensation? $_____

(if part-time, mark what full-time equivalent would be)

Are you automated?

catalog	___yes	___no	___planned
circulation	___yes	___no	___planned
acquisitions	___yes	___no	___planned
other	___yes	___no	___planned

Do you do online searching?   ___yes ___no

on which vendor(s)? _____

Do you have CD-ROMs?   ___yes ___no

if no, do you plan to add them in the next 2 years?   ___yes   ___no

Now, for how you feel about being a solo:

How did you become a solo?

___by choice?

___by circumstances?

___other? (explain)_____

How do you stay in contact with other librarians?

___membership in prof's societies (circle all that apply)

(SLA, ALA, MLA, AALL, ASIS, other_____)

Are your dues paid by your employer?   ___yes ___no

___local networks (consortia, user groups, etc.)

(explain_____)

___online (e-mail, listservs, newsgroups, Internet surfing)

(explain_____)

What do you wish you'd known before you went solo?

How do you think library schools can prepare solos better?

What do you like most about being a solo?

What do you like least?

Other comments?

Appendix IV

Demographics: Results of Surveys

	Carol 1992	Judy 1993	Judy 1995	Medical 1996	Public 1996	Law 1996	German 1996	Australia 1996	South Africa 1996
STAFF									
# profs									
zero		6	4	21				0	0
<1		86	11	74			2	1	1
1		0	89	0	100		25	5	3
>1			0				4	1	1
non prof									
zero		51	61	66			18	4	5
<1		15	16	13			4	2	0
1		22	16	13			5	0	1
>1		12	7	9			4	1	0
HOLDINGS									
volumes									
mean		4,434	5,515	1,742	40,000	10,385	22,500	3,400	2,017
range				350–14,000	4,000–24,5000	750–40,000	3,000–50,000	280–8,000	20–6,000
journals									
mean		278	205	128	104	256	196	173	78
range				6–350	5–850	5–1500	10–20001	45–400	52–120
PATRONS									
# in co.	4,340	4,847	2,253	1,391	16,000	625	276	241	313
# served	625	268	268	271		106	475	42	290

	Carol 1992	Judy 1993	Judy 1995	Medical 1996	Public 1996	Law 1996	German 1996	Australia 1996	South Africa 1996
MONEY									
budget	56,000	85,090	89,053	47,000	199,000	220,000	DM 52,500	A 65,700	R 8,000
salary	32,500		37,021	35,000	25,000	43,000	DM 41,000	A 37,150	R 52,000
figures below here are in percentages:									
AUTOMATION									
circulation		27	31	47	30	49	71	57	40
catalog'g		55	65	17		17	23	86	80
acns		20	21	17		29	32	29	60
CD now		42	63				39	86	40
CD 2 yrs		33	60						50
TO SOLO?									
choice	29		29	40		39	55	57	20
circum	67		65	79		56	39	43	80
DUES PD?				66		76	48	40	60
SOCIETIES:									
SLA				45		71	84		
ALA				26		20			
MLA/AALL				94		68			
n =	150	327	123	47	209	41	31	7	5

Public Library Demographics:
DIALOG file 460, American Library Directory, 1995, as of 3/29/96

total staff = 1 = 2,540
professional staff = 1 = 2,804
professionals = 1 and type – public – 808
professionals = 1 and type = special = 1,273
professionals = 1 and type = medical = 397
professionals = 1 and type = law = 182
professionals = 1 and type = religious = 149

	responses	25th %ile	mean	75th %ile	range
non-prof'l staff	193	4	15	21	0-33
population served	179	5,000	16,000	22,000 89,000	<1,000-
circulation	164	29,000	79,000	100,000 565,000	2,000-
circulation per person	153		7.2		0.5-27.5
budget	136	$72,000	$199,000	$262,000 $802,000	$5,000-
for books	111	$8,000	$24,000	$32,000 $124,000	<$1,000-
for subscriptions	92	$2,000	$4,000	$5,000 $17,000	<$1,000-
for audiovisual	73	$1,000	$4,000	$5,000 $17,000	<$1,000-
for maintenance	76	$8,000	$28,000	$38,000 $150,000	<$1,000-
for all salaries	128	$37,000	$104,000	$148,000 $451,000	<$1,000-
salaries as % of budget	126		52%		20%-56%
book volumes	188	20,000	40,000	49,000 245,000	4,000-
periodical subscriptions	168	50	104	123	5-850
audiovisual total	127	335	1,273	1,500	24-9032
automated?	62 (30%)				
member of network?	122 (58%)				
librarian's salary	90	$18,000	$25,000	$30,000	$<$1,000- $55,000

Bibliography

This list represents my list of sources with comments on particular books or articles of interest. In order for you to find or order these sources, I have also included ISBN numbers for some of them, as well as some annotations.

Acton, Patricia. 1986. Alternative career? *Canadian Library Journal* 43(6): 385-387.

Ahlrichs, Ruth, and Priscilla Harms. 1988. Iowa small library association survey. *Iowa Library Quarterly* 25:28-45.

Allen, Lawrence A. 1974. *Continuing Education Needs of Special Librarians*. New York, NY: Special Libraries Association (SLA State-of-the-Art Review 3).

Alsop, Stewart. 1995. If you think information is free, you must have stolen this column from someone (Column: Distributed Thinking). *InfoWorld* 17(49):126.

Anderson, M. Elaine, and Patricia T. Pawl. 1979. When you are the staff: Tips for managing a small library/media/learning center. *Wisconsin Library Bulletin* 75:271-274.

Anonymous. 1993. The incredible shrinking staff: Supervisors deal with downsizing. *Library Personnel News* 7(6):3-4. From ALA/LAMA sessions at annual conference.

Appel, L. 1996. Personal communication.

Baker, Brian L. October 2, 1995. Librarians online might get entangled in the Web. *National Law Journal* B13-14.

Barter, Richard F., Jr. 1994. In search of excellence in libraries: The management writings of Tom Peters and their implications for library and information services. *Library Management* 15(8):4-15.

Bauwens, Michel. 1993. The emergence of the "cybrarian": A new organizational model for corporate libraries, *Business Information Review* 9(4):65-67.

———. 1994. The BP nutrition virtual library: A case study. *Information for Management: A Handbook*, Washington, DC: Special Libraries Association 159-165.

————. 1996. Marketing the cybrary. *Marketing Library Service* 10(4):1-3.

Belanger, David. 1995. Board games: Examining the trustee/director conflict. *Library Journal* 120(19):38-41.

Bender, David R. 1994. A study of the continuing education needs of SLA members and education activities at SLA conferences. Special Libraries Association Board Memorandum.

Bennett, Kitty. 1995. Whose job is it anyway? *Online* 19(5):7-8.

Berk, Robert A. 1989. *Starting, Managing, and Promoting the Small Library.* Armonk, New York: M.E. Sharpe, Inc.

Berkman, Robert I. 1995. *Rethinking the Corporate Information Center: A Blueprint for the 21st Century.* New York: Find/SVP Inc. ISBN 1-56241-0.

Berner, Andrew, and Guy St. Clair. 1990. *The Best of OPL: Five Years of The One-Person Library.* Washington, DC: Special Libraries Association. ISBN: 0-87111-438-0.

————. 1996. *The Best of OPL, II: Selected Readings from The One-Person Library: A Newsletter for Librarians and Management,* 1990-1994. Washington, DC: Special Libraries Association. 1996.

Berry, John. 1993. The two crises in library education. *Library Journal* 118(14):102.

Bierbaum, Esther G. 1986. Professional education doesn't stop with your MLS. *The One-Person Library* 2(12):2.

————. 1996. Museum libraries: The more things change . . . *Special Libraries* 87(2):74-8.

Boaz, Martha T. 1981. Strengthening the profession: A plea for national certification. *Wilson Library Bulletin* 55:767.

Bolef, Doris. 1988. The special library. In *The How-to-do-it manual for small libraries,* edited by Bill Katz. New York: Neal-Schuman Publishers, 54-61. Author is at Rush-Presbyterian-St. Luke's Medical Center, Chicago.

Brandt, D. Scott. 1996. Evaluating information on the Internet. *Computers in Libraries* 16(5):44-46.

Brees, Mina Akins. 1973. The challenge for library schools: A student's view. *Special Libraries* 64(10):433-438.

Bryant, Sue Lacey. 1995. *Personal Professional Development and the SOLO Librarian (Library Training Guides).* London: Library Association Publishing. 1995. ISBN 1-85604-141-7.

Burton, Ken. 1995. The road to 2001. *InfoManage* 2(7):supplement 3.

Byrne, John A. 1996. Has outsourcing gone too far? *Business Week* (April 1): 26-28.

Campbell, William D. 1987. *A Budgeting Manual for Small Public Libraries.* Clarion, PA: Center for the Study of Rural Librarianship.

Canale, Debra, and Colleen Meeker. 1995. Librarians in competitive intelligence: A profile and ranking of entry-level competencies. Paper presented to SLA/Cleveland Chapter. Based on a survey of those who were members of both SCIP and Special Libraries Association.

Carns, Brenda. 1989. Locked up libraries. *Colorado Libraries* 15(3):17-18.

Chao, Juli. 1995. Internet pioneers abandon world they create. *Wall Street Journal* (June 7):B1, B6.

Chris Olson & Associates. 1995. Packaging the Internet as a new library service. *Marketing Treasures* 8(3): 1,3.

Citron, J. Wesley. 1992. *Time Management Handbook for Librarians.* New York: Greened Press. ISBN 0-313-27842-3.

Cochran, J. Wesley. 1992. *Time Management Handbook for Librarians.* New York: Greenwood Press. ISBN 0-313-27842-3

Collins, Boyd R. 1996. Web watch (column). *Library Journal* 121(6):27.

Corporate Library Update:

1. Internet is "overhyped" editor tells librarians, 3(24):2-3, 1995.

2. Library spending by 55 firms to drop seven % in five years, 4(1):1, 1995.

3. Be consultants, not brokers, independent librarians told, 4(2):2,4, 1995.

4. Librarians, paper will survive, Opperman tells online audience, 4(5):4-5, 1995.

5. Corporate librarians in top 25 of working woman job survey, 4(10):1, 1995; Surveys show 54-65% of lawyers don't call librarians for aid, 4(10):1-2, 1995.

7. Speed, information retrieval valued in corporate librarians, 4(10):4,6, 1995.

8. Advice offered for survival: Find partners, survey needs, 4(15):2,5, 1995.

9. Outsource in 1995? Teltech's take on the benefits, 4(13)4, 1995.

10. Will Brown Bros. NYC library run itself after staff is gone? 4(14):1, 1995.

Cortez, Edwin M. 1986. Developments in special library education: Implications for the present and future. *Special Libraries* 77(4):198.

Crawford, Walt, and Michael Gorma. 1995. *Future Libraries: Dreams, Madness, and Reality.* Chicago: ALA Editions. ISBN 0-8389-0647-8.

Cronin, Blaise, Michael Stiffler, and Dorothy Day. 1990. The emergent market for information professionals: Educational opportunities and implications. Library Trends 42(2):262.

Cronin, Blaise, K. Overfelt, F. Foucheraux, T. Monzvanzvike, M. Cha, and E. Sona. 1994. The Internet and competitive intelligence: A survey of current practice. *International Journal of Information Management* 14(3):204-222.

Cronin, Blaise, and Williamson, Joan. 1988. One person libraries and information units: Their education and training needs. *Library Management* 9(5):1-72.

Coutts, Margaret M. 1991. New professionals: Training for the present and the future. *Library Review* 40(2/3):10.

Davidson, Ann C. 1996. Obedience to the unenforceable: The ethics of outsourcing. *Searcher* 4(4):28-30.

Detlefsen, Ellen Gay. 1993. Library and information science education for the new medical environment and the age of integrated information. *Library Trends* 42(2):359.

Dickerson, Mary E. 1992. *Report, Presidential Study Commission on Professional Recruitment, Ethics, and Professional Standards*. Washington, DC: Special Libraries Association.

DiMattia, Susan. 1995. When the "dumb" increases, increase the smarts, sci-tech news. *Corporate Library Update* 4(15):4.

Doms, Carol. March 20, 1996. Internet post, BUSLIB-L.

Doran, Kirk. 1996. The Internet: Its impact, import, and influence. *Computers in Libraries* 16(3):8-10.

Drake, David. 1990. When your boss isn't a librarian. *American Libraries* (February):152-153.

Duranceau, E. 1994. The balance point: vendors and librarians speak out on outsourcing, cataloging and acquisitions. *Serials Review* 20(3):69-83.

Ebbinghouse, Carol. 1995. Information professionals face the Internet: The Ninth Annual SCOUG Retreat, *Searcher* 3(8):48-56.

Eiblum, Paula. 1995. The coming of age of document delivery. *Bulletin of the American Society for Information Science* 21(3):21-22.

Eide-Jensen, Inger. 1977. The one-man library. *Scandinavian Public Library Quarterly* 10(1):15-17.

Eismark, Henrik. 1995. The business of entrepreneurship in Europe: Would-be information brokers click here. *Searcher* 3(10):18-22.

Ellis, Albert, and Robert A. Harper. 1977. *A New Guide to Rational Living*, North Hollywood CA: Wilshire Book Company. ISBN 0-87980-042-9, originally published by Prentice-Hall.

Ertel, Monica. 1994. How to make information technology work for you. In *Information for Management: A Handbook*, edited by J.M. Matarazzo and M.A. Drake. Washington, DC: Special Libraries Association.

Everett, John H., and Elizabeth Powell Crowe. 1994. *Information for Sale: How to Start and Operate Your Own Data Research Service*, 2nd ed. New York: Windcrest/McGraw-Hill. ISBN 0-070199507.

Ferguson, Elizabeth, and Emily R. Mobley. 1984. *Special Libraries at Work*. Hamden, CT: Library Professional Publications. ISBN 0-208-01939-1.

Ferguson, Tony. 1996. The "L" word. *Against the Grain* 8(2): 80, 89.

Field, Judith J. 1995. Downsizing, reengineering, outsourcing and closing: Words to lose sleep over. *Library Management Quarterly* 18(4):4.

————. 1996. Continuing our professional growth: A rational. *Business Information Alert* 8(6):8. Adapted from talk at Betty Burrows Memorial Seminar, Cleveland, 4/19/96.

Fletcher, Lloyd Alan. 1996. The new economics of online. *Searcher* 4(5):30-44.

Foster, Allan. 1994. Information technology: Impact on our future. *InfoManage* 1(6):6-7.

Gagliardi, Anna. January, 17, 1996. Library/departmental collaboration, Internet post, MEDLIB-L. Reference librarian at Health Sciences Library, St. Michael's Hospital, Toronto.

Garman, Nancy. 1996. Be a savvy online consumer. *Online User* (July-August): 5.

Garrou, Sharon M., Katharine. Winter 1996. *Sharp Review* 2: http://edfullis.uiuc.edu/review/winter1996/garrou.html.

Gelfand, Julia, ed. 1996. Does CD-ROM have a future?—Some opinions from the field. *Across the Grain* 8(2):17-21.

Gervasi, Anne, and Betty Kay Seibt. 1988. *Handbook for Small, Rural, and Emerging Public Libraries*. Phoenix: Oryx. ISBN 0-89774-303-2; excellent, very detailed.

Gervino, Joan. 1995. Establishing fees for service. *Marketing Treasures* 8(3):4-6.

Gilder, George. 1996. Feasting on the giant peach. *Forbes ASAP* (August 26): 85-96.

Gilman, Debra. 1 May 1996. Summary of responses. PACS-L.

Gilson, Tom. 1996. The Infofilter Project. *Against The Grain* 8(1):58.

Gilton, Donna J. 1992. Information entrepreneurship: Sources for reference librarians. *Reference Quarterly* 31(3):346-355.

Going, Mona E., and Jean M. Clarke. 1982. *Hospital Libraries and Work with the Disabled in the Community*. 3rd ed., London: Library Associations. History of hospital libraries in the United Kingdom.

Gorman, Michael. 1996. Dreams, madness and reality: The complicated world of human recorded communication. *Against the Grain* 8(1):1,16-18.

Gothberg, Helen M. 1991. Time management in public libraries. *Public Libraries* 30(6):350-357.

Griffiths, Jose-Marie, and Donald W. King. 1986. *New Directions in Library and Information Science Education*. White Plains, NY: Knowledge Industry Press, Inc. for American Society for Information Science.

————. 1993. *Special Libraries: Increasing the Information Edge*. Washington, DC: Special Libraries Association.

Gurley, William. 1996. It's the end of the Net as we know it. *Fortune* 133(8):181-186.

Hahn, Harvey. 1987. *Technical Services in the Small Library*. Chicago: ALA/ LAMA Small Libraries Publication 13. Mostly on cataloging, only ten pages.

Hardsog, Ellen L. 1992. The small town library: Discovering relevancy. *The Reference Librarian* (38):31-39.

Harvey, John, ed. 1980. *Church and Synagogue Libraries*. Metuchen NJ: Scarecrow. ISBN: 0-8108-1304-1.

Hayes, Suzi. 1994. Technology and collaboration. *InfoManage* 1(4):4-5.

Hennen, Thomas J., Jr. 1986. Attacking the myths of small libraries. *American Libraries* 17:803+.

Henri, James and Roy Sanders, eds. 1987. *Libraries Alone: Proceedings of the Rural & Isolated Librarians Conference. Wagga Wagga*. Wagga Wagga NSW Australia: Libraries Alone. ISBN 0-7316-1766-2; 170 participants from all over Australia and New Zealand, keynote from Bernard Vavrek.

Hill, Julianne. 4 December 1995. untitled Internet post, LIBREF-L.

Hill, Linda. 1993. Education for library and information management careers in corporate environments. *Library Trends* 42 (2):225-368.

Holt, Vickie L., and Verna Pugnitore, compiler. 1990. Life in small public libraries of Indiana. *Indiana Libraries* 9(1):23-37.

Hoffman, Herbert. 1986. *Small library cataloging*. Metuchen, NJ: Scarecrow. ISBN 0-8108-1910-4; for those with no formal cataloging training, simplified, with examples.

Hofstetter, Janet. 1991. The one-person manager. *Book Report* 9:16-17. School librarian in Missouri.

Horton, Forest Woody, Jr. 1994. *Extending the Librarian's Domain: A Survey of Emerging Occupational Opportunities for Librarians and Information Professionals*. Washington, DC: Special Libraries Association Occasional Papers Series 4. ISBN: 0-87111-419-4.

Kadanoff, Diane G. 1986. Small libraries—no small job! *Library Journal* 111:71-73.

Kalba, Kas. 1977. Libraries in the Information Marketplace. In. *Libraries in Post-Industrial Society*, edited by Leigh Estabrook. Phoenix: Oryx. ISBN 0-912700009.

Katz, Bill. 1985. Perspective: the delights of the small library. *Collection Building* 7:32-34.

Katz, Bill, ed. 1988. *The How-to-Do-It Manual for Small Libraries*. New York: Neal-Schuman Publishers. ISBN 1-55570-016-0.

Khan, Marta. 1987. Successful downsizing strategies. *Canadian Library Journal* 44:393-399.

Kinder, Robin. 1988. Agreeing to disagree: The relationship between librarians and brokers. *The Reference Librarian* (22):1-3.

King, G.P. 1971. Problems in the one-man electronics library. *Library Association Record* 73(4):1-2.

Koenig, Michael E.D. 1980. *Budgeting Techniques for Libraries & Information Centers*. Washington, DC: Special Libraries Association Professional Development Series 1.

Kramer, Pamela K., 1989. Salute to the "super SOLOs"—school librarians who do it all. *Illinois Libraries* 71:282-283. By a non-SOLO.

Kristensen, Kurt. 1985. The Norwegian library service: The advantages and disadvantages of small units. *Scandinavian Public Library Quarterly* 18(3):71-73.

Krumenaker, Larry. 1996. Surveyors of cyberspace. *Internet World* 7(6):69-74.

Ladner, Sharyn J., and Hope N. Tillman. 1993. *The Internet and Special Librarians: Use, Training, and the Future*. Washington, DC: Special Libraries Association. ISBN 0-87111-413-5.

LaForte, Susan R. 1982. Information brokers: Friend and/or foe? *Public Library Quarterly* 3:83-91.

Lee, Don. 1980. One-man operated: Running an Information unit for management in the public transport industry. *ASLIB Proceedings* 32(3):114-117.

Luther, Judy, and Diane Graves. 1996. A not-so-modest proposal (with apologies to Jonathan Swift)—Library education: The cutting edge? *Across the Grain* 8(2):25-26.

Lynch, Mary Jo. 1991. *Some Basic Figures and Who Works in Libraries? The Whole Library Handbook: Current Data. Professional Advice, and Curiosa about Libraries and Library Services*. Chicago, IL: American Library Association.

Mackenzie, Alec. 1990. *The Time Trap*. New York: Amacom.

Marshall, Joanne, et al. *Competencies for Special Librarians of the 21st Century*. Submitted to the SLA Board of Directors by the Special Committee on Competencies for Special Librarians.

Martin, Christine. 1996. Response to Katharine Garrou. *Sharp Review* 2. http://edfullis.uiuc.edu/review/winter 1996/garrou.html

Martin, Murray S., ed., 1983. *Financial Planning for Libraries*. New York: Haworth Press. ISBN 0-86656-118-8.

Matarazzo, James M. 1990. *Corporate Library Excellence*. Washington, DC: Special Libraries Association. ISBN 0-87111-367-8; profiles of thirteen corporate libraries voted outstanding by the boards of six Special Libraries Association chapters.

Matarazzo, James M., and Miriam A. Drake. 1994. *Information for Management: A Handbook.* Washington, DC: Special Libraries Association.

McMichael, Betty. 1984. *The Church Librarian's Handbook: A Complete Guide for the Library and Resource Center in Christian Education.* Grand Rapids MI: Baker Book House. ISBN 0-8010-6166-0.

McQueen, Judy and N. Bernard Basch. 1991. Negotiations with subscription agents. *American Libraries* 22:644-647.

Merry, Susan A. How to talk to senior management. In *Information for Management: A Handbook,* edited by James M. Matarazzo and Miriam A. Drake. Washington, DC: Special Libraries Association.

Metcalfe, Bob. 1995. Predicting the Internet's catastrophic collapse and ghost sites galore in 1996. *InfoWorld* 17(49):61.

Meylor, Elizabeth. 30 March 1996. Personal communication.

Miller, Kathy, and Dorothy Pike. 1996. Computers in Libraries '96 shatters attendance and exhibitor records. *Computers in Libraries* 16 (4): 20.

Mount, Ellis, ed. 1993. *Opening New Doors: Alternative Careers for Librarians.* Washington, DC: Special Libraries Association. ISBN 0-87111-408-9; profiles of twelve entrepreneurs and sixteen workers in nontraditional positions.

Murphy, Marcy. 1988. *The Managerial Competencies of Twelve Corporate Librarians.* Washington DC: Special Libraries Association. (SLA Research Series No. 2)

Nicholls, Paul. 1996. Why did you think they called it the World Wide Web? *Searcher* 4(5):20-27. Good list of international Web sites.

Nichols, Jim. Response to Katharine Garrou. *Sharp Review* 2. Winter 1996. http://edfullis.uiuc.edu/reveiw/winter1996

O'Donnell, William S. 1976. The vulnerable corporate special library/information center: Minimizing the risks. *Special Libraries* 67:179-187.

O'Leary, Mick. 1987. The information broker: A modern profile. *Online* 11:24-30. Eleven interviews.

O'Toole, Susan, Charles Knuth, and Kellee Selden-Althouse. 1995. Automated alternatives are alluring. *National Law Journal.* (October 2):B9-10.

Panella, Deborah S. 1991. *Basics of Law Librarianship.* Binghamton, New York: Haworth Press. ISBN 0- 86656-989-8.

Paris, Marion, and Herbert S. White. 1986. Mixed signals and painful choices: The education of special librarians. *Special Libraries* 77(4): 207-212.

Parris, Lou B. 1994. Know your company and its business. In *Information for Management: A Handbook,* edited by James M. Matarazzo and Miriam A.

Drake, Washington, DC: Special Libraries Association.

Paul, Meg, and Sandra Crabtree. 1995. Strategies for special libraries. *SMR Special Report* 1, New York: SMR International.

Piggott, Sylvia. 1996. Charting the course to the 21st century: Managing your career and your profession. *LMD Quarterly* 19(1) 4-6. Summary of findings from workshops held October–November at Eastern Canada, Baltimore, and Washington SLA chapters.

Pitts, Roberta L. 1994. A generalist in the age of specialists: A profile of the one-person library director. *Library Trends* 43(1):121-135.

Prusak, Laurence. 1994. Corporate libraries: A soft analysis, a warning, and some generic advice. In *Information for Management: A Handbook*, ed. by James M. Matarazzo and Miriam A. Drake. Washington, DC: Special Libraries Association.

Prusak, Laurence and James M. Matarazzo. 1990. Tactics for corporate library success. *Library Journal* 115(15):45-46. Survey of 164 larger U.S. companies

———. 1995. The value of corporate libraries: The 1995 survey. *SpeciaList.* (November): 9, 15.

Pungitore, Verna, compiler. 1990. Life in small public libraries of Indiana. *Indiana Libraries* 9(1):23-37. Essays by four small public librarians.

Quint, Barbara. 1991. *Wilson Library Bulletin* (November): 59.

———. 1995. Competition. *Searcher* 3(10):1.

———. 1996a. Disintermediation. *Searcher* 4(1):4,6.

———. 1996b. Professional associations react to the challenge. *Searcher* 4(5):8-18.

———. 1996c. The best defense is a good offense: Interview with AALL's Mark Estes. *Searcher* 4(7):12-17.

Raitt, D., ed. 1994. The future of libraries in the face of the Internet. *Electronic Library* 12(5):275-276.

Rich, Jane L. 1994. Effective information delivery. In *Information for Management: A Handbook*, edited by James M. Matarazzo and Miriam A. Drake. Washington, DC: Special Libraries Association.

Riggs, Donald E., and Gordon A. Sabine, eds. *Libraries in the Nineties: What the leaders expect.* Phoenix, AZ: Oryx Press, 1988. (ISBN 0-89774-532-9)

Rose, Lindy. 1988. We're more than books. *Marketing Treasures* 9(4):1,3.

Rosen, Linda. 1993. The information professional as knowledge engineer (Part II). *Information Today* 10(5):47-49. An interview with Sue Rugge, Miriam Drake, James Matarazzo, Reva Basch, and David Bender.

Rosenbaum, Howard, and Gregory B. Newby. 1990. *An Emerging Form of Human Communications: Computer Networking*. Toronto: ASIS '90: Proceedings of the 53rd ASIS Annual Meeting.

Rothstein, Samuel. 1985. Why people really hate library schools. *Library Journal* 110(1):41-48.

Rubin, Rhea J., and Daniel S. Suvak. 1995. *Libraries Inside: A Practical Guide for Prison Libraries*. Jefferson NC: McFarland.

Rugge, Sue. 1993. Focus on information brokering. *Information Today* 10 (5):15.

Rugge, Sue, and Alfred Glossbrenner. 1995. *The Information Broker's Handbook*. New York: McGraw-Hill. ISBN 0-07-911878-X.

Sager, Donald J. 1992. *Small Libraries: Organization and Operation*. Fort Atkinson, WI: Highsmith Press. ISBN 0-917846-16-8.

St. Clair, Guy. 1976. The one-person library: An essay on essentials. *Special Libraries* 67(3):233-238.

———. 1987. The one-person library: An essay on essentials re-visited. *Special Libraries* 78(4):263-270.

———. 1989. Interpersonal networking: It is who you know. *Special Libraries* 80(2):107-112.

———. 1993. *Customer Service in the Information Environment*. Information Services Management Series. London: Bowker-Saur. ISBN 1-85739-004-0.

———. 1994a. *Power and Influence: Enhancing Information Services within the Organization*. Information Services Management Series. London: Bowker-Saur. ISBN: 1-85739-098-9.

———. 1994b. A tale of two corporate libraries, *InfoManage* 1(3):6-7.

———. 1994c. Meg Paul. *InfoManage* 1(5):1-4. Freelance Library and Information Services, Camberwell, Victoria, Australia.

———. 1995a. Who's doing what? and how well are they doing it? *InfoManage* 2(3):6-7.

———. 1995b. When you downsize: Focus, connect and network. *InfoManage* 2(6):8.

———. 1995c. Trish Foy: Matching corporate information services to corporate information needs. *InfoManage* 2(11):1-5.

———. 1995d. Looking at that volatile "vendor/senior management/information practitioner" relationship. *InfoManage* 2(12):6-7.

———. 1995e. The one-person library in the organization. *SMR Special Report* 2. New York: SMR International.

———. 1995f. One-person librarianship: The authority of the customer. *SMR Special Report* 3. New York: SMR International.

————. 1995g. What the one-person library does. *SMR Special Report* 4. New York: SMR International.

————. 1995h. Finances and value: How the one-person library is paid for. *SMR Special Report 5*, New York: SMR International.

————. 1995i. The InfoManage editor talks about librarianship. *InfoManage* 2(2).

————. 1996a. Joan Williamson. *The One-Person Library* 12(9):1-5. Royal Automobile Club, London.

————. 1996b. Real estate management: When it's part of your job. *InfoManage* 3(2):6-7.

————. 1996c. "Adding value"—what's it mean? (Column: The Practical Information Manager), *InfoManage* 3(3):6-8.

————. 1996d. The seven deadly sins of entrepreneurial librarianship. *InfoManage* 3(4):5-6.

————. 1996e. Dealing with downsizing: A guide for the information services practitioner. *SMR Special Report 6*. New York: SMR International.

————. 1996f. To partner or not to partner? *The One-Person Library* 13(1):1-3.

————. 1996g. 1996. *Entrepreneurial Librarianship: The Key to Effective Information Services Management.* Information Services Management Series. London: Bowker-Saur. ISBN 1-85739-014-8.

St. Clair, Guy, and Andrew Berner. 1996 Insourcing: The evolution of information delivery (new management trends for OPLs). *The One-Person Library* 13(4):1-4.

St. Clair, Guy, and Joan Williamson. 1986. *Managing the One-Person Library.* Stoneham, MA: Butterworth. ISBN 0-408-01511-X.

————. 1992. *Managing the New One-Person Library.* New York: Bowker Saur.

Schement, Jorge Reina. 1996. A 21st-century strategy for librarians. *Library Journal* 121(8):34-36.

Schwartz, Candy. 1994. Records management and the corporate library. In *Information for Management: A Handbook*, edited by James M. Matarazzo and Miriam A. Drake. Washington, DC: Special Libraries Association.

Searfossa, Steven. 1995. Internet isolates libraries: It's lonely in the stacks, *Cleveland Plain Dealer* (July 9): 5I.

Secor, John R. 1996. Why some vendors will endure and others will not, *Against the Grain* 8(1):20-24.

Sellen, Betty-Carol, ed. 1980. *What Else You Can Do With a Library Degree.* Syracuse, New York: Gaylord Professional Publications. ISBN 0-915794-40-3.

Sellen, Betty-Carol, and Dimity S. Berkner. 1984. *New Options for Librarians: Finding a Job in a Related Field.* New York: Neal-Schuman. ISBN 0-918212-73-1.

Shaffer, Roberta. 1996. The future of the law library and law librarian, *Lexis-Nexis Information Professional Update* (3):37.

Sheridan, John H. 1993. The new breed of M.B.A. *Industry Week* 244 (19):14.

Shuter, J. 1984. *The Information Worker in Isolation.* Bradford, England: MCB University Press.

Sickles, Linda. December 1995. Personal communication.

Siess, Judith. 1995. The MLS is not enough: One SOLO librarian's view. *The One-Person Library* 12(5):4-7.

Sih, Julie. 1995. Are we mice, or are we marketers? *Trends in Law Library Management and Technology* 7(4):1-4.

Sinclair, Dorothy. 1972. *Administration of the Small Public Library.* Chicago: American Library Association.

Sineath, Timothy W., ed. 1995. *Library and Information Science Education Statistical Report.* Raleigh NC: Association for Library and Information Science Education. ISSN 0739-506X.

Skapura, Robert. 1988. The school library. In *The How-to-Do-It Manual for Small Libraries*, edited by Bill Katz. New York: Neal-Schuman Publishers, 14-26.

Smith, G. Stevenson. 1983. *Accounting for Librarians and Other Not-for-Profit Managers.* Chicago: American Library Association. ISBN 0-8389-0385-1.

Smock, Raymond W. 1995. What promise does the Internet hold for scholars? *The Chronicle of Higher Education.* (September 22): B1-2.

Stathis, Andrew L. 1995. Technology offers incentive to downsize law libraries. *The National Law Journal.* 18(5):B9, B11. President of architectural design firm specializing in law offices, not a librarian.

Stear, Ed. 1996. The Internet has no clothes. *Bulletin of the Fairfield County Chapter/SLA* 14(2).

Stipek, Kathleen. 1988. The public library. In *The How-to-Do-It Manual for Small Libraries*, edited by Bill Katz. New York: Neal-Schuman Publishers, 3-13.

Strable, Edward. 1992. Special libraries: What's the difference? Report from the Presidential Study Commission on Professional Recruitment, Ethics, and Professional Standards. Washington DC: Special Libraries Association.

Svoboda, Olga. 1991. The special library as a competitive intelligence center. *Electronic Library* 9(4/5):239-244.

Synar, Bohdan S., ed. 1994. *Recommended Reference Books for Small and Medium Sized Libraries and Media Centers.* Englewood, CO: Libraries Unlimited.

Tees, Miriam. 1986a. New roles for library school graduates. *Canadian Library Journal* 43(6):372-336.

———. 1986b. Graduate education for special librarians: What special libraries are looking for in graduates. *Special Libraries* 77(4):190-197.

Thompson, Sherry. 1996. CD-ROMs and the future—Some publishers talk. *Against the Grain* 8(2):22-24.

Tillman, Hope. 1995. The Internet in your library. Presentation to New England Library Association Annual Conference.

Tooley, Jo Ann. 1996. Library and information science, 1996 America's best graduate schools. *U.S. News & World Report*. (Special issue): 54-55.

Trefethen, Dan. 28 January 1996. Downsizing. Personal communication via the Internet.

U. S. Department of Labor, Bureau of Labor Statistics. *Occupational Outlook Handbook (Bulletin 2450)*, 1994-95.

Vavrek, Bernard. 1987. Libraries alone: The American experience. In *Libraries Alone: Proceedings of the Rural & Isolated Librarians Conference*, edited by James Henri and Roy Sanders. Wagga Wagga NSW, Australia: Libraries Alone, 5-13.

———. 1993. *Assessing the Role of the Rural Public Library*. Clarion, PA: Clarion University of Pennsylvania.

Voges, Mickie A. 1988. *Building Your Law Library: A Step-by-Step Guide*. Chicago: American Bar Association. ISBN 0-89707-361-4; videotape also available.

Walker, M.E. 1994. Maslow's hierarchy and the sad case of the hospital librarian. *Bulletin of the MLA* 82(3):320-322.

Warner, Alice Sizer. 1987. *Mind Your Own Business: A Guide for the Information Entrepreneur*. New York: Neal-Schuman, 1987. ISBN 1-555-70014-4.

Warnken, Kelly. 1981. *Information Brokers: How to Start and Operate Your Own Fee-Based Service*. New York: Bowker. ISBN 0-8352-1347-1.

Washburne, Nancy G. 30 October 1995. Training issues for SOLOs. Internet posting, SOLOLIB-L.

Weingand, Darlene E. 1994. Competence and the new paradigm: Continuing education of the reference staff. *The Reference Librarian* (43):173-182.

Weinsoft, J. 1990. Commitment at high level: Management strategies for the one-person library. *Pacific Northwest Library Association Quarterly* 54(4): 30-31.

Weitzen, H. Skip. 1988. *Infopreneurs: Turning Data into Dollars*. New York: Wiley. ISBN 0-471-63371-2.

Westwood, Karen. 1994. Prison law librarianship: A lesson in service for all librarians. *American Libraries* 25:152-154.

White, Herbert S. 1984. *Managing the Special Library: Strategies for Success within the Larger Organization.* White Plains, NY: Knowledge Industry Publications.

————. 1988. Basic Competencies and the Pursuit of Equal Opportunity. *Library Journal* 113(12):56-57.

————. 1989. *Librarians and the Awakening from Innocence: A Collection of Papers.* Boston: G.K. Hall.

————. 1994. Small public libraries—Challenges, opportunities, and irrelevancies. *Library Journal* 119(7):53- 54.

————. 1995. *At the Crossroads: Libraries on the Information Superhighway.* Englewood CO: Libraries Unlimited. ISBN 1-56308-165-2; a collection of his writings from 1980-1994.

White, Herbert S., and Sarah L. Mort. 1995. The accredited library education program as preparation for professional library work. *At the Crossroads: Libraries on the Information Superhighway.* Englewood, CO: Libraries Unlimited, 211-236.

Williams, W.W. 1994. Library journal career survey part 3: Alternative careers: You can take your MLS out of the library. *Library Journal* 119(19):43-46.

Williamson, Joan. 1984. How to be an OMB. *Information and Library Manager* 4(2).

————. 1990. One person libraries and information units: Their education and training needs. In *The Information Professional: An Unparalleled Resource,* Papers Contributed for the 81st Annual Conference, Washington DC: Special Libraries Association, 189-199. ISBN 0-87111-355-4; also published as *Library Management* 9 (5):1-72, 1988.

Willner, Richard A. 1993. Education for library and information management careers in business and financial services. *Library Trends* 42 (2):232-248.

Wright, Susan L. 1996. Reap the benefits of volunteering for SLA. *SpeciaList* 19(4).

Wooley, Marcus. 1988. The one-person library: professional development and professional management. *Library Management* 9(1). One British SOLO's first year, written for his certification.

Young, Peter R. 1994. Changing information access economics: New roles for libraries and librarians. *Information Technology & Libraries* 13(2):103-144.

Zimmerman, Judy, ed. 1989. The one person library. *Colorado Libraries* 15(3).

Index

AAIP
  See Association of Independent
  Information Professionals

AALL
  See American Association of Law
  Libraries

ALA
  See American Library Association

American Association of Law Libraries,
  55, 57, 61–62, 100, 139

  Task Force on the Value of Law
    Libraries in the Information Age,
    61

American Library Association, 21, 44, 46,
  86, 141

American Society for Information
  Science, 2,4

Americans with Disability Act, 34

annual report, 30

Appel, Linda, 130

ASIS
  See American Society for Information
  Science

ASLIB
  See Association of Libraries and
  Information Bureaux

Association of Independent Information
  Professionals, 57, 123

Association of Libraries and Information
  Bureaux, 9, 57, 136

Austin, Rhea, 129

Australia, 75–77, 155–156
  OPAL, 75

Backbone Network Service, 115

Bates, Mary Ellen, 129

Bauwens, Michael, 48, 105-106, 127
  See also cybrarian

book jobber, 56

sale, 47

Bender, David, 57, 59

Berkman, Bob, 108-109, 131

Berner, Andrew, xi, 37-39

book jobbers, 56, 170-172

book sale, 47

Brazil, 82, 159–160

budgeting
  capital, 33
  director's salary, 34
  functional, 33
  librarian's salary, 34
  line-item, 33

CAMLS
  See Cleveland Area Metropolitan
  Library Systems

Canada
  library schools, 154-155, 158

CD–ROM, 103, 118

CE
  See continuing education

Center for the Study of Rural
  Librarianship, 21

certification, 99–101

charging back, 35

church librarians, 23, 186, 197-198, 308
CIO, 123–124
Clarion University of Pennsylvania, 21
Cleveland Area Metropolitan Library
    System, 44
competencies, 89–93
competitive intelligence, 24, 110, 173
Computer Select CD–ROM, 12
continuing education, 51, 98–100, 126,
    162–165
copyright statements, 33
corporate culture, 28
Covey, Stephen, 33
customer service, 5–6, 32
cybrarian, 48, 105, 127–8

Dale, Georgina, 75, 138
DataTimes, 69
Daulong, Renee, 56
DIALOG, 14, 37, 46, 69, 107–108
director's salary
    See budget
Dobbs, James, 58
disintermediation, 60
distance education, 85, 95, 148, 152,
    160–162
document delivery, 173–175
    See also outsourcing
Dow–Jones, 46, 107
downsizing, 53, 59–64, 131
    Australia, 75
    case studies, 61, 65–69
Draper, Norma, 68-69

Education, 83–101, 94
    listing of schools, 98–100
    proficiency exams, 97
    See also distance education and contin-
    uing education

"Four Hard Truths," 27
Free-Nets, 216–217
fund raising
    book sales, 34
    Friends group, 34

Garman, Nancy, 111
Germany, 73–75, 81
Gervino, Joan, 35
Griffiths, Jose-Marie, 104–105, 115

"hot buttons," 28

ILL
    See interlibrary loan
infopreneur, 24
Information Advisor, 109
information brokers, 24–25, 58, 81, 87,
    191
Information Handling Services, 12
Infoseek, 107
insourcing, 128
interlibrary loan, 12, 34, 42, 93, 108, 130
Internet, 11, 37, 44, 93, 106–113, 118
    books, 189-191
    future issues, 115, 123–124
    job descriptions, 123
    listservs, 201–217
    search engines, 112, 201–202
internships, 93, 95, 97

job security, 124

law libraries, 14, 21–22, 192, 197,
    208–209
LEXIS–NEXIS, 46, 107–108
library committee, 30
library evaluation, 36
library of the future, 121–122
library schools, 125–126
    course offerings, 86, 94–97
    credit hour requirements, 86
    entry level requirements, 126
    ideal program, 84
    future curriculum, 125

listings, 144–167
reasons for selection, 85
survey, 86, 219–223
Louw, Anna, 79

Mackenzie, Alex, 39–40
Marshall, Joanne, 90
medical libraries, 15, 22, 209–211
Medical Libraries Association, 22, 44,
    100, 140, 141
Meylor, Elizabeth, 69
Middle Management Institute, 98
Miller, Jane, 59
mission statement, 30–31
MLA
    See also Medical Libraries Association
MLS degree, 84, 96–98
Morgenstern, Evelin, xi, 73
museum libraries, 15, 23, 186

National Library Week, 46
networking, 43–45, 103

OCLC, 12, 43, 103
One-Man-Band, 9, 71–75
    See also United Kingdom
OPAL (One-Person Australian Libraries),
    75, 138
open house, 11, 46–47
Opperman, Vance, 118
organizational behavior, 28–31
outsourcing, 44, 53–59, 62–63, 93
    books, 191
    cataloguing, 56
    document delivery, 56
    online searching, 57
    subscriptions
Outsourcing Institute, The, 54n.
Owens, Gil, 78, 80

Paul, Meg, 75

performance review, 43
PR
    See public relations
PREPS Commission, 87
prison librarians, 22, 186
professional image, 48–51
public librarians, 15, 19–21
    books, 185–196
    director, 49, 125
public relations, 45–48, 90, 93

Quint, Barbara, 13, 107

Rhine, Martha, 9
Rose, Linda, 46–47

St. Clair, Guy, ix–x, xi, 9, 31–32, 41–42,
    63–64, 75, 128, 130
saving money, 34–35
school librarians, 23
self-assessment, 30
SLA
    See Special Libraries Association
Small Library Development Center, 21
SOLO Librarians Division, 4, 9, 16, 87,
    129, 136, 207
SOLOLIB–L listserv, 18, 169
South Africa, 77–81
Special Committee on Competencies for
    Special Librarians, 90
Special Libraries Association, 4, 16,
    43–44, 59, 83, 87, 94, 97–98, 136, 199
subscription services, 172–173
    See also outsourcing
Sweden, 82

time management, 37–43, 90, 93
time wasters, 39–40
Toastmasters, 99
Tracy, Morgan, 19–20
transformational librarianship, 36
Trefethen, Dan, 67–68

United Kingdom, 71–75
   ASLIB, 71
   British library, 81
   continuing education, 99
   library schools, 157–158
   networking resources, 72
Vavrek, Bernard, 21

virtual library, 105–106, 118

Wall Street Journal, 11
White, Herb, 36, 50, 64
World Wide Web, for business research,
   108–109
Zieselman, Paul, 65